THE COMPLETE IDIOT'S GUIDE®

Dream Dictionary

by Eve Adamson and
Gayle Williamson (a.k.a. Dream Genie)

ALPHA

A member of Penuin Group (USA) Inc.

ALPHA BOOKS

Published by the Penguin Group

Penguin Group (USA) Inc., 375 Hudson Street, New York, New York 10014, U.S.A.

Penguin Group (Canada), 10 Alcorn Avenue, Toronto, Ontario, Canada M4V 3B2 (a division of Pearson Penguin Canada Inc.)

Penguin Books Ltd, 80 Strand, London WC2R 0RL, England

Penguin Ireland, 25 St Stephen's Green, Dublin 2, Ireland (a division of Penguin Books Ltd)

Penguin Group (Australia), 250 Camberwell Road, Camberwell, Victoria 3124, Australia (a division of Pearson Australia Group Pty Ltd)

Penguin Books India Pvt Ltd, 11 Community Centre, Panchsheel Park, New Delhi—110 017, India

Penguin Group (NZ), cnr Airborne and Rosedale Roads, Albany, Auckland 1310, New Zealand (a division of Pearson New Zealand Ltd)

Penguin Books (South Africa) (Pty) Ltd, 24 Sturdee Avenue, Rosebank, Johannesburg 2196, South Africa

Penguin Books Ltd, Registered Offices: 80 Strand, London WC2R 0RL, England

International Standard Book Number: 978-1-59257-575-6
Library of Congress Catalog Card Number: 2006932987

09 08 07   8 7 6 5 4 3 2

Interpretation of the printing code: The rightmost number of the first series of numbers is the year of the book's printing; the rightmost number of the second series of numbers is the number of the book's printing. For example, a printing code of 07-1 shows that the first printing occurred in 2007.

Printed in the United States of America

Note: This publication contains the opinions and ideas of its authors. It is intended to provide helpful and informative material on the subject matter covered. It is sold with the understanding that the authors, book producer, and publisher are not engaged in rendering professional services in the book. If the reader requires personal assistance or advice, a competent professional should be consulted.

The authors, book producer, and publisher specifically disclaim any responsibility for any liability, loss, or risk, personal or otherwise, which is incurred as a consequence, directly or indirectly, of the use and application of any of the contents of this book.

Most Alpha books are available at special quantity discounts for bulk purchases for sales promotions, premiums, fund-raising, or educational use. Special books, or book excerpts, can also be created to fit specific needs.

For details, write: Special Markets, Alpha Books, 375 Hudson Street, New York, NY 10014.

Publisher: *Marie Butler-Knight*
Editorial Director: *Mike Sanders*
Managing Editor: *Billy Fields*
Senior Acquisitions Editor: *Randy Ladenheim-Gil*
Book Producer: *Lee Ann Chearney/Amaranth Illuminare*
Development Editor: *Lynn Northrup*
Production Editor: *Kayla Dugger*

Copy Editor: *Krista Hansing Editorial Services, Inc.*
Cover Designer: *Bill Thomas*
Book Designers: *Trina Wurst/Becky Harmon*
Layout: *Becky Harmon*
Proofreader: *Aaron Black*

Contents

Introduction

Dreaming is so *personal* it can be hard to explain to someone else. How many times have we been beside ourselves with excitement to tell someone about a dream, only to get blank stares back. And you can't even say, "I guess you had to be there." This is why we wrote *The Complete Idiot's Guide Dream Dictionary* which you hold in your hands. There is a language for each dreamer, yet there are universal truths to our individual dreams.

Everyone dreams, and each of us has a distinctive dream style. Whether you're the kind of dreamer who remembers every dream moment in high-definition detail and with instant recall; who gets flash insights and remembers vivid visuals strung together piecework by waking memory; or whether all you can bring back from your dreams are a few colors, a bunch of numbers, a face, a voice, or a fast-action download blur shorter than your digital camera's video memory capability, it doesn't matter. Whatever kind of dreamer you are, you're just like everyone else who is dreaming: fascinated, curious, and eager to figure it all out. *What do your dreams mean?*

How to Use This Dictionary

Dreamers love to read dream dictionaries, and we're guessing that you may have a collection of them—always looking for new insights, combinations, and interpretations. *The Complete Idiot's Guide Dream Dictionary* arranges more than 1,500 entries in A to Z format, covering topics of interest for dream interpretation as far-ranging as dreams themselves—everything from specifics such as **butterfly, best friend, cell phone,** or **fast food** to concepts such as **breaking up, dropping the ball,** or the **wrong size.** Dreamers also find entries for the usual dream suspects from flying to falling, numbers, colors, body parts, animals, celebrities, seasons, money, and more. Plus, *The Complete Idiot's Guide Dream Dictionary* showcases the most up-to-date vocabulary of dream symbols and dream meanings—stuff older, outdated references either don't include at all, or can't interpret in a way that's so, well, *now.*

Dream Words: A to Z Entries

Each A to Z dream dictionary entry is defined, and its dream interpretive meanings fully explored. Where appropriate, cross-references to related entries will appear. For example, the entry on **ringtone** includes the tag **See also** *cell phone, phone.* Blind entries lead dreamers to core concepts; for example, **lottery: See** *winning.* All of the entries in *The Complete Idiot's Guide Dream Dictionary* focus on dream symbols and their interpretations to allow dreamers to reach for the fullest selection of extrapolated dream meanings possible. The content of A to Z entries provides hands-on instructional insight leading to innovative dream interpretation. This dictionary will not include entries on the science of sleep or the psychology of dreaming; only symbols, meanings, interpretations, and much more!

At the end of each A to Z dream entry, *The Complete Idiot's Guide Dream Dictionary* includes two great features: Yin/Yang Dream Shadows and the Dream Themes Index.

Yin/Yang Dream Shadows

Psychologist Carl Jung often wrote about the challenge of acknowledging our shadow, that is, of recognizing and embracing the darker or flip side of our emotions and experiences. Dreams often show us seemingly confusing images, and it is up to dreamers to puzzle out the full dream meaning. That can include exploring both light and dark, yin and yang possibilities. When you see the symbol ☽, following it you'll find a list of opposite or complementary dream dictionary entries to explore. For example, the yin/yang shadow of **girl** is **boy,** or for **glass,** it is **rock.** In Eastern philosophy, balance and understanding are achieved by considering opposites, united in harmony. Dreamers may be surprised at what can be seen in dream shadows!

Dream Themes Index

The Dream Themes Index lists collections of dream dictionary entries by topic of interest, allowing dreamers to search quickly and easily for deeper, more resonant dream meanings. Dreamers can access Dream Theme power in two ways: 1. by looking at the Dream Themes Index at the back of the dictionary, where all the Dream Themes are collected; and 2. by looking for the Dream Theme symbol ℂ in the A to Z entries to find a list of Dream Themes to explore.

For example, looking in the Dream Themes Index at the back of the dictionary, here are the entries linked to the Dream Theme for "Color":

> **Color:** artist, black, blonde hair, blue, brunette hair, green, jewels, pink, purple, red, red hair, yellow.

Turning to the A to Z entry for **artist,** the Dream Themes of **beauty, color,** and **creativity** are listed. The more connections dreamers look up, the more dream insights and interpretations become possible.

Plus More!

In addition to the Dream Themes Index, a complete listing of the more than 1,500 A to Z entry words is included in a Dream Words appendix to help dreamers locate entries at a glance. We've included a Tuck-in Time appendix to help dreamers invite, induce, and remember dream messages. A Dream Interpretation Checklist details how dreamers can interpret dreams step-by-step.

Put it all together and *The Complete Idiot's Guide Dream Dictionary* is a dream come true. From teenagers to New Agers, from students of dreams and dreaming to each of us who just wants to understand a little bit more about ourselves—all kinds of dreamers can enjoy this dictionary and find something new, fun, and informative to reveal, stimulate, and provoke insight and understanding about dreams and what they might mean. We're all dream genies!

Acknowledgments

From Eve:

"You're writing a dream dictionary? Let me tell you my dream ..." So many people spoke these words to me during the course of writing this book, and so many of these dreams provided even deeper insight for me into how dream interpretation works. Thanks to all of you who shared your dreams, good and bad, scary and hilarious, and everything in between. It has been, and continues to be, a fascinating dream journey. Thanks also to my family, so often a part of my dreams; and to Ben, who laughs in his sleep.

From Gayle:

My dreams have saved me a ton of money I would have spent at the psychiatrist's office, seriously. I'm convinced my mind sorts my problems out at night and presents solutions to me wrapped in pretty dream packages. Well ... they're not all pretty. Remember, this dictionary is a tool, and you are your own best interpreter because you know what's causing you to dream this weird stuff. Also, pay attention to your daydreams. They're the ones that will really get you in trouble. And speaking of trouble, all my thanks to Lee Ann.

Trademarks

All terms mentioned in this book that are known to be or are suspected of being trademarks or service marks have been appropriately capitalized. Alpha Books and Penguin Group (USA) Inc. cannot attest to the accuracy of this information. Use of a term in this book should not be regarded as affecting the validity of any trademark or service mark.

abandonment Hey, where did everybody go? Many people have deep, even subconscious fears of abandonment, and these often surface in our dreams, but exactly who or what abandons you in your dream can symbolize what you really feel about your own life. Fear of abandonment means you lack confidence or control. Sadness from abandonment means you are mourning the loss of something. Anger at abandonment means you have someone you need to forgive. **1.** If you dream that you have been abandoned by your family or friends, you don't feel like you have a reliable network of support in your life. You might take some concrete steps to establish firmer ties with the people you rely on. **2.** Who has abandoned you? A parent abandoning you may mean you feel the adult world has abandoned you. A spouse or partner abandoning you may mean you feel you will never find true love. A friend abandoning you may mean you are not being enough of a friend to yourself. **3.** If you have abandoned someone in your dream—a child, a spouse, a parent, a friend—then examine your relationship with that person or with the group that person symbolizes. You might feel neglectful in real life or too overwhelmed to give someone or something necessary attention. **4.** Abandoning someone can also represent your own feelings of loss toward a part of yourself. Abandoning a child may symbolize the loss of your own inner child or sense of youth. Abandoning a parent might mean you are neglecting your own need to be more mature. Abandoning a friend may mean you have betrayed yourself or your personal ideals in some way. ☯ **crowds, public places** ℂ *anger, anxiety, fear, feelings, isolation, relationships.*

abdomen Oomph! The abdomen is a highly personal and sensitive spot, and dreams about this body part signify highly personal, sensitive subjects. **1.** If you've just been punched in the abdomen in your dream, something in your real life has knocked the wind out of you. **2.** If you dream your abdomen has been cut open, you are hiding something from yourself. Or you just started your period, girls. **3.** An injured abdomen means someone has hurt you

deeply. **4.** A swollen or shrunken abdomen means you are overindulging or neglecting your personal care needs. If only we could do sit-ups in our sleep, how sweet that would be. See also *stomach*.
☽ **back** ☾ *body parts, injuries, pain, personal power, repression, vulnerability.*

abduction   So aliens took you to their ship for some tests, or a masked stranger stole you, or someone you love whisked you away in the middle of the night? **1.** If someone or something abducts you, you might wish to escape your life but don't want to take responsibility for leaving. **2.** You may be hiding fear of the world and its sinister elements. **3.** You feel like someone else controls your life. **4.** If someone abducts your child or other family member, you fear a loss of power over those you love. Get more involved in their lives. Spend more time and be present with them to resolve this anxiety. "Abduct them" for a picnic and concert in the park. See also *aliens, escape.* ☽ **taking responsibility** ☾ *anxiety, caretaking, control issues, family, fear, responsibilities, trust issues.*

abnormal   Whoa, dude, what's up with *that?* Dreams about the abnormal are totally normal, just in case you were worried. If you dream something about you, someone else, or your environment that is abnormal—a strange face, missing body parts, everything upside down, things not quite like

they should be—your subconscious might be trying to shake you out of your rut. Maybe you need to change something about yourself or your life to get back on the right track. If you find the abnormality disturbing in your dream, you resist change and don't like to face unpleasantness (who does?). Acknowledge this about yourself, and gently encourage yourself to open your mind a bit.
☽ **monotony** ☾ *anxiety, body parts, confusion, transformation.*

abortion   No, you probably aren't pregnant, and unless you are reliving a past experience, dreams of an abortion represent something entirely different. **1.** An idea, plan, or path you've chosen might not be the right one for you. Your subconscious is telling you to go another way. Reconsider your options before it's too late to change your mind. **2.** A relationship is ending and you need to let it go. **3.** If you *are* pregnant and dream of an abortion, it doesn't mean anything is wrong. You are experiencing typical pregnancy anxiety, and, just like everyone does, you are questioning whether you can handle parenthood. This is completely normal. **4.** If you are reliving an actual experience from your past in your dreams and feel disturbed by the dream, especially if it is recurring, you probably haven't fully dealt with or processed the experience yet, no matter how long it has been. Consider talking to a professional to help you manage your feelings.
☽ **birth, pregnancy** ☾ *changing course, loss, relationships, transformation.*

abstinence If you dream of something you've given up, like smoking, drinking, intimacy, or some kind of food, your body may just be telling you it misses your previous addiction, but you might also be craving nourishment in some other form: love, security, human touch, or communication. See also *alcohol, eating, smoking.* ◐ **bingeing, decadence** ℂ *food and drink, relationships, repression, sexual activity.*

accelerator The accelerator makes the vehicle go, and pushing on one shoots you off in a very particular direction. But are you in control? **1.** Pushing on the accelerator on purpose so you can drive faster, faster, faster, means you are, or would like to be, speeding through life right now. You are on the fast track and loving it. You go! **2.** If you can't help pushing on the accelerator, or the pedal is stuck with you the unwitting and frightened passenger, you need to get off the fast track now. Slow down and take it easy. Why are you in such a hurry? Your life is getting a little bit out of control, and you are missing out on some important things. Your body knows it, so pay attention to this dream. See also *car, car accident.* ◐ **paralyzed, repression** ℂ *control issues, travel, vehicles.*

accident Uh oh. Accident dreams signal anxiety and the fear that something will go wrong. They could hint at a mistake you are making or a lack of self-confidence in your current project. If you are injured in an accident, you don't feel safe. See also *airplane crash, car accident, falling.* ◐ **rescue** ℂ *accidents, anxiety, death, disaster, fear, injuries, vehicles.*

acid Acid eats away at surfaces. You might need to take some aggressive action to get to the bottom of what's really going on, and you might have to cause some damage to do it. ◐ **healing** ℂ *message, repression, subterfuge.*

acne A sudden case of dream acne means something is coming to the surface, and it's not going to be pretty. You might as well wash your face and come clean. See also *skin.* ◐ **health** ℂ *body parts, secret, subterfuge.*

ad See *advertisement.*

addiction See *bad habits.*

adolescence Pulsing with hormones, rebellion, and righteous indignation, adolescents represent the adolescent part of you that still rages within. And you thought you were done with puberty. When an adolescent appears in your dream—either you or someone else—it means you need that part of yourself to deal with a current issue. Are you settling? Have you fallen into a monotonous routine? Are you letting The Man get you down? Let your inner adolescent free in your waking life and find out why you need to remember those tumultuous times *right now.* ◐ **child,**

children; grown-up ℂ *feelings, freedom, rebellion, transformation.*

adoption   Dream you are adopted, and you feel like you don't belong in some group—family, colleagues, or friends. Do you want to fit in better? Dream you adopted a child, and you are looking for someone or something to nurture. Does someone need your parental guidance? See also *child or children, maternal instinct.* ☯ **abandonment** ℂ *caretaking, family, relationships.*

adultery   Don't panic! Dreams of adultery don't mean you have any intention of breaking your vow—or that your partner is straying. More likely, you are feeling stifled or unable to fully express yourself to your partner, and in your dream you are exploring symbolic ways of regaining your freedom, personal power, or autonomy. You might need to improve communication or gain more intimacy with your partner. The person in your dream might actually symbolize your partner. You might also be feeling like you can't be sexually free with your partner and you can only imagine really expressing yourself with someone you don't know—it might feel safer or less vulnerable or intimate to you. If you feel guilty in your dream, the dream might symbolize your feelings that you have betrayed your partner in some other way, even if it just means saying something negative about him or her to someone else. If you feel exhilarated and enjoy the adultery

in your dream, you are simply expressing a desire for excitement and daring, which you can, of course, exercise without cheating. If you dream about an actual adulterous relationship you or your partner had in the past, you are still working through your feelings about this. You may not have forgiven yourself or your partner yet. ☯ **isolation** ℂ *communication, desires, freedom, forgiveness, guilt, personal power, risky behavior, sexual activity, trust issues.*

adventure   Epic adventure dreams can be a blast, even when parts of them get scary. To embark on an adventure means you are feeling courageous and able to take on new challenges. Time to book a trip abroad or read an adventurous book. Are you finally ready to make that career move? ☯ **monotony** ℂ *adventure, career, changing course, courage, freedom, opportunity, risky behavior, transformation, travel.*

advertisement   Place an ad, and you've publicly declared what you want. Read an ad, and you've told yourself what you need. ☯ **closet** ℂ *communication, message, opportunity.*

advice   "If I were you …." We don't always want advice from others, but pay attention to dream advice, which comes directly from your subconscious, no matter who the dream advice-giver is. **1.** If you get advice, consider following it or doing what it symbolizes. **2.** If you are giving someone else good advice, you are getting ready for a leadership position. Step up to the plate. **3.** If you give someone bad advice and it goes horribly wrong, you have been overstepping your boundaries lately. Hang back and keep your mouth shut, literally or metaphorically. ☯ **mute** ℭ *communication, listening, message, support.*

affair   See *infidelity.*

Africa   Life began in Africa, and dreams of Africa take us back to our origins. Some primal instinct within you struggles to be free. Go on safari and discover what it is. ☯ **monotony** ℭ *places, instincts, repression, travel.*

> Dreams of a particular place you've never actually visited usually signify an untapped part of you that is ready to be explored. The jungle might be a wild side you never knew you had, the tropics a relaxed or super-heated passionate side, the frozen tundra a part of you that can control your emotions better than you think. Imagine your individual potential as a giant map. Where does your dream point you?

aggression   Most people have the occasional aggressive instinct, but if you behave aggressively in a dream, hurting someone, destroying things, or yelling, you have pent-up frustration you don't feel you can release in the real world. Find a way

to let it out, or it might just keep recurring in your dreams, and that's no way to get a good night's sleep. (Avoid feather pillows for midnight punching bags—what a mess!) ☯ **nonviolence** ℭ *anger, feelings, frustration, violence.*

AIDs   As a culture, we have become so familiar with AIDs that it sometimes infiltrates our dreams. Dreaming of AIDs does not mean you have AIDs, but it can mean you feel vulnerable. **1.** If you have AIDs in your dream, you haven't been protecting yourself or taking care of yourself, or you feel that others aren't protecting you. Have you been engaging in risky behavior? Neglecting your health? Isolating yourself from friends? Time for some self-care, and now. **2.** In your dream, if you fear letting people know you have AIDs, you've hidden something personal, perhaps even from yourself. **3.** If you dream someone else has AIDs, you worry about that person or whomever they represent. Someone needs your nurturing. See also *disease.* ☯ **health** ℭ *caretaking, fear, health and hygiene, reputation, risky behavior, secrets, sexual activity.*

air conditioner   Time to chill out! Sitting in front of an air conditioner means you are either having a hot flash in your sleep, or: **1.** You have been getting too intense, angry, or hot-under-the-collar about something. Back off and cool off, or you might overheat. **2.** You are purposefully cooling off a sexually intense

situation. Time for a cold shower?
◑ **heat** ℭ *anger, sexual activity.*

air force   See *military.*

airplane   Buckle your seatbelts, it's
time for take-off. Dreaming of an
airplane means you have the power
to rise above your situation or move
on to new freedoms and frontiers.
Is it time to change the scenery?
If you dream of an airplane being
refueled while in flight, you are
considering procreating … really.
See also *airplane crash, flying.*
◑ **falling** ℭ *personal power, freedom,
transformation, travel, vehicles.*

airplane crash   The oxygen mask
drops down in front of you and
you try to remember how to use
your seat cushion as a flotation
device …. We've all imagined it,
and many of us dream about it. An
airplane crash symbolizes loss of
control and the anxiety that you are
plummeting toward disaster and
you can't do anything about it. It
may be too late to step off the plane
in your dream, but what disaster
looms in your real life? Time to
look closely at your ticket and do
some rescheduling, no extra charge.
See also *accident, falling, flying.*
◑ **flying** ℭ *accidents, anxiety, control issues, disaster, fear, vehicles.*

alcohol   You can't get a citation
for drunk driving in your dreams,
but dreaming of alcohol—drinking
it, not drinking it, or getting drunk
from it—can signal several things.
1. If you dream of drinking alcohol
and enjoy it, you desire a temporary

escape. **2.** If you drink alcohol and
feel guilty about it, you fear you are
losing control of your life. What
does alcohol represent here? Bad
habits, or someone who is a bad
influence? **3.** If you see and choose
not to drink alcohol, even though
you want to, you are reigning yourself in and might need to cut loose
a little (not necessarily by drinking,
however). **4.** If you dream everyone
else is drinking alcohol and you
aren't, either you feel left out of
a social circle or you feel morally
superior to your less self-controlled
friends. **5.** Enjoying an abundance
of wine and food means you embrace life with delightful abandon.
Good for you! Just be careful not
to get so hedonistic that you let the
important things or people in your
life suffer. Moderation in all things,
you god or goddess of wine. See
also *bad habits, beer, champagne, wine.*
◑ **abstinence** ℭ *addictions, celebration, desires, escape, food and drink,
hedonism, pleasure, risky behavior.*

aliens   Aliens infiltrating your
home, abducting you, or simply
waving as they zoom by in their
flying saucers signify your fear
of or interest in the unknown. **1.**
Frightening, invasive aliens mean
you are struggling with a change in
your life and don't want to accept it.
2. Pleasant exchanges with aliens,
or seeing them from afar without
fear, mean you have the potential to
push your boundaries and venture
out into new territory. 3-2-1, blast
off! ◑ **friends** ℭ *adventure, changing course, characters, fear, myths and
legends, threats.*

alligator or crocodile Animals represent some part of you, usually some aspect of your instincts or more primal side. Alligators usually signal distress or a conflict. **1.** If you are attacked by an alligator, your problem is overwhelming and you must wrestle to get control. The stress is getting to you! You might even be in danger. **2.** If you run from and escape an alligator, you are narrowly avoiding problems, but they are still after you and you need to address them before they catch up to you. **3.** To befriend an alligator means you are in control of your problems. Congratulations! **4.** To kill an alligator means you are threatened enough to consider drastic action in solving your problem. ◐ **calm** ℂ *animals, anxiety, crawling creatures, danger, nature, threats.*

alone If everybody finally leaves you alone in a dream and it's the best dream you ever had, wake up and smell the coffee! Call the spa, right now. If you're alone and lonely, frightened, or abandoned, you aren't getting enough support in your life. Call a friend, right now. If you leave someone else alone by mistake, you feel like you've abandoned someone. Call that person just to make sure everything is okay. ◐ **crowd** ℂ *abandonment, freedom, isolation, support.*

Alzheimer's disease See *senile.*

ambulance Dial 911! You've been careless, and if you don't know it,

your subconscious mind does. An ambulance coming for you means you aren't being careful with yourself—your health, your safety, your reputation. An ambulance coming for someone else means you are neglecting others, or you fear you aren't doing enough for others. Don't shirk your responsibilities, or someone really could get hurt. Even if you think you are doing all you can, someone needs to know you really are there for them, flashing lights and all. ◐ **caution** ℂ *accidents, risky behavior.*

amnesia Who hasn't wished they could blame amnesia for another fine mess they've gotten themselves into? Dreams of amnesia mean you are avoiding something. What don't you want to remember? This dream also presents a unique opportunity for reinvention, asking you to consider who you might become if you could start from scratch. Let that inspire you. ◐ **remembering** ℂ *identity, memory, repression, secrets, subterfuge, transformation.*

amputation No matter what body part it is, somebody has dreamt that somehow it was cut off. This very common dream seems to symbolize the loss of something very important (an arm, a leg, a head, even genitals!), but amputation dreams can also mean "use it or lose it." **1.** If you dream your legs have been cut off, you need to move more—walk, run, or metaphorically walk or run out of a situation. **2.** Amputated arms mean you aren't embracing something important. Who needs a hug? What ideas or plans should you welcome with open arms? **3.** Amputated fingers mean you are missing out on the details. **4.** An amputated head means you aren't thinking. Use your head while you still have one! **5.** Amputated genitalia mean you aren't making sex an important enough part in your life or relationship, or you feel sexually ignored. For men, castration dreams can symbolize a loss of personal power—someone has made you feel less than manly. Castration dreams can also symbolize the need to start over sexually from the beginning. Have you gone too far? Are you feeling guilty about something you've done? ☽ **arms, legs, sex organs** ℭ *accidents*, *body parts*, *freedom*, *loss*, *medicine and surgery*, *pain*, *personal power*, *sexual activity*.

amusement park Like a roller coaster heading over the crest of a hill, amusement park dreams show you how you see the life immediately ahead of you. **1.** If you dream of a vast, limitless amusement park with fantastic rides, amazing games, magical elements, and never-ending entertainment, you see your life right now as full of exciting possibilities, adventure, and glorious fun. **2.** If you dream of a run-down, sad little carnival, you have compromised and see your life as small, uninteresting, even tacky. **3.** Dreaming a carnival ride has gone awry represents your life, too: a stuck Ferris wheel means you

are caught in a precarious position and feel you don't have any choices, while a roller coaster or other ride that is off its track or coming loose and crashing means you are headed for disaster if you don't slow down. Be a little more discerning with your tickets, will ya? Maybe you shouldn't have gotten on that ride in the first place. ☽ **monotony** ℭ *adventure*, *freedom*, *fun*, *places*, *risky behavior*.

ancestors A dream visit from your ancestors once would have been considered a message from the spirit world, and who says it isn't? It could be some of that good ol' DNA talking to you. Ancestors help you relocate your place in the larger scheme of generations, advising you on your career, your partner choice, your obligation to family, even your role in the world. Ancestors may offer some very good advice. ☽ **future** ℭ *characters*, *family*, *history*, *messages*, *people*.

androgyny Are you a boy or a girl? If you aren't sure in your dream, don't worry. You're just getting in touch with both sides of yourself. We all have both genders within us. **1.** If you are androgynous in your dreams—you have male and female sex organs or no sex organs at all—you are on the verge of understanding something new about yourself. **2.** If you meet an androgynous person, you are exploring your feelings about the balance between male and female energy, in yourself or in the world.

3. If you dream you have an androgynous baby or child, you have the potential to appreciate a wide range of abilities in those you nurture. And good luck figuring out what to wear today. ☉ **heterosexuality, man, woman** ℂ *balance, gender issues, yin-yang.*

anesthesia   To dream you are under anesthesia means you want to remain numb to something right now. Give yourself time before forcing yourself to deal with any issues. See also *surgery, paralyzed.* ☉ **pain** ℂ *feelings, medicine and surgery, pain.*

angel   People used to think angels visited dreams to bring important messages from God. Maybe so! Just in case, give them a listen. They may be telling you, or showing you, something you need to know or do for your spiritual self. They might have a divine mission for you! Angels may also appear in dreams if you have been neglecting your spiritual side. A gentle reminder from the powers that be? See also *ghost.* ☉ **devil** ℂ *characters, divine power, myths and legends, spirituality.*

anger   Why, I oughtta …. People often dream they are angry when they won't let themselves be angry in real life. Getting angry in your dreams doesn't hurt anybody, so this is the time to let 'er rip. **1.** If you dream of an angry outburst, you are releasing a repressed feeling. **2.** If you dream of suppressing anger, something is trying to come out, but you aren't letting it free. Maybe it was something you ate.

3. If someone else is angry at you, you feel guilty about something and your dream is punishing you. Can you make it right? **4.** Anger resulting in violence means your feelings have gotten intense. What's got you so worked up? Can you inject a dose of objectivity into the situation? ☉ **calm** ℂ *anger, communication, feelings, relationships, repression, violence.*

animals   Animals represent your deepest emotions, instincts, and desires. When an animal appears to you in a dream, you are sending yourself an important message about who you are right now and where you are going. To dream of many animals together suggests your instincts have overcome your ability to be civilized. To see animals in cages suggests you've reigned in your instincts, perhaps too far. Sick or dying animals suggest you've lost touch with your instincts almost entirely. See also *dead animal,* and individual types of animals. ☉ **brain** ℂ *animals, birds, crawling creatures, freedom, instincts, nature, repression.*

When an animal appears in a dream, some cultures believe it is a spirit messenger or your own personal totem animal delivering a life lesson. If an animal communicates with you in a dream, pay special attention. Such a message might hold particular significance about what you have been doing or what you can expect.

ankle   Twist an ankle, and you're likely to go down. If you dream you hurt or twist your ankle, you feel vulnerable or in-the-wrong, and you won't be able to hide it much longer. ◔ **wrist** ℂ *body parts, insecurity, stability, work.*

anorexia   See *starvation.*

answering machine   If you let the answering machine get it in your dream, you don't want to face something or take responsibility. If you get a message on an answering machine, your subconscious is trying to tell you something and can't seem to reach you. Listen to the message! ◔ **mute** ℂ *communication, inanimate objects, messages, technology.*

antidote   Taking an antidote for poison or venom means you are on the verge of a solution to that problem. Can't find the antidote? You fear you won't solve the problem in time. ◔ **poison** ℂ *solutions and remedies.*

antiques   A room full of antiques urges you to look at stories from the past for help in the present. Breaking an antique means you are moving on. ◔ **future** ℂ *history, inanimate objects, messages.*

ants   If you dream of ants in nature, you are working hard and getting the job done. You are a team player, or you need to be. If ants come into your house, you are losing control of your home situation. If you don't do something, it could all fall apart. ◔ **lazy** ℂ *animals, crawling creatures, nature, work.*

apartment   See *house.*

apocalypse   See *end of the world.*

applause   You rock! To dream of applause means to pat yourself on the back. You've done a good job, and even if you don't consciously acknowledge it, you know it's true, and your self-esteem is soaring. Go, you! See also *audience.* ◔ **booing** ℂ *celebration, personal power, success.*

apple   Hey, Adam, take a bite, you're going to *love* this. Dreams of apples may be filled with biblical or fairytale symbolism (look before you crunch, Snow White!), or your body might just be telling you to watch your health. **1.** If you eat and enjoy an apple, you may actually need more fruit in your diet. Listen to your body's wisdom, and you'll keep that proverbial doctor away. Apples may also symbolize cleansing. Do you need physical, emotional, or spiritual purification? **2.** If you eat but don't enjoy an apple, you are trying to escape reality. Are you looking for a perfect partner to kiss you to rescue you? Life in a glass coffin isn't all it's cracked up to be. It may be time to add some fairytale elements to your reality. Treat yourself like the royalty you know you are: The Fairest of Them All. **3.** If someone hands you an apple, you are facing temptation in your life. Best consider the consequences before you take a bite. **4.** If you see an apple tree, you have

A

the opportunity to gain important knowledge. **5.** Sharing an apple or any round, full, sensuous fruit symbolizes seduction. Do you have your eye on someone? **6.** If you bite into an apple and find a worm, you are hiding something from yourself: a bad feeling about someone, reservations about a situation, or a deep unhappiness. It's time to 'fess up. See also *fruit.* ☯ **resistance** ℭ *desires, food and drink, fruit, love, myths and legends, sexual activity.*

aquarium   A beautiful habitat enclosed in glass, filled with creatures that breathe water instead of air …. Aquariums symbolize the small realities we keep self-contained within us: our fantasy lives, our dreams for the future, our separate worlds of work, family, and love. **1.** Aquarium dreams celebrate these inner worlds, but also show us how we limit ourselves by our own rules and preconceived notions about the world. You can't swim past that glass wall. **2.** To break an aquarium means your neatly compartmentalized realities are breaking down. Time to integrate some parts of your life? **3.** To dream you are inside an aquarium means you limit yourself, or someone else limits you. If you don't like it, take a deep breath and step out into the open air. ☯ **breaking free** ℭ *animals, freedom, inanimate objects, repression.*

archaeologist   Chip away at that layer of rock, and you might just uncover buried treasure, an undiscovered civilization, a frozen caveman. To dream you are an archaeologist means you have serious unearthing to do. Something waits under the surface—*your* surface—for discovery. To dream you are with an archaeologist means a mentor will help you uncover your inner treasure. But like Indiana Jones or Lara Croft, you must be very careful—treasure can be dangerous. Remember the Ark? Pandora's box? Acknowledging your own inner treasures is a responsibility. Can you use your gifts wisely when you find them? Then start digging! ☯ **future** ℭ *career, characters, history, people, secrets, subterfuge, travel.*

archery   Hit a bull's-eye, and you've got the right idea. Keep missing the target? Be the arrow in your waking life and you'll improve your aim. ☯ **asking for directions** ℭ *competition, direction, intuition, sports and games.*

argument   Why can't everybody just get along? Because humans argue, and to argue in your dream means you need to work through a problem. **1.** If you pick a fight, you need to get something out of your system. **2.** If someone picks on you, you lack confidence in your current direction. Find a better way to defend your position, or change it. **3.** If you argue violently, you aren't thinking rationally about a problem. Step back and get some perspective before you tackle this one. ☯ **nonviolence** ℭ *anger, communication, relationships, violence.*

Armageddon   See *end of the world*.

arms   Arms hug, care for others, or hold people back. To hold something or someone in your arms shows how well you nurture others. To injure your arms means your caretaking abilities need some work, or you may feel unable to care for others or yourself. See also *amputation*. ☽ **legs** ☾ *caretaking, peacemaking, relationships*.

army   See *military*.

arrested   Drop your weapon and put your hands up! **1.** Dreaming you've been arrested means that somewhere inside, you think you've done something wrong and someone in an authority position ought to do something about it. Confess! **2.** Dreaming you've been unjustly arrested suggests people don't really understand your motives. Maybe you need a lawyer. **3.** Resisting arrest means you plan to fight an unfair situation. **4.** Arresting someone else means you see yourself as an authority figure responsible for other people. See also *bad behavior, crime, citizen's arrest*. ☽ **award** ☾ *anxiety, authority, guilt, injustice*.

arson   Fire consumes and destroys, and arsonists instigate that destruction. **1.** Committing arson in a dream means you want or need to obliterate something in your life. What needs to be metaphorically burned away? **2.** Seeing someone else commit arson means you fear others will destroy something in your life, or that you wish you could effect a major change but don't feel able to do it yourself. On the other hand, you might want to check the wiring in your electric blanket. See also *crime, fire*. ☽ **building** ☾ *changing course, destruction, risky behavior, transformation*.

In Ayurveda, an ancient Indian system of health (yoga is a part of this practice), fire is associated with the second chakra, an energy center behind the naval. This is where *agni* burns, the digestive fire within the body that takes in and consumes. Consider all these symbols and meanings when interpreting any dream you have about fire.

arthritis   Painful, sore joints make it hard to move, and dreams of arthritis mean you can't move, either—what has got you all stiff and inflexible? Take a metaphorical aspirin and consider what's slowing you down in your waking life. What do you refuse to accept or change about yourself? Or are you just afraid you're getting old? ☽ **flexibility** ☾ *age, body parts, pain, resistance*.

artist   Put on your beret and grab that paintbrush. Words can't express the masterpiece you have in mind. You're ready to show, not tell, so paint that picture. To dream you meet an artist means you may want to collaborate with others to materialize your great vision. ☽ **author**

ℭ *beauty, career, characters, color, creativity, people.*

ashes   You've moved on. Scatter those ashes to the wind and get ready for something new.   ☽ **birth** ℭ *death, freedom, transformation.*

Asia   Asian mystique fascinates Westerners, who envision this far-away land as full of spiritual wisdom. Dreams of Asia signify: **1.** a quest for meaning; **2.** a desire to escape from the daily monotony; or **3.** an untapped part of your personality trying to emerge.   ☽ **monotony** ℭ *places, spirituality, travel.*

asking for directions   Are you lost? You must be, or you wouldn't be asking for directions. Your dream is, quite literally, seeking direction in life. Consider where you are lost and who might be able to direct you. See also *lost.*   ☽ **wandering** ℭ *changing course, direction, relationships, travel.*

assassin   Time to dodge some bullets. **1.** To dream someone is trying to kill you means you feel insecure in your present situation. Who is "killing" your plans, your ambitions, your fun? Who is "shooting you down"? **2.** If you are the assassin, you are stronger and more resourceful than you think, and you have the power to do great—or terrible—things. Remember what Spider-man's uncle said: "With great power comes great responsibility." Your dream urges you to use your skills and charisma to make changes in your life.

☽ **nonviolence** ℭ *career, characters, control issues, death, insecurity, people, personal power, relationships, violence.*

asteroid   See *meteors and meteorites.*

astronaut   Houston, we have no problem at all! To dream you are an astronaut means you have great self-confidence and the ability to explore unknown territory. Even if something goes wrong in your astronaut dream, you are courageous enough to venture into space. If you meet an astronaut, your mind seeks vast unexplored frontiers. You seek a guide.   ☽ **fear** ℭ *career, characters, courage, opportunity, people, personal power, technology.*

asylum   See *insane asylum.*

atomic bomb   See *nuclear bomb.*

attacked   Run for your life! To dream you are attacked signifies anxiety. **1.** If a person attacks you, you don't trust someone. You might not even realize who it is until you think about it, but your dream tells you to watch your back. **2.** If an animal attacks you, your baser instincts—appetites, desires, aggressive impulses—are getting the best of your more logical mind, and you aren't comfortable with this imbalance. You need some structures in place to reign yourself in. **3.** If aliens or monsters attack you, your current situation feels insecure. You're nervous. You need to change something so you don't feel threatened. See also *aliens, intruder.*

◕ **security** ☾ *anxiety, insecurity, trust issues, violence.*

attic   Houses symbolize your personality, and attics symbolize your subconscious mind. What's hidden up there? **1.** Interesting attics filled with fascinating objects you never knew you had, secret passages, hidden doors, chests full of treasure, cool vintage clothes, or irresistible antiques mean you've got great untapped potential in that brain of yours. Something—hidden talents, unrealized energy, an illuminating idea—waits for you to discover it. Bring it out of the attic and make it part of your waking life. **2.** Scary, dark, musty, run-down, or cobwebby attics mean there are parts of your mind you'd rather not visit right now. That's fine. Save it for another day, when the attic might look more inviting. **3.** Locked attics or pitch-black attics mean your subconscious mind is hiding something from you. **4.** Dreaming you live in your major professor's attic means you are ready to graduate. See also *house, darkness.* ◕ **basement** ☾ *buildings and rooms, home, intuition, places, repression, secrets.*

audience   Dream of an audience watching you and you feel like you are in the spotlight. **1.** If an audience cheers, claps, or otherwise gives you positive reinforcement, you have courage and strong personal energy right now. You might even be pretty proud of yourself about something and your dream is patting you on the back. **2.** If the attention of an audience fills you with fear, you feel you aren't up to the task you've been given, or you wish you were getting less attention. **3.** If an audience ignores you, you aren't getting sufficiently recognized for your efforts. See also *applause, booing.* ◕ **invisible** ☾ *control issues, courage, ego, image, insecurity, people, personal power, success, support.*

audition   You mean you don't have a monologue prepared? But you're on in 3, 2, 1 …. Dreaming of an audition means you are trying out another role or idea for yourself—marriage, a new job, a new haircut, a tattoo? Who are you thinking of becoming? Your confidence about the audition reflects your confidence about the life change you are considering. A teleprompter sure would be handy. See also *play acting.* ◕ **monotony, security** ☾ *changing course, characters, transformation.*

Aurora Borealis   Nature has an inspirational message about your inner light and personal power. Tune in to your natural environment right now to help find your spiritual truth. ◕ **darkness** ☾ *messages, nature, personal power, spirituality.*

Australia Your rebellious spirit seeks release, and a dream of Australia tells you to let go and get a little wild, mate. You are ready for adventure. ☯ **conformity** ℭ *adventure, places, rebellion, travel.*

author You may never write the Great American Novel, but dreaming you are an author means you have a story to tell, and now is the time. Just start, and see what comes out: "Once upon a time, there was a …." To dream you meet an author means you seek someone to help you tell your story. ☯ **reading** ℭ *career, characters, communication, messages, people, personal power, work.*

autopsy The coroner has some information for you: that relationship failed because … your dream will fill in the blank. If *you* perform the autopsy, you simply must know what went wrong with a situation that didn't work out, and you have the motivation to get to the bottom of it. ☯ **birth** ℭ *body parts, death, relationships, subterfuge.*

autumn If the leaves are falling, you are leaving a stage of your life behind, and this is the natural order of things, so it will work out just fine. ☯ **spring** ℭ *age, changing course, nature, transformation, weather and seasons.*

Seasons symbolize the cyclical stages of life. Spring represents birth, summer growth, autumn maturation, and winter death; but then, of course, spring comes again. Dreams about seasons may represent your actual place along the continuum of your life, but they can also represent the stages you go through in the smaller moments—the birth of a new relationship, your growth in a new position at work, the way you've been able to handle a situation more maturely after a lot of practice, or the death of an idea you've finally realized won't ever come to fruition. Dreams about seasons changing signify that a major life change is happening to you.

avalanche When it all comes tumbling down, your dream realizes your worst fears for you. That doesn't mean your situation is as unstable as a shaky mountain of snow, but you fear it is. Get on stable footing—and don't yell so much! ☯ **security** ℭ *anxiety, disaster.*

award And the winner is … *you!* **1.** To dream you win an award means you have great confidence in your abilities and you are about to finish something important. It's going well. **2.** To dream someone else wins an award you think you should have won means you believe someone is taking credit for your work. **3.** To present an award to someone else means someone needs to hear what a good job they are

doing. Speak up! ☛ **punishment**
℃ *caretaking, celebration, desires, personal power, success.*

axe   Who uses an axe anymore? You do, and here's why. **1.** Chopping wood with an axe means you have hard work to do and you need to do it yourself. **2.** Attacking someone with an axe means you need to get inside a relationship situation or you won't ever understand it. **3.** If someone attacks you with an axe, you feel vulnerable and fear someone sees more about you than makes you comfortable. ☛ **lazy**
℃ *destruction, inanimate objects, relationships, solutions and remedies, subterfuge, violence, vulnerability, work.*

baby   Baby dreams come in all shapes and sizes, but they usually represent your feelings about your own nurturing abilities—toward yourself or others, or your general feelings about innocence. **1.** If you care for a baby in your dream, someone needs your nurturing skills. It might even be you. **2.** You might also have a strong desire to offer your nurturing skills to a child, or someone or something else, and the baby in your dream is fulfilling your desire. **3.** If you neglect, lose, or forget about a baby in your dream, you haven't—or you fear you haven't—been giving someone the nurturing they need. This might also be *you*. **4.** If you are pregnant and you dream of any kind of baby (normal, abnormal, strange-looking, boy, girl), you are simply wondering what your baby will be like, and what you will be like as a parent. **5.** If you dream you are a baby, your basic needs aren't being met and you need to take better care of yourself, or seek out someone who can give *you* a little nurturing. **6.** If you dream of a sick or injured baby, you've lost some part of your own innocence, or seen

someone else lose their innocence. ☯ **old person** ◐ *age, caretaking, comfort, desires, family, hopes and dreams, innocence, people, relationships, vulnerability.*

baby animal   Roly-poly puppies, fuzzy kittens, tiny baby rabbits, helpless baby birds … baby animal dreams represent undeveloped emotions or unexplored instincts that need careful nurturing to "grow up" in a healthy way. **1.** Finding a healthy baby animal means you have discovered new feelings about something or someone and you want to explore them. **2.** Finding a sick, injured, or dead baby animal means your recent feelings about something or someone aren't healthy. **3.** Accidentally or purposefully injuring or killing a baby animal means you know you must put a stop to a new emotion or instinct you've been exploring, even if you don't want to. **4.** Giving birth to a baby animal means you are just beginning to explore a new emotion or instinct, and you have great potential to take it in many directions. 5. If you are pregnant, dreaming about giving birth to a baby animal *doesn't* mean your baby will be born with a tail or any other abnormality. This very common dream simply means you can't quite imagine the child as a human being yet and you are wondering what it will be like. It can also mean parenting will be different than you expect. ☽ **death** ℭ *caretaking, feelings, innocence, instincts, opportunity, vulnerability.*

bachelor Ah, the single life. **1.** To dream you are a bachelor if you are actually married or in a long-term relationship means you could use a little more freedom, even if you are perfectly happy in your relationship. How about a night out with the guys? **2.** To dream of a bachelor if you are woman suggests you are accessing the male side of yourself that wishes to be left unencumbered by responsibility. See also *divorce, single.* ☽ **marriage** ℭ *characters, escape, family, freedom, people, relationships.*

back It's right behind you! Dreams of your back represent what follows you or lies hidden. **1.** Back injuries or abnormalities mean something unexpected could hurt you. **2.** Someone or something riding on your back indicates a burden you carry. Do you enjoy it, or wish you could throw it off? See also *paralyzed, spine injuries.* ☽ **abdomen** ℭ *addictions, burdens, injuries, pain, responsibilities, stability.*

backpack What do you have in there? Backpacks represent your resources. How good of a Boy Scout are you? **1.** Carrying a back-pack means you have the necessary resources to handle an upcoming problem. **2.** Looking inside a back-pack means you are exploring your own inner resources. Is it full of helpful tools, or things you wouldn't ever use? **3.** An empty backpack means you feel unprepared. **4.** A too-heavy backpack means you carry too much responsibility. Can you let someone else share the burden? Hey, take a load off, Fanny. ☽ **empty** ℭ *inanimate objects, responsibilities, solutions and remedies.*

backward Walking backward means you aren't making any prog-ress. Wearing your clothes backward means you don't feel comfortable in your current role. Are you acting like someone else in a relationship, environment, or job, and the new persona isn't really you? Driving backward means you need to go back and look at something you thought was finished. ☽ **success** ℭ *direc-tion, frustration, identity.*

bacteria See *disease, food poisoning.*

bad behavior Bad behavior, from the slightly illegal to the truly dan-gerous, doesn't signal any real inten-tion to cause trouble, but it can indi-cate your own feelings about your instincts or past actions. **1.** Mild bad behavior—insulting someone, playing pranks, minor vandalism— means you've been feeling a bit too buttoned up lately and your dream is helping you loosen up without actu-ally getting in trouble. **2.** Very bad behavior—crimes, hurting others,

B

killing—indicates your own fear of your natural instincts. If you let go just a little, you wonder if you'll go too far. **3.** Getting in trouble for bad behavior means you feel guilty and think you deserve punishment for something. See also *arrested, bad habits, crime.* ☾ **citizen's arrest** ☾ *authority, guilt, instincts, rebellion, risky behavior, rules and laws, violence.*

bad habits Biting your nails, twisting your hair, popping your gum. Bad habits may be hard to break, but dreams about them tell you about the parts of yourself you fear might get the better of you. **1.** If your bad habit goes horribly wrong in your dream—your nails break off, your hair comes out, your gum explodes—you're way too stressed about things you can't control. Ease up on yourself and take a deep breath now and then. **2.** If you enjoy your bad habit in your dream, you're enjoying a bit of relief from the strictures of your life. It's nothing to feel guilty about. **3.** If your bad habit is more of an addiction, you are struggling to control it in your subconscious mind. The addiction you dream about might not be the addiction you actually struggle with in life—dreaming about an addiction to drinking, smoking, or drugs may represent an addiction to food, the computer, or even a person. **4.** If you feel empowered to conquer your addiction in your dream, you are having success at overcoming your addiction in life. **5.** If you feel helpless in the face of your addiction in your

dream, your mind is telling you that you need some outside help with an addiction, even if it isn't the same addiction you dream about. (For a little extra help with your bad habits, check out *The Complete Idiot's Guide to Breaking Bad Habits*; Alpha Books, 1998.) See also *alcohol, drugs, smoking.* ☾ **abstinence, self-control** ☾ *addictions, control issues, guilt, risky behavior.*

baggage See *suitcase.*

bait Putting bait on a hook means you've got an idea about how to lure in something you want. Is that cologne or stinkbait you're wearing? Putting out bait to kill pests like bugs or rodents means you've got an idea about how to get rid of something you don't want. See also *fishing, poison.* ☾ **curse** ☾ *control issues, opportunity.*

bakery You can smell the bread rising, taste the sweet doughnuts, gawk over the beautiful cakes. Bakeries can be filled with delights or fearful temptations, depending on your state of mind. **1.** If you are trying to lose weight or have recently lost weight and you dream of guiltily eating sweets in a bakery, you fear you might lose control of your new health habits. Are you being too strict in your diet? Or are you just craving carbs? **2.** Bingeing in a bakery can signal a food addiction you can't control, or this dream might be telling you that you've been too hard or strict on yourself lately and your body is trying to rebel. **3.** If you delight in your bakery experience and savor every bite of baked goods without guilt, you know how to enjoy yourself and take full pleasure in life. **4.** If you are inside or outside a bakery but you can't get to any of the food, you want something that you can't have, or you haven't figured out how to get it. Consider what, in your waking life, holds such appeal. You might not even have realized you wanted it. See also *baking, dessert*. ☽ **abstinence, self-control** ☾ *addictions, comfort, control issues, food and drink, places, pleasure, rebellion.*

baking   The process of baking symbolizes domesticity. Baking in your dream means you have gotten back in touch with your home-body self, or your dream is telling you that this is just what you crave. Maybe stay in tonight, do a little nesting? See also *bakery, dessert*. ☽ **party** ☾ *comfort, family, food and drink, home, pleasure.*

balcony   To look down from a balcony means you have gained perspective on a situation that has troubled you. To look up at a balcony means you have an important goal you want to reach. ☽ **basement** ☾ *buildings and rooms, goal-setting, places.*

baldness   No, you aren't foretelling a hairless future. **1.** To dream you are bald means you have made

yourself vulnerable by revealing your inner thoughts to someone. This might not be a bad thing. **2.** To be upset about your own baldness means your ego has been damaged. **3.** To dream you like being bald means you have nothing to fear about revealing your thoughts. **4.** To dream your hair is falling out means you have lost power to someone or something. **5.** To dream someone else is bald means that person, or someone that person represents, has become vulnerable to you. You have the advantage because you can tell what they are thinking. The exception is to dream that someone is bald and looks fabulous that way. This indicates that you admire or feel jealous of the candor and communicative abilities of a friend. ☽ **hair** ☾ *body parts, control issues, ego, insecurity, vulnerability.*

ball   A ball bouncing or rolling means you have somewhere to go. A ball in your hands (or in your court) means it's your move. Go! ☽ **stop sign, stoplight** ☾ *competition, inanimate objects, opportunity, personal power, sports and games.*

ballerina   To be a ballerina means you feel powerful, beautiful, and feminine. To watch, meet, or talk to a ballerina means you seek more power and femininity or grace in yourself. ☽ **clumsy** ☾ *beauty, career, characters, femininity, people, personal power, sports and games.*

B

Aerobic exercise, like running or dancing, early in the day can help you sleep better at night, but aerobic exercise right before bed can make it more difficult to fall asleep. However, more relaxing evening exercise, such as yoga, can help lull you into the right frame of mind for sleeping.

ballet   A ballet, or any other dance performed for others or even in rehearsal, represents the way you currently "choreograph" your life. **1.** A beautiful, flowing ballet filled with talented dancers means things are running not only smoothly, but beautifully for you right now. **2.** If you are one of the dancers in a ballet, your place in the show represents how you see your place in your current life situation—are you the lead dancer or someone stuck in the back of the chorus? **3.** A ballet gone wrong, with accidents, falls, and mistakes, means things in your life aren't going very well right now. You might need to rechoreograph your current situation by getting more organized or replacing a few key cast members. See also *ballerina, dancing.* ☾ **clumsy** ☾ *creativity, identity, sports and games, success.*

balloon   Balloons represent your hopes and dreams. **1.** If you let a balloon free, you have given up a hope, but this has been an important step for your growth. Be happy you have set this free. **2.** If a balloon pops, a hope has burst and you weren't ready for it. You may need to spend some time mourning the loss of this dream. **3.** If you carry a balloon proudly, you still hold on to a particular dream with pride and joy. If people admire your balloon, you feel confident that you will achieve this dream. ☾ **disappointment** ☾ *goal-setting, hopes and dreams, inanimate objects, personal power, wishes.*

banana   This classic phallic symbol represents the male sex organ. Do you relish the taste? Can't stand it? Peel it lovingly? Or has it gone rotten? All these attitudes reveal how you feel right now about masculinity in general, either your own or masculinity in someone else. If you are currently involved in a passionate relationship, your attitudes and actions toward the banana might affect your feelings toward that person. Or maybe you just need to eat more fruit. See also *fruit.* ☾ **doughnut** ☾ *food, fruit, masculinity, sexual activity, yin-yang.*

band   Music moves the world, and to play in a band for an audience means you want to make a positive impact on the world, either in a subtle way as a back-up singer, or in a big way as a singer or lead guitarist. **1.** To play the drums in a band means you set the pace for everyone around you. **2.** To play in a marching band means you need to go somewhere to deliver your message. **3.** To listen to a band means something or someone has made an impact on you, possibly changing your perceptions about life. ☾ **silence** ☾ *changing course, music and sound, personal power.*

bandages You've been wounded. Can you bandage yourself, or do you need a nurse? Bandages symbolize the need for healing, and your dream begs you to take care of yourself or let someone else help you to heal. ◐ **wounds** ℭ *accidents, body parts, healing, inanimate objects, injuries.*

bank Something's up with your financial situation or with your work life. **1.** If you withdraw money from a bank, you are worried about having enough money or enough credibility at work. **2.** If your bank account is empty, you've lost your leverage. You need to start living within your means before you've lost all credibility. **3.** If you rob a bank, you aren't sure whether what you are about to do is the right thing. **4.** If you dream the ATM is giving you more money than you actually have, someone is trying to tell you how much you mean to them. See also *money.* ◐ **bankruptcy** ℭ *buildings and rooms, financial issues, places, reputation.*

bankruptcy You're worried you're losing it all—money, perhaps, but bankruptcy dreams often represent spiritual bankruptcy. Do you feel you've compromised? Sold out? It's not too late to start saving again for a better future. See also *bank, poverty.* ◐ **rich** ℭ *ethics and morals, financial issues, loss, reputation.*

baptism Hallelujah, you want to start over with a clean slate. Forgive yourself and move on. See also *religious ceremonies.* ◐ **bad habits**

ℭ *changing course, forgiveness, solutions and remedies.*

bar What kind of bar did you dream about? Hanging around in a neighborhood bar means you crave a sense of community and belonging. A nightclub represents your desire to let loose and go a little crazy. Getting drunk in a bar means you fear loss of control in public. ◐ **privacy** ℭ *buildings and rooms, communication, places, relationships, reputation.*

bar fight Did you start it or just get caught in the middle? Or are you hiding under a table hoping nobody sees you? Bar fights represent a loss of control, either in you or in others. The real fight exists somewhere in your waking life. What role will you play? Be careful. ◐ **nonviolence, self-control** ℭ *control issues, violence.*

Barbie doll See *doll.*

barefoot Take off your shoes and feel the earth under your feet. Going barefoot in a dream means you need to get out of your head and into your body, and feel your own two feet on the ground. **1.** Going barefoot outside calls you to spend more time close to the earth. **2.** Going barefoot in public means you should approach a situation more honestly and naturally. Stop putting on such a show. **3.** Embarrassment about being barefoot in a situation where everybody else wears shoes means you are self-conscious about being less prepared than others. Dig your toes into the sand and get up to speed. ☾ **shoes** ☾ *body parts, embarrassment, nature, vulnerability.*

barricade   See *barrier.*

barrier   A barrier can take many forms: a wall, a roadblock, a fence, even a velvet rope like they use in movie theaters. But barriers in dreams all mean the same thing: something holds you back. Is it something you did, something someone else did, a situation, money, status, your own sense of decency? Think about what you want and what really is holding you back in your waking life. Should you get rid of the barrier or go a different route? The situation surrounding the barrier in your dream will give you clues. ☾ **running** ☾ *direction, frustration, impediments, journeys and quests, resistance, travel.*

baseball   This all-American sport represents wholesome values. **1.** If you play baseball and you do well or enjoy yourself, your life satisfies you on a deep emotional level. **2.** If you get benched or make errors in the game, you feel compromised in some way in your life. How can you get out of that slump and back in the game? **3.** If you watch a baseball game, you have a plan for feeling more comfortable with your life. ☾ **crime** ☾ *comfort, competition, ethics and morals, goal-setting, inanimate objects, play, sports and games, success.*

B

baseball bat   Baseball bats symbolize the action we take to make things happen. **1.** Swinging a baseball bat means you are ready to take action. **2.** Hitting the ball means your current plan will be successful. **3.** Hitting a home run means you are right on target and your success will be dramatic. **4.** Missing the ball means, metaphorically, that you have "missed the ball" and are interpreting or doing something wrong. It's time to try a different approach, or bat. ☾ **pillow** ☾ *inanimate objects, journeys and quests, personal power, play, sports and games.*

basement   The basement of a house symbolizes your hidden inner desires and your deep-seated instinctual (what's that smell?) side. This is the *you* you don't show the world but that lurks within, for better or for worse. The condition of the basement represents the current condition of your instinctual (there's that smell again) side, your deepest urges and desires. **1.** A dark, frightening basement signifies your recognition that parts of you scare even you. That's okay; that's why you keep them in the basement. Look at them when you are ready. **2.** A pleasant, clean, lighted, well-organized basement means you have nothing to hide. **3.** A basement you didn't know was there means you have the potential to feel things you haven't felt before. You may be about to discover new emotions and strong urges or desires you've always kept hidden away. It's time to go down there and explore. See also *house.* ☯ **attic** ℭ *buildings and rooms, fear, home, instincts, places, repression, secrets.*

basketball Basketball dreams symbolize engagement in life—the way you coordinate all your efforts to reach your goals, particularly in your career or primary work. **1.** Making baskets means you are right on target and what you do right now works. **2.** Missing baskets means your aim is off. Can you create a new play for your current project or goal? This one isn't working. **3.** Watching basketball means you are considering strategies for handling a new project or goal, and you have ideas but you haven't settled on a plan just yet. It might help to get up off the couch. ☯ **fired from a job** ℭ *career, competition, goal-setting, inanimate objects, play, sports and games, success.*

bath See *showers and baths.*

bathing suit See *bikini.*

bathroom Keep the door closed, will ya? Bathrooms symbolize hygiene, health, and bodily functions best kept private. **1.** Dreaming of a dirty bathroom means you need to clean up your act, physically or morally. **2.** Clean, sparkling bathrooms mean you have squeaky-clean habits or morals. **3.** Flushing something down a toilet shows a desperate attempt to separate yourself from an association. If the toilet overflows, your attempts aren't working. Whatever it is has come back up so you can deal with it. **4.** If people can see you while you are in the bathroom, you are self-conscious about what you have done or who you are. 5. To dream of "going to the bathroom" (urinating or defecating) represents letting something pass through you. You've gotten rid of something unpleasant. It's gone, and you feel better and 10 pounds lighter. ☯ **dirt** ℭ *buildings and rooms, dirt, ethics and morals, health and hygiene, home, places, water.*

bats Dark and scary, out-of-control flapping overhead, potentially blood-sucking … most people fear bats, and bats in dreams represent fear. We all have fears, and bat dreams can help you recognize the place these fears play in your waking life. **1.** If you are attacked, bitten, or touched by a bat, you don't feel safe. Your fears directly affect you right now. **2.** If you see a bat but don't feel afraid, or you have a bat as a pet, you are mastering your fears. **3.** Seeing bats in a cave means you've put your fears somewhere for safe-keeping, but they still exist within you and could flap out, screeching, at any time. **4.** To see bats flying overhead means your fears remain active in your life but don't immediately threaten you. ☯ **doves** ℭ *animals, crawling creatures, fear, nature, threats.*

battery Dream of this compact energy source, and you'll get clues to where you can get more energy.

1. Finding a battery means you have recently found a new source of energy. You might not realize what it is until you look at where you found the battery in your dream. **2.** If you have a battery inside you, you've been running like the Energizer bunny and you need to slow down. Find your off switch. **3.** Seeing or installing a battery in a toy signifies your discovery of how to make a situation work better. **4.** Dreaming of something running out of batteries means you've exhausted a current resource and you'll need to change something if you want the situation, or person, to keep working. ☯ **lazy** ℂ *electronics, health and hygiene, inanimate objects, solutions and remedies, technology.*

beach   The warm sand, sun, and soothing water portray the ultimate escape and represent the way you handle stress. **1.** If you relax on a beach, you have good stress-management skills and you are actively employing them. **2.** If you are buried in sand, you are protecting yourself from something to avoid the stress. If someone else buries you, someone else is protecting you. **3.** If the beach is stormy, dark, or dangerous, or a tidal wave or hurricane threaten, you are feeling stressed out by a recent change or impending life change. Do you run for it, are you most worried about protecting others, or do you stand up and wait for it to hit you full force? These are clues about how you have decided to handle the stress of this change. See also *coastline, rip tide, storm, surfing, tidal wave, water, waves.* ☯ **job** ℂ *electronics, health and hygiene, places, solutions and remedies, technology.*

bear   Bears mean danger to some, the wild adventure of nature to others, but if a bear attacks you, you are grappling with a difficult issue. Did you conquer, or did the bear get the best of you? To see a bear from far away means you have avoided a problem so far, but keep paying attention so it doesn't surprise you. Remember to treat all bears as individuals. ☯ **rabbit** ℂ *adventure, animals, danger, fear, impediments, nature, threats, violence.*

beard   Grow a beard, and you've been acting more mature lately. Shave a beard, and you've moved on to something new. ☯ **baldness** ℂ *age, changing course.*

beauty contest   If you are in one, you have great concern for your appearance right now and you've been spending too much time comparing yourself with others. **1.** If you win, you have high self-esteem but you might be focusing a little too obsessively on superficial things. **2.** If you lose, you feel unattractive, physically or emotionally. See also *contest.* ☯ **ugliness** ℂ *anxiety, beauty, ego.*

beauty pageant   See *beauty contest.*

beauty parlor   See *salon.*

bed   See *bedroom, furniture.*

bedroom   Your bedroom is your sanctum of intimacy, where you can undress; unwind; be passionate; or just relax, read a good book, and fall asleep. Bedroom dreams reveal your relationship with yourself and with those you are most intimate with. In the best of dreams, bedrooms reveal the source of your inner creativity. **1.** To dream you are in bed and comfortably relaxed means you feel comfortable in your current situation and your creativity is flowing. **2.** To dream of having pleasurable sex in the bedroom means you feel comfortable and contented with your intimate relationships right now. **3.** Dreams of extremely passionate sex in the bedroom can indicate that your creative power is particularly high right now. You are capable of greatness. **4.** High anxiety, insomnia, restlessness, violence, nightmares, invasions of privacy, or other unpleasant experiences in the bedroom indicate intimacy problems. You aren't getting enough, or you aren't getting intimacy that makes you feel safe. **5.** A locked bedroom symbolizes your inability or unwillingness to feel intimacy at this point in your life. Are you pulling the covers up over your head? See also *sex.* ☽ **living room** ☾ *buildings and rooms, comfort, creation, furniture and appliances, home, places, pleasure, protection, sexual activity.*

beer   Drinking beer in your dream means you feel a part of the group and you enjoy spending time with your friends. Have you been neglecting them lately? Beer dreams urge you to reach out and spend time with others. However, watching others drink beer means you feel left out, and if you drink beer in your dream but you don't drink alcohol in waking life, you want to cross a line you've established for yourself. It may have nothing to do with drinking. Make sure it's a good idea before you compromise your personal code. Binge-drinking dreams mean you need to reign yourself in a little bit. Maybe you've been seeing *too* much of your friends. See also *alcohol, bingeing.* ☽ **abstinence, loneliness** ☾ *addictions, desires, ethics and morals, food and drink, fun, pleasure, relationships, risky behavior.*

Dried hop flowers give beer its pleasantly bitter taste, but did you know they might just help you sleep? An old folk remedy for helping to encourage a good sound night's sleep is to fill a pillow with flowers from the hop vine and sleep on it. Drinking a beer beforehand can actually cancel out the effect because alcohol can sometimes make sleep more restless and increase wakefulness during the night.

bees   Hard work and team spirit produce the sweetness of life, and dreams about bees show your own ability, or desire, to emulate these qualities. However, if a bee stings you in your dream, you've been lax in your duties and other people are having to pick up your slack. ☽ **lazy** ☾ *animals, crawling creatures, nature, pain, responsibilities, work.*

beggar   See *homeless person*.

belly button   Are you an innie or an outtie? Dreams of this vulnerable spot reveal how well your most intimate needs are being met. **1.** If you show off your belly button, you feel ready to be openly vulnerable in an intimate relationship. **2.** If something is wrong with your belly button, or it is missing, nobody is meeting your needs. You feel emotionally and physically neglected. **3.** If you dream that you have a pierced belly button, or see someone else with a pierced belly button, you have the courage and desire to explore more daring and exciting contact in your intimate relationships. ☽ **brain** ☾ *body parts, caretaking, sexual activity.*

berries   Luscious and juicy, berries represent pleasure, passion, and simply joy. **1.** Eating or picking berries symbolizes your quest for pleasure. **2.** Spilling or overflowing containers of berries, or berries bursting open from juiciness, means you have indulged yourself plenty and it might be time for a little restraint. **3.** Dry, withered, or rotten berries mean you've denied yourself pleasure for too long. ☽ **deprivation** ☾ *food and drink, hedonism, pleasure, sexual activity.*

best friend   Together forever, blood brothers, pinky sisters, the person who knows more about you than you know about yourself .... Your best friend represents your ability to bond with another human being. **1.** A best friend standing up for you means you feel supported in the world. **2.** Your best friend betraying you means you sense instability in your current situation. Watch your back. **3.** If your best friend is a dog or cat, you are a natural leader and people look to you for guidance. **4.** If your best friend in your dream is someone you've never actually met, your current project has great potential to succeed. See also *betrayal, dog, friends, love.* ☽ **enemy** ☾ *caretaking, characters, comfort, loyalty, people, relationships, social life.*

betrayal   To dream someone betrays you means you don't trust that person, or someone that person represents. To betray someone else means you don't trust yourself. ☽ **best friend** ☾ *anxiety, ethics and morals, fear, loyalty, relationships, risky behavior, trust issues.*

bicycle   See *bike*.

Big Foot   Saskwatch, Yeti, the Abominable Snowman—large apelike creatures walking on two legs have been spotted all over the world for many years, although nobody has ever proved what these mysterious skulking creatures really are. To dream of them represents a huge and hidden secret, either yours or someone else's. **1.** If you pursue Big Foot, you want to let the secret out or find out what it is. **2.** If you run or hide from Big Foot, you aren't ready for this secret to come out. **3.** If you see Big Foot momentarily but then he is gone, you think you know someone else's secrets, but you aren't sure. We're talkin' *big* secrets. ☻ **naked** ℂ *animals, characters, fear, myths and legends, nature, people, secrets.*

bike   Riding a bike means getting somewhere on your own steam, and bicycle dreams mean you have the power to make it happen, whatever it is, in your waking life. **1.** To ride through beautiful countryside on a bike symbolizes your own personal power to harness the beauty and wonder of the world around you. You don't just move through life unaware; you really live it. **2.** To crash on a bike means you have experienced a setback. **3.** To work on fixing a bike means you can fix this problem you've been dealing with. **4.** To win a bike race means you can go all the way with this. **5.** To ride on an exercise bike inside means you succeed at fulfilling your responsibilities, but you don't feel you are really going anywhere in your current situation. ☻ **paralyzed** ℂ *competition, control issues, direction, goal-setting, inanimate objects, journeys and quests, personal power, play, sports and games, travel, vehicles, work.*

bikini   Bikinis show almost everything, and they symbolize how revealing you want to be, either physically or emotionally. **1.** If you wear a bikini and feel great in your dream, you are enjoying self-confidence and personal power right now. You want the world to see how fantastic you are. **2.** If you wear a bikini and feel self-conscious and embarrassed, you want to keep your private life to yourself. You aren't ready to share certain things. **3.** To look at other people in bikinis means you find the private lives of others very interesting. ☻ **blanket** ℂ *clothing and accessories, personal power, protection, vulnerability.*

billboard   These mega-signs send messages in the least subtle way, and billboards in dreams do the same. Whatever words or pictures show up on a billboard in your dream represent something your subconscious mind insists that you know, even if you don't quite yet know that you know it. Read the billboard! See also *sign.* ☻ **secret** ℂ *communication, inanimate objects, messages, shapes and symbols.*

bills and debts   Whether or not you feel burdened by bills and debts in your waking life, dreams of these burdens symbolize any burden you currently carry. You may be stretched too thin emotionally, physically, or financially. In any case, you need to replenish whatever savings account you've drained. See also *credit card.* ☻ **rich** ℂ *burdens, financial issues, responsibilities.*

bingeing   Whether you've spoiled your diet or fallen off the wagon, dreams of bingeing—on food, alcohol, drugs, sex, or any other indulgence—don't doom you to binge in real life. Instead, they suggest that you feel drastically deprived of something. This might not be the thing you binge on in your dream, but whatever that thing represents. Find those voids in your life and fill them in healthful ways before you find yourself bingeing for real. ❧ **deprivation** ❧ *abundance, addictions, extremism, food and drink, greed, hedonism, risky behavior.*

bird flu   See *disease.*

birds   Birds represent many things, depending on their numbers, color, and placement in your dream, but in general, birds represent freedom from the bounds of earthly existence. **1.** A flock of soaring birds represents your desire to break free from your obligations and burdens to be more than you feel you are right now. **2.** A flock of birds that follows you or gathers around menacingly means you are afraid of something you can't control. **3.** White birds symbolize peace and goodwill. **4.** Black birds symbolize a message, either good or bad. **5.** Blue birds point you to what will make you happier. **6.** Red birds symbolize where your heart is. **7.** Yellow birds demonstrate how you can express your joyful feelings. **8.** Tropical birds symbolize your desire to travel. **9.** Birds of prey, like eagles, hawks, and falcons, represent your ambition and your survival skills, showing you how to get what you need and want. How high can you fly? What do you think that mouse represents? See also *chicken, dove, duck, flying, pigeon.* ❧ **turtle** ❧ *birds, control issues, escape, fear,*

freedom, happiness, success, travel, wishes.

B

birth   Dreaming of birth symbolizes a new beginning. You've already started something, or you are ready to start something in your life. Birth dreams can also symbolize the desire to take care of something or to become a parent. In some cases, dreaming of giving birth can mean you are pregnant, but more often, it means you would like to be, or feel ready to try. **1.** If you dream you are giving birth, you've created something amazing, or you are ready to create something. Your creative energy is strong right now. **2.** If you dream of giving birth and you really are pregnant, you are trying out various birth scenarios in your dreams to mentally prepare yourself for the real event. If something bad happens during your birth dream, fear not. You are just acting out your fears, not predicting anything dire. **3.** If you dream of having a Cesarean section or other birth process with medical intervention or emergency, your current creative process might take some forcing or be emotionally painful. **4.** If you dream of watching someone else give birth, you are aware of, or envious of, someone else's creative potential. If you help with the birth, you are part of a creative process that involves others. **5.** If you dream of an animal giving birth, the natural world has something to teach you right now. See also *baby, baby animal, child or children, in vitro* *fertilization.* ☽ **death** ☾ *caretaking, changing course, creation, creativity, desires, family, fear, hopes and dreams, medicine and surgery, personal power, transformation.*

birth control   See *contraception.*

birthmark   Birthmarks, like signatures on your body, represent a message from your body to you. **1.** To dream you have a birthmark you don't actually have means you need to pay attention to a change in your body or health. Have you been ignoring some symptoms? It's probably nothing serious, but you should have it checked out. Your body is wise, and it's smart to listen. **2.** If you dream that a birthmark you do have is gone, you've recently left a part of yourself behind and you are ready for a change. ☽ **blanket** ☾ *body parts, health and hygiene, messages.*

bisexuality   Some people think everyone is a little bit bisexual, but dreams of being bisexual, or encountering a bisexual, or having or seeing someone with both male and female sex organs, doesn't mean you really are bisexual. No, not even if you enjoy the dream. These totally normal and common dreams more likely indicate that you have tapped into both the male and female energies within yourself or others (we all have them), and that makes you a more well-rounded, understanding, and internally balanced person. See also *androgyny, sex.* ☽ **heterosexual, homosexual**

☾ *balance, feminine, masculine, sexual activity, yin-yang.*

bite   Biting is an instinctual, animal reaction signaling fear or desperation. **1.** To bite someone means you feel the need to defend yourself on an instinctual level, out of self-defense and fear. What are you afraid of? **2.** To be bitten by a person means you fear someone on an instinctual level. **3.** To be bitten by an animal means you are feeling anxiety about a problem and you don't know how to solve it. See also *attacked, vampire.* ☽ **kissing** ☾ *animals, anxiety, danger, fear, instincts, violence, vulnerability.*

black   Black can take many forms in dreams, but it usually represents leaving something behind, a major change, or, in some cases, sadness and depression. However, it depends on what is black. **1.** A black animal—cat, horse, dog, bird—is a sign that you have experienced or are soon to experience a major change and you have some anxiety about what it will be like. Black animals can also sometimes deliver important messages from your subconscious. **2.** Black sky, black water, and black or dark rooms, houses, and furniture represent sadness, depression, or an oppressive fear or anxiety you feel unable to conquer. **3.** Black objects—tools, weapons, household items—represent a job you have to do that you don't want to do. **4.** Black masks, disguises, capes, and clothing represent something you want to hide from others, or even yourself. **5.** Black put together with white represents balance, equality, and a new vision of how things work together. See also *cat, darkness, dog, horse, storm, water.* ☽ **white** ℭ *anxiety, balance, changing course, clothing and accessories, color, messages, secrets, subterfuge, weather and seasons, yin-yang.*

black horse   See *horse.*

blackout   If all the lights go out, you can't or don't want to see something in your waking life that is keeping you from functioning at your best. If the blackout is caused by a disaster like a nuclear explosion or invasion, what you don't want to see is causing you great anxiety. See also *black, darkness.* ☽ **light** ℭ *anxiety, confusion, danger, disaster, fear, secrets, subterfuge.*

blaming others   **1.** If you dream of blaming others for something you actually did, you are trying to shift the focus away from yourself because of something you know you have done but don't really want to face. **2.** If you dream of blaming others for something others did, you feel powerful and capable of exerting your own authority and sense of right and wrong upon others. If in your waking life such finger-pointing would be inappropriate, you may be acting out these self-righteous feelings in your dream. ☽ **guilty conscience** ℭ *dishonesty, ethics and morals, guilt, relationships, repression, subterfuge.*

blank screen   To dream of a blank screen means you feel stymied by a situation. You don't know how to react, what to say or do. Blank screens can also symbolize a snag or problem you didn't expect to encounter. You might have to start over. ☽ **fixing something** ℭ *communication, confusion, inanimate objects, technology.*

blanket   Blankets keep you warm, but they also cover you up, and blanket dreams represent either the need for comfort and nurturing or shame. You want to feel safe, or you don't want anyone to see you. Or both. ☽ **naked** ℭ *caretaking, comfort, inanimate objects, insecurity, protection, subterfuge, vulnerability.*

blender or food processor   You have everything you need, but you need to mix them all up to get what you want. **1.** Making something in a blender or food processor means you know how to put it all together. You are managing things. **2.** Food exploding out of a blender or food processor means you are losing control of a situation you are supposed to be managing. **3.** Getting injured, or injuring someone else, with a blender or food processor means you don't feel confident in your current role and you fear you might damage someone or something. Maybe it's time to ask for some help. ☽ **lost** ℭ *accidents, control issues, food and drink, furniture and appliances, inanimate objects, injuries, responsibilities, success.*

blindness   See *vision problems.*

bling   Bedecked with bling, you feel valuable and confident. Envying someone else's bling? Someone else has something you want. See also *gold, jewelry.* ☾ **poverty** ℂ *abundance, beauty, envy, financial issues, happiness, inanimate objects.*

blister   You've overdone it. A blister means you've said or done too much and you need to stop so things get back to normal. **1.** A blister on your foot means things are moving too quickly. **2.** A blister on your hand means you should stay out of something you've been interfering in. **3.** A blister on any sexual organ means you have been flirting (or more) with someone you shouldn't. Your dream is telling you to back off or risk a problem. See also *disease.* ☾ **privacy** ℂ *body parts, control issues, injuries, relationships, risky behavior, sexual activity, solutions and remedies.*

blizzard   See *snow, storm.*

blond hair   No jokes, please. Blond hair represents beauty, lightness of thought, innocence, and passion. **1.** To dream you are blonde when you aren't actually means you feel lighter, freer, and younger, possibly because you have recently forgiven yourself for something or shed a great burden. **2.** To dream of someone with blond hair means you see that person, or someone that person represents, as physically and spiritually attractive.

3. Hair obviously dyed blond, either on you or someone else, represents a trick. Someone (is it you?) isn't as innocent as they pretend to be. ☾ **darkness** ℂ *beauty, body parts, color, forgiveness, happiness, innocence, pleasure.*

blood   The vital essence flowing through your veins, pumped by your heart and delivering nutrients to your entire body, is an important part of what keeps you alive, and dreams about blood usually indicate something equally vital about survival or passion. **1.** Bleeding in your dream represents the passion and creativity you give to the world. You live what you believe, possibly to the extreme. **2.** To have blood on your hands means you feel guilty about something you did. **3.** To see blood on someone else, or cause someone else to bleed, means someone is sacrificing something for you, or giving everything they have to a situation in which you are involved. **4.** To see words written in blood symbolizes something very important you must admit or understand. **5.** Blood associated with a traumatic accident means you or someone else has given up too much. It's time to replenish inner resources. See also *injuries, menstruation.* ☾ **water** ℂ *accidents, creation, extremism, guilt, injuries, messages, sacrifice.*

blue   Blue signifies inner tranquility, calm, and contentment. **1.** Blue animals reveal what makes you happy. **2.** Blue sky means you feel optimistic and you have bound-less opportunities. **3.** Blue water suggests you have a satisfying and nurturing relationship with others. ☻ **red** ☾ *caretaking, color, happiness, opportunity, relationships, water.*

Studies show that color affects mood. According to color researchers, blue has a soothing effect and people can actually experience a drop in blood pressure just by looking at blue.

---

boat   Water represents passion, sex, and the fluid movement of your life's journey. A boat is your tool for navigating these conditions. **1.** A boat moving freely through calm waters signifies your steady progress in the pursuit of your passions—career, hobby, or rela-tionship. **2.** Struggling on a boat through stormy waters or crashing a boat means you are fighting against what feels natural to you. You need to reassess how you approach the things that matter most to you right now. **3.** A boat stranded on dry land means you've lost the way. You've forgotten what truly excites and motivates you, or the passion has left your relationship. See also *storm, water.* ☻ **camel** ☾ *inanimate objects, journeys and quests, travel, vehicles, water.*

body   The body is your own per-sonal vehicle through life, and any body part, in a dream, represents some part of your life. Look up individual body parts for the mean-ings of these. Your entire body represents your life's purpose. **1.** To dream your body is stronger, taller, or more perfect than in real-ity means you have clear goals and you feel good about achieving them. **2.** To dream your body is injured means you have suffered a setback. Your life isn't going the way you thought it would, or you have been hurt or affected by something in a way that has deeply altered your view of your own life. **3.** To dream you have someone else's body or body parts means you don't feel some part of your life fits. Are you pretending to be someone you're not? Remember Frankenstein? See also *amputation, injuries, piercing.* ☻ **soul** ☾ *body parts, journeys and quests, personal power.*

body piercing   See *piercing.*

bomb   See *explosion.*

bones   Your bones give you struc-ture, stability, and mobility, and dreams of bones offer clues about how structured and stable your life is. **1.** If you see your bones in a dream but you aren't injured, you have imposed a strict structure on your life. **2.** If your bones break, your stability has been threatened. You might need to change the way you've structured your life—how much you work, how you take care of yourself, your priorities—before it all comes crashing down. **3.** If you see someone else's bones or a skeleton, you can see right through someone else. You know exactly what they're up to. See also *body, injuries, skeleton.* ☽ **skin** ☾ *body parts, injuries, stability.*

booing   What could be more humiliating? Just when you think the crowd loves you, the booing and hissing begin. **1.** If you dream you're being booed, you feel embarrassed or insecure about something, even if nobody knows about it. You've suffered a blow to the ego and you're extra vulnerable right now. **2.** If the booing makes you angry, you feel like you've been treated unjustly in your waking life. **3.** If you feel you deserve the booing, then you are feeling guilty. **4.** If you boo someone else in a dream, you haven't been very nice lately. Who have you been picking on? Do they really deserve that kind of treatment? See also *audience.* ☽ **applause** ☾ *anxiety, embarrassment, ego, failure, injustice, insecurity, vulnerability.*

book   Books tell your story, and when you dream about books, you dream about the story of your own life, direction, and the entire cast of characters that give your life color and meaning. **1.** Reading a book means you see your life as an interesting adventure. **2.** Writing a book means you feel engaged in the creation of your own life and being. **3.** Destroying a book means you don't like the way your life is going and you want to shift direction. What would you title a book about you? ☽ **painting** ☾ *adventure, changing course, characters, decisions, inanimate objects, journeys and quests.*

boots   Dreams about work boots mean you are working hard. Dreams about cowboy boots mean you crave adventure and freedom. Dreams about fashionable boots mean you don't want someone to know where you are going. ☽ **shoes** ☾ *adventure, clothing and accessories, freedom, inanimate objects, subterfuge, work.*

border   Crossing a border means you've made an important change or transition in your life. Sneaking across a border illegally means you aren't sure this change will go over well with others, or you aren't quite ready to reveal the new you to others. Or maybe the others aren't ready for the new you? ☽ **circle** ☾ *adventure, changing course, decisions, journeys and quests, places, transformation.*

boredom   See *monotony.*

boss   Who's the boss? If you dream of your boss, you might really be dreaming about yourself, or you could be dreaming about what direction you want or need to take in your career. **1.** If your boss praises you, you are on the right track and you might just be ready to move up. **2.** If your boss yells at or criticizes you, you just might be criticizing yourself for something. Consider the context to see what it is. **3.** If your boss ignores you, you feel unappreciated in your work life. **4.** If you yell at or criticize your boss, you feel frustrated with authority and would like to have more control over your own life. **5.** If you have a romantic or sexual dream about your boss, you desire more power in your working life. (Or you really do desire your boss.) **6.** If your boss is someone other than your boss in waking life, that person, or someone that person represents, has some power over you in a different area of your life. ☻ **servant** ℂ *authority, career, characters, control issues, ego, people, work.*

bowling   Did you get a strike or a gutter ball? Bowling symbolizes how successful you are, or how successful you feel. If you watch other people bowl, you feel like you aren't even in the game. ☻ **fired from a job** ℂ *career, competition, goal-setting, personal power, play, sports and games, success.*

box   Whatever is inside a box in your dream is important to you. You want to protect it, or you want to keep it away from you. An empty box symbolizes the loss of something important. Your car keys? Your ideals? ☻ **escape** ℂ *caretaking, fear, inanimate objects, loss, protection.*

boy   Dreams about boys signify youthful power and energy. **1.** If you are a girl and you dream you are a boy, you have accessed your inner male. You need extra energy and strength right now, so your dream has summoned it up for you. **2.** If you dream you meet or talk to a boy, you are seeking your own inner power. **3.** If a boy acts violent, mean, or out-of-control, you fear what might happen if you really tap

into your own power. See also *child or children, man.* ☻ **girl** ℂ *age, body parts, gender issues, masculine, people, personal power.*

boyfriend   Support, affection, a steady date on Friday nights … boyfriends in dreams usually represent this kind of underlying support, although this theme can vary depending on who he is and what he does. **1.** If you dream about your actual boyfriend, he is an important part of your life and comfortably nestled inside your subconscious (and if you never dream about your actual boyfriend, you may not be all that deeply committed). **2.** If you have a good dream about a boyfriend you don't actually have, you crave that falling-in-love feeling, or maybe just more amorous physical contact. **3.** If you dream a boyfriend is unpleasant, rude, cruel, or violent, someone you trust has betrayed you. **4.** If you dream of having sex with your boyfriend, the environment and whether you enjoy the experience in your dream can clue you in to how you really feel about your sexuality. **5.** If you dream you steal someone's boyfriend, or someone steals your boyfriend, or you or your boyfriend cheat on each other, you don't trust yourself or someone else to be loyal. **6.** If you are a heterosexual male and you dream you have a boyfriend and the dream bothers you, you feel overpowered or submissive in your current relationship. If you enjoy the dream, this does not necessarily mean you actually desire a boyfriend. This dream means you are balanced in your male-female energies in a healthy way. ☽ **girl-friend** ℂ *characters, comfort, gender issues, guilt, identity, love, loyalty, masculine, people, sexual activity, support, trust issues.*

bra It's underwear, it's lingerie, but most important, it's *support* where you really need it. **1.** Dreaming about wearing a bra or putting on a bra means you need more support related to a subject very close to you. **2.** If you are a man and you dream of wearing a bra, you have been feeling burdened by responsibilities and you wish someone would share the load. **3.** If you dream that people see you in your bra, you feel exposed and insecure. You wish people didn't know quite so much about you. If you enjoy being seen in your bra, however, you feel so emotionally supported that you can dare anything. **4.** If you take off someone else's bra, you want to be closer to someone else's heart. Or thereabouts. ☽ **falling** ℂ *burdens, caretaking, clothing and accessories, comfort, feminine, inanimate objects, love, support.*

bracelet If you dream someone gives you a bracelet, that person, or someone they represent, means well but wants to control you. ☽ **escape** ℂ *control issues, clothing and accessories, inanimate objects.*

braces Braces straighten your teeth, and dreams of braces symbolize the rules you make for yourself—your health habits, your ethics, your personal code. **1.** To dream you have braces means you feel the need to more closely follow the straight-and-narrow path. You feel you've been too loose and careless in your words or actions lately, and your dream is telling you to enact some structure. Can you be more precise about just what your own personal code really says? **2.** If braces hurt or cut your mouth, you've recently spoken words that have hurt someone else. **3.** If you dream you have your braces removed, your rules for yourself might be a little too constraining and you can afford to loosen up. See also *teeth.* ☽ **decadence** ℂ *body parts, clothing and accessories, control issues, ethics and morals, health and hygiene, inanimate objects, pain, rules and laws.*

brain What were you thinking? Dreams about the brain signify your intellectual side. **1.** An exposed brain means you feel like others around you might be smarter. **2.** Dreaming you have a brain tumor or need brain surgery symbolizes that you might not be giving enough attention to your intellectual side. Have you been too emotional lately? **3.** Dreaming your brain is larger than normal means you might be giving *too* much attention to your intellectual side. You can't rationalize everything. ☽ **belly button** ℂ *ego, insecurity, intelligence, medicine and surgery.*

Changes in brain waves indicate when people are dreaming, as well as other stages of sleep and wakefulness. Scientists can measure this brain activity with an electroencephalograph, or EEG. This device showed sleep scientists in the 1950s that dream sleep was actually a period of very high brain activity rather than low brain activity, as they previously believed.

brakes not working   This common dream can be frightening and symbolizes that something has gotten out of control. You might be intimidated by a new situation—are you afraid you have more responsibility than you can handle? Or you've set something in motion that is now rolling along without you and you couldn't stop it if you tried. See also *car accident*. ◐ **stop signs and stoplights** ℂ *accidents, control issues, fear, responsibilities, technology, vehicles.*

branches   See *trees.*

bread   They call it the staff of life, and bread is one of humankind's most basic foods, even if low-carb diets frown on it. Dreams of bread symbolize nourishment at its most basic. **1.** To dream of eating bread means you feel like you have what you truly need in your life right now. **2.** To dream of sharing bread means you find your relationship with someone deeply rewarding. **3.** Moldy, stale, or otherwise spoiled bread signifies a relationship gone

bad. See also *bakery, baking.* ◐ **water** ℂ *food and drink, health and hygiene, relationships.*

breakfast   Start your day out right with a good dream about breakfast, which symbolizes beginnings. **1.** A pleasant, hearty, or refreshing breakfast symbolizes an auspicious beginning to a progress. **2.** Dreams of an unpleasant, tension-ridden breakfast means things have gotten off to a bad start. **3.** Skipping breakfast means you've missed something. Go back and look again. ◐ **dinner** ℂ *creation, food and drink, goal-setting.*

breaking free   Breaking free in a dream, whether from prison, a trap, a locked room, or someone else holding you, symbolizes your desire to break free from a situation or relationship in your waking life. ◐ **imprisoned** ℂ *courage, desires, escape, freedom.*

breaking something   Broken objects in dreams signify broken dreams, broken promises, and broken convictions. **1.** Broken dishes, cups, glasses, and chipped pottery suggest you've compromised your morals or beliefs. **2.** Broken toys suggest you've lost your youthful spirit. **3.** Broken glass or a broken window means your illusions have shattered and you have a clearer vision of the truth. **4.** Breaking electronic equipment or technology symbolizes your desire to get back to a more basic, less complicated way of life. **5.** Breaking a promise means you didn't really mean what you said to someone. **6.** Broken bones mean your inner stability has been compromised. **7.** If you break something while in a rage, you've lost control of a situation. See also *bones, breaking up, glass, promise, toys*. ☽ **fixing something** ℭ *accidents, anger, ethics and morals, frustration, injuries, pain, technology*.

breaking up   Breaking up with your boyfriend, girlfriend, or spouse in a dream can signal your wish to break up, your fear that you could break up, or simply the need for a change in your relationship. Break-up dreams can also symbolize anger you have been hiding, even to yourself, or trust issues you have. If you dream of breaking up with your partner, it might symbolize your desire for payback or your fear that your partner will break up with you and your desire to do it first, to save your own feelings. What does your intuition tell you? Break-up dreams can also signify the end of one stage and the beginning of another in your relationship to others, not necessarily your romantic partner. ☽ **marriage** ℭ *anger, changing course, decisions, escape, fear, freedom, love, relationships, trust issues*.

breasts   Nourishers and nurturers, breasts symbolize both maternal and passionate nurturing. **1.** To dream you have larger breasts than you actually do means you have the capacity and desire to nurture others even more than you are doing right now, or you have recently been doing more nurturing than usual. **2.** To dream you have breasts if you are a man means you have the opportunity to nurture someone right now, but you will have to tap into your softer side. Don't tell that person what to do. Try listening. **3.** To dream of breastfeeding a baby means your maternal instincts have been activated. To dream of breast-feeding an adult means someone feels helpless and needs you. **4.** To dream of breasts in a sexual context means you desire more nurturing in your sexual relationships. You want to take care of your partner, or you want your partner to take care of you. ☽ **baby** ℭ *body parts, caretaking, feminine, protection, sexual activity*.

breathing   To take deep breaths in a dream symbolizes a desire for healing or cleansing. To hear someone breathing in your dream means someone in your waking life has gotten too close for comfort. Snoring? Roll over …. See also *breathing problems*. ☽ **suffocating** ℭ *health and hygiene, healing, relationships*.

breathing problems   If you have trouble breathing or can't breathe in your dream, you feel suffocated in life. Your rules are too strict or a person or situation has been inhibiting you to the point of anxiety. Is your boss too demanding? Do you feel compelled to act like someone you aren't? Has a relationship become oppressive and stifling? If someone else has trouble breathing in your dream, you have the opportunity right now to set someone or something free. Are you doing the suffocating? ◑ **freedom** ℭ *anxiety, authority, control issues, fear, freedom, identity, impediments, personal power, repression.*

bribing someone   You want something, but you don't know how to get it. To dream of bribing someone symbolizes your belief that you should be able to get whatever you want, and the ends justify the means. **1.** If you bribe someone and it works, you are on your way to a solution for that problem, but be sure you're really okay with your methods. You might be feeling guilty. **2.** If you try to bribe someone but they refuse to accept the bribe, you are taking the wrong approach to a problem. **3.** If someone bribes you and it works, you have the unpleasant feeling you've sold out for material gain. **4.** If you refuse to be bribed, you've recently stood up for something important even though it wasn't easy, and your dream is giving you a pat on the back. ◑ **gift** ℭ *ethics and morals, financial issues, guilt, personal power, rules and laws, solutions and remedies.*

brick wall   See *barrier.*

bride   A Cinderella story, or the woman trapped behind the veil? Examine the imagery and feelings surrounding being a bride or seeing a bride in your dream for clues about how you really feel about commitment in general or your own relationship in particular. Is it all romance and flowers or a gothic horror story? **1.** To be a beautiful, happy bride means you have optimistic expectations for your relationship, even if they don't actually include marriage. **2.** If you aren't in a relationship, being a bride indicates your desire for someone to take care of you. **3.** To be an anxious, unhappy bride or a bride dressed in black means you have a feeling of foreboding about a commitment you've made. **4.** To be a bride running away from a wedding means you feel trapped and you want more freedom. **5.** To marry a bride means you have recently taken on a big responsibility. How do you feel about it? See also *marriage, ring.* ◑ **divorce** ℭ *beauty, burdens, caretaking, celebration, characters, feminine, freedom, happiness, innocence, people, relationships, responsibilities, rules and laws, transformation.*

bridge   Bridges offer passage across a difficulty—a river, a chasm, a busy road—and bridge dreams symbolize a solution to a problem. **1.** If you dream of crossing a bridge, you already know the solution, even if you aren't aware of it yet. **2.** If a bridge is broken or impassable, you need to take a different approach because what you are doing now isn't working. **3.** If you see a bridge in the distance, the answer is out there but you haven't found it yet. ◑ **barrier** ℭ *places, solutions and remedies.*

brother   See *sibling.*

bruises Bruises symbolize hurt inflicted on you or someone else. You still feel the pain. See also *injuries.* ❧ **healing** ℭ *pain, healing, injuries, relationships.*

brunette hair Brunette (or dark) hair represents mystery, drama, and passion. **1.** To dream you are brunette when you aren't means you feel more dramatic and mysterious lately. Have you tapped into your inner vamp? Someone new might see you in this way, and it has helped you to see that part of yourself. **2.** To dream of someone with dark hair means you see that person, or someone that person represents, as attractively mysterious and enigmatic. You are fascinated. ❧ **blond hair** ℭ *beauty, body parts, color, love, mystery, personal power, transformation.*

bugs To dream of an insect, spider, or other creepy-crawly bug means something has been bothering you and you've been trying to ignore it, but this is only making the problem worse. Face it or risk an infestation. To dream you are being bugged with an electronic spying device means you feel your privacy is being invaded. **1.** To dream a bug crawls on you means something you don't like has invaded your life—a bad habit, an intrusive person, a disturbing situation. **2.** To be bitten by a bug means you've been obsessing over something and you can't seem to let it go. It isn't good for you. **3.** To

keep a bug as a pet means you see the details others miss. **4.** To dream of huge numbers of bugs symbolizes great anxiety and fear about what has infiltrated your private life. See also *disease.* ❧ **birds** ℭ *addictions, animals, anxiety, crawling creatures, destruction, fear, nature, threats.*

Many people claim that they wake up at night in a panic because they see spiders, snakes, or insects in their bed, in the room, even on their bodies. These people often jump out of bed and tear the covers off the bed, run from the room, or at least wake up panicking. These experiences are probably the result of hypnagogic or hynopompic hallucinations, images people experience just as they are falling asleep (hypnagogic) or waking up (hynopompic). Other examples are the sensation of falling and consequent jerking of limbs to catch oneself, or thinking you hear someone calling your name.

building Are you in one, or are you making one? **1.** To dream about a building represents your life, with the quality and character of the interior space representing all the parts of your life, and the exterior representing the way you present yourself to the world. **2.** To dream you are building something shows you are oriented toward creative action right now. This is the time to make it happen. See also *house.* ❧ **destruction** ℭ *buildings and rooms, creation.*

B

bull   Dreaming of a bull means you have tapped into your masculine energy. You have strong personal power and charisma right now, and the result is a swelling of material wealth. You are a success. To fight a bull signifies an excess of masculine energy. Men will admire you, but women may find you remote. ❧ **cow** ℭ *abundance, animals, financial resources, masculine, nature, personal power, success.*

bullet   See *gun.*

bully   Someone is picking on you, and you feel insecure and unsafe. If you conquer a bully, you are experiencing a wave of personal power. ❧ **best friend** ℭ *anxiety, characters, control issues, fear, insecurity, people, personal power.*

bungee jumping   Did you jump out of bed this morning with new vigor? You want to take a big risk, but you still want to know someone's got hold of that bungee cord. **1.** If you enjoy bungee jumping in your dream, you feel prepared to take a risk. **2.** If you jump but find it terrifying, you have been under too much stress lately. **3.** If you get hurt while bungee jumping or see someone else get hurt, you fear you might be taking too much of a risk. **4.** If you can't get yourself to jump, you aren't ready yet for a major change you've been considering. **5.** If you watch someone else bungee jumping, you feel the urge to take more risks in your life, but you're still in the "watch and think about it" stage. ❧ **caution** ℭ *adventure,*

anxiety, changing course, decisions, fear, risky behavior.

buried alive   Who turned off the lights? A common but terrifying nightmare, buried-alive dreams signal anxiety, dread, or fear about something. You feel so oppressed or overwhelmed by a person or situation that you don't think you can get out. This dream begs you to take steps in your waking life to reduce stress and change something about your situation. See also *coffin, grave.* ❧ **escape** ℭ *anxiety, changing course, control issues, danger, death, fear, freedom, frustration, impediments.*

burns   See *fire, injuries.*

bus   Someone else drives, but you still get somewhere. Bus dreams indicate movement, but not of your own making. **1.** If you ride on a bus, you are part of a plan that is working just fine. Sit back and enjoy the ride. **2.** If you drive the bus, you have taken responsibility for the lives of others. **3.** If a bus ride is scary, the bus drives itself, or the bus crashes, you are involved in something others control, and you fear it isn't going well or you don't like having so little control. Maybe you should get off the bus before it's too late. **4.** If you dream you are on a school bus, you've been feeling the weight of authority lately, and perhaps a little rebellion? ❧ **car** ℭ *accidents, authority, control issues, rebellion, responsibilities, travel, vehicles.*

butterfly   Did you cut your hair?
Have you lost weight? Whatever
it is that you've recently done to
transform yourself, it's fabulous,
so keep it up! Your dream is telling
you it's working. Or maybe you are
considering a major life change.
This dream says, "Do it." Dreams
about butterflies might also mean:
1. You seek some sort of transformation or wish to be something
other than what you are. **2.** You
want freedom from the bonds of
your life. How might you break out
of that cocoon? **3.** You are just coming into the fullness of your own
beauty and the peak of your potential. Spread your wings and make
the most of it. **4.** Something will
happen soon that makes you both
nervous and excited. You'll flutter
right through it. **5.** You love beauty
and pleasure. But you already knew
that. ☽ **ugliness** ☾ *beauty, crawling creatures, freedom, transformation.*

C

cabin Houses represent you, and cabins represent your natural self—the part of you that feels a connection to nature. The surroundings and feeling of the cabin and its contents reveal the way you feel about your own relationship to nature. **1.** A clean, comfortable cabin means you feel comfortable in nature and you have a strong connection to the natural world. **2.** A dirty, dark, or neglected cabin symbolizes a separation from the natural world and a feeling of isolation and desolation because you've lost touch with Mother Earth. See also *house*. ☽ **city** ℂ *buildings and rooms, nature, places.*

cabinet See *storage*.

cactus Step back. Cactus dreams suggest you feel guarded or protective and you don't want anyone near. ☽ **flowers** ℂ *nature, plants, protection, threats.*

cage Cages in dreams are metaphors for feeling trapped. **1.** If you are in a cage, that's just how you feel in your waking life—locked into a relationship, a job, or a situation. **2.** If you see someone else in a cage, you have inadvertently put someone in a difficult situation, or you are aware of a difficult situation that you might be able to do something about. **3.** An animal in a cage represents something you've tamed—an instinct, an impulse, a bad habit? **4.** An empty cage represents your recent freedom. ☽ **breaking free** ℂ *animals, burdens, changing course, control issues, escape, places, responsibilities, rules and laws, stasis.*

cake The ultimate sweet indulgence, cake symbolizes happiness, celebrations, hedonism, and, in the diet-conscious, temptation. **1.** If you dream of eating and enjoying cake, you enjoy your life right now. You're happy! **2.** If you eat cake but feel guilty about it because you are supposed to be on a diet, you've been overly restrictive with yourself. Give yourself some waking-life rewards, even if they don't involve food. You can't deprive yourself *all* the time. **3.** If you dream of watching someone else eat cake, somebody has something you desire. **4.** If a cake gets smashed, dropped,

or ruined in a dream, you've been denied something you hoped for.
☾ **vegetables** ℂ *celebration, desires, food and drink, guilt, happiness, hedonism, inanimate objects, pleasure, sacrifice.*

camcorder   If you find a camcorder or videotape a movie with a camcorder in your dream, you want to remember this time in your life—an event, a person, a feeling. If someone videotapes you with a camcorder or gives you a camcorder, you've made a memorable impression on someone. Someone may also want to be like you.
☾ **amnesia** ℂ *electronics, history, inanimate objects, memory, technology.*

camel   You can't get across the desert without a camel. The dry, mundane parts of life may not seem worth dreaming about, but camel dreams tell you that you've found an effective way to get through those dry spells in your life. You've got inner resources, and you know how to use them. You'll survive.
☾ **boat** ℂ *animals, burdens, creativity, journeys and quests, nature, travel, vehicles, work.*

camera   Cameras record a moment you might otherwise forget. If you dream of a camera, you want to remember something specific: a face, a comment, a feeling. **1.** If you take a picture with a camera or find a camera, you want to remember something. It means a lot to you. **2.** Looking through a camera lens or looking at a picture means you suddenly "see" or

understand something you didn't understand before. **3.** If you dream someone takes a picture of you, someone wants to remember you in your waking life. You've become important to them in some way. **4.** To break a camera means something has happened that you want to forget, but you can't seem to get the image out of your head. Your dream is trying to do it for you. ☾ **vision problems** ℂ *electronics, history, inanimate objects, memory, technology.*

camouflage   Finding it hard to blend in, or is it too easy? **1.** If you dream you are wearing camouflage or hiding in a camouflaged location, you need to hide from someone or something right now. Don't force yourself to come out or draw attention to yourself just yet. You aren't ready. **2.** Dreams of wearing camouflage during a war or while in the military mean you either desire (if the dream is good) or fear (if the dream is bad) authority, rules, and being part of an organized group. **3.** Dreams of being camouflaged in some way but trying to be seen without success mean you feel like nobody notices you. ☾ **celebrity** ℂ *authority, clothing and accessories, fear, identity, insecurity, rules and laws, secrets, subterfuge.*

camping   Dreams of roughing it in the great outdoors often come after a memorable brush with the natural world. Have you recently witnessed some natural beauty or had a frightening encounter with an animal? Camping dreams symbolize a desire to get closer to nature, or in the case of scary camping dreams, fear of the power and mystery of the natural world. If your dream involves an exciting adventure out in the wilderness, you crave a challenge and the independence to be out on your own in the world, battling the elements and proving yourself. Camping dreams can also symbolize the desire to escape civilization and technology, to live on instinct, or to get away from crowds. Nature is calling you. See also *bear, cabin, tent.* ☾ **city** ℭ *adventure, animals, courage, danger, escape, fear, happiness, instincts, isolation, nature.*

cancer   To dream you have cancer most likely doesn't mean you actually have cancer. Instead, cancer dreams may symbolize something inside you or in your immediate environment or situation that you feel has gone wrong; that is causing you grief, pain, or an experience of loss of potential. This could be physical, emotional, even moral. Is it your health, or a relationship, or a job that isn't right for you anymore? Whatever it is, it's eating away at you from within, and you need to find it and make a change. See also *disease.* ☾ **health** ℭ *anxiety, body parts, changing course, ethics and morals, failure, fear, healing, health and hygiene, impediments.*

candle   This little light can symbolize celebration, as in a birthday; romance, as in a candle-lit dinner; passion, as in a bedroom lit with scented candles; or religious symbolism. Candles in general signify

the light of understanding, discovery, and enlightenment. Holding one means you seek the answers. Blowing one out means you don't want to know. ☾ **darkness** ℭ *celebration, divine power, heat, inanimate objects, intuition, knowledge, love, sexual activity, spirituality.*

candy   Candy symbolizes the sweetness in life, reward, indulgence, or something you wish for. Candy also suggests your own childlike joy in the simple pleasures of the world. **1.** Getting or eating candy and enjoying it means you deserve a reward or your wish has been granted. **2.** Guilty candy dreams and dreams of bingeing on candy or of poisoned or spoiled candy symbolize temptation, hedonism, and a loss of self-control or moral strength. See also *dessert.* ☾ **punishment** ℭ *abundance, comfort, control issues, desires, ethics and morals, extremism, food and drink, happiness, hedonism, innocence, pleasure, wishes.*

People on strict diets as well as low-carb diets sometimes have dreams of eating candy and other sweets, sometimes in large amounts and with a sense of urgency. These dreams act out the body's cravings during sleep.

cane   Canes represent aging, a loss of stability, and the need for help. **1.** If you dream you are walking with a cane, you've been feeling off-balance and you need a stabilizing force. Are you feeling old and need to feel young? Unsteady in your life's direction and you need advice? Weak in body and you need more exercise or better health habits? **2.** If you see someone else walking with a cane, you've perceived someone else's need. Can you help them? ☾ **roller skates or inline skates** ℭ *age, balance, caretaking, healing, health and hygiene, inanimate objects, injuries, stability, vulnerability.*

canyon   Seeing a canyon in a dream means you have room to move and vast untapped possibilities for your life right now. You can go anywhere, but such freedom also comes with the risk of falling. If you stand in a canyon and look up, you feel your options are limited. See also *falling*. ☾ **mountain** ℭ *adventure, changing course, freedom, journeys and quests, opportunity, places.*

car   Perhaps because we spend so much time in our cars, car dreams are common and symbolize where you are going and how you are getting there. **1.** Enjoyable dreams of driving through beautiful countryside suggest your life is going well right now and you are making progress. **2.** Losing control of the car, or the car driving without you, or being unable to stop the car, reveal your anxiety about losing control of a situation. Things are getting out of hand. **3.** If you buy a new car, you have decided to approach a situation in a new way. **4.** If your car gets ruined in some

way, the path you've been traveling isn't working and you need a new approach. See also *car accident*. ☾ **backward** ℭ *anxiety, changing course, control issues, goal-setting, inanimate objects, journeys and quests, travel, vehicles.*

car accident   Car accident dreams can be frightening, or you may experience them as if removed from the situation, as an observer. In either case, they represent something gone wrong. **1.** If you've been in a car accident and you relive the experience in your dreams, you still feel anxiety or residual stress from the event. Your dream is helping you to work through your feelings. **2.** If you haven't been in a car accident but you dream of one, you are under stress and you fear a current situation will end badly. **3.** If you get injured in a car accident, you have been hurt, or fear you will be hurt, by someone's carelessness— possibly your own. See also *car, injuries.* ☾ **mountain** ℭ *adventure, anxiety, changing course, freedom, injuries, journeys and quests, opportunity.*

cards   Playing cards have probably been around for centuries, and fortune tellers have used them at least since Victorian times to tell the future. **1.** If playing cards show up in your dream, you may be getting a glimpse into your own future. Examine the context for clues. You may be picking up on sensory clues about what's in store for you without realizing it.

2. If you play a game of cards in your dream, you need to use more strategy and organized thinking to deal with a current situation. **3.** If you get a greeting card in a dream, someone has a message for you. Are you listening? **4.** If you give someone a greeting card, you want to tell somebody something, but you are afraid to do it directly. ☮ **silence** ℭ *code, competition, inanimate objects, intuition, messages, play, sports and games.*

carnation   Carnations symbolize nonmaterialism, and seeing them in a dream means you embrace life's deeper joys. If someone gives you carnations, someone has sacrificed something for you. See also *flowers.* ☮ **greedy** ℭ *beauty, happiness, nature, plants, sacrifice.*

carnival   Carnivals represent childhood and fun, but also decadent revelry à la Mardi Gras. **1.** If you have fun at a carnival riding the rides and eating kid food, you are in touch with your inner child and you know how to find innocent joy in everyday life, or you miss the feeling you had during those childhood days and want to relive them. **2.** A carnival that turns frightening—scary clowns, out-of-control carnival rides, dangerous people—symbolizes bad habits that have gotten out of control, or a situation that once was fun but has now crossed the line into uncomfortable or morally questionable. Have you been breaking the rules? Is it time to go home? **3.** Flirting or being romantic with someone at a carnival

symbolizes your desire for the early, carefree stage of a relationship. You may be considering getting into a relationship, or you miss this stage in your current relationship. **4.** Seeing yourself in a funhouse mirror at a carnival means you have recently seen a side of yourself that surprised you, in either a good way or a bad way. ☮ **monotony** ℭ *adventure, escapism, fear, fun, identity, innocence, love, places, play, pleasure, relationships, risky behavior, rules and laws, wishes.*

carpal tunnel syndrome   See *wrist.*

carpenter   You are trying to build or construct something in your waking life if you dream of a carpenter. Who can help you? If you are the carpenter in the dream, you've taken on your own remodeling project. Are you trying to create a new you, a new job, a new look, a whole new life? See also *construction.* ☮ **destruction** ℭ *buildings and rooms, career, changing course, characters, creation, creativity, identity, people, transformation.*

carry   Carrying something in a dream represents a burden or dependent. Consider what you are carrying—a package, a child, a basket of flowers, a bomb? Whatever it is suggests your responsibility in your waking life. ☮ **dropping something** ℭ *burdens, caretaking, responsibilities.*

cartoon   Dreaming in animation must be rare. Cartoons show us

C

comically or tragically exaggerated versions of our life. Watching cartoons in your dream means you have been making a big deal about something that isn't really so important, or you have been making a joke out of something you should take more seriously. If a cartoon character comes to life in your dream, you have been taking someone too seriously. If the cartoon character is threatening or frightening, you haven't been taking someone seriously enough. ☾ **monotony** ☾ *anxiety, characters, extremism, fun.*

cartwheels   Turn cartwheels in your dream, and you're feeling lighthearted. Injure yourself turning cartwheels, and you've been recently unpleasantly surprised at signs of aging. ☾ **grown-up** ☾ *age, fun, play, pleasure.*

cash register   Cha-ching! You've got money issues. A cash register full of money means money is coming to you or you've got control of your financial situation. An empty cash register means you are worried about your financial situation or face a financial loss. ☾ **poverty** ☾ *abundance, financial issues, inanimate objects, loss.*

casino   See *gambling, poker.*

casket   See *coffin.*

castle   Houses represent who you are, and castles represent who you'd like to be: your wishes and your inner knowledge of your own potential for greatness. **1.** A magnificent castle filled with riches and luxurious furnishings means you have a high self-image and great optimism about your future. **2.** A castle filled with exciting people, dragons, knights, princesses, or other interesting characters symbolizes the importance of other people in your ultimate plan. You see an exciting and adventurous life ahead of you filled with stimulating relationships with others and with the world. **3.** A scary, haunted, or dark castle means you fear your future and what you might become. **4.** An empty or run-down castle means you don't see any opportunities for yourself. You feel stuck, or without potential. ☾ **house** ☾ *adventure, characters, creation, desires, goal-setting, journeys and quests, identity, personal power, places.*

castration   See *amputation.*

cat   Dogs symbolize devotion, but cats symbolize independence and your mysterious, hidden side. In dreams, cats represent secrets and autonomy. Only you can solve a current dilemma, but first you will need to figure out something you already know, but don't know you know. This will take some creativity. ☾ **dog** ☾ *animals, creativity, nature, personal power, secrets.*

According to folklore, the color of the cat in your dream indicates different things. Dreaming of a black cat means you will have bad luck. Seeing a white cat means you love someone deeply and purely, and seeing a two-colored cat means your feelings are more carnal. Seeing multiple cats means someone is cheating on you.

caterpillar Caterpillars don't look like much, but they have the potential to become amazing butterflies, and dreams about caterpillars represent potential. You have yet to achieve your full glory, and your dream urges you to start spinning that cocoon in preparation for your transformation. ☽ **butterfly** ℂ *animals, crawling creatures, creation, goal-setting, identity, nature, transformation.*

caution Being cautious in a dream means your subconscious mind is telling you to be careful about something in your waking life. To see a caution sign is an even more obvious warning to you from yourself. ☽ **ambulance** ℂ *caretaking, control issues.*

cave Caves represent unknown places. **1.** To dream about going into a cave represents courage, an adventurous spirit, and the need to find out something. **2.** If you are too afraid to enter a cave in your dream, you aren't ready to go to that hidden place just yet. **3.** Getting lost inside a cave symbolizes

your fear that something—a relationship, a project, an obsession—could take over your life too completely and you'll lose track of your goals. Shall we send out a search party? ☽ **sun** ℂ *adventure, control issues, courage, danger, places, secrets, subterfuge.*

CDs and DVDs Those shiny discs filled with music, movies, and information symbolize the stories you make about yourself. To see or use a CD or DVD in your dream means you've decided to see a past event in a particular way that helps you make sense of it. It may not be exactly the way it happened, but it works for you. To dream of a CD or DVD player means you are particularly creative right now. All you need to do is turn it on. ☽ **silence** ℂ *communication, creativity, electronics, inanimate objects, knowledge, memory, technology, transformation.*

ceiling You've reached the top. Is this as far as you can go? To dream you're touching or pressing against a ceiling means you've maximized the potential of a current situation and you can't go any farther, at least not in this direction. If you need to keep moving, you'll have to go a different way. ☽ **floor** ℂ *buildings and rooms, career, changing course, direction, goal-setting, impediments, journeys and quests, stasis*

celebrity Almost everybody with any access to the media has had a celebrity dream. These symbolic brushes with greatness reveal a desire to be involved in something that gets recognition. **1.** To dream you are a celebrity means you've been getting a lot of recognition lately. If you enjoy the dream, you like being the center of attention. If you don't like your celebrity status in your dream, you haven't been getting enough privacy. **2.** To dream you meet, talk to, or hang out with a celebrity may just mean you've recently seen that celebrity's image somewhere, or it could mean you have something in common with that person, or what that person represents. **3.** To have a romantic, passionate, or sexual dream about a celebrity means that celebrity represents something you desire: The ultimate mate? Wealth? Beauty? Power? Fantastic athletic ability? More drama in your life? ☽ **invisible** ℂ *beauty, characters, desires, ego, identity, people, reputation, sexual activity, success, wishes.*

celibacy   Sex dreams are common, but what about dreams of *not* having sex? If you dream you are celibate, you may desire a reprieve from sex—you've had enough, for goodness sake! Or you may fear you'll never have sex again. It depends on how you feel about being celibate in the dream: relieved or frustrated? If you dream someone you desire is celibate, you fear you'll never really connect with that person on a deeper level. ☽ **sex** ℂ *burdens, freedom, love, relationships, responsibilities, sexual activity.*

cell phone   Can you hear me now? Dreaming of a cell phone might just mean you spend way too much time talking on that thing, but cell phones also symbolize some unique aspects of our technological age. **1.** If you dream you are talking on a cell phone, you need to tell somebody something. Speak up! You have four bars! **2.** If people keep calling your cell phone, you feel overextended. Everybody needs to go through you. How can you delegate some of this responsibility? **3.** If you travel while talking on a cell phone, you feel free and important. If you get in a car crash while talking on a cell phone, you are letting social obligations or work get in the way of your life. Slow down and hang up the phone. **4.** If your call gets dropped while on a cell phone, someone is keeping something from you. You are out of the loop. **5.** If you receive cryptic text messages, you aren't getting the message someone is trying to send to you. **6.** Caught in the act? Cell phone snapshots can be invasions of privacy, or might show a need to investigate or document the truth as it occurs in the moment. See also *camera, car accident, phone, ringtone.* ☽ **silence** ℂ *accidents, communication, electronics, inanimate objects, technology.*

cemetery   Walking through a cemetery symbolizes all the things you've let die or moved on from in your life. You still think about them, even though they are only part of your past. To be frightened, chased, or scared in a cemetery means you haven't let something go after all, even if you thought you had. Something still haunts you.

See also *buried alive, grave*. ❧ **birth** ℂ *fear, memory, places, repression.*

chain   Chains bind you to something or someone, or they represent a heavy load, like the chains ghosts rattle. **1.** To carry a chain means you have a responsibility you resent. If the chain has a ball on it, you fear or resent marriage. **2.** To be chained up means you feel stifled and repressed, or can't escape something unpleasant. **3.** To be chained to someone else means you feel obligated to someone. **4.** To break a chain means you are ready to make a drastic change in your life, in the name of freedom. ❧ **breaking free** ℂ *burdens, freedom, impediments, inanimate objects, relationships, responsibilities.*

chainsaw   See *power tools.*

chair   Take a load off. To see or sit in a chair in your dream means you need to stop and think about something. Quit moving so fast and sit down. You need to regroup. See also *furniture*. ❧ **running** ℂ *furniture and appliances, inanimate objects, intelligence, stability, stasis.*

chalk   Chalk communicates a message but is easily erased, and dreaming of chalk means someone is trying to tell you something and you don't have long to get the message. Chalk also symbolizes school and teachers. Someone might be trying to teach you something or serve as a mentor. What does the chalk say? ❧ **silence** ℂ *communication, inanimate objects, knowledge, messages, relationships.*

chameleon   Chameleons symbolize the adaptive ability to change in order to blend in with any environment. To dream of a chameleon means you need to do this. Something in your life demands that you adapt to it right now. See also *camouflage*. ❧ **celebrity** ℂ *animals, crawling creatures, identity, nature, transformation.*

champagne   Champagne symbolizes celebration, abundance, and the good life. **1.** Dreaming of drinking champagne means you appreciate fine things and have a natural sense of style. If you drink too much, however, you've been living beyond your means. **2.** Toasting with champagne means something has happened worth celebrating. **3.** Spilling champagne means you risk ruining something important. Be careful and show some restraint. See also *alcohol, wine*. ❧ **abstinence** ℂ *abundance, celebration, food and drink, financial issues, hedonism, pleasure.*

chasing   Run for your life! **1.** Chasing something in a dream symbolizes something you desire but haven't been able to get. If you catch the thing you chase, you're finally within reach of your desires. **2.** If you dream you are being chased, you really are being pursued by something: guilt, a debt, an obligation, an addiction, or fear of something. If you get caught, you fear that the thing that pursues you really will get the best of you. ☾ **stop signs and stoplights** ℭ *anxiety, desires, fear, guilt, wishes.*

chat room   Dreams about chatting in chat rooms on the Internet may just mean you've been spending too much time chatting in chat rooms on the Internet. However, these dreams can also symbolize a dueling force within you: the desire for a relationship and the fear of getting too close. Memorable messages you get from chat rooms in dreams might also mean something important for your waking life. Your subconscious is trying to bring something specific to your attention whenever you see written words in a dream, and that includes dreams of written words on computer screens, too, especially if they pop up on the screen as an instant message. Pay attention! ☾ **silence** ℭ *communication, messages, places, relationships, technology.*

cheating   Cheating in a dream means you feel guilty about cheating in some way in your waking life, or you are looking for a shortcut. **1.** To cheat on your romantic partner or spouse in a dream could mean you like the fantasy of cheating but wouldn't actually do it, or it could mean you have done something else to hurt your partner and the cheating dream plays out your guilt. **2.** If you dream of cheating in a game, you thought you wanted recognition at any cost, but if you

feel guilty in the dream, your dream asks you to reexamine how you feel about your methods. **3.** If you cheat someone out of money or other resources, you've taken something away from someone in waking life, and it's still in your mind. ☾ **confession** ℭ *anxiety, desires, dishonesty, fear, guilt, trust issues, wishes.*

cheerleader   You can do it if you put your mind to it! **1.** To dream of a cheerleader means you need a pep talk and your dream is giving you one. **2.** To dream you are a cheerleader means somebody needs *your* optimistic take on things. Cheer them on. **3.** To dream of getting romantic or sexual with a cheerleader means you crave more positive reinforcement in your sex life. Your dream is giving you an ego boost. ☾ **teasing** ℭ *characters, ego, fun, people, personal power, sexual activity, sports and games.*

cherry   Eating a cherry means you desire passion, love, and, sure, we'll say it: sex. Seeing a cherry but not eating it means you don't want to—or are afraid to—spoil the thing you desire. ☾ **celibacy** ℭ *food and drink, fruit, pleasure, sexual activity.*

chess   Playing chess in a dream reveals that you have a strategy. How you do in the chess game tells you how well you think your own strategy is going to work. ☾ **stop signs and stoplights** ℭ *career, competition, goal-setting, play, solutions and remedies, sports and games.*

> Any dream about a game suggests a current dilemma or problem in your life that you are attempting to conquer or figure out. How you do in the game suggests how you feel about your ability to solve your problem.

chest To dream of your own chest means you've met the world with your heart forward. You've taken a risk. If you injure your chest or have chest surgery in a dream, you've taken a risk and gotten hurt. Now you feel vulnerable. To dream of a chest of drawers or a treasure chest means you're ready to realize or unlock some important information you've kept hidden from yourself. ☽ **stop signs and stoplights** ☾ *body parts, courage, furniture and appliances, inanimate objects, knowledge, secrets, vulnerability.*

chewing gum See *gum.*

chicken Chickens might represent cowardice. But seeing a chicken in your dream can also signify a craving for rural life or a more simple life. Are you spending enough time at home? **1.** If you see chickens contentedly pecking at the ground, your life is getting too complicated or materialistic and this makes you uncomfortable. **2.** If chickens chase you or run wildly around, you're afraid or nervous about something. **3.** Sick or dead chickens mean you are losing money. **4.** If you dream of eating chicken, your body may be telling you to scale back to a more basic diet. See also *birds.* ☽ **binge-ing** ☾ *animals, anxiety, birds, fear,*

food and drink, financial resources, happiness, nature, solutions and remedies.

child or children Dreams of children symbolize innocence, playfulness, simplicity, and also a sense of caretaking and responsibility. **1.** If you see a child in your dream, you have to take care of something. It might be you who needs your nurturing right now. **2.** If you dream you are a child, you struggle against an impulse to grow up. *I am the child I always wanted!* You want someone else to take responsibility. **3.** If you see a child in trouble or you rescue a child, someone feels helpless and needs you to take care of them right now. **4.** If you dream of your own, actual children, something is going on with them that you aren't seeing. **5.** If you dream you have children but you don't actually have children, you are ready to take on a new responsibility. See also *baby.* ☽ **grown-up** ☾ *age, caretaking, comfort, family, intuition, people, responsibilities.*

China See *Asia.*

chiropractor Dreaming of being adjusted by a chiropractor means you're bent out of shape and you need to realign your goals and priorities. Dreaming of being injured by a chiropractor means you are letting someone influence you too much, and you're losing sight of what you really need. ☽ **straight line** ☾ *goal-setting, health and hygiene, healing, people, stability.*

C

chocolate   See *candy.*

choir   See *singing.*

choking   Dreams of choking mean you've done or said something and you wish you hadn't. ◗ **eating** ℂ *communication, food and drink, health and hygiene, regret.*

christening   See *baptism, religious ceremonies.*

Christmas   Christmas means different things to different people, so dreams about Christmas—the tree, Santa Claus, Christmas cards, or the day itself—symbolize a desire or nostalgia for whatever Christmas invokes for you, personally. If your Christmas dream is happy and magical, Christmas still holds spiritual meaning for you, whether or not you consider yourself religious. If your Christmas dream is unpleasant, past memories from the holiday still linger within you. You haven't let them go yet. ◗ **Halloween** ℂ *caretaking, celebration, comfort, family, relationships, weather and seasons.*

church or synagogue   To dream of a house of worship symbolizes your desire for more spiritual structure in your life, even if that means taking just a few minutes every day for quiet contemplation. If the dream frightens or disturbs you in some way, you may have had a bad experience with organized religion. ◗ **nature** ℂ *buildings and rooms, divine power, places, spirituality.*

cigar   See *smoking.*

cigarette   See *smoking.*

cinema   See *theater.*

circle   Circles are powerful symbols that represent the cyclical nature of all things: birth and death, creation and destruction, all flowing into each other and back around. **1.** If you dream of drawing or otherwise making a circle, you feel integrated into your own life cycle and you feel confident that things will be okay. **2.** If you dream of standing inside a circle, you feel protected. **3.** If you walk, run, or drive in a circle and feel frustrated or angry, you aren't making any progress in your life right now. **4.** If you are moving in a circle without feeling any particular emotion, and/or you see other objects or people moving in a circle or on a wheel, you are experiencing karma: what goes around comes around. **5.** Circles can also represent female energy, and if you dream of giving someone a circular object like a ring, key chain, or hula hoop, you are expressing your love or sexual desire. ◗ **straight line** ℂ *creation, destruction, direction, feminine, frustration, journeys and quests, karma, love, protection, sexual activity, shapes and symbols.*

circumcision   If you dream of getting or being circumcised when you are not circumcised (or are not a man), you feel the need to make a fresh start because things didn't go the way you wanted them to go. If you dream of getting circumcised and you are already circumcised, you may be experiencing a residual memory reframed for your adult mind to understand. Or you may believe you need spiritual guidance right now. ◐ **erection** ℂ *body parts, changing course, health and hygiene, masculine, medicine and surgery, solutions and remedies.*

circus   Circus dreams symbolize the way you've organized all the different parts of your life. You are the ringmaster and all the different acts, rings, and events are parts of your daily existence. Examine your dream circus to discover which parts of your life you find most entertaining and interesting, and which parts aren't working very well. Is your circus fun or ridiculous? Are the people talented and amazing or frightening? See also *clown.* ◐ **movie** ℂ *career, characters, family, fun, personal power, places, relationships.*

citizen's arrest   Stop in the name of the law! To dream you, as a civilian, arrest someone means you feel responsible for the moral lives of others and you have the confidence to make rules for others even if you don't have the authority. You have a strong sense of right and wrong. To dream someone else places you under citizen's arrest means you fear nobody is monitoring your behavior but you wish someone would. You aren't sure you're capable of following the rules on your own. ◐ **crime** ℂ *authority, control issues, ethics and morals, responsibilities, rules and laws.*

city   Tall buildings, busy streets, traffic and crowds …. Cities have a lot of energy and development. Dreams of cities can represent your desire for more excitement, more social interaction, or more culture. They can also symbolize your detachment from the natural world, your isolation in a crowded place, or stress at having too much to do all the time. **1.** To dream of having fun in a city means you crave stimulation and you want people around you. **2.** To dream of being scared or lost in a city symbolizes your feeling of isolation from the social world. You don't feel like you belong, and you don't know how to find your way back into the group. **3.** To dream of being angry or irritated in a city or to see small signs of nature in a city, such as a tree or a bird, suggests you haven't been getting enough of the natural world. You need more nature in your life to feel balanced. **4.** To dream of a city that has been destroyed means your social connections may be falling apart. Are you neglecting your friends? See also *disaster.* ◐ **farm** ℂ *buildings and rooms, destruction, isolation, people, places, relationships.*

clapping   See *applause.*

claustrophobia   To feel claustrophobic in a dream represents your feelings of limitation and being trapped or stifled in your waking life. What has got you closed into such a small space? Your relationship? Your job? Your social network? Somebody else's rules or morals? The bed sheets? If the dream feels truly terrifying, it's time for action in your waking life. The situation is causing you anxiety. See also *buried alive, crowd, suffocating, trapped*. ☾ **breaking free** ℭ *anxiety, authority, control issues, ethics and morals, fear, freedom, impediments, responsibilities, rules and laws*.

> Mary Shelley wrote the novel *Frankenstein* after having a nightmare that gave her the idea. Maybe your next dream will inspire you to write a great book—just one more reason to record your dreams every morning.

claws   To see claws in your dream means you feel threatened by something. To have claws means you are on the defensive. ☾ **arms** ℭ *animals, body parts, danger, fear, insecurity, nature, threats*.

cleaning   Cleaning your house in a dream symbolizes a need for cleaning out your life. Do you need to rethink some of your habits, your old patterns, or even your attitude? **1.** Cleaning a bathroom means you have been neglecting health issues. **2.** Cleaning a kitchen means you need to eat better. **3.** Cleaning a bedroom means you need a fresh take on your love life. **4.** Cleaning

your desk means you need to clean up your act at work. **5.** Cleaning your child's room means you need to pay more attention to your family. **6.** Cleaning someone else's house means you feel an obligation to someone, or you think someone can learn from you. **7.** Cleaning yourself means you are trying to make amends for something you did that you regret. **8.** Cleaning up the yard around your home means you need to clean up your reputation. What will the neighbors think? ☾ **dirt** ℭ *caretaking, ethics and morals, family, health and hygiene, home, reputation, solutions and remedies, transformation*.

cliff   Stand on the edge of a cliff, and you see vast and unlimited possibilities for your life. Jump off, and you're ready to make a change. See also *falling*. ☾ **canyon** ℭ *adventure, changing course, freedom, journeys and quests, opportunity, places, transformation*.

climbing   Dreams of climbing signify a difficult passage that leads to an improved situation. If you climb something—a tree, a ladder, a wall, a cliff—you are ready to do the work necessary to get somewhere better. If you dream of watching someone else climb, you are working out how to get somewhere by watching the example of others. If you fall or someone else falls when climbing, you fear failure. ☾ **falling** ℭ *adventure, changing course, direction, failure, goal-setting, journeys and quests, opportunity*.

clock Seeing a clock or hearing a clock ticking in your dream means you feel the pressure of time passing, getting older, or not having enough time to finish something. **1.** An alarm clock represents a task you must do in a timely manner. Don't forget because this is important. If the alarm goes off in your dream, now is the time for action. **2.** A grandfather clock signifies that you must respect time right now. It matters. **3.** A broken clock means you should take a break from your strict schedule. Relax and take some time off. **4.** A clock running backward means you can operate outside of time. The rules don't apply to you right now. See also *time travel.* ☻ **running late** ℭ *age, goal-setting, inanimate objects, music and sound, time.*

closed door They say when one door closes, another opens. Seeing a closed door in your dream means something has ended or is no longer available. If you open a closed door, you have found a way around an obstacle. ☻ **open door** ℭ *changing course, impediments, inanimate objects.*

closet Maybe you don't have a skeleton in there, but if you dream about a closet, you are hiding something (or you want to). Rooms represent some aspect of you, and closets represent the parts of you hidden from others. Whatever qualities your dream closet shows you, pay attention. This is your inner life speaking. ☻ **exhibitionism** ℭ *buildings and rooms, home, places, repression, secrets, subterfuge.*

clothes Dreaming of clothes symbolizes the way you make yourself up to appear to others. **1.** New clothes symbolize a new image. You're looking good and your reputation has improved. **2.** Old, tattered, or dumpy clothes suggest you feel insecure about the way you look or seem to others. **3.** If you are missing some clothes in public—pants or underwear, or you are wearing your pajamas—you feel self-conscious about something you did. If nobody notices, you've gotten away with it. **4.** If you dream of formal clothes—a tuxedo or ball gown—you feel more sophisticated or well-off than others, or you wish you did. **5.** If you dream of a dress, you project a soft, feminine image (even if you are a man). **6.** If you dream of a suit or boyish clothes, you project a masculine image (even if you are a woman). See also *shoes, wrong size.* ☻ **naked in public** ℭ *beauty, clothing and accessories, identity, image, inanimate objects, reputation.*

clouds Clouds block the sun but soften the light, and cloud dreams can symbolize barriers to a goal or protection. **1.** If you dream of storm clouds, you are worried about something. **2.** A soft, cloudy sky means you can relax. Nobody is watching you right now. **3.** Clouds that get in the way of something you want to see suggest that you're up against an obstacle. See also *sky*. ☽ **sun** ☾ *feelings, impediments, nature, weather and seasons.*

clown　Funny clowns mean you feel lighthearted and silly about a current relationship, or you would like to have a better sense of humor. Scary, evil clowns symbolize a childhood fear that still haunts you, or a feeling that you have lost control and anarchy rules. See also *circus*. ☽ **working hard** ☾ *career, characters, control issues, fear, fun, play, people.*

club　**1.** Dreaming you've been admitted into a private club means you've recently been granted a privilege or upgrade in status. **2.** Dreaming of a nightclub means you have been too work-oriented or isolated from your friends lately and you need to let yourself go a little. Enjoy a night on the town. **3.** Getting into trouble in a club symbolizes your fear that you might not have control over your own behavior. Do you tend to go too far? **4.** Not being allowed into a club suggests that you don't feel like part of the group. Groucho Marx quipped, "I refuse to belong to any club that will accept me as a member." See also *nightclub*. ☽ **loneliness** ☾ *buildings and rooms, celebration, conformity, ethics and morals, fun, hedonism, image, peer pressure, places, relationships, risky behavior, rules and laws, social life, success.*

coastline　The coastline symbolizes the dividing line between earth and sea, or intellect and emotion, and dreams of seeing or walking along the coastline suggest a conflict between mind and heart. If you find yourself walking on sand but gazing at the water, you may need to use your heart more. If you find yourself swimming or wading and looking at the beach, you might be wise to use your head. Going back and forth between land and water suggests you are doing a good job of balancing both head and heart, or that you can't quite decide which force within you knows what's best. If you see a coastline from far above, you have recently gained insight into how you balance your own intellect and emotions. ☽ **mountain** ☾ *balance, changing course, decisions, feelings, intelligence, nature, places.*

coat　Cover up, it's cold outside. Coats protect us, keep us warm, and symbolize that protection in dreams. **1.** If you dream of putting on a coat, you need to feel sheltered from something in your waking life. **2.** Wearing a coat but still feeling cold means someone has treated you coldly and you haven't yet recovered from feeling neglected or snubbed. **3.** If you put a coat on someone else, you feel the impulse to protect or nurture someone. **4.** If you see a coat hanging in a closet or on a coat rack, you have many forces protecting you, and you feel safe. ☽ **underwear** ☾ *caretaking,* *clothing and accessories, cold, comfort, inanimate objects, protection, vulnerability.*

cobwebs   Dreaming of cobwebs in corners or hanging from ceilings symbolizes being stuck. You haven't been moving, changing, or feeling like a vital and active part of your own life. You might also be neglecting your health. Is it time for a fresh start and some internal spring cleaning? ☻ **cleaning** ℂ *health and hygiene, stasis.*

cockroach   To see a cockroach in a dream means your life has become infested with something that could compromise your health, happiness, or safety. You've let yourself get to a place you don't want to be, and you need to look closely at what you are doing and how you can purge yourself of this influence, whether it is a bad habit, a relationship, a dangerous situation, or even chronic negative thinking. ☻ **butterfly** ℂ *addictions, anger, anxiety, changing course, crawling creatures, danger, ethics and morals, fear, health and hygiene, impediments, regret, risky behavior, threats.*

coffee   Coffee stimulates and sharpens the senses and can generate a feeling of excitement and optimism or, in excess, nervousness and anxiety. **1.** If you dream of drinking coffee, you are thinking hard about something and trying to solve a problem or come to a solution. Keep thinking because you don't have it quite yet. **2.** If you dream

of drinking too much coffee, you need to slow down. You are obsessing over something and you aren't seeing the situation clearly. **3.** If you drink coffee with someone else, that person, or someone they represent, excites you. **4.** Drinking coffee in a group or in a café with other people symbolizes your desire for more social interaction with friends, neighbors, or the community in general. **5.** Drinking espresso, lattes, or other fancy coffee drinks symbolizes your developed sense of culture and the arts. You've got your finger on the pulse. ☻ **tea** ℂ *anxiety, comfort, decisions, desires, food and drink, relationships.*

coffin   Coffins don't foretell actual death, but they do foretell the death of something, or a major change. **1.** To see a coffin in a dream means you've accepted the end of something—a relationship, an idea, a part of yourself you've grown out of—and you are ready to see it buried for good. **2.** If you dream you are in a coffin, you've made a major change in your life. You may still feel in transition, but the new you will soon emerge. **3.** If you see someone you love in a coffin, you fear someone is in danger or you fear your recent neglect or falling-out with someone has changed your relationship forever. See also *buried alive, cemetery, grave, funeral.* ☻ **raft** ℂ *changing course, danger, death, decisions, destruction, fear, inanimate objects, places, relationships, subterfuge.*

People like to tell the story that shortly before his assassination, Abraham Lincoln had a dream that foretold his impending death. In the dream, Lincoln was in the White House, where he saw a coffin containing a body. He asked someone nearby who was in the coffin, and the person answered, "The president." Nobody can prove (or disprove) this story, but it does suggest that our dreams can clue us in to things we might sense, even if we don't logically know them.

coins   See *money*.

cold   To feel cold or experience cold weather in a dream might just mean you've kicked off the covers, but it can also signal that you've lost interest in something or someone, and you've withdrawn your emotional investment. You've cooled off. To be uncomfortably cold may mean you've withdrawn too much and isolated yourself from something or someone, or someone has withdrawn from you, and now you are suffering because of it. You feel alone. See also *snow*. ☾ **heat** ℭ *cold, death, isolation, loss, relationships, weather and seasons*.

collapse   If you dream of a person collapsing, somebody needs your help. If you dream of a structure collapsing, such as a building or a bridge, your world is changing and you feel like everything is falling apart. ☾ **building** ℭ *anxiety, buildings and rooms, caretaking, changing course, destruction, disaster*.

college   If you see a college or university in a dream, you have plans to improve your situation. To dream you are attending a college or university means you've already taken steps to improve yourself, or you've been learning a lot of new information lately. ☾ **playing hooky** ℭ *buildings and rooms, changing course, intelligence, knowledge, places*.

coma   To dream that you are in a coma and can see and/or hear people but can't respond to them means you feel unable to act in a current situation. You feel like everyone else is making all the decisions and you have no say or influence. Depending on how the dream makes you feel, you might be frustrated by this, or you might find it a welcome relief. To see someone else in a coma suggests that someone in your life feels powerless, and you might feel responsible for this situation. ☾ **waking up** ℭ *communication, control issues, isolation, personal power, stasis*.

comet   See *meteors and meteorites*.

commercial   See *advertisement*.

communion   See *religious ceremonies*.

compact disc   See *CDs and DVDs*.

compass   Read a compass in a dream, and you are looking for direction, trying to decide which way to go. You've got a decision to make, but you need to read all the signs first. ☽ **lost** ☾ *decisions, direction, inanimate objects, journeys and quests, travel.*

competition See *contest.*

compliment Dream of giving a compliment, and you have figured out how to get what you want. Dream of getting a compliment, and you're enjoying high self-esteem right now. ☽ **insult** ☾ *desires, image, personal power, reputation.*

computer Computers represent the way many of us interface with the world today, and the benefits and problems that can cause. **1.** If you use computers often and you dream of a computer, you are probably just reliving aspects of your day. **2.** If you rarely use a computer but you dream of a computer, you may find the answer to a current problem within the world of technology. **3.** If you dream of getting a new computer, you will benefit from updating an old attitude. It isn't serving you well anymore and a fresh approach will make things clearer. **4.** If you dream of a computer having problems, getting a virus, or losing important information on a computer, it's time to get back to basics. Try a face-to-face encounter. Technology isn't the way out of your current situation. **5.** If you dream of a message popping up on your computer, somebody is trying to tell you something. See also *blank screen, chat room, cybersex, Internet dating, Internet surfing, key-*

board. ☽ **nature** ☾ *communication, electronics, inanimate objects, messages, solutions and remedies, technology.*

concentration camp Dreams of seeing or being in a concentration camp signify fear on a deep level. You don't feel safe or in control of your own life, and you feel that those in control of you have evil or dangerous intentions. ☽ **utopia** ☾ *anxiety, authority, control issues, danger, death, fear, places.*

concert To play in a concert symbolizes your need to express your creativity to others. To watch a concert suggests you have recently gained a greater appreciation for the creativity of others. ☽ **silence** ☾ *communication, creativity, music and sound.*

condom See *contraception.*

confession Dreaming of admitting you did it suggests you have feelings of guilt and you want to alleviate them by confessing, even if you don't really plan to confess anything. To confess to a priest means you need someone to forgive you for something. Some stuff you can just forgive yourself for and get on with your life and try not to do it again. To hear someone else confess suggests you've been a guiding force to someone who needs you to set a good example. ☽ **crime** ☾ *guilt, regret, solutions and remedies.*

confetti You've got something to celebrate if you dream of confetti.

Let go and enjoy the moment! ☾ **rain** ☾ *celebration, fun.*

constellation   See *stars.*

construction   Dreams of construction mean you are building something for yourself. Is it a new relationship, a new persona, a new attitude? Whatever it is, you are heavily into the creation phase and your life is full of possibility. ☾ **destruction** ☾ *buildings and rooms, creation, creativity, opportunity.*

contact lens   Contact lenses symbolize the way you see the situation you are in. **1.** Dreaming of putting in a contact lens means you are ready to give a troubling situation or relationship a closer look. The details have been eluding you, but no more. **2.** Dreaming of losing a contact lens means you've lost perspective and you aren't seeing what's really going on. **3.** Dreaming of wearing colored contact lenses so your eyes look different symbolizes how you have recently seen yourself in a new way. ☾ **vision problems** ☾ *clothing and accessories, image, impediments, inanimate objects, relationships, solutions and remedies.*

contest   Win, lose, or draw … whatever the situation, dreaming of a contest or competition means you aren't the only one going after a goal, and you can sense that the race has begun. In your dream, the contest might be a race, a lottery, a reality show, or some other test

of knowledge, skill, power, or ability. What are you competing for in your waking life? The details surrounding the contest or competition in your dream will give you clues. How you feel about the contest also symbolizes how confident you are in your ability to get what you need or want. Good luck. See also *beauty contest, losing, race, reality show, test, winning.* ☾ **quitting** ☾ *competition, desires, goal-setting, image, opportunity, personal power, sports and games.*

contraception   Sex dreams are common, and these often include the issue of contraception. Condoms, birth control pills, or any other form of birth control can represent mastery of the mind over the passions to achieve a goal, or a reluctance to experience the consequences of your actions. **1.** If you use contraception in a dream and this seems natural, you have a firm control over your future. **2.** If you use contraception but you aren't sure how it works or whether it will work, or you almost forget to use it, you feel like a victim of fate and you don't really believe you have control over what happens to you. **3.** If you dream your contraception fails (such as a condom breaking), you feel guilty about something you've done. **4.** If you forget to use contraception in a dream, you blame yourself and your own carelessness for a bad situation. ☾ **pregnancy** ☾ *control issues, guilt, regret, sexual activity, solutions and remedies.*

According to folk medicine, caraway seeds and their essential oils can help you to remember your dreams better. If you want to try it, wrap a small handful of caraway seeds in a square of fabric and keep it under your pillow.

contract   Signing a contract in a dream represents a decision you've made. Refusing to sign a contract also represents a decision. If you debate about signing a contract or read but don't understand a contract in your dream, you aren't yet ready to make that decision. ❧ **breaking something** ℂ *decisions.*

convertible   To see a convertible with the top down in your dream means you've loosened up and decided to enjoy life lately. You're feeling free and easy. If the top is closed on the convertible, you've decided not to say or do something, against your first impulse, and your restraint is probably a smart move right now. See also *car.* ❧ **SUV** ℂ *freedom, happiness, pleasure, vehicles.*

convict   Unlike a criminal, a convict is serving or has served time in jail for a crime, and dreams about convicts symbolize guilt, punishment, and retribution. **1.** If you dream about a menacing or frightening convict, you feel threatened by a bad influence. **2.** If you dream of befriending a convict, you want to forgive someone or you want to believe that others have made the

same mistakes you have made. **3.** If you dream you are a convict in jail, you feel guilty about something and you fear having to fess up to an authority figure. **4.** If you dream you are a convict released from jail, you've done your time but you still feel a mark on you from a past mistake. You feel judged. ❧ **police officer** ℂ *authority, characters, danger, fear, guilt, people, punishment, rules and laws, threats.*

cooking   Cooking symbolizes creativity and sensual pleasure. To cook is to create something for the world, made out of things from the world. Cooking also represents the potential for pleasure, but the cooking itself represents the plan. The eating represents the pleasure. **1.** To dream you are cooking means you are enjoying a period of creativity and you are ready to create something wonderful. You have the power right now. **2.** To dream you've burned or ruined a meal while cooking means you might experience some setbacks but you are still ready to create something. If your plan doesn't work, start over. **3.** To dream someone else is cooking something good means you have pleasure or beauty in store for you. You plan to enjoy sensual pleasures. **4.** To dream someone else is burning or ruining a meal means somebody has been spoiling your well-laid plans for having a good time. Can you uninvite them? See also *eating.* ❧ **starvation** ℂ *creation, creativity, food and drink, hedonism, pleasure.*

cop   See *police officer.*

copy machine   You've done something worth repeating. Dreams of making copies on a copy machine symbolize success and the potential to profit from that success. Can you market that idea? If you dream a copy machine breaks down, your idea has limited appeal to others. ☽ **one-of-a-kind** ☾ *electronics, financial resources, inanimate objects, opportunity, technology.*

corner   Turn a corner in a dream, and you've changed direction, made an important decision, quit a bad habit, or improved something significant about yourself. To see a corner but be afraid to look or go around it symbolizes your fear of change. ☽ **wall** ☾ *buildings and rooms, changing course, decisions, fear, places, transformation.*

corpse   See *dead body.*

corsage   To wear a corsage in a dream means someone considers you a prize or a beautiful possession. To give someone a corsage means you want to mark that person, or someone they represent, as belonging to you. If someone gives you a Venus Fly Trap corsage, *run!* ☽ **rejection** ☾ *beauty, clothing and accessories, love, relationships.*

cosmetics   See *makeup.*

costume   To dream of wearing a costume means you want to appear to be something you aren't—maybe for fun, to try on a different persona, or to hide. **1.** To try on a costume suggests you are thinking about making a change in yourself or in your image. **2.** To wear a costume to a party or for a holiday like Halloween symbolizes your fun-loving and celebratory nature. You want to have a good time by temporarily trying on another persona. **3.** To wear a costume when nobody else is wearing a costume means you don't want people to know something about you, or you feel inauthentic and you fear everybody knows you aren't really who you pretend to be. See also *disguise.* ☽ **mirror** ☾ *celebration, characters, clothing and accessories, creativity, fun, guilt, identity, image, secrets, subterfuge, transformation.*

cotton candy   Dreaming of cotton candy means your life is sweet, just like when you were a child, and you're enjoying every sticky moment. ☽ **vegetables** ☾ *food and drink, fun, innocence, pleasure.*

couch   To see a couch in a dream represents relaxation, slowing down, and leisure time. **1.** To lie on a couch means you need to think things over. **2.** To sit on a couch with someone else means you feel emotionally intimate with someone. **3.** To sit on a couch alone suggests that you need some space. See also *furniture.* ☽ **stress** ☾ *freedom, furniture and appliances, healing, home, relationships, time.*

C

coughing   To cough in your dream symbolizes a blockage in communication. You want to say something, but you can't get it out. Coughing in a dream can also be a sign from your body that you are having a health problem related to your throat or lungs. Have it checked out if you are worried. ☻ **yelling** ℂ *communication, health and hygiene, relationships.*

counselor   See *therapist.*

counterfeiting   If you dream of counterfeiting money, or having and spending counterfeit money, you have an issue with your resources, financial or otherwise. You need more of something, but you feel you don't have any legitimate way to get it. In your dream, you've resorted to breaking the law, but in your waking life, this suggests that you find a less expected or typical way of getting what you need. Use your creativity—within legal boundaries, of course. ☻ **money** ℂ *creativity, financial resources, risky behavior, rules and laws, solutions and remedies.*

court   The court represents authority, punishment, and justice. If you dream you are in court, you may feel you deserve justice or have the authority to dispense justice. **1.** If you see a courthouse in your dream, rules or laws can guide you toward an answer to a current dilemma. **2.** If you dream you are in court as a defendant, you feel guilty about something and you expect to be judged. **3.** If you dream a court convicts you of something but you are innocent, you fear that others have judged you unfairly. **4.** If you dream you are in court as a judge or member of a jury, you have already passed judgment and your dream is further validating, or possibly questioning, the way you've decided to see another person or situation. Have you been fair? ☻ **jail** ℂ *authority, ethics and morals, guilt, injustice, innocence, places, punishment, rules and laws.*

cousins   Dreaming of your cousins connects you to other people, as part of a family or social network. **1.** To dream of your own cousins signifies that you feel a part of something bigger, even if you don't necessarily get along with your cousins. You are integrated into a social network. **2.** To dream of cousins you don't actually have represents a desire to be a part of a larger social network. You crave closer or more numerous connections with people. **3.** To dream of romantic involvement with cousins doesn't mean you actually want to get involved with your relatives. Instead, "kissing cousin" dreams mean you desire more romance in your life, but you would like your potential romantic partner to be someone you can trust and understand. See also *family.* ☻ **stranger** ℂ *family, people, relationships, social life.*

cow   The cow is a powerful and ancient symbol for fertility and nurturing. **1.** If you see a cow in your dream, you need nurturing or you have the impulse to nurture others. **2.** Cow dreams can also symbolize a desire for pregnancy. **3.** Dreaming of a herd of cows tells you that you have been following the crowd instead of making decisions for yourself. Are you being a passive follower? Are you sure the group is doing what's best for you? **4.** Dreaming of a very large cow means you are enjoying material wealth or have it coming to you. **☯ bull** *☾ abundance, animals, caretaking, desire, conformity, feminine, financial resources, nature, relationships.*

> In several ancient cultures, the cow was sacred and Hathor, the sacred cow goddess, symbolized nurturing, abundance, and fertility. Seeing a cow in your dreams might just mean a message from Hathor, a sign of happiness and abundance in your home, or your fertility.

cowboy   Cowboys symbolize independence, mastery over nature, and rebellion. **1.** If you dream you are a cowboy, you have an independent and self-sufficient nature. You see life as an adventure, and your dream is telling you that this quality can serve you well right now. **2.** If you dream you are a cowboy in a rodeo, you have been drawing attention to yourself lately by being rebellious and rowdy. Is getting attention the only reason you've

been kickin' up dust? **3.** If you dream of roping or lassoing an animal, you not only feel comfortable in the natural world, but you know how to use it to your own benefit. **4.** If you see or interact with a cowboy in your dream, someone in your waking life is pointing the way to a more independent and self-sufficient existence, or might be encouraging you to question authority.   **☯ crowd** *☾ adventure, characters, control issues, nature, people, rebellion.*

co-worker   Dreaming of your co-workers symbolizes the social support you enjoy or desire in your working life. **1.** If your co-workers treat you with respect in your dream, you've done something at work to increase your good reputation. **2.** If you dream co-workers threaten or fear you, you've recently done something to make others look bad, perhaps for your own benefit. You fear their retribution. **3.** If you dream of friendly interactions with co-workers, you feel comfortable and socially satisfied in your work life. **4.** If you dream of romantic or sexual interactions with a co-worker, you are letting your work relationships get too personal, physically or emotionally. Romantic dreams about co-workers could also signal a true devotion to your work. **5.** Pleasant dreams of co-workers you don't actually have demonstrates your desire for more friendly interactions or emotional support in your work life. You feel isolated or left out. Too bad you can't get paid overtime for dreaming about work! ☾ **boss** ☽ *career, characters, desires, image, opportunity, people, relationships, reputation, work.*

coyote Coyotes symbolize the need to be alone, isolated, and in close communion with nature. To see a coyote in your dream means you've begun to compromise your principles and only a withdrawal from the civilized world, no matter how temporary, will help you to find your path again. To be chased by a coyote means your need to change direction has become urgent. See also *animals.* ☾ **crowd** ☽ *animals, ethics and morals, instincts, isolation, nature.*

crab Dreaming of a crab represents excessive materialism, saving money, even hoarding resources. Your dream may be telling you that you've become too materialistic, or it may be that you need to be a little more thrifty. Are you thinking about your future? See also *animals.* ☾ **abundance** ☽ *animals, financial resources, ethics and morals, instincts, nature.*

cradle To dream of a cradle symbolizes innocence and your desire to nurture and protect it. To dream of a cradle tipped over or broken means something innocent has been corrupted. See also *baby.* ☾ **decadence** ☽ *age, caretaking, furniture and appliances, innocence, vulnerability.*

crawling To dream of crawling means you've had to go back to

the beginning. Forget what you've learned; it isn't relevant. Ominous dreams of crawling creatures or crawling children symbolize a broken promise or total disregard for rules and civilized behavior. ☾ **running** ☽ *changing course, crawling creatures, ethics and morals, instincts, risky behavior, rules and laws.*

crazy See *insane.*

cream See *milk.*

credit card Credit cards (or debit cards) in dreams symbolize financial issues, or debts you owe that don't necessarily involve money. **1.** Using credit cards to buy things in a dream suggests you might be taking on more debt than you can handle or making promises or plans you can't keep. **2.** Losing a credit card symbolizes a loss of control over your financial situation or loss of your good reputation. **3.** Cutting up a credit card in a dream suggests an inner resolve to regain control over your personal resources. ☾ **rich** ☽ *ethics and morals, financial resources, inanimate objects, relationships, reputation.*

cremation To dream of someone being cremated, or seeing a crematorium, symbolizes your desire to end something completely, with closure and finality. You don't ever want to go back to that relationship or situation. ☾ **reincarnation** ☽ *changing course, death, destruction, relationships.*

crib　See *cradle*.

crickets　Dreaming of a single cricket chirping symbolizes good luck and a happy home life. Dreaming of lots of crickets symbolizes the subtle infiltration of an idea into your life. Something has changed you so gradually you don't even realize you've changed. ☾ **monotony** ☾ *animals, changing course, crawling creatures, happiness, nature, transformation.*

crime　If you commit a crime in your dream, you feel guilty about something you did, you are worried about something you might do, or you just want to let off some steam and break the rules in a way that won't get you in trouble. It certainly doesn't doom you to involvement in a bank heist. **1.** To dream of getting caught committing a crime symbolizes your anxiety at breaking the rules. **2.** To dream of committing a petty crime like vandalism or shoplifting symbolizes your rebellious side. Have the rules governing your life been overly repressive lately? **3.** To dream of committing a violent crime represents repressed energy. You've been denying your instincts and they are trying to come out in a way you will remember when you wake up. Can you let off steam in a way that won't land you in jail or hurt others? **4.** To stop a crime in your dream symbolizes your vigilant fight against injustice and anarchy. You believe the rules matter. **5.** To dream you are watching a crime but remain uninvolved shows your

ambivalence about a recent restriction in your life. You aren't sure it's right, but you aren't sure it's wrong, either. **6.** To be a victim of a crime in a dream symbolizes your feelings of helplessness and fear in the face of forces you can't control. See also *cheating, murder, rape, stealing.* ☾ **confession** ☾ *anxiety, control issues, danger, desires, ethics and morals, fear, frustration, guilt, punishment, rebellion, risky behavior, rules and laws.*

criminal　See *crime*.

crocodile　See *alligator or crocodile*.

cross　Crosses represent many different things throughout ancient history. The cross, today a Christian symbol, was originally a pagan symbol, but dreaming of a cross today often symbolizes spiritual love and sacrifice or religious questioning. But crosses can have more ancient symbolism in dreams. They can represent spiritual protection, male power (in some cultures, the cross is a phallic symbol), creation, or the cycles of nature: life and death, the changing of the seasons, or the connection between Earth and heaven. Consider the context of the cross in your dream to discover what it means for you. Seeing or wearing a crucifix (a cross with the crucified figure of Jesus Christ on it) is more obviously a Christian symbol denoting sacrifice and forgiveness. **1.** To wear a cross in your dream means you have been forgiven. **2.** To see a cross over or

C

on top of something suggests that you need protection from what that object or person represents. **3.** To see a cross in nature, formed by trees or clouds or animals, means you can find spiritual meaning for your life in the natural world. Nature is an important spiritual source for you right now and is worth exploring. **4.** To witness the crucifixion of Christ or of someone else suggests that someone has made a very important sacrifice for you. **5.** To dream you are being crucified or carrying a cross suggests that you have a martyr complex. Are you comfortable wearing that cross? ☽ **circle** ℂ *code, creation, divine power, forgiveness, inanimate objects, masculine, nature, protection, sacrifice, shapes and symbols, spirituality.*

cross-dressing Dreams of cross-dressing don't mark you as a cross-dresser, necessarily. More likely, cross-dressing in a dream indicates dishonesty. You aren't being authentic, or a situation isn't what it seems. Cross-dressing dreams can also indicate an imbalance within you. We all have a mix of feminine and masculine energies within us. Have you been forcing yourself to be more feminine or more masculine than is really you? **1.** Dreaming of the process of putting on clothes belonging to the opposite sex suggests you have been wearing a guise that isn't really you. Are you being honest with yourself and others? **2.** To dream of being out in public in clothes belonging to the opposite

sex suggests you've been stifling your true desires, which may have nothing to do with gender or sexual issues. **3.** To dream of getting sexually aroused by clothing suggests that appearance is very important to you and you use it to judge yourself and others. **4.** If you dream of someone else being a cross-dresser, someone or some situation in your waking life isn't what it seems. ☽ **telling the truth** ℂ *balance, characters, clothing and accessories, desires, dishonesty, feminine, gender issues, identity, masculine, secrets, sexual activity, subterfuge, transformation, trust issues, yin-yang.*

Dreams about sexuality can frighten and confuse people, but dreaming of doing or being something or someone doesn't mean that is really who you are. Many people have dreams about being attracted to, or having a physical relationship with, someone of the same sex. No cause for alarm! While such dreams can be acting out your desires, in many cases, sexual dreams really symbolize something else, such as an emotional intimacy, a wish for friendship, admiration for someone, curiosity, or attraction to an idea, place, or principle rather than an actual person. The object of your desire or your actions or feelings in your dream might very well also symbolize somebody or something entirely different than it seems on the surface of your dream.

crossroads To come to a crossroads in a dream means you face an important decision. You recognize on a deep level that this decision will have a major impact on your life. If you choose a path in your dream, you already know what your decision will be. If you hesitate, you are still thinking. ☾ **speeding** ℭ *changing course, decisions, opportunity, places.*

crossword puzzle   It's a cipher! You're working out how to make things all go together. It's a complex puzzle of interlocking ideas, people, and problems, but you'll figure it out. Your crossword puzzle dream shows you've got strategic plans, an intellectual approach, and the big picture in your mind. ☾ **numbers** ℭ *code, intelligence, responsibilities, solutions and remedies.*

crowd   To be part of a crowd in a dream represents conformity to mass opinion or your attitude about people in general. **1.** To have fun in a crowd or be at a crowded party shows your enjoyment of social interaction. You like to be with people, and people energize you. **2.** To be in a crowd but not know anyone suggests you feel out of place. You don't belong in any group and you are lonely, even when people surround you. **3.** To feel suffocated or claustrophobic in a crowd reveals your need for some time off. People drain your energy, and you need to replenish it with a retreat from the masses. Can you take a day off? **4.** To be in a crowd that causes trouble or a riot, or breaks the law, suggests that your friends or social network has been leading you astray. Is the

group getting you to do something against your own personal code? ☾ **alone** ℭ *anxiety, conformity, ethics and morals, fun, hedonism, isolation, people, rules and laws.*

crown   To see a crown in your dream indicates the presence in your life of a highly respected authority figure. To wear a crown symbolizes your new responsibility or position of authority. People respect you. Are you comfortable wearing that crown? See also *king, queen.* ☾ **baldness** ℭ *authority, clothing and accessories, image, inanimate objects, reputation.*

crucifix   See *cross.*

cruise   To dream of going on a cruise suggests the desire for or fear of a relaxing escape or break from your ordinary life. **1.** If the cruise is pleasant, exciting, fun, luxurious, or romantic, you're having a wish-fulfillment dream. You are ready for some time off from your regular existence. The Love Boat awaits you. **2.** If you dream of a boring or silly cruise, or a cruise you feel is a waste of time, you may have been recently encouraged to take some time off, but you don't need it. You're too interested in your work right now. **3.** If something goes wrong on the cruise—the ship sinks, fellow travelers become dangerous, wild animals attack—you have some reservations about taking time off. You fear consequences if you relax too much. ☾ **job** ℭ *adventure, career, disaster, fun, hedonism, places, travel, work.*

C

crutches   To see crutches in a dream symbolizes a bad habit you haven't been able to kick or a loss of stability in your life. **1.** To dream of using crutches means you need help with something you can't do alone. Are you afraid to ask? **2.** To dream of someone else using crutches means somebody in your waking life is having a problem. Your dream may be telling you to help. ☉ **running** *€ frustration, health and hygiene, impediments, inanimate objects, injuries, pain, risky behavior, stability, vulnerability.*

crying   **1.** To dream you are crying means you need emotional release you haven't allowed yourself in your waking life. **2.** To dream someone else is crying means someone needs your empathy right now. **3.** To wake up actually crying suggests you are still in mourning over a loss, even if you haven't consciously admitted you feel any sadness at all. ☉ **laughing** *€ feelings, loss, pain, repression.*

crystal ball   In gypsy folklore, a crystal ball shows the future, and dreams of gazing into a crystal ball tell the future, too—or at least, what you believe the future has in store for you. If you see an image in the crystal ball, what you see represents what you expect or intuit will happen. If you see nothing in a crystal ball, you feel anxiety about not knowing what to expect. If you see your own reflection, you are the one in control of your destiny. See also *fortune teller.* ☉ **past life**

€ anxiety, code, goal-setting, inanimate objects, myths and legends, predictions.

cult   Cult dreams are fairly common and represent fear and anxiety about getting into a situation you can't control. **1.** If you dream of getting kidnapped and forced to join a cult, you've been feeling peer pressure to do something you don't really want to do. You feel like you might not have a choice. **2.** If you dream of voluntarily joining a cult and then realizing after it's too late that you can't get out, you've got an instinct that you're headed in a direction in your waking life that you might regret. **3.** If you dream of joining a cult and enjoying it, you haven't been getting enough support from others. You lack the feeling of being in a family, and you wish for this security. **4.** If you dream of getting rescued from a cult, you depend on others to help you set your personal boundaries. **5.** If you dream someone you know joins a cult, you have a suspicion that someone you care about is headed in a bad direction. **6.** If you dream of trying to rescue someone else from a cult, you have the desire to save someone in a dramatic fashion. Does the person you want to rescue really want to be saved? ☉ **loneliness** *€ anxiety, caretaking, family, fear, peer pressure, regret, risky behavior, spirituality, vulnerability.*

cup or glass   Cups and glasses symbolize what you take in, take to heart, or believe. **1.** If you dream of drinking from a cup, you've recently learned something new that you consider important. **2.** If you spill the drink, you don't believe something you've just been told. **3.** If you give someone else a cup or glass, you are trying to convince someone else of something important. **4.** If the cup or glass is cracked, chipped, or broken, you've lost faith in something. ☽ **lying** ☾ *communication, food and drink, inanimate objects, messages.*

cupboard   See *storage.*

curling iron   See *hair.*

curse   **1.** To curse or swear in a dream suggests pent-up anger or frustration with your inability to communicate something. **2.** If you dream someone is cursing or swearing at you, you feel like you've done something wrong and you fear getting admonished for it. **3.** To dream that someone has put a curse on you symbolizes your anxiety about your past behavior and how it will affect your future. **4.** To dream of putting a curse on somebody else means you haven't forgiven somebody for something, and you don't particularly want to be forgiving. ☽ **compliment** ☾ *anger, anxiety, communication, fear, guilt, regret, threats.*

curtains   **1.** Closed curtains symbolize something you are hiding, or something hidden from you. **2.** Open curtains symbolize your readiness to reveal what's up with you or to see what's really going on.

☽ **window** ☾ *buildings and rooms, home, impediments, subterfuge.*

cut   **1.** To dream of cutting something in a dream with scissors, a knife, or another sharp object symbolizes your wish to get beneath the surface to discover what's really going on. **2.** If you cut yourself, you have been hiding your feelings and you are ready to let them out. **3.** If you cut your fingers by mistake, you should be more careful. You've been careless. **4.** If someone else cuts you, you feel betrayed. **5.** If you cut someone else, your actions or words have caused damage to someone. **6.** If you cut fabric, you want to change something about yourself. **7.** Cutting food means you should be more careful about what you eat. See also *injuries.* ☽ **bandages** ☾ *accidents, body parts, destruction, health and hygiene, injuries, risky behavior, secrets, subterfuge.*

cybersex   To dream of having sex over the Internet removes you several times over from actual human contact, and cybersex dreams suggest both a desire for sexual release and a reluctance to get too emotionally involved with an actual human being. You want connection, but not intimacy. Also, your cyber connection may be with someone who is masking his or her true identity (or you could be masking *yours*). Is your partner in waking life wearing a brilliant disguise? Cybersex dreams can also symbolize an obsession with technology. ☽ **love** ☾ *communication, hedonism, sexual activity, technology.*

D

daffodil Dreams of daffodils suggest the presence of beauty, innocence, joyfulness, and fresh starts in your life. Dreaming of wilted daffodils means you've just learned something that has made you feel older and wiser. See also *flowers*. ◑ **decadence** ℂ *beauty, creation, happiness, innocence, nature, plants.*

daisy Seeing daisies in a dream represents a celebration of your feminine side, sweetness, innocent love, and the beginnings of relationships. To give daisies to someone in a dream means you have a crush on that person, or someone that person represents. If someone gives daisies to you, you feel pretty. See also *flowers*. ◑ **ugliness** ℂ *beauty, feminine, innocence, love, nature, plants.*

dancing Dancing symbolizes the joyful embrace of existence, living in the moment, pleasure, and freedom. **1.** If you dream of dancing alone, you feel independent and whole. **2.** If you dream of dancing with someone, you are happy and secure in a relationship or friendship. **3.** If you dream of dancing in a big crowd, you feel like celebrating. **4.** If you dream you dance awkwardly or keep stepping on someone's feet, a current relationship or situation isn't working very well. See also *ballet, ballerina, club*. ◑ **depression** ℂ *celebration, freedom, happiness, music and sound, pleasure.*

dandelion 1. To dream of this pretty and sunny-looking weed suggests that you've recently made the best of a bad situation. **2.** To give dandelions to someone means you understand that person, or someone they represent. **3.** If you dream someone gives dandelions to you, you have a realistic view of your relationship with that person, or someone they represent. **3.** To pull out dandelions from the ground in your dream means you've become particularly fastidious about making sure everything goes right in a recent endeavor. **4.** Dreaming of spraying dandelions with weed killer symbolizes your recent campaign to eliminate an imperfection in your life. But cut yourself some slack. Some people see dandelions as weeds while others see them as flowers. See also *flowers*. ☾ **grass** ☽ *creativity, goal-setting, nature, plants, relationships.*

> Dreaming of flowers with six petals has special significance. Six was the sacred sexual number for the goddess Aphrodite, and her flower had six petals. Dreaming of six-petalled flowers or the number six symbolizes sacred feminine power and an intense sexual energy with the associated link to fertility and motherhood. Six is a powerful number for women.

dandruff   Dreaming you have dandruff symbolizes embarrassment. You've done something you're ashamed of or you're just feeling generally embarrassed in a certain area of your life. You fear people are laughing at you. Dreaming you see dandruff on someone else indicates a feeling of superiority over someone you know, even if you feel sympathetic toward that person or try to help him or her. ☾ **baldness** ☽ *body parts, embarrassment, image, personal power.*

danger   Dreams about being in danger can frighten and terrify or thrill and excite, but they come for a reason. Your subconscious mind has picked up subtle cues in your life and wants to warn you of something. **1.** Frightening dreams about being in danger suggest you need to be careful in your waking life. The danger might not be nearly as dramatic as in your dream, but something lurks. Pay attention. **2.** Dreams in which you are in danger but the dream is exciting, even thrilling, act out your sense of adventure and craving for more excitement in your life. Risk-taking in dreams gives you a real thrill, even if it doesn't happen much in your waking life, and you might even have sensed something is about to happen. You look forward to the thrill and the risk. **3.** To dream someone else is in danger and you must rescue him or her suggests your intuition that someone really does need your help, or at least your protection, just in case. Your dream shows that you are aware of your responsibility. **4.** To dream you see someone else in danger but you don't or can't do anything about it symbolizes generalized anxiety about life in this sometimes dangerous world. You feel anxious or even depressed about your helplessness, and you carry with you a fear that something bad is going to happen. See also *dangerous person, disaster*. ☾ **stability** ☽ *accidents, adventure, anxiety, caretaking, control issues, danger, death, disaster, fear, intuition, predictions, responsibilities, risky behavior, threats, vulnerability, weather and seasons.*

dangerous person   Someone dangerous threatens or pursues you. What do you do? The way you react to or feel about dangerous people in your dream indicates what the dream means for you. **1.** If you get chased, assaulted, or threatened by a dangerous person, you're plagued with worry about a problem or situation and the dangerous person represents the thing that troubles you. **2.** If you escape a dangerous person, you feel confident in your abilities to solve your current dilemma. **3.** If you feel excited and challenged by involvement with a dangerous person, or get involved romantically with a dangerous person in your dream, you crave more excitement or greater challenges to your abilities in your waking life. **4.** If the dangerous person in your dream is you, you've been repressing some urge, thought, or feeling in yourself that threatens to come out. You might as well face it. **5.** If someone you love or trust in your waking life becomes a dangerous person in your dreams, you've become distrustful and you suspect someone is hiding something from you. **6.** If a dangerous person pursues or assaults a family member or friend, you have been worrying about someone else and feeling responsible for their safety. See also *crime, danger.* ◐ **mother** ☾ *adventure, anxiety, caretaking, characters, control issues, danger, fear, people, relationships, responsibilities, risky behavior, threats, trust issues, vulnerability.*

darkness Darkness can take on many guises in dreams but generally symbolizes the unknown, mysterious, unexplored, or unacknowledged parts of your own psyche. Darkness shows up in dreams for a reason. It can surround something you fear and don't know, something you don't want to know or aren't ready to face, or something mysterious and exciting in a compelling way. Pay special attention to the things in your dreams shrouded in darkness and the way you react to them. Adventurous exploration means you feel strong and confident, ready to face the unknown with bravado. Fear, shrinking away, or anxiety in the face of darkness usually signifies fear and anxiety about something unknown. Your dream acts out your anxiety, but it can also help you to prepare for the inevitable when you face a significant change or discovery. ◐ **light** ☾ *adventure, anxiety, courage, danger, fear, journeys and quests, mystery, subterfuge, yin-yang.*

darts and dartboards Did you hit a bull's-eye, or are there more holes on your wall than in your dartboard? Dreams of throwing darts or playing darts symbolize the project you are currently working on, and how well your aim has been in planning and instituting the plan. ◐ **lost** ☾ *career, competition, direction, goal-setting, inanimate objects, play, sports and games.*

dating Dreaming of dating can be wish fulfillment, a safe and non-threatening escape from reality for those in a long-term relationship, or it can symbolize your desire to try out anything new in your life: a new look, a new job, even a new persona. **1.** If you enjoy dating in your dream, you are probably experimenting with the idea of changing something. **2.** If dating in

D

your dream becomes all about sex, you are passionate about something new you've been doing. **3.** If dating in your dream turns out to be an unpleasant experience, you may be faced with a change you don't want to make. ☾ **divorce** ℭ *adventure, anxiety, changing course, relationships, transformation.*

daughter   1. To dream of your actual daughter means she needs your attention. Something requires a parent's guidance. **2.** To dream of a daughter you don't actually have usually symbolizes the younger you. Are you feeling in need of a parental figure? Or maybe you feel rebellious. Think of the daughter in your dream as yourself, and you should recognize what the dream is about. ☾ **mother** ℭ *age, caretaking, family, people, relationships.*

dead animal   1. You've thoroughly squelched a troublesome instinct, or you've lost a more innocent part of yourself, when you dream of a dead animal. **2.** Seeing a dead animal can also represent separation from the natural world, or the end of something meaningful, like a relationship or a dream. **3.** If you killed the animal in your dream, accidentally or on purpose, you've taken control of something in your life that required your mastery, but you aren't entirely comfortable with this change just yet. **4.** If someone else kills an animal in your dream, you feel disillusioned with the world. **5.** If the dead animal is your pet, you are in mourning for an important loss, even if you don't fully realize

it in your waking life. See also *animals.* ☾ **birth** ℭ *animals, birds, control issues, crawling creatures, death, instincts, nature, transformation.*

dead body   **Something you thought was dead and buried—a feeling, an opinion, a habit—has surfaced in your dream if you find a dead body. If the dead body comes to life, this thing you had buried has been banging against your conscious mind, trying to get back in. If you see a dead body and are filled with grief or you admit that you were responsible in your dream, you really are ready to move on from this thing that used to be part of your life. ☾ **birth ℭ *characters, creativity, goal-setting, relationships.*

dead end   **To dream of coming up against a dead end suggests the path you have chosen in your life right now isn't working. You might have to turn around and go back, or try a new direction. ☾ **street ℭ *changing course, direction, failure, frustration, impediments, journeys and quests, travel.*

deafness   1. To be deaf in a dream signifies your unwillingness or inability to recognize something important. Someone is trying to tell you something, but you won't listen. **2.** To meet or talk to a deaf person in a dream means you will have to try some alternative methods of communication to get your point across. ☾ **noise** ℭ *communication, relationships.*

death   Just as the death card in a tarot card reading represents change rather than literal death, dreams of death also represent significant change. **1.** To dream someone or something close to you (a child, a friend, a family member, or a pet) dies means you face a major change in *your* life. **2.** If the death of the person is particularly traumatic or you remember it vividly when you wake up and still feel upset about it, you may be predicting a change in that person's life, or in the life of someone that person represents. **3.** To dream someone who has died comes back as a ghost to tell you something could, according to some, actually be a message from that person. Or it can be your subconscious self missing that person and wishing to hear from them, or projecting what you think they would say to you now. **4.** To dream of a wild animal's death means you've mastered instincts that had been getting out of control. **5.** To dream that you die in your dream means you've already made an inner change and you are now working on reinventing some part of yourself. **6.** To dream you meet the figure of death symbolizes your own personal power. You've been granted a glimpse into the spirit world and given access to unseen forces of change. Use this knowledge wisely! See also *dead animal*. ☽ **birth** ☾ *changing course, characters, courage, creativity, death, myths and legends, transformation.*

debit card   See *credit card*.

debts   See *bills and debts*.

decadence   Dreams of decadent behavior can be fun or naughty in a thrilling way, or they can symbolize a loss of innocence and wonder. They can also symbolize struggles with self-control. Of course, what constitutes "decadence" differs from person to person. Dreams of indulging in chocolate may be decadent to you, while to someone else, decadence might be engaging in an all-night bender or seducing that adorable-but-married co-worker, so interpreting dreams of decadence often hinge on what the behavior is and how you feel about it. **1.** If you dream of your own decadence, you struggle to control a behavior and you're letting loose in your dreams. Or you fear you will lose control and behave in a decadent way in your waking life, and this fear plays out in your dream. **2.** If you truly enjoy your decadent dream, you may be too strict on yourself, and you could stand to let up a little and have some more fun. A little decadence can be part of a healthful lifestyle. **3.** Dreams of decadence can be pure entertainment without any indication that you are seriously considering acting on them. These dreams are like watching movies—escapism, pure and simple, and no threat to your personal life. **4.** If the decadent behavior involves an addiction you have in your waking life, your dream is your addiction banging on your mind to have its way. Consider it a subconscious temper tantrum. **5.** If someone else

D

behaves in a decadent way in your dream and tries to get you to go along with it, someone is tempting you to do something you aren't entirely comfortable about in your waking life. **6.** If someone behaves in a decadent manner and you shun or judge him or her, you're feeling like you've got firm control over your own behavior, but you might also be judgmental toward others. Are you feeling a mite superior? ☽ **modesty** ℂ *abundance, fear, food and drink, freedom, fun, greed, guilt, hedonism, impediments, instincts, pleasure, regret, relationships, repression, reputation, risky behavior, sexual activity, wishes.*

According to many people who have experienced them, dreams sometimes warn of an impending event and it pays to take precautions. One famous example is that of a woman on the *Titanic* who dreamed the ship would sink. Her husband didn't take the dream seriously, but she felt so strongly about the dream that she put her children to bed dressed in their warmest clothes. When the ship struck the iceberg, the woman whisked her children out of bed and was able to make it onto a lifeboat. Her husband went down with the ship.

decapitation   To see someone decapitated in your dream symbolizes a loss of good sense. Are you using your head, or being careless and thoughtless? Decapitation dreams, when graphic and gory, can also represent the fear of losing control. Are you thinking with other parts of your body? ☽ **headache** ℂ *accidents, body parts, intelligence, risky behavior.*

deer   Deer have acute senses, startle easily, and are hunted by many animals, including humans. **1.** To see a deer in your dream can mean you should tune in to your environment. Pay very close attention, and you'll pick up subtle cues about what's really going on. **2.** To chase a deer on foot symbolizes a desire to escape society and develop a more intimate relationship with nature. **3.** To dream of communicating or having some interaction with a deer represents a recent awareness of your own sensitivity. You might be surprised by how strongly you feel an emotion, or how quickly you reacted to something you didn't realize you feared. **4.** To dream of shooting a deer and feeling triumphant or excited about it represents a mastery over nature or instincts you've struggled to control. It can also symbolize your self-sufficiency. **5.** To feel guilty or sad about shooting a deer represents guilt and anxiety about the way you've treated someone. Maybe you didn't realize someone was quite so sensitive. **6.** To dream of hitting a deer with a car symbolizes a major obstacle in a plan. You might have to change direction. See also *dead animal.* ☽ **lion** ℂ *animals, anxiety, control issues, danger, fear, instincts, intuition, nature, vulnerability.*

deformity   **1.** To dream you have a deformity means that some part of you hasn't developed the way you want it to, or in a way you feel is normal. You feel self-conscious about this, or you feel different from everyone else. **2.** To dream you see a deformity on someone else means that something in your life isn't working the way it's supposed to work. What has gone awry without your attention? ☻ **monotony** ℭ *accidents, body parts, image, responsibilities.*

deity   See *gods, goddesses.*

dementia   See *senile.*

demons   See *devil.*

dentist   If you visit the dentist in a dream, you need help communicating with someone. Dreams of oral surgery or other dental procedures symbolize attempts to fix communication problems. The dentist represents the action you will need to take to get your message across. See also *teeth.* ☻ **silence** ℭ *body parts, career, characters, communication, messages, medicine and surgery, people.*

depression   **1.** If you dream you are depressed when you aren't depressed during your waking life, you are playing out an internal desire to escape your responsibilities. You wish you had an excuse to let it all go. **2.** To dream someone else is depressed could be a sign that you are actually the one who is depressed but you've had difficulty

admitting it to yourself. **3.** Dreams of a depressed person can also mean that someone needs your help because they are losing the ability to cope with something. ☻ **happy** ℭ *burdens, caretaking, desires, feelings, vulnerability.*

deprivation   **1.** To dream of being deprived of something can represent resentment regarding a sacrifice you've made or envy toward someone else. **2.** To dream someone else suffers from deprivation means you have an opportunity right now to be a good Samaritan and help someone who needs it. ☻ **bingeing** ℭ *envy, ethics and morals, financial resources, sacrifice, solutions and remedies.*

desert   **1.** The long, dry desert represents a dry spell in creativity, sexual activity, or passion for life. **2.** Wandering in a desert suggests you feel like you are wandering in life without a meaningful purpose. **3.** Being lost in the desert suggests you see no end to your current mundane existence. **4.** Traveling through the desert on an adventure, however, can mean that you desire new experiences or a change of scenery. ☻ **flood** ℭ *adventure, danger, direction, feelings, heat, journeys and quests, nature, places, repression, threats, travel.*

desk   Your desk represents your work life and/or your financial situation. **1.** To dream of a messy desk means you feel disorganized, scattered, or overextended at work or you aren't in control of your finances. **2.** An empty desk suggests you don't feel fulfilled by your working life or you are lacking in financial resources. **3.** A neat, well-organized desk or a new, fancy desk that pleases you symbolizes success in your work life and the potential to go even further. You may just get that promotion or raise. ☻ **fired from a job** ℂ *career, financial resources, furniture and appliances, goal-setting, work.*

dessert   To dream of beautiful, delicious desserts symbolizes luxury, decadence, and indulgence, or in the case of dieters, guilt. **1.** If you eat and enjoy dessert in your dream, you know how to appreciate pleasures in your life, and the occasional sensual indulgence fills you with joy. **2.** If you overindulge in desserts and feel guilty, you might be depriving yourself too much in your diet, or you might be busy kicking a sugar habit and your body is rebelling, in which case these dreams will pass once you've kicked the habit. **3.** To dream of *not* eating dessert but feeling deprived or resentful about it symbolizes your resentment about the things you are missing because of an obligation. **4.** To dream of not eating dessert and feeling empowered by it symbolizes a habit you've successfully overcome, or having the power to overcome a habit. See also *bakery, baking.* ☻ **deprivation** ℂ *abundance, comfort, food and drink, guilt, happiness, hedonism, personal power, pleasure, sacrifice.*

destruction   Knock it down, blow it up, burn it to the ground. To dream of destruction symbolizes major change in your life: the end of the old, in order to start over and build something new. **1.** To cause or engage in destruction symbolizes your personal role in revamping your life. You can make it happen. **2.** To watch destruction symbolizes your feeling that life is changing and you have no control over it. **3.** To be caught in the middle of destruction and to feel unsafe symbolizes your anxiety and insecurity about changes in your life. You aren't comfortable with an impending change. ☻ **construction** ℂ *accidents, anxiety, buildings and rooms, changing course, death, destruction, disaster, transformation.*

detective   **1.** If you dream you are a detective, you have been relishing the process of uncovering a mystery: a new love, the best way to solve a problem, even the mystery that is you. **2.** If you dream you hire a detective, you should enlist someone else to help you solve a problem. **3.** If you are interrogated by a detective, you feel guilty about something and you suspect someone is on to you. ☻ **hiding** ℂ *career, characters, guilt, identity, knowledge, mystery, people, personal power, solutions and remedies.*

detour   You'll have to go another way. Dreams of detours symbolize a setback that requires extra creativity. You'll still get there, but it might take a little longer. ☻ **shortcut** ℂ *changing course, direction,* *frustration, impediments, journeys and quests, travel.*

devil Dreams about the devil, demons, demonic possession, or other religious symbols of evil symbolize anxiety over an inner moral conflict. This could be linked to your religious experience, but more often, dreams about the devil symbolize anxiety about bad influences in your life or fear of the unknown. You may have become overly influenced by a person or situation and you don't like how this influence has affected you. Your dream plays out your fear. See also *possessed by demons.* ❂ **angel** ℭ *anxiety, characters, control issues, danger, death, ethics and morals, fear, myths and legends, risky behavior, spirituality, vulnerability.*

diamond To dream of diamonds suggests wealth, luxury, and a future commitment. Diamond rings symbolize the desire for a commitment in a relationship, but if the ring is missing diamonds or you lose the diamonds out of the ring in your dream, you aren't ready for a commitment yet, or you have become disillusioned about a relationship. Give it more time before you make any promises. See also *jewelry, ring.* ❂ **breaking up** ℭ *abundance, desires, financial resources, inanimate objects, love, relationships.*

diet Dreaming you are on a diet symbolizes a subconscious dissatisfaction with your appearance. You think you need to look like, or

even be, someone else. Dreaming of breaking a diet symbolizes feelings of oppression and a desire to break the rules. ❂ **bingeing** ℭ *food and drink, health and hygiene, image, rebellion, rules and laws.*

digging To dream of digging suggests you are working hard to discover something. If you dig and discover treasure, you almost have the answer to your question. See also *dirt.* ❂ **hiding** ℭ *mystery, secrets, solutions and remedies, subterfuge.*

digital camera See *camera.*

dinner **1.** To dream of eating dinner symbolizes contentment with family, home, and happiness. **2.** To dream of eating dinner alone symbolizes your independence, which you relish, flavored with loneliness, which you could do without. **3.** If you enjoy a dinner alone in peaceful reflection, you could use some time alone to nourish your inner resources. **4.** To dream of skipping dinner means you feel emotionally or spiritually starved. ❂ **breakfast** ℭ *caretaking, food and drink, family, happiness, home, stability.*

D

Mealtime in dreams represents a particularly vulnerable time. As you consume food in a dream, you take the ideas, emotions, and actions of others into you. You are open to influences. What you eat in a dream symbolizes what you've allowed yourself to absorb, believe, or feel.

diploma   See *graduation*.

dirt   **1.** Digging in dirt symbolizes a search for an answer, or for the origin of something. Why do you always *do* that thing? **2.** Getting dirt on you symbolizes a mistake you've made. **3.** Washing dirt off symbolizes a new beginning and a fresh start. **4.** Moving dirt with heavy equipment symbolizes major reconstruction of your environment or opinions. Something has happened to change your perceptions. **5.** Dirt falling on you suggests anxiety about an entirely new situation. Everything seems upside down and you aren't sure which way is up. See also *buried alive, digging*. ☻ **cleaning** ☾ *adventure, anxiety, changing course, mystery, transformation*.

disappearing   **1.** Dreams of disappearing that feel empowering can be an important sign that you are able to do something unnoticed right now. **2.** Disappearing dreams that feel frustrating or scary suggest you feel invisible and nobody notices you. You've learned to blend in a little too well. **3.** To dream someone else disappears symbolizes someone's recent absence, permanent or temporary, from your life. To dream objects disappear signifies a change in your material or financial situation. **4.** You may be simplifying, or you may be suffering losses. ☻ **celebrity** ☾ *anxiety, conformity, control issues, insecurity, secret, subterfuge, transformation*.

disappointment   **1.** To dream of disappointment symbolizes foiled expectations in your waking life. The person or situation that has disappointed you in your dream—it may be yourself—will clue you in to what has disappointed you in waking life. **2.** To disappoint someone else in a dream suggests you have actually disappointed yourself. ☻ **success** ☾ *burdens, embarrassment, failure, feelings, image, impediments, insecurity, loss*.

disaster   Dreams of disaster can sometimes be prophetic. Many people claim they really did dream of a disaster before it happened, and sometimes the dream actually warned them, causing them to decide to change course and stay out of harm's way. If you dream of a disaster, pay attention. If you truly feel a sense of foreboding when you wake up, it wouldn't hurt to take some precautions. More often, however, dreams of disaster signal a desire for excitement, anxiety about your responsibility to protect others, or fear of an impending change in your life. See also *airplane crash, car accident, earthquake, flood, storm, tidal wave, tornado*. ☻ **superhero** ☾ *adventure, anxiety, changing course, courage, danger, destruction, disaster, fear, journeys and quests, travel, violence, vehicles, weather and seasons*.

disease   Dreams of diseases don't mean you've got one, but they do ask you to pay attention to your physical or emotional health. Because we hear about so many diseases these days, people often dream they've been diagnosed with cancer, AIDs, bird flu, or other diseases in the news, and this can signal a generalized anxiety about health and safety, but specific disease dreams can also mean more. **1.** Dreaming you have cancer suggests something has infiltrated your life that makes you uncomfortable or that you consider bad for you. Is it a person, a job, a friend who is leading you down a path that doesn't benefit you? **2.** Dreams of heart disease or heart attacks symbolize being hurt in love. A recent break-up of a relationship can trigger heart disease dreams, but so can long-term disappointment or lack of love. If your heart isn't filled with love, you might dream you've got heart disease. **3.** Dreams about AIDs can signal anxiety about sexual behavior, sexual identity, or reputation. Are you worried about what people think of you? **4.** Dreams about sexually transmitted diseases suggest you worry about your sexual behavior and safety. Have you been engaging in risky behavior? It's making you nervous, so listen to your body and do what makes you comfortable and keeps you healthy. **5.** To dream about bird flu, swine flu, or other diseases in the news, including plagues and pandemics, symbolizes your anxiety about the state of the world. Do you fear the human race has run its course? These dreams sometimes turn into end-of-the-world dreams, which symbolize your insecurity at a very basic level. You don't feel safe right now, perhaps because your life is changing. **6.** To dream someone close to you has a disease suggests you have worry and anxiety for

someone else. You feel responsible for someone, but you also feel like you can't control what happens to that person, and this causes you to worry. **7.** Dreams about someone close to you with a disease can also symbolize something wrong with *your* health. See also *AIDs, cancer, epidemic.* ☾ **health** ☾ *anxiety, body parts, caretaking, changing course, danger, ethics and morals, failure, fear, health and hygiene, impediments, love, relationships, reputation, risky behavior, sexual activity.*

disguise If you put on a disguise in your dream, you are hiding something or pretending to be someone you aren't in some area of your waking life. This may be for your benefit if the dream is fun and interesting, or it may be because you feel you have no other choice if the dream is anxious, guilty, or fearful. If you dream of someone else in a disguise, somebody is not who they pretend to be or someone is lying to you, and you can sense it. See also *costume, mask* ☾ **mirror** ☾ *celebration, characters, clothing and accessories, creativity, fun, guilt, identity, image, secrets, subterfuge, transformation.*

dishes Dishes represent how you perceive the world and your place in it. **1.** If you dream of dirty, cracked, or broken dishes, you have been feeling down or pessimistic. **2.** If you dream of beautiful, clean dishes, you feel optimistic and content. **3.** Dishes piled with delicious food mean you are enjoying a bountiful period—money or other things

you want are coming your way.
4. Dishes stacked neatly in a cupboard, unused, mean you are good at saving up your resources, but you may have been a little stingy lately. **5.** If you dream of throwing dishes, you are angry at someone for disillusioning you. Your expectations have been shattered. **6.** If you dream of accidentally dropping dishes, you are aware of a mistake you've made that may have deep consequences for your life. **7.** If you dream of delicate, expensive, or rare China, your life feels meaningful to you. ◐ **utensils** ☾ *anger, financial resources, food and drink, inanimate objects, loss, personal power, regret.*

diving into water   Water represents passion, sex, and the body. **1.** Dreaming you are diving into water symbolizes your desire to immerse yourself in bodily pleasures right now. **2.** Dreaming of watching someone else diving into water suggests that you admire someone else's physical, sensual beauty, or that you wish you could be as sensual and free in your body as someone you know in your waking life. **3.** To dream of diving in an athletic competition means you feel sexually competitive. ◐ **desert** ☾ *beauty, competition, desires, feelings, pleasure, sexual activity, sports and games, water.*

divorce   **1.** Dreaming that you are getting a divorce or that you are divorced suggests that a change in your relationship is underway. This doesn't mean you will break

up, but it does mean something is different than it was—possibly even much, much better than it was. **2.** Dreaming that your parents are getting divorced suggests that you have considered ending a relationship but you don't want to admit it to yourself, or you fear that you won't be able to hold on to your relationship. **3.** Dreaming of someone's divorce that has already happened (including your parents') suggests you either haven't recovered from the experience yet and you are working through it in your dream, or that your dream wants to remind you of the experience because something about it will be instructive to your current situation. **4.** To dream friends or siblings are divorcing suggests you've sensed a change in someone else's relationship. **5.** To dream someone is divorcing who isn't actually married signifies that you sense a major life change for someone that person represents. See also *single, bachelor.*
◐ **marriage** ☾ *changing course, decisions, desires, destruction, failure, family, fear, love, relationships, transformation.*

doctor   Dreams about doctors can signal something in your health you should pay attention to. **1.** If a doctor gives you advice in a dream and it feels right or makes sense to you, pay attention. Your body—your most knowledgeable doctor, after all—may be trying to tell you something. **2.** If you have a bad encounter with a doctor in your dream, you may have anxiety about a medical condition and you fear modern medicine can't help you. Or maybe you have an intuition about your own doctor and it's time to get a second opinion. **3.** Dreams that a doctor ignores you may be your body telling you to get out of the way (by improving your health habits) and let it heal itself. ◐ **disease** ☾ *career, characters, healing, health and hygiene, intuition, medicine and surgery, people.*

dog   Loyal and faithful, dogs symbolize devotion. **1.** Dreaming of a good dog, or your own dog, means you have fans and high self-image. **2.** Dreaming of scary or attacking dogs means you feel anxious and unsafe in your environment. Is something tracking you? Don't be so obvious. Stay downwind. **3.** Hearing a dog barking means someone is trying to tell you something and you aren't hearing them. ◐ **cat** ☾ *animals, comfort, communication, injuries, loyalty, nature.*

doll   Dolls represent childhood, or you as a child. **1.** To dream of playing with dolls symbolizes a return to youthful thinking or a refusal to face adult responsibilities. **2.** Watching children play with dolls represents your evolution from child to caretaker. **3.** Breaking a doll symbolizes a recent event that has forced you to grow up in some way. **4.** Dreaming of a Barbie doll or other teen or adult doll symbolizes your feelings about cultural ideas of femininity. Is the Barbie something to emulate, or are you

throwing it away or ignoring it? **5.** If someone treats you like a doll or thinks you are a doll in your dream, you feel objectified by someone. They want to possess you and care for you, but you feel they are mostly concerned with how you look and not the real you. **6.** Dressing or undressing a doll symbolizes your focus on appearance. What are you trying to accomplish? Who do you want to resemble? **7.** If you have a nightmare that a doll comes alive and becomes evil, a bad memory from childhood may be surfacing, triggered by something in your current life. **8.** Friendly dolls coming alive suggest your inner child is still alive and well and helping you retain a joyful innocence in your adult life. **9.** Dreaming of a dollhouse represents the environment you wish you lived in, or the environment you feel stuck inside and unable to escape. ◐ **grown-up** ☾ *age, characters, clothing and accessories, comfort, feminine, fun, identity, image, innocence, play, relationships.*

dollhouse   See *doll.*

dolphin   Considered by some to be the wisest and most spiritual of animals, dolphins may appear in dreams to deliver important messages about your spiritual life. Dolphins also represent freedom, passage into another realm, nurturing, and personal power of a spiritual nature. ◐ **camel** ☾ *animals, freedom, masculine, personal power, spirituality.*

In ancient Greek, the word for "dolphin" was *delphinos,* which was also the word for "womb," and dolphins were one of the earth goddess Demeter's totem animals. Male gods were also sometimes depicted in ancient art riding on the backs of dolphins, as were sea nymphs. These sea-faring allies to deities also helped people pass into the spirit world after death.

door   See *closed door, open door.*

dorm room   Dreaming of a dorm room represents your current situation, even if you aren't in college. The state of the dorm room represents the state of your life right now, and the fact that you've dreamt of a dorm room instead of an apartment or a house suggests that you are at a transitional stage of life during which you are learning a lot. **1.** If the room is messy and unkempt, you are losing control of things. You have too much going on and the basics are getting away from you. **2.** If the room is neat and orderly or luxuriously furnished, you have got a firm handle on your everyday life and you are profiting from what you learn right now. **3.** If the dorm room is empty, you need more fulfilling social interactions. **4.** If you dream of a dorm room full of people, you've been socializing a lot lately—maybe too much? Are you getting distracted from your purpose? ☽ **homeless person** ☾ *buildings and rooms, home, identity, journeys and quests, knowledge, places.*

doughnuts   Doughnuts represent temptation, indulgence, and, in some cases—like any circular object—love and/or sexual desire, especially for women. If you dream of eating doughnuts, life is sweet, pleasurable, and fulfilling. If you dream of looking at doughnuts but not eating them, you are being tempted, or denied the object of your desire. See also *bakery, baking.* ☽ **banana** ☾ *feminine, food and drink, love, pleasure, relationships, sexual activity.*

dove   Symbols of peace and pacifism, spiritual messages, and freedom, doves in your dream may be delivering a message to you. You are forgiven, or set free, or deeply loved. ☽ **bats** ☾ *animals, birds, comfort, divine power, freedom, love, messages, peacemaking, spirituality.*

drafted   Dreaming that you have been drafted into the military symbolizes either your anxiety about war, fighting, and death; or your patriotic spirit, depending on how you feel in your dream about being drafted. Common in times of war, dreams of being drafted can also represent anxiety about a loved one—a child, a sibling, a friend—getting drafted and sent away to fight. ☽ **nonviolence** ☾ *adventure, anxiety, authority, journeys and quests, peacemaking, protection, rules and laws, violence, war.*

dragon   Wow, how lucky is this? Very. Dragons represent danger, adventure, and the opportunity to display courage. **1.** To dream of fighting a dragon symbolizes a major challenge you are facing. If you win, you feel confident about your ability to meet the challenge head-on. If you run away or get captured by the dragon, you aren't sure you can handle the challenge. **2.** To dream of seeing a dragon flying overhead but not interacting with it signifies your instinct that something perilous or exciting is about to happen. **3.** To dream you are a dragon symbolizes a position of authority you are in. You feel powerful—perhaps *too* powerful. Are you intimidating or undermining others? ☯ **dove** © *adventure, animals, authority, courage, danger, disaster, instincts, personal power, predictions.*

drain **1.** Dreaming of watching liquid go down the drain represents the end of something, such as a relationship or a plan. **2.** A clogged drain represents stagnation. You can't seem to get moving. **3.** Losing something of value down a drain, such as an earring or a ring, signifies the loss of something important to you. Is the object gone forever in the dream, or are you able to recover it, give it a good polish, and put it back into your life? ☯ **fountain** © *loss, regret, stasis.*

drawers See *storage.*

drawing Dreaming of drawing represents your creativity and the way you've chosen to create your current situation. You are the artist. What have you drawn? ☯ **disappearing** © *code, communication, creativity, messages, shapes and symbols.*

dreaming that you are dreaming and dreaming that you wake up Many people dream that they awake from a dream, then fall back into the dream again, without ever actually waking up. People often report dreaming that they say or think, "That was just a dream!" This common occurrence represents the many levels of reality and understanding we experience as humans. If you dream that you are dreaming, or dream that you wake up, your subconscious mind is exploring the possibilities of awareness and testing the boundaries of reality. This is an especially creative time for you right now, but you also risk fooling yourself about what's real and what's not real in your waking life. ☯ **sleeping** © *confusion, creativity, identity, intuition, mystery.*

> Some people think they never remember their dreams, or even that they don't dream at all. Everyone dreams, and remembering your dreams more often is easy. Keep a dream journal by your bed; every morning, as soon as you wake up, write down everything you remember, before you get out of bed or even talk to anyone. Soon the dream images will be easy to pluck out of those first moments of wakefulness.

drinking Dreaming of drinking something represents a thirst for knowledge or experience. It can also represent the body's need for more water. Are you a little dehydrated? See also *alcohol, beer, coffee, tea, water, wine.* ☽ **thirsty** ☾ *food and drink, desire, knowledge, health and hygiene.*

driver's license or ID card   Who are you? Your ID card or driver's license gives you an easy answer, and to dream of these forms of identification symbolizes your quest to discover who you *really* are. Is it that person on the card, represented by those numbers and one-word descriptions, or are you searching for clues to a deeper, more significant you? ☽ **disappearing** ☾ *identity, inanimate objects, journeys and quests.*

driving   Driving symbolizes the direction you are going. Are you in control? Are you lost? Did you get into an accident? Pay attention to how you drive and where you are going for clues about the path you are currently taking in your life. See also *bus, car, speeding, trucks and semis.* ☽ **backward** ☾ *changing course, control issues, direction, journeys and quests, vehicles.*

dropping something   **1.** Drop an object, and you've lost track of something important. **2.** Drop a baby or child, and you feel you've been neglecting someone who depends on you. **3.** Drop someone from a great height, and you've put a friendship at risk. See also *dropping the ball.* ☽ **carry** ☾ *burdens,*

failure, relationships, responsibility, risky behavior.

dropping the ball   What have you been letting slide? Have you let the important things, people, or responsibilities get away from you lately? Reexamine your commitments and pick up the ball again! **1.** If you dream of dropping a ball in a game, you have let down your friends or colleagues. **2.** Drop a ball at home, and you feel you have disappointed your family or are not living up to their expectations of you. **3.** You feel incompetent or out of your league in your work or life. **4.** You have lost track of your childlike side. ☽ **child, success, win** ☾ *failure, family, play, sports and games, work.*

drought   A drought symbolizes a loss of emotions, sexual feelings, or opportunity for emotional intimacy. If you dream of a drought, you feel drained of emotion. ☽ **flood** ☾ *feelings, sexual activity, water, weather and seasons.*

drowning   **1.** To dream of drowning symbolizes being overwhelmed by emotions or sexual feelings. Your excessive emotions have made you vulnerable. **2.** If you dream someone is trying to drown you, you feel overwhelmed by a relationship in your life. Your emotions or desires have kept you from seeing the situation clearly. **3.** To dream someone else is drowning means your feelings may be overwhelming someone else, or someone may need support because of an emotional upheaval. See also *underwater*. ☾ **thirst** ℭ *accidents, feelings, love, relationships, sexual activity, vulnerability, water.*

drug store See *pharmacy*.

drugs **1.** To dream of doing illegal drugs represents a risk you might take or have recently taken. You aren't sure you should have done it, but how you feel about the drugs in the dream represents how you feel about this risk. Did you enjoy it? Was it worth it? Do you fear the consequences? **2.** If you dream of doing drugs when you are trying to kick a drug habit, your body is rebelling against the new restriction, like a troublesome toddler who isn't getting its way. **3.** If you dream of doing drugs when you would never actually consider doing drugs, you are in the mood to be a little daring. Can you exercise your adventurous spirit without compromising your health or breaking the law? **4.** If you dream of taking legal drugs for a medical condition, you seek a remedy for a problem and you are hoping for a quick fix, but watch out for the side effects. See also *alcohol, bad habits, medicine, pills, smoking.* ☾ **health** ℭ *addictions, authority, guilt, health and hygiene, rebellion, rules and laws, solutions and remedies.*

drum **1.** To dream of playing a drum suggests you are hitting your stride and finding a rhythm for your life that makes sense for you and feels comfortable and unique. **2.** To dream of listening to drums symbolizes a deep desire emerging. ☾ **silence** ℭ *desire, happiness, inanimate objects, instincts, music and sound.*

drunk See *alcohol*.

duck Ducks represent passion, fertility, and a happy home life. **1.** If you see a duck in your dream, you may be fertile right now, or you feel contented at home with your family. **2.** If you dream of shooting a duck, you are doing something to put your happy home life at risk. **3.** If you dream of eating duck, you lust after someone. ☾ **dove** ℭ *animals, birds, happiness, home, love, pleasure, risky behavior, sexual activity.*

DVDs See *CDs and DVDs*.

dynamite See *explosion*.

D

E

ear **1.** Dreaming of a problem with your ear, like ear pain or hearing loss, means you haven't been hearing something important. **2.** Dreaming you are looking at or touching your ear suggests you've been listening too much to what other people say and you are letting it get to you. **3.** Dreaming of getting your ear pierced suggests you place a lot of importance on what people say. **4.** Dreaming of adorning your ear with jewelry symbolizes the value you place on listening to others. You care. **5.** If you see something wrong with someone else's ear in your dream, you aren't being heard. **6.** Ear dreams can also signify a health problem with your ear. If you suspect this, get it checked out. See also *deafness, piercing.* ☽ **eye** ☾ *communication, health and hygiene, image, listening.*

earrings See *ear, jewelry.*

earthquake Earthquakes shake the very foundation, the ground we stand on, even split the earth apart, and dreams of earthquakes represent just this kind of life-quaking feeling. Something big has changed, something has changed your whole point of view, and it might be scary or it might be wildly exciting. Who will you be when your dream stops shaking? That's the exciting part. How you react to the earthquake in your dream and what your priorities are—getting to safety, saving others, going out to see as much as you can see—symbolizes how you have been handling this drastic outer or inner change. See also *disaster.* ☽ **mountain** ☾ *adventure, anxiety, changing course, courage, creation, destruction, disaster, nature, transformation.*

earwig This long, skinny bug with the pinschers on its rear end doesn't actually burrow into your brain via your ear canal, but people have believed it does since probably the year 1000 C.E., according to some sources. That means people sometimes dream about earwigs (or other bugs) going into their ear and causing no end of madness and distress. But a dream about an earwig can represent more than a fear of close encounters with the insect world. It can indicate an insidious or irrational fear that plagues you. ☽ **butterfly** ☾ *animals, crawling creatures, fear.*

Easter Easter symbolizes different things to different people, so what a dream about Easter means to you depends, to a large extent, on what Easter itself means to you. However, in general, dreams of Easter mean you have fresh hope, you can make a fresh start, and you feel as if you've been released from a terrible burden. All your mistakes have been forgiven. Easter also symbolizes childlike joy, innocence, and birth. ☾ **Halloween** ☾ *celebration, creation, forgiveness, happiness, innocence, journeys and quests, weather and seasons.*

eating Eating symbolizes all that you take in from the world around you—what you see and hear, feel and smell, as well as taste. You take in feelings from your experience and relationships, and eating can also symbolize what you swallow emotionally. Eating too much in a dream means you feel like you have lost control over your behavior. Eating healthy food in a dream symbolizes your resolve to take care of your health or emotional well-being. See also *bingeing, dessert, fruit, meat, vegetables.* ☾ **vomiting** ☾ *abundance, desires, ethics and morals, food and drink, fruit, greed, guilt, happiness, health and hygiene, hedonism, pleasure, senses.*

echo Dreaming of hearing an echo of your own voice symbolizes your feeling of isolation or loneliness, or being misunderstood or rejected. You have been trying to reach out to others, and all you can hear is the sound of your own voice. You can't get satisfaction. To hear someone else make an echo in your dream suggests there is a great chasm between you and someone else, but they are trying to reach across it. Will you answer? *Will you answer?* ☾ **silence** ☾ *communication, isolation, love, relationships.*

E

In Greek mythology, Echo was a nymph who loved to talk. Once when Zeus was amusing himself with some of her nymph friends, Echo distracted Juno with excessive chatter until the goddess realized the trick and cursed Echo so that she could always have the last word but never the first, only echoing what others said. When Echo later fell in love with the beautiful boy Narcissus, he shunned her advances. She fled into the mountains and caves and wasted away, pining after him. The myth says she still lives in the mountains and caves today, only a voice, and will answer any who call out for her.

eclipse Dreaming of unusual natural phenomena may portend some future event. You may be catching a glimpse of a future world event: dark times are coming, but they will be followed by light and a return to normal. For women, eclipse dreams can also signal a hormonal fluctuation: PMS, pregnancy, perimenopause. This spike or drop in hormones will eventually be back to normal, but it may not feel so normal right now. If you feel hormonally unstable or are worried about your health or condition, have a doctor check you out. ☾ **sun** ☾ *anxiety, changing course, creation,* *destruction, feminine, health and hygiene.*

ecstasy   Dreaming of feeling ecstasy can be a simple energy release or a glimpse of a wonderful direction for your life. Even if it comes from something in the dream that would never actually happen, such as flying or enjoying a crush on someone you don't actually like, ecstatic dreams feel great and will keep you smiling all day when you remember them. Some people believe dreams of ecstasy are glimpses into spiritual enlightenment. See also *drugs.* ☽ **depression** ℂ *divine power, feelings, freedom, fun, happiness, hedonism, love, pleasure, spirituality.*

egg   Eggs symbolize fertility, creation, and perfection. **1.** Dreaming of eating an egg suggests you have been busy internalizing everything you need to create something truly amazing. You're almost ready to start producing … Art? Offspring? A really great idea? **2.** Dreaming of breaking eggs means you are already in the process of creating. You are making something happen. **3.** Dreaming of a hen laying eggs, or collecting eggs from a nest, symbolizes your quest for ideas. You are looking for inspiration. **4.** Finding an egg and keeping it warm or hatching it suggests you are ready to become responsible for someone. Your nurturing skills are blossoming. ☽ **breaking something** ℂ *caretaking, creation, creativity, feminine, relationships.*

elbow   **1.** You're flexible. Dreaming of your elbow means you can bend according to the situation. You've got support and you won't be compromising your principles if you give a little. **2.** To dream of breaking your elbow means you've been giving in too often and it's time to be a little set in your ways. ☽ **knee** ℂ *body parts, changing course, control issues, injuries.*

election   Elections symbolize a choice that can have significant future repercussions. **1.** To dream you are voting in an election means you already know your decision about an important issue in your life. **2.** To dream you are running for election means you are seeking an elevated position—a promotion, a commitment in a relationship, or recognition for your work. **3.** To dream you win an election symbolizes your self-confidence in your current task. You will prevail. **4.** To dream you lose an election symbolizes your insecurity about a current decision or course. You may regret previous choices, or you feel as if nobody understands what you are trying to do. To dream you voted for Richard Nixon is (almost) never good. ☽ **king** ℂ *authority, career, changing course, control issues, decisions, personal power.*

electric guitar   See *musical instrument.*

electrocution   **1.** To dream you've been jolted by a bolt of electricity suggests you've been struck with

an absolutely brilliant idea, one so far-reaching in its implications that it just might change the world. It could certainly change your perceptions of the world, your life purpose, and your relationships. **2.** To dream someone else has been electrocuted symbolizes your anxiety that danger is all around you. You don't feel safe. See also *lightning*.
◐ **monotony** ℂ *accidents, anxiety, changing course, creation, danger, injuries, intuition, transformation.*

elephant This lumbering and highly intelligent giant mammal symbolizes rationality, a long memory, or a force too great for you to control. **1.** To dream an elephant charges toward you symbolizes your anxiety about an imminent event you couldn't stop if you wanted to. You feel like closing your eyes and hoping for the best. **2.** To dream of riding an elephant symbolizes your ability to see a complicated situation with serene good sense. People ought to ask you what to do because you've got special insight right now. **3.** To watch elephants from a distance in their natural habitat suggests you are going through an introspective time right now. You have been looking back over your life and surveying your many memories and experiences to understand what they mean and how they have influenced the person you are today. This is an important time to spend some time alone rummaging through your trunk of life.
◐ **mouse** ℂ *animals, anxiety, changing course, fear, intuition, journeys and quests, knowledge, personal power.*

elevator 1. The common and frightening dream of being inside an elevator as it shoots uncontrollably upward or, even more common, plummets down through the elevator shaft to your certain doom, symbolizes anxiety about your lack of control in a situation. You feel things are happening whether you want them to or not and you are trapped, a helpless victim of circumstances. **2.** If you dream of taking an elevator—getting in, going to another floor, getting back out—you have decided to make a change in your life. You're taking it to another level. **3.** If you dream you are trapped in an elevator and the elevator is stuck between floors, you feel similarly stuck in your personal life. Something isn't moving along the way it should, and you don't know how to get going again. Are you in a rut? Caught in the throes of a bad habit? Or just not going anywhere in your job? **4.** Dream of being trapped in an elevator with an elephant? Are you claustrophobic? Avoiding an inescapable truth? Trying to stuff something big into a small space? ◐ **breaking free** ℂ *accidents, anxiety, buildings and rooms, career, changing course, control issues, direction, fear, places, technology.*

eloping What will your parents say? **1.** Dreaming that you are eloping means your relationship has become too complicated, and while you don't want to end it, you are looking for ways to simplify. **2.** If your elopement doesn't work in your dream—you get caught or somebody stops you—then you aren't sure about a recent decision. It might not be the right one. ☾ **marriage** ☾ *adventure, decisions, escapism, love, relationships.*

e-mail   To receive any message in your dream symbolizes a message someone is trying to send you in your waking life. An e-mail message to you or from you symbolizes a message to or from someone who is close to you—but not *too* close to you. Either you, the other person, or both of you like it that way. ☾ **mute** ☾ *communication, messages, relationships, technology.*

embarrassment   Feeling embarrassed in your dream symbolizes self-consciousness. If you do something stupid, find yourself in public wearing little or no clothing (a very common dream!), or put your foot in your mouth, as they say, you have been particularly aware of how you look or seem to others lately. See also *naked in public.* ☾ **exhibitionism** ☾ *accidents, anxiety, embarrassment, feelings, image.*

emotional   If you feel emotional in your dream, you may be experiencing a physical hormonal surge in your body. Or you may be repressing your actual feelings about something and they are sprouting up in your dream where you aren't as likely to hold them down. Emotional feelings in dreams about water symbolize meaningful sexual feelings. ☾ **numb** ☾ *control issues, feelings, loss, love, relationships, sexual activity.*

empty   1. To see an empty container in your dream symbolizes loss or finishing. You've let something slip away or you've used up all your resources. **2.** To pour or dump something out of a container to make it empty suggests you might need to "dump" the current project, relationship, or idea and start all over again. **3.** To feel empty in your dream—your stomach, your heart, your head—symbolizes some part of you that you've been neglecting. What needs filling up again? **4.** If you dream the gas gauge says your car is empty of fuel, you have worn yourself out. You're "running on empty" and you need to replenish your inner resources if you expect to do your best. See also *running out of gas.* ☾ **full** ☾ *changing course, feelings, food and drink, loss, relationships.*

end of the world   The sky is falling! If, like Chicken Little, you are sure the world is ending in your dream, you may have anxiety about a major change in your life. You feel as if your own personal world really is ending. End-of-the-world dreams can be highly detailed and realistic, leaving you with a feeling of doom long after they end, but even if terrifying, these dreams don't foretell doom—only your own fear of change. If the dream is exciting and vivid and you get to test your courage in an extreme situation, an end-of-the-world dream means you crave drama and adventure in your life. ☾ **birth** ☾ *adventure, anxiety, changing course, courage, death, destruction, disaster, fear, transformation.*

enemy   To dream of an enemy means you sense someone is plotting against you—or just plain doesn't like you. Enemy dreams can also mean you are being an enemy to yourself. Have you been "mean" to your body, your mind, or your heart? ☻ **friend** ℭ *anxiety, characters, fear, health and hygiene, people, relationships, threats.*

engine   **1.** Engines deliver the power. If you dream of an engine, you're enjoying a newfound source of energy. You can get this job done, no problem. Just keep on chugging. **2.** If something is wrong with the engine you dream about, your energy is lagging. You need a rest—or a tune-up. At least get your oil checked. ☻ **running out of gas** ℭ *health and hygiene, inanimate objects, personal power, technology, vehicles, work.*

enter here   To dream of seeing a sign that asks you to enter symbolizes an opportunity that has arisen. Your dream is telling you to take it. How exciting! ☻ **exit sign** ℭ *opportunity, places.*

epidemic   **1.** To dream of being part of the spread of an epidemic represents your fear that a recent event involving you will hurt others. **2.** To dream that an epidemic will cause the end of the world may be an insight into a major change or upheaval imminent in your own life. **3.** To dream of an epidemic in which you aren't infected symbolizes your anxiety about the world or the state of your life. You fear you

won't have any control over the bad influences or bad habits that have recently become more influential in your life. See also *disease.* ☻ **health** ℭ *anxiety, changing course, disaster, fear, health and hygiene.*

E

Everybody worries about epidemics, plagues, strange new diseases, and the latest flu in the news. Worrying about disease isn't always unfounded, however. In the Middle Ages, the Bubonic plague killed 20 million people in Europe—almost a third of the population. However, even this devastating disease didn't kill as many people as the influenza pandemic that occurred between 1918 and 1919. This flu killed more people than World War I (20 million to 40 million people) and is considered the biggest epidemic in history and a truly global catastrophe. Could it happen again? Sure it could. We recommend washing your hands before you eat. (Not that we want to give you nightmares ....)

erection   **1.** Dreaming you have an erection means you feel powerful and action-oriented. **2.** Dreaming you see someone else's erection and it excites you symbolizes your sensual nature and sexual desire. If you are a man and heterosexual, seeing someone else's erection symbolizes your own sexual and personal power. **3.** Dreaming you see someone else's erection and it upsets or disgusts you symbolizes your anxiety about someone else's power. You don't agree with the way things are being managed, or you fear that powers beyond your control will cause trouble for you. ☯ **impotence** ℭ *authority, personal power, sexual activity, vulnerability.*

escalator **1.** Going up on an escalator symbolizes going to the next level, getting promoted, getting a raise, or advancing to a new level of knowledge or spiritual awareness. **2.** Going up an escalator but looking down below means you can rise above a situation right now and see things from a more objective place. **3.** Going down on an escalator symbolizes getting to the root of a problem, finding out privileged information, or finally uncovering the reason for something. You are getting down to it. **4.** A broken escalator suggests your progress has stalled. You won't get anywhere until a problem gets fixed. ☯ **stop signs and stoplights** ℭ *direction, knowledge, places, spirituality, subterfuge, technology.*

escape Dreaming you escape from any sort of captivity symbolizes your feelings of repression and your desire to break out of your situation. **1.** To escape from someone who has kidnapped you symbolizes your desire to break out of a current relationship with someone who has too much power over you. **2.** To escape from a place, like a prison or a locked room, suggests your desire to get out of your current situation. Your living conditions or your job has become too restrictive. **3.** To escape from restraints, like handcuffs, rope, or a straitjacket, suggests you are about to solve a particularly difficult problem. **4.** To dream you escape from authority figures like the police or governmental figures represents your anxiety that you could be in trouble or wrongly accused by those in charge. **5.** To dream someone escapes from you symbolizes your fear that someone important to you might be ready to move on. **6.** To dream of ripping off all your clothes is (most of the time) just fun. See also *breaking free, handcuffs, jail, kidnapping.* ☯ **imprisoned** ℭ *anxiety, authority, changing course, control issues, rebellion, threats.*

espresso See *coffee.*

evacuation **1.** Dreaming you must evacuate because of a disaster symbolizes the desire to avoid an imminent conflict, problem, or confrontation. **2.** Feeling safe during an evacuation means you've found a solution to a problem in your waking life, or you have found a way to protect yourself from something and you have confidence your plan will work. **3.** To evacuate and be panicked or afraid symbolizes your worry that a situation has gone bad and the only way you can avoid the consequences is to run from it. See also *disaster.* ☯ **storm** ℭ *disaster, escapism, fear, protection, solutions and remedies.*

eviction **1.** To dream of being evicted means you feel banished from some area of your life you previously enjoyed. Who has kicked you out of what circle? **2.** To dream you have evicted someone means you have decided not to tolerate someone's behavior or a particular situation any longer. You are taking action. Sleep-walk right outta there. See also *landlord or landlady, tenant.* ❧ **moving** ℭ *anxiety, changing course, decisions, home, isolation, places, taking action.*

evil   When someone or something evil lurks in your dreams, you may be fighting your natural instincts and this manifests in your dream as an evil force. Devils and other evil religious symbols often represent unresolved morality issues. Are you still feeling like it is wrong or sinful to enjoy sex, indulge your senses, or be who you really are? Dreaming that someone else is doing evil things or has supernatural powers to do evil also symbolizes your fear that your natural instincts will take over your rational self and hurt others. Can you pinpoint exactly what you are fighting within yourself? If you accepted it, would it seem less dangerous? ❧ **angel** ℭ *anxiety, burdens, danger, desires, divine power, ego, fear, instincts.*

ex   Wow! Who needs lawyers? Let's settle this over a good night's sleep. To dream of an ex-spouse or ex-boyfriend or ex-girlfriend doesn't mean you want to get back together, but it does signal your resolution, or lack of it, about this relationship from your past. **1.** If the interaction in your dream is upsetting or unpleasant, anxious or unsettling, you may have yet to resolve issues from this past relationship. **2.** If the interaction is pleasant and satisfactory, your dream may be helping

you to resolve and have closure about the relationship. **3.** Pleasant interactions with an ex in dreams can also represent your fondness for the memory of that relationship. It means you really are over it and you can see the experience in perspective, appreciating how it helped you to grow. ❧ **husband, wife** ℭ *people, relationships.*

ex-boyfriend/girlfriend   See *ex.*

ex-husband/wife   See *ex.*

excrement   See *bathroom.*

exercise   See *working out.*

exhibitionism   Sleep streaker strikes again. **1.** Dreaming you are showing it all off and enjoying it, or getting a thrill from it, symbolizes your self-confidence or your body-confidence. Dreaming of exhibitionism can also suggest that you have been focusing too much on external appearances lately. Are you really so obsessed with how you look that you feel compelled to show everybody everything? **2.** To dream of witnessing someone else's exhibitionism suggests that you've learned a little too much about someone or something. Are you fascinated to watch, or do you wish someone had kept the curtains closed? See also *naked in public.* ❧ **hiding** ℭ *desires, ego, embarrassment, image, knowledge, personal power, pleasure.*

exit sign   To see an exit sign in a dream means you know, deep down, that it's time to get out of a situation. Your dream is literally giving you a clear sign. ❧ **enter here** ❦ *changing course, places, solutions and remedies.*

explosion   To dream you see an explosion symbolizes a dramatic and jarring change of course, either for you or affecting you in some way. Something is ending with a bang. This change may involve some suffering, pain, loss, maybe even some extensive reconstruction of your emotions and understanding of yourself, but the only way to make it happen is to make it happen in a big way. To dream you are setting off an explosion using a bomb or dynamite or other explosive means you are ready to make that change happen for yourself. Just don't wake up the neighbors. ❧ **whispering** ❦ *anxiety, changing course, creation, decisions, destruction, loss, violence.*

extreme sports   Dude! That was radical! **1.** If you dream of doing any kind of extreme sports, even if you never have in your waking life, you have a daring *joie de vivre* and you want to get the most out of every moment of life. This is a time to take risks and dare to step out and change your life for the better. **2.** If you dream of extreme sports and you actually do extreme sports in your waking life, you are mentally refining your technique. This will show up in your waking life as improved performance. **3.** To dream of getting injured doing extreme

sports of any kind is a warning: you are trying something risky. You could get hurt. Is it worth the thrill? Did you have trouble getting out of bed this morning? See also *skateboarding, snowboarding, surfing.* ❧ **fear** ❦ *adventure, competition, courage, opportunity, risky behavior, sports and games.*

eyeglasses   See *glasses.*

eyes   The eyes are the windows to the soul. To dream of your own eyes symbolizes a need to look deep inside yourself for the answers right now. You will know what to do if you use your intuition. To dream something is wrong with your eyes means you aren't using your intuition to see what's going on. If you look harder, you'll see what you've missed. To dream of looking into someone else's eyes suggests a deep spiritual connection with someone. ❧ **vision problems** ❦ *body parts, intuition, relationships.*

Ancient Eastern traditions teach that humans possess a third eye in the middle of the forehead, the center of intuition and psychic power. To see with your intuition is to see with your third eye. Modern practices like yoga and ayurveda also talk about the third eye, sometimes referring to it as the sixth chakra, a potent energy center in the forehead related to intuition.

F

face **1.** Dreaming of looking at or touching your own face and admiring it, or noticing how good you look, symbolizes a strong feeling of personal power based on your good image or reputation. **2.** If you dream of injuring your face or you dream your face suddenly looks different than usual, you feel insecure about who you really are or how you appear to others. You recognize that you aren't showing others your true self. **3.** If someone else's face gets injured or looks different in your dream, you suspect someone isn't what he or she appears to be. ☽ **faceless** ☾ *body parts, ego, identity, image, insecurity, personal power, reputation.*

face lift See *plastic surgery.*

faceless **1.** If you look in a mirror and your face is gone, you are wondering who you really are. You've been playing a role, or wearing a metaphorical mask, for so long that you've started to forget who you really are. All of our senses involve the face. Are you becoming an unemotional zombie? **2.** To dream someone else doesn't have a face means that someone you thought you knew has suddenly done something to make you question whether you know who he or she really is after all. ☽ **face** ☾ *body parts, identity, image, repression, reputation, subterfuge.*

failure Dreams of failure symbolize anxiety about something important you fear you won't accomplish. You aren't feeling secure or confident enough to make it happen. **1.** Almost everyone has dreamed of failing a test or assignment in school. This suggests you forgot to do something in your waking life and you are worried about it. **2.** To dream of failing at a relationship symbolizes worry that things aren't working out with someone. Can you intervene before things really go wrong, or should you let them go? **3.** To dream of failing at something related to your job means you worry that you aren't really qualified, or that you don't really have a handle on what you are supposed to be doing. **4.** Failing in front of others means you worry about your image. ☽ **success** ☾ *anxiety, embarrassment, failure, image, impediments, insecurity, loss, reputation, relationships.*

fainting **1.** If you dream of fainting, you don't feel prepared for an upcoming challenge. You don't think you can handle it. **2.** If you dream of fainting in response to an attractive person, you are so intimidated by someone that you don't have the slightest idea how to communicate intelligently. **3.** Fainting dreams can also signal circulation problems. ☽ **success** ☾ *desires, embarrassment, health and hygiene, insecurity, love, opportunities, relationships, vulnerability.*

fairy Lucky you! In dreams, fairies represent the spirits of nature, mischief, and all the little things you can't explain. Fairies may bring you good news or cause trouble in little, frustrating ways. **1.** If fairies try to lead you somewhere in dreams, follow them. They may have a message for you. **2.** If fairies play tricks on you, you aren't living in accordance with your natural impulses. **3.** If a fairy grants you a wish or gives you a power, things are going your way and you have a lot of charisma right now. This is the time to go for it. All in all, fairies are fun! ☽ **ghosts** ☾ *characters, frustration, instincts, journeys and quests, messages, mystery, myths and legends, nature, opportunity, personal power, wishes.*

fall See *autumn.*

falling Oh no, you've totally lost control! But you won't really die if you don't wake up before you hit the ground, so don't sweat dreams about falling. Falling dreams are among the world's most common, which sometimes result in a sudden violent awakening just before landing. Falling dreams symbolize anxiety, fear, insecurity, and indiscretion. If you dream about falling, slow down and take a look at your obligations and your abilities. What is going on in your life that is causing you anxiety? Where and how you fall can offer some clues. **1.** If you fall down stairs at home, you are insecure about your family life. Or your kids have been leaving their toys on the stairs. **2.** If you fall off a building, you feel you have lost control of your life's direction. If the building is your place of work, you have lost control of your professional life. Time to hit the want ads? **3.** If you fall from a dramatic craggy cliff, you are anxious about who you are, where you are going in life, and what it all means. Time for some soul searching—or at least a pedicure. **4.** If you are in a falling elevator, you feel boxed into a certain role from which you can't escape. For goodness sake, take the stairs next time! **5.** If you fall into water, you have fallen for *someone* or fear your passions or sexual impulses may get the best of you. This may be a time to be prudent—or a time to let yourself fall and enjoy the swim. ☽ **flying** ☾ *accidents, anxiety, control issues, disaster, failure, fear, loss, personal power.*

family You love them, you hate them, you can't do much about them. Families are such an important part of life, like it or not, that most people are bound to dream about them. Even those who aren't close to their families usually have some kind of support system of friends that stands in for a family. But what does your dream tell you about your relationship with your family, your view of yourself, and your approach to life? **1.** If you dream of having a good time with your family, you feel secure and supported in your social network. **2.** If you dream of fighting with your family, you are uneasy about some aspect of yourself that you consider to be inborn. Is it that negative attitude you got from your mother, or that judgmental streak from your father? Whatever it is, you have felt it within and you don't like it, so you are fighting with your dream family to deny it. Accepting it as part of yourself might be a more helpful strategy. **3.** If you dream that your family is in trouble and you have to save them, you feel a strong responsibility for the health and welfare of the people you care about. They are lucky to have you. Dreams of a family in trouble can also symbolize real waking-life problems you might have sensed but not consciously noticed. Check into it. You might be able to help. **4.** Dreams that you have a different family than you do in your waking life suggest that you feel more comfortable and understood by another group of people, and you don't always understand your actual family. Sometimes they seem like strangers. Remember, the family that dreams together stays together. See also *cousins, grandparents, parents, sibling.* ☽ **orphan** ☾ *caretaking, characters, comfort,*

communication, control issues, embarrassment, family, forgiveness, happiness, identity, love, people, relationships, responsibilities, stability.

famous person   See *celebrity.*

farm   **1.** If you see a farm in your dream, you crave a simpler existence in tune with the seasons, your natural instincts, and Mother Nature. **2.** If you dream of working on a farm, you desire a more hands-on approach to your work. Your dream might be telling you to take up a more physical hobby. How about gardening or woodwork? **3.** If the farm in your dreams is spooky or threatening, you aren't comfortable with a recent feeling or occurrence that taps into your instincts. Does your own animal nature seem foreign or frightening to you? Grab hold of your animal nature, wrestle it. You'll feel like you're down on the farm. ☽ **city** ☾ *animals, career, happiness, instincts, nature, places, work.*

farsighted   See *vision problems.*

fast food   Ah, the pleasures of greasy food delivered instantly. You crave more decadence in your life, or feel guilty about too much indulgence. Time to join a gym? Certainly time to slow down; return to natural, organic foods; and look to reestablish a healthy mealtime. Just don't associate food with your car, and you'll be okay. ☽ **deprivation** ☾ *food and drink, eating, hedonism, pleasure.*

F

fat **1.** Is that really you in the mirror? People often dream they are fatter than they really are, and this can feel very disturbing but is usually the result of being overanxious about diet or hyperconscious of appearance, or a sign of anxiety that a recent weight loss won't "stick." If you have lost weight recently and you have begun to gain some back, your body might be calling this fact to your attention, especially if you haven't wanted to admit this is happening. You are what you see, and that's the truth. **2.** To carefully examine fat areas on your own body in a dream, such as a spare tire or a jiggly thigh, means you are overly concerned with your appearance. Know what? Our whole society is making a buck off your appearance. You have been micromanaging your body out of a fear that you might lose control of what your body does. You are putting your appearance above your health. **3.** If you see a fat person in your dream, someone has made himself out to be bigger and more important than he really is. This person is much less confident than he pretends to be. Be compassionate; be kind. ☾ **thin** ☾ *anxiety, body parts, control issues, ego, embarrassment, health and hygiene, image.*

father Dreaming about your father signals an issue you are having with an authority figure, which may or may not be your actual father. It could be a boss, a supervisor, a partner, or a friend who always takes charge and tells you what to do, or even another family member who has been a father figure to you. **1.** If you argue with your father, you are rebelling against an authority figure in your waking life, or you wish you could. A dream of arguing with your father could be the only safe way you know how to rebel against this authority. **2.** On the other hand, a happy, positive, or affirming dream about your father means you have a balanced, well-adjusted relationship with the authority figures in your life. **3.** To dream of having sexual contact with your father signals your own inner confusion about your relationship with authority; or you see yourself as an equal to those who are, at least technically, "above" you. You don't recognize their "presumed" superiority. **4.** Intimate father dreams can also signal confusion about how to deal with authority figures. You may have a tendency to "seduce" or charm authority figures to get what you want, or to be seduced or overly influenced by authority figures into giving them what they want. This conflict is best resolved early in life. Go ahead and figure this one out, getting professional help if needed. **5.** Incest dreams can also signal a desire for more intimacy with people close to you. See also *family, incest.* ☾ **mother** ☾ *authority, comfort, control issues, family, love, masculine, people, personal power, punishment, relationships.*

faucet See *plumbing.*

fax machine **1.** Dreaming of receiving a fax means someone is trying to tell you something. **2.** Dreaming of sending a fax means you want to tell somebody something, but you are afraid of the response, so you are looking for an indirect way to do it. **3.** If you dream a fax machine is beeping but it is out of paper, you have nothing left to say, and you aren't listening anymore, either. **4.** If you keep trying to send a fax but it doesn't go through, you aren't getting your message across. If your dreams of fax machines continue, get rid of your fax machine ... easy! ❧ **mute** ℭ *communication, electronics, inanimate objects, listening, messages, technology.*

fear Feeling fear in a dream can be an upsetting experience, but usually the cause of fear in a dream represents something in your waking life that is causing you stress, and you are trying to release or understand those stressful feelings through your dream imagery. This may be something you don't want to acknowledge, and your lack of dealing with it in waking life has caused it to pop up in your dreams. Look to your dream for specific images to give you clues about what is causing you so much stress. Generalized feelings of fear without any obvious cause in a dream are also often a physical reaction to too much stress, acknowledged or unacknowledged, in your waking life. Stress management techniques such as exercise, meditation, and talking to someone about your feelings can often help fearful dreams disappear. If you dream about a particular phobia you have, such as about spiders, speaking in public, or small spaces, you are again most likely under stress and tapping into your phobia is an easy way for your dream to send you a message that you are overloading your brain and body and you need to do something about it. ❧ **hero** ℭ *anxiety, communication, confusion, danger, death, disaster, fear, feelings, impediments, pain, repression, senses, threats, vulnerability.*

feather **1.** To dream of a feather means you need a lighter touch. You've been too heavy-handed or obvious. Subtlety, even a little lighthearted teasing, will work better now. **2.** Feeling a bird's feathers or seeing feathers falling from a bird symbolize your desire to escape a situation. **3.** Feathers are also good medicine. To dream of a feather means you are able to fly above your present situation. Look down and learn. ❧ **rock** ℭ *animals, birds, communication, escapism, inanimate objects, love, relationships.*

feet Your feet symbolize all that you stand on, what holds you up and gives you stability, and what gives you the ability to move. **1.** If you dream of looking at your feet, you have recently questioned where you are going. What direction do you want to take? **2.** To dream your feet are injured or damaged symbolizes a problem with something that you consider to be important. Your very foundation has suffered damage. **3.** To dream of someone else's feet means that you seek direction from someone else regarding where you are going in your life or who you want to become. **4.** Dreaming of tickling or playing with someone's foot suggests not only that a new relationship will become pleasurably intimate, but that you and this other person are going in the same direction in your lives. This could be a great match in that sock drawer of your life. See also *running problems.* ❧ **hand** ☾ *body parts, changing course, direction, journeys and quests, personal power, relationships, sexual activity.*

fence A fence is a barrier or a dividing line, keeping you safe or keeping you out. Fences in dreams represent protection from something or a barrier to progress. Do you stay on your side or ignore the boundaries and climb over? ❧ **trespassing** ☾ *impediments, isolation, protection.*

ferret See *weasel.*

Ferris wheel **1.** Dreams of enjoying a ride on a Ferris wheel suggest you have recently been able to look at things from a more objective, far-off perspective. You've risen above a problem to see the big picture. **2.** To dream of getting stuck on a Ferris wheel suggests you are too removed from a situation. You need to get more involved or you won't ever understand what's really going on. **3.** To dream of being on a Ferris wheel when it breaks or goes too fast, or to dream you are falling off a Ferris wheel, symbolizes anxiety that you have gotten into a situation that has become too

big to handle. You've lost control. **4.** To watch a Ferris wheel from a distance suggests a recent spiritual insight into the cycle of life and an understanding of karma: what goes around comes around. See also *circle, wheel.* ❧ **straight line** ☾ *control issues, karma, knowledge, solutions and remedies, spirituality.*

ferry Ferries aren't for pleasure cruising, but specifically to take people from one spot to another as quickly as possible. To dream of riding on a ferry symbolizes your desire to get somewhere, and fast. This passage could involve an actual physical journey or a metaphorical one. You may need to get to an entirely new place in your thinking or feelings in order to progress. Dreaming of a ferry can also signify a major life change. You may be ready to move on in a big way. ❧ **shipwreck** ☾ *changing course, journeys and quests, transformation, travel, vehicles.*

According to Greek mythology, when someone died and was properly buried or cremated, a spirit named Charon came on his ferry to take the deceased across the River Styx into the underworld. For this service, the spirit charged a coin, which people often placed in the mouth of the deceased before burial or cremation.

fetus The unborn child represents potential. To see a fetus on an ultrasound suggests that a new idea or notion gestates in your mind but hasn't been born yet. To see a fetus that has been born or to see an aborted fetus symbolizes a premature ending to something. It's over before it started. ☽ **old person** ☾ *changing course, creation, family, hopes and dreams, karma, transformation.*

fever If you dream you have a fever, or feel feverish in a dream, you may really have a fever and your body is letting you know. Or, you may be feeling hot because an attraction to someone has become too intense. Fever dreams can also represent the need to purge or purify yourself, physically or emotionally, of something you feel is unhealthy for your body or mind. Dreams of being feverish and having someone care for you can mean you feel like you desire someone to sweep in and take care of a problem you don't feel capable of handling on your own. ☽ **lazy, snow** ☾ *caretaking, desires, healing, health and hygiene, heat, sexual activity.*

fight 1. To fight in your dream suggests pent-up energy and anger. You want to release this energy, and dream-fighting is a safe way to do it, but it probably won't be an effective way unless you figure out what you are really angry about. 2. To dream of getting injured in a fight suggests that you wish you could resolve a problem but you are fearful of confrontation because you might get hurt. 3. To watch a fight in a dream symbolizes your feelings of removal from an explosive situation. You know it's going on, but you aren't

really involved. See also *aggression, argument.* ☽ **nonviolence** ☾ *anger, communication, desires, frustration, injuries, relationships, violence.*

film 1. Getting film developed in a dream means you are waiting to find out how something you have said or done will affect future events. How will it all turn out? 2. Destroying film suggests a desire to erase something you've done in the past. See also *camera, movie.* ☽ **future** ☾ *predictions, regret.*

finding something You've searched and searched, and at last, success! Dreams of finding something you've lost symbolize a recent success or triumph over a bad situation. Finding something valuable reveals that you are on the right path to success. ☽ **losing something** ☾ *inanimate objects, journeys and quests, opportunity, solutions and remedies, success.*

finger Hey, you! Yes, you! Fingers point to what we mean and also help us manage the world with delicate dexterity. 1. If you dream of pointing at someone, you may be looking for someone to blame. Are you sure you shouldn't be pointing at yourself? 2. If someone points at you, you feel guilty about something. What are you hiding from yourself? 3. If you use your fingers to do something difficult, you have great confidence in your abilities. You have more skill than you think. 4. If you flip off someone with your middle finger, you are repressing anger at someone, but not necessarily the

F

person in your dream. If someone flips you off, you feel like a helpless victim. How can you regain control of your situation? **5.** If you injure or cut off your finger, some small part of your life is going badly. See also *fingernails, hand.* ◐ **amputation** ℂ *anger, body parts, direction, goal-setting, guilt, injuries, loss.*

fingernails **1.** To dream of looking at or cleaning your fingernails means you notice the details, and quality has helped define you to others. **2.** To dream of breaking a fingernail symbolizes a superficial loss that pains you nevertheless. **3.** To dream your fingernails are ragged and dirty means you've been trying too hard lately. Ease up. **4.** To dream that you have beautiful, perfectly manicured fingers means you have a good reputation. See also *finger.* ◐ **toes** ℂ *body parts, career, image, loss, reputation.*

fire Fire destroys, transforms, and purifies. Dreams of fire signal all these things in your waking life—something has changed, transformed, been radically purified, or been lost forever. **1.** Dreams of getting burned by fire symbolize the strong feelings and emotional scars you still have because of a radical change in your life. **2.** To dream your house is on fire suggests a major change underway in your domestic situation. **3.** To dream you see a person on fire is a sign that you should pay attention to what your friends are doing. See also *arson.* ◐ **water** ℂ *buildings and rooms, changing course, danger,* *death, destruction, disaster, health and hygiene, injuries, nature, transformation.*

fire engine To see a fire engine in your dream symbolizes that help is on the way. Hold on a little longer. ◐ **shipwreck** ℂ *courage, solutions and remedies, vehicles.*

firecrackers See *fireworks.*

fired from a job Dreaming you've been fired from your job can mean several things, depending on how you feel about getting fired in your dream. **1.** If you don't mind getting fired in your dream, or even feel a sense of relief, your dream symbolizes a desire to be released from a situation or to be released from responsibility. **2.** If you feel anxiety about getting fired, you may harbor the fear that you might not deserve the things you have or the position you hold. **3.** If you get fired and mostly worry about not having a source of money in your dream, you could be responding to shaky financial footing in your personal or professional life. You don't feel prepared in case of a financial emergency. **4.** To dream of firing someone else from a job means you are ready to end an association with someone. ◐ **hired** ℂ *anxiety, career, changing course, desires, escapism, failure, financial resources, loss, responsibilities, work.*

firefighter To dream of a firefighter symbolizes your desire to be saved, or your intuition that someone is already on their way to save you. ☽ **arson** ☾ *career, characters, courage, intuition, people, protection, solutions and remedies.*

firefly Fireflies represent spirits of those who have passed away, or messages from the spiritual realm. To see many fireflies in the dark means many voices seek to connect with you. Perhaps some come from the "other side"? To catch a firefly in a jar means that someone is acting as a spiritual messenger to you, even though they might not even realize it. See also *bugs.* ☽ **worm** ☾ *animals, communication, crawling creatures, divine power, messages, spirituality.*

fireman See *firefighter.*

fireplace The fireplace and its hearth symbolize the warmth of home, family, and domesticity. **1.** Dreaming of a fireplace suggests a craving for or appreciation of your own home life. **2.** If the fire has gone out or the fireplace is dirty or broken, you've been neglecting your home or your family. ☽ **jungle** ☾ *family, happiness, home.*

fireworks Beautiful explosions of light, fireworks symbolize a revelatory burst of understanding or a mind-blowing burst of passion. **1.** To dream of watching fireworks alone means you've become enlightened about something—like the proverbial light bulb going off in your head, but much, much bigger. **2.** To dream of watching fireworks with someone else suggests that a recent relationship—not necessarily with the person you dream about—has potential to be truly passionate and exciting. It may not have long-term potential, but it will certainly be an adventure. **3.** To dream of setting off fireworks yourself suggests that your own efforts have, or will, pay off in a big way. You worked hard to reach this "aha" moment, this spectacular idea, or this great explosion of passionate fulfillment. ☽ **darkness** ☾ *intuition, knowledge, love, pleasure, sexual activity, spirituality.*

fish Fish symbolize your deepest emotions, feelings you might not even realize you have. **1.** To see fish swimming in your dream symbolizes desires and urges you've recently begun to feel. They may be rising up to the surface, looking for light. **2.** To be pursued or attacked by a fish suggests anxiety connected to an emotion you are having. You fear it might overwhelm you. **3.** To dream of eating fish means someone has been very emotional with you, and you have taken in these emotions and felt true empathy in order to help this person make it through a difficult time. See also *dolphin, fishing, shark, snorkeling and scuba diving.* ☽ **birds** ☾ *animals, anxiety, fear, desires, feelings, instincts, relationships, repression, sacrifice, water.*

fishing **1.** To dream of fishing symbolizes your search for meaning. You seek a deeper relationship, a more relevant or important job, or something that will connect you

F

to a higher purpose. **2.** To catch a fish in your dream means you've hit on a great idea or you've recently met someone with relationship potential. **3.** To let a fish go in your dream represents sacrifice. You've given up something you want to help someone else. See also *bait, fish.* ☽ **swimming** ☾ *journeys and quests, knowledge, love, opportunity, relationships, sacrifice, water.*

fixing something Dreaming you are repairing something that has broken symbolizes something you have worked to fix in your waking life—a relationship, an idea that didn't work, a family problem. You are determined to make this situation work again. ☽ **breaking something** ☾ *caretaking, creativity, healing, solutions and remedies.*

flag **1.** Waving a flag means you feel compelled to participate in supporting your country or other authority figure. **2.** Saluting the flag symbolizes your deep respect for the values and freedoms your country stands for, or for the values represented by some other institution you support. **3.** Burning a flag symbolizes your anger at what your country, or some other authority figure, has been doing. **4.** Waving a white flag symbolizes your willingness to surrender to a situation. **5.** Seeing someone else wave a white flag means you sense someone is about to give up. You've won. ☽ **revolution** ☾ *authority, ethics and morals, loyalty, rebellion.*

In waking life, flying a flag upside down is a signal that you need help and is considered appropriate only in true emergencies. Dreaming of an upside-down flag may also symbolize a call for help.

flat tire See *tires.*

fleas Yikes! **1.** If you dream your pet has fleas, or you see fleas in your house, some small but insidious influences have invaded your home life. **2.** If you dream of finding fleas on you, you may be neglecting some area of your health, and your immune system may not be operating at peak capacity. ☽ **cleaning** ☾ *crawling creatures, health and hygiene, risky behavior, threats, vulnerability.*

flexibility Who knew you were that "bendy"? Dreaming you are super flexible means you have an open and flexible mind, and you might just need to use it right now to deal with a difficult person. Consider it a gift to someone, the way you can bend without breaking. ☽ **arthritis** ☾ *body parts, caretaking, relationships.*

flies They buzz around your head and drive you crazy. They crawl on your food and suddenly you aren't hungry. Flies represent all that is disgusting, unpleasant, and annoying. Are they fascinating creatures to biologists? Sure, but at a basic dream level, flies represent rot, filth, and neglect. **1.** To dream of flies in your house symbolizes neglect of your home and family, and guilt and hopelessness at being unable to change. You've really let things get out of hand. **2.** To dream of flies on your food represents a lack of personal hygiene. You've slid into some bad health habits and your body is sending you a warning. **3.** To dream of flies buzzing around you or following you, or being chased or surrounded by a swarm of flies, means you have been compromising your ethical principles or you have become financially irresponsible and you are suffering from the effects. You're starting to get a bad reputation, and it's time to clean up your act and turn things around before it goes any further. **4.** To swat or kill flies in your dream means you've decided to do something about the problem. ❧ **butterfly** ℂ *animals, crawling creatures, ethics and morals, family, financial resources, guilt, health and hygiene, home, reputation.*

flirting Who doesn't love flirting dreams? You get the whole rush of pleasure and desire without actually committing any transgression. You don't even have to wake up startled by some weird dream-sex memory. It's all lighthearted fun. **1.** If you flirt with someone you are attracted to in your waking life, your dream is acting out your attraction and your sense of excitement and fun. You might also be practicing, in your mind, for real-life future flirting. **2.** To dream of flirting with someone you aren't attracted to in

your waking life does not mean you really are secretly attracted to that person. That person may represent someone or something else that you want to know better, or the flirting actually symbolizes a desire to develop a professional relationship or friendship with that person. Perhaps you connect on some level, even if it's not romantic. **3.** To dream someone is flirting with you suggests you are particularly charismatic lately. Everybody wants to be around you. ❧ **insult** ℂ *communication, desires, fun, love, pleasure, relationships.*

floating See *flying.*

flood **1.** If your house floods in a dream, you are completely overwhelmed by emotions connected with your family or home life. You may have so many responsibilities that you feel like you are metaphorically drowning in your to-do list, or you might just be unable to cope with other people's problems because you just can't get control of your strong feelings. **2.** If all your stuff—furniture, carpets, clothing, household items—gets ruined in a flood, you've gotten too attached to material possessions. Your subconscious is telling you to let some of that stuff wash away. It's dragging you down. **3.** If your street or town floods in your dream, you feel like your whole life has gotten out of control and you wish you could just start over. **4.** If you struggle in the water during a flood, you are under too much pressure in your life. You can't get control of yourself, and you need someone to throw you a life preserver. Can you ask for help? The stress is too much. **5.** If your primary concern in your dream is to save other people such as family members or friends from the flood, you have been feeling a lot of pressure lately as a caretaker. Your responsibilities are taking an emotional toll on you. **6.** If you float calmly on a boat or other floatation device during a flood, or swim effortlessly through the floodwater, you don't feel sucked in to the stress and anxiety you see happening all around you. You've mastered your emotions and you can just go with the flow. See also *tidal wave.* ☾ **desert** ☾ *anxiety, burdens, caretaking, control issues, danger, destruction, disaster, feelings, relationships, responsibilities, water.*

floor   To notice the floor in your dream is a sign that you need to get back to reality. Put your own two feet on the ground and pay attention to the foundation. What is really supporting you? If you dream the floor is shaking, moving, or breaking open, you face a major life change and you feel your very foundation has cracked. ☾ **ceiling** ☾ *buildings and rooms, changing course, stability, support.*

flowers   Flowers represent beauty, romantic love, passion, and sexual attraction. **1.** To dream of budding flowers symbolizes new beginnings, youth, and young love. **2.** Flower buds can also symbolize male or female genitalia. To see them in your dream represents just where your mind is regarding someone who attracts you, or simply your appreciation for the beauty of those body parts. **3.** Seeing a flower opening in your dream means you are becoming more and more passionate about someone or something and opening yourself to a deeper and more intimate relationship. **4.** Dreaming of giving flowers to someone symbolizes your love for or attraction to that person, or someone or something that person represents. **5.** If someone gives flowers to you in your dream, you suspect someone has a crush on you. **6.** To see dead flowers in your dream represents depression, feeling your age, or the end of a passionate relationship. **7.** Dead flowers can also represent impotence and frigidity. You just don't feel passionate lately, and you don't see this as a good thing. You see it as a sign of something else that is going wrong in your life. See also *carnation, daffodil, daisy, dandelion, lily, rose, tulip.* ☾ **vegetables** ☾ *age, beauty, body parts, desires, love, innocence, nature, plants, relationships, sexual activity.*

flying   Oh, to be like a bird, soaring through the sky, free of earthly bonds and obligations. Flying dreams can mean many things, depending on how you fly, where you fly, and how you feel about it. **1.** To fly (or float) with feelings of joy or ecstasy means you have a strong inner self-confidence. Life is good. If the sky is blue or sunny

when you fly, you are on the right track. Keep going! **2.** Pleasant flying dreams can also mean you deeply crave an escape from your mundane life and responsibilities. Think about how you could relieve your boredom and routine, capturing the temporary freedom of flight in your waking life. You might desperately require a vacation right about now. Tahiti, anyone? **3.** If you are a bird in your dream, you have tapped into your inner avian, and such dreams signify a leap in spiritual growth. Some Native American cultures believe you are actually having an out-of-body experience, getting to travel by bird. Being a bird can also mean that, deep down on an instinctual level, you crave more freedom. **4.** If you look down and see the ground far below when flying and find it interesting or beautiful, you have the ability to see things from an overarching perspective. The dream may also be telling you to step back and look at the big picture for the answer to a current dilemma. **5.** To fly but feel fearful about it, unsteady in the air, or to be afraid of falling from your shaky flight means you feel you have taken on more than you can handle, but so far, you are still airborne. You need a shot of self-confidence. Flex those wings and take control, in your real life if not in your dream. **6.** To fly in a vehicle like a plane, hot air balloon, hang glider, helicopter, and so on means you have taken the wheel of your life and are navigating yourself. If the vehicle seems to steer without you, or the balloon or hang glider blows off course and you can't control it, external forces control you. Think about how you can take back the wheel. It's your life! **7.** If the sky is dark or stormy when you are flying, you may be headed in a dangerous direction. Best to land and watch out for lightning. **8.** Watching someone else fly, or watching birds fly, while you remain grounded, means you have the desire to escape but you don't know how to find the inner resources to make it happen.
◗ **falling** ☾ *animals, birds, control issues, fear, freedom, happiness, hopes and dreams, personal power, risky behavior, vehicles.*

Flying dreams may just be the world's most sought-after dreams, and often the stuff of *lucid dreams*, those dreams in which you realize you are dreaming and can control the action. Children often get to enjoy dreams of flying, adults less often. Nobody knows why, but a dream of flight as an adult is a rare and wonderful treat. Enjoy it!

flying saucer   See *UFO*.

fog   Fog shrouds the truth, and dreams of fog symbolize that which is being hidden from you and that which you really just don't want to see. That fog hides something. You can count on it. ◗ **sun** ☾ *impediments, mystery, secrets, subterfuge, weather and seasons.*

F

following   To dream of following someone suggests that someone has something you want. To dream of being followed suggests that someone wants something from you. Either way, you aren't in this alone, but be careful. This isn't a relationship of equality, and everyone has their own best interests in mind. ☽ **leader** ☾ *desires, danger, direction, relationships.*

food   Food is the subject of many a dream because it is so integral to our lives and to keeping us alive. Your attitudes about food can flavor your dreams about food, but food dreams often represent other bodily urges or sensual pleasures. **1.** To dream of eating and enjoying food means you enjoy the sensual pleasures in life and appreciate subtle sensual stimuli. You are passionate, interested, and appreciative of the physical world around you. **2.** To dream of eating or bingeing on food and feeling guilty about it suggests that you put so many restrictions on yourself or engage in sensual pleasures so mindlessly that your body has forgotten how to read its own cues. You've lost your organic connection to your physical self. **3.** To dream that you see food and want to eat it but don't suggests that there is some sensual pleasure or desirable person you want but haven't been able to have. **4.** To dream that you see food and appreciate its beauty but don't want to eat it suggests that you are in good balance right now. You have an appreciation for beauty in the world

or in other people without the anxious desire to consume everything. You know how to step back and see. **5.** To dream of rotten or spoiled food symbolizes some pleasure gone bad. Once you got something you thought you wanted, you realized it wasn't as good as you imagined it would be. See also *cooking, food poisoning.* ☽ **drinking** ☾ *addictions, balance, comfort, desires, extremism, food and drink, happiness, health and hygiene, hedonism, pleasure, sexual activity.*

food poisoning   To dream you get food poisoning means you've been doing something you know isn't good for you. That thing you love really could hurt you, and your body is trying to tell you to stop before you really do become injured, ill, or spiritually lost. ☽ **food** ☾ *danger, food and drink, health and hygiene, risky behavior.*

food processor   See *blender or food processor.*

football   **1.** To dream of playing football means you enjoy a combative and competitive relationship with others. You are physical and like to make a big impression, but you work well with others. You are a team player. **2.** To dream of watching football means you have a good understanding of how teams and groups work and you are, or would be, a good manager. ☽ **following** ☾ *adventure, career, competition, inanimate objects, play, relationships, sports and games, success.*

foreign language   1. Dreaming you speak a foreign language symbolizes your wide range of interests. You have an open mind and an incessant curiosity for the unknown. You probably spend a lot of time Googling things you just have to know on the Internet. **2.** To dream someone else is speaking a foreign language suggests that a new acquaintance seems strange and mysterious to you. You want to know more. **3.** If you dream that everyone around you speaks a foreign language, you face a new and unfamiliar situation, or you may soon be traveling to a far-away place. See also *foreigner*. ☽ **homebody** ℂ *adventure, communication, journeys and quests, knowledge, mystery, travel.*

foreigner   1. Dreaming you meet a foreigner means you have recently encountered something unusual and new to you in your life, or you soon will. **2.** Dreaming you are a foreigner suggests that you don't feel comfortable in your current environment. You aren't at home. See also *foreign language*. ☽ **family** ℂ *adventure, characters, insecurity, people.*

forest Forests represent spiritual crisis, confusion, or lack of a clear life purpose. **1.** If you are lost in a forest in your dream, you really are wondering where you should be going in life. You are looking for direction. You may also feel morally or ethically confused and you aren't sure how to think about something

or don't know what the right thing to do is. **2.** If you wander through a forest purposefully or enjoy being in a forest without being lost, you enjoy the mysteries of life and you don't mind being a little lost. You don't always want to know where you are going, and you may have a bit of the gypsy in your soul. **3.** If you encounter animals in your dream forest, these messengers might be trying to give you a sign about what direction you should head. ☽ **desert** ℂ *adventure, animals, anxiety, changing course, danger, decisions, direction, ethics and morals, impediments, instincts, journeys and quests, loss, nature, places, plants, spirituality, threats, vulnerability.*

forgetting   See *amnesia*.

forgiving   If you dream of forgiving someone, you are probably ready to forgive someone in your waking life, but the person you need to forgive might not be the person you forgive in the dream. It might be someone that person represents. It might even be yourself. ☽ **anger** ℂ *changing course, comfort, communication, courage, decisions, desires, feelings, forgiveness, freedom, happiness, love, peacemaking, relationships, solutions and remedies, taking action.*

fork   See *utensils*.

fork in the road   See *crossroads*.

fortune teller   Fortune tellers appear in your dreams when you

F

really do seek to know what life has in store for you. What the fortune teller tells you is probably a reflection of what you hope or fear might happen, but it could also be a sign based on your own intuition about what really will happen to you, so listen carefully. Your dream might help you decide what to do or where to go. See also *cards, crystal ball, palm reading, gypsy.* ☽ **past life** ☾ *career, characters, changing course, mystery, people, predictions, solutions and remedies.*

Some people believe you can use your dreams as your own personal fortune teller. You can certainly use dreams to help you make decisions. Before you go to sleep, concentrate very specifically on your question. Say it out loud or think it in your mind as if you were saying it out loud. Then relax and try to clear your mind. If you find yourself thinking about something else, gently guide your mind back to your question until you fall asleep. As soon as you wake up, write down all the dreams and images you can remember. Your answer may well be right there in front of you.

fossil   To dream of digging up or finding a fossil symbolizes something you've recently discovered about the past. It's given you a new perspective. ☽ **future** ☾ *history, knowledge, nature.*

fountain   Water symbolizes emotion and fountains shoot water high into the air or let it bubble gently out for the world to see and enjoy. **1.** If you dream of a fountain, you are ready to let your feelings flow, and you are in the right frame of mind to communicate beautifully. **2.** If you dream of a dry or broken fountain, you are having trouble expressing your feelings. **3.** If you dream of an overflowing, flooding fountain, you have been letting your emotions take over and speak for you. You might be wise to practice a little restraint. Your feelings are so strong right now that you aren't quite prepared to express them in a way others can really appreciate or understand. ☽ **drought** ☾ *communication, feelings, water.*

four-leaf clover   You got lucky! Dreaming of finding a four-leaf clover means you are living a charmed life right now. Take full advantage of your good luck. Buy a lottery ticket, go to the races, or cut your hair! You never know how long your luck will last. ☽ **omen** ☾ *nature, opportunity, personal power, plants.*

free stuff   Whether it's coins on the sidewalk, all the designer clothes and shoes you can carry, or free food at the best buffet in the world; dreams of free stuff symbolize possibilities in your life and your positive feelings that the world is full of abundance. Dreams about free stuff can also symbolize desire when you have been under a lot of financial pressure and you haven't been able to feel easy about money for awhile. Your dream is giving you a break and letting you enjoy some unbridled dream materialism. ☻ **giving away possessions** ☾ *abundance, desires, financial resources, opportunity.*

freedom See *breaking free.*

freezer 1. To dream of a freezer means you've cooled off significantly lately. You just aren't hot for something, or someone, anymore. That's a chilling thought. 2. Freezer dreams can also convey emotions you've purposefully stowed away where they can't affect you. 3. If you dream of a freezer filled with food, you are enjoying a time of material or emotional abundance. You have everything you need, and more. ☻ **fire** ☾ *abundance, changing course, cold, feelings, food and drink, furniture and appliances, protection, relationships, repression.*

friends Your friends support you, tell you what you need to know, and spend time with you. To many people, their friends play an even more significant role in their current lives than their families, so this important social group says a lot when its members show up in your dreams. 1. To dream of having fun with friends means you feel supported and protected by the very presence of your social network. 2. To dream your friends reject you or ignore you symbolizes your fear that you might have lost a connection with your group or with an individual friend. 3. To dream your

friends try to get you to do something you don't want to do suggests that you feel pressure within your social network. Didn't your friends use to make your life easier? 4. To dream a friend has betrayed you is a warning. You might not have even realized that you have trust issues with someone. 5. To dream of a particular friend could mean you need to spend more time with that person, or that person has become particularly important to you. 6. To dream of sexual contact with friends simply means you feel a strong connection. Don't let it freak you out! 7. To dream of having a friend or group of friends you don't actually have—dream friends—symbolizes your desire to broaden your social network. You may be ready for some new influences, even if you still cherish the old ones. ☻ **enemy** ☾ *communication, comfort, fun, happiness, love, loyalty, peer pressure, people, protection, relationships, social life, support, trust issues.*

frog See *reptiles and amphibians.*

fruit Fruit symbolizes beauty, pleasure, and sexual fulfillment. To dream of eating fruit symbolizes your desire to experience these delights. See also *apple, banana, grapes, pear.* ☻ **vegetables** ☾ *beauty, food and drink, fruit, hedonism, pleasure, sexual activity.*

full Are you full of it? Dreaming you, or something else, is full symbolizes abundance, plenty, or excessive consumption. 1. If you dream you are pleasantly full of food, you are satisfied and happy with your life. You have enough, and you don't crave more. **2.** To be unpleasantly full, or to be full and to keep eating and drinking, suggests you are saddled with cravings, addictions, and desires that rule your behavior. You always want more, but when you get more, you still feel you don't have enough. **3.** To see a container that is full or overflowing means you have enough—enough to do, enough to think about, enough confidence, enough charm, enough beauty, enough stuff. You can stop trying so hard. ☯ **empty** ℂ *abundance, addictions, food and drink, happiness, pleasure.*

full moon　See *moon.*

funeral　**1.** Dreaming of a funeral doesn't necessarily portend death, but it could. Some people claim to dream of a relative's or friend's funeral, only to find out shortly after that the person has died. **2.** In most cases, dreaming of a funeral signifies a loss or other major change in your life. You are mourning what is gone in order to move on to what is next. **3.** To see someone you know in a coffin at a funeral symbolizes your recent neglect of, harsh treatment of, or disagreement with someone who means a lot to you. You fear your relationship has changed forever. See also *coffin.* ☯ **birth** ℂ *changing course, death, loss, transformation.*

furnace　The furnace heats the house and is the heart of the home.

1. To dream of looking at the furnace and seeing the pilot light burning represents a happy and satisfactory home life. All is running smoothly and you truly treasure your home and family. **2.** To dream of furnace problems symbolizes problems at home. Family members have cooled off toward one another and relationships may be suffering. Are people moving apart? What happened to family solidarity? ☯ **freezer** ℂ *comfort, family, furniture and appliances, heat, home, love, loyalty, relationships, stability.*

furniture　Furniture represents our external environment, comfort, and lifestyle. **1.** To move furniture around suggests that you want to change your environment without changing it *too* much. Maybe you just need a change of scenery. **2.** To buy furniture means your lifestyle has recently become more comfortable. **3.** To sell furniture means you know how to make other people more comfortable and you do so regularly. **4.** Broken furniture symbolizes decadence that has gone too far. Your pursuit of pleasure is undermining your basic needs, but who has time to sit when you are pursuing your pleasures? ☯ **homeless person** ℂ *buildings and rooms, comfort, furniture and appliances, home.*

future　Dreams of the future help you to prepare and project ahead to what you want and where you are going. What is your dream future like? **1.** If your dream of the future is fun, interesting, adventurous, or full of positive changes, you have an optimistic view of your life and where you, and even the world as a whole, are going. **2.** To dream of just a short time in the future, such as the next few hours or the next few days, may predict that something important is about to happen. Be ready. Your instincts can sense a change coming. **3.** If you dream of a high-tech, sci-fi sort of future, you are fascinated with progress and have a sense of adventure. You have the potential to create a truly exciting life for yourself because you understand progress in the larger sense. **4.** If your dream of the future is frightening, stressful, or otherwise unpleasant, you worry about what will happen and tend to be pessimistic about the future. Are your fears realistic, or are you worried over things you can't possibly control? Time will tell. ☻ **archeologist** ℂ *adventure, changing course, creation, instincts, opportunity, places, predictions, technology, time, transformation.*

F

G

galaxy See *space.*

gambling You like to take risks, but is it worth it? **1.** To dream of gambling suggests a risk you are taking. Whether you win or lose in your dream could show you what you really think of your odds. **2.** To gamble and win a lot of money in your dream can represent your wish or desire to win, or your desire to get a lot without much effort. **3.** To dream you are gambling and losing a lot of money warns you to be careful at something you've been doing. You suspect this risk might not pay off. **4.** If you have a gambling problem and you dream of gambling, your body is playing out your addiction. When the dreams stop, you'll know you've really kicked the habit, and good luck with that. ☽ **caution** ☾ *addictions, adventure, financial resources, play, risky behavior.*

gaming system See *video game.*

gang **1.** To dream you are in a gang symbolizes your wish to belong to a group. You feel too isolated and you crave interac-

tion with people who actually "get" you. **2.** To dream you are in a gang and they try to get you to do things you don't want to do, or you do things you feel guilty about because everyone else in your gang was doing them, symbolizes your fear that your friends have been influencing you in a way that makes you uncomfortable. Are you losing your identity to the group or compromising your principles due to peer pressure? **3.** To dream you are harassed or victimized by a gang symbolizes your fear of a certain type or group of people. Your dream might be clueing you in to a personal prejudice or reflecting your fear based on a past experience. ☽ **loneliness** ☾ *decisions, family, fear, identity, peer pressure, people, relationships.*

garbage **1.** To dream of garbage symbolizes something you feel you've wasted or a fear that your morals have been declining. Why are you throwing everything away? **2.** To dream of picking up garbage symbolizes a recent inclination toward self-improvement. That, or you need to take the garbage out, phew! **3.** Throwing away something in particular as garbage symbolizes something you don't value, or have decided you no longer value. ☾ **cleaning** ℭ *ethics and morals, extremism, failure, fear, guilt, health and hygiene, inanimate objects, transformation.*

garden Perennial dreams? **1.** Getting back to nature in your dreams through gardening symbolizes your desire to touch the earth, be self-sufficient, and reintroduce yourself to your authentic self, without the distractions of modern life, technology, and complicated relationships. **2.** Seeing a garden in your dreams symbolizes an appreciation of beauty. **3.** Dreaming of weeding a garden symbolizes your recent quest to improve your health and simplify your life by getting rid of extraneous influences. ☾ **machinery** ℭ *balance, beauty, creation, health and hygiene, identity, nature, plants.*

garlic **1.** Dreaming of eating or cooking with garlic symbolizes your quest for more flavor and zest in life. You want adventure and exciting experiences! **2.** Dreaming of wearing or displaying garlic means you fear a bad influence and you want to protect yourself with good intentions and strong principles. **3.** Smelling garlic on someone's breath means you would like a little distance from that person, or you think they might like a little distance from you. ☾ **desserts** ℭ *adventure, desires, food and drink, ethics and morals, plants, protection, relationships.*

In traditional gypsy folklore, garlic is one way to repel a vampire. This belief has existed for centuries, but when Bram Stoker wrote about it in his novel, *Dracula*, the idea of garlic and vampires became part of the popular imagination. In the novel, Dr. Van Helsing rubs garlic on the curtains and puts a wreath of garlic around Lucy's neck to protect her from further vampire attacks. If you've been having vampire dreams, perhaps a nice garlicky evening snack might help to ward them off.

gas **1.** To dream of filling up your car with gas symbolizes the need to replenish your inner resources. You need some you-time or you won't be able to keep going, and you definitely have things to do, places to go, and people to see, so you need to take care of yourself now. And those gas prices aren't gonna come down again. **2.** To dream of running out of gas suggests you've already run yourself down, or you will very soon. Take a break. ☾ **water** ℭ *health and hygiene, travel, vehicles.*

gate **1.** To open a gate means you have an exciting opportunity. **2.** To close a gate means you are finished and ready to move on. **3.** To encounter a locked gate means you've got to contend with a problem before you can go any further in your current project. ☾ **breaking free** ℭ *changing course, impediments, opportunity.*

gay See *homosexuality.*

genitals See *sex organs.*

G

germs **1.** To dream of catching germs or being germ-obsessed or fearful of germs suggests perfectionism that has gotten out of hand. Are you being too hard on yourself or others? Probably. Are you letting the little things overwhelm the more important things? **2.** Being acutely aware of germs in your dream can also symbolize a moral failing. You might have done something you think is "dirty" and now you feel "infected" by what you did. See also *disease, epidemic.* ☾ **health** ℭ *control issues, crawling creatures, ethics and morals, fear, health and hygiene.*

ghost Ghost dreams represent people, ideas, or feelings you thought were dead and buried (at least, metaphorically) but that have risen up again into your life. **1.** If you meet a ghost and interact with it in your dream but you aren't scared of it, something has come up from the past that interests or intrigues you. Maybe you'd forgotten all about it, but whatever it is, it has come back into your consciousness for a reason. **2.** If you fear or feel threatened by a ghost in your dream, some memory or guilty feeling has cropped up that you don't want to remember or face, but you carry it like a ghost carries a chain and your mind is trying to help you relieve the burden. **3.** If you feel only mildly anxious about seeing the ghost but also compelled to look or communicate with it, you are ready to explore a past experience that you haven't resolved. **4.** If you dream you see a ghost of someone who is still living, that person holds some fascination for you. You are "haunted" by them, either because of guilt or because of an attraction. **5.** If you dream a ghost is trying to tell you something, your subconscious is sending you a message. Or you just might be getting a message from the spirit world. Either way, pay attention to what the ghost tells you. It probably has important meaning for your current situation. **6.** If you dream of a child ghost, the dream relates to a memory from your own childhood. **7.** If you dream of a ghost of someone you know, you may be trying to resolve something you weren't able to resolve during that person's life, or tell that person something you never got to say. Or perhaps that person's spirit really is paying you a visit. ☾ **angel** ℭ *burdens, characters, fear, guilt, memory, messages, myths and legends, people, repression, spirituality.*

gift **1.** To dream of giving a gift symbolizes your desire to give something of yourself to someone else. Your gift represents your time, your help, your heart, or something else you want to give. **2.** To dream of receiving a gift from someone means you recognize that someone has given you something of him- or herself, or you wish that person would. **3.** To receive a gift you didn't want symbolizes your discomfort with a current relationship. You would rather not be the object of that person's attention. ☾ **stealing** ℭ *desires, relationships, wishes.*

girl Dreams about girls represent feminine energy, beauty, and cycles of change. **1.** To dream of meeting a girl you don't know represents meeting your feminine side, or getting a message from your feminine side. Have you been neglecting your feminine self? Or overindulging it? **2.** To dream of having a crush on a girl suggests you are yearning for sweet, innocent youth, or that you need to indulge your feminine side a little more. Let yourself be softer, for balance. **3.** To dream of a mysterious or elusive girl suggests a change is coming, and this is all part of the natural process of your development. **4.** To dream you are a girl when you are actually a boy symbolizes your need to get more in touch with your feminine side, or your fear that you aren't in enough touch with your masculine side. Seek balance. See also *child or children, woman*. ◖ **boy** ◗ *beauty, changing course, desires, feminine, gender issues, people.*

girlfriend Support, affection, unconditional love, ego-boosts …. If you are a guy, dreaming of a girlfriend represents your satisfied feeling that you are in balance with another human being, or that you wish to be. If you are a girl, dreaming of a girlfriend may be a sign that person needs support right now, or you need that person right now. Positive dreams mean you cherish your friends. Negative dreams mean you have an issue to resolve. **1.** If you have a good dream about your actual girlfriend, you feel supported and bolstered by the knowledge of her presence. **2.** If you dream of arguing with your girlfriend or trading insults, you fear your connection with your girlfriend may be weakening. **3.** If you are a guy and you have a good dream about a girlfriend you don't actually have, you crave the excitement of meeting someone new and falling in love, or your body craves physical contact. Or both. **4.** If you dream a girlfriend betrays you, you sense you shouldn't trust someone in your waking life. (It might not be your girlfriend.) **5.** If you are a guy and you dream of having sex with your girlfriend, the details of the dream will offer you clues about the state of your intimate relationship. **6.** If you are a guy and you dream of flirting or having sex with someone else's girlfriend, or you dream that your girlfriend cheats on you, you don't trust yourself or you don't trust someone else's loyalty. **7.** If you are a heterosexual girl and you dream of having sex with a girlfriend, you are simply expressing a close feeling of intimacy with your friend. (It doesn't mean you have suddenly and mysteriously turned into a lesbian.) If you feel disturbed by the dream, you may not feel balanced in a current romantic relationship. Are you taking all the power or giving all the power? If you enjoy the dream, this does not mean you actually desire a girlfriend. Instead, you appreciate and cherish your own female energy. You are your own girlfriend! (Even if you also have a boyfriend.) ◖ **boyfriend** ◗ *characters, comfort, ego, feminine, gender issues, guilt,*

G

identity, love, loyalty, people, sexual activity, support, trust issues.

giving away possessions **1.** To dream of giving away your possessions signals a desire for a less materialistic existence. Have you been accumulating too much stuff? Feeling weighed down by owning and buying? Maybe it's time to lighten your material load. **2.** Dreaming of giving things away may also signal an impending change in your life or a desire for a more spiritual existence. ☽ **shopping** ℂ *abundance, changing course, solutions and remedies, spirituality.*

giving up See *quitting.*

glacier Glaciers and icebergs represent emotions you've kept locked up, or frozen, so you don't have to face them. **1.** To dream of glaciers or icebergs means these emotions still float icily in your awareness. **2.** To step on glaciers or icebergs symbolizes your cautious exploration of these locked-up feelings. **3.** To dream an iceberg hits your boat, à la the *Titanic*, tells you that the feelings you have frozen up are impacting your life in a negative way. An iceberg can't damage a ship once it has melted. ☽ **water** ℂ *disaster, feelings, repression.*

glass **1.** To dream of looking through a pane of glass symbolizes a gentle barrier you've erected between yourself and a situation. You still want to be involved, but not directly. **2.** To dream of breaking glass symbolizes your need to

speak up or act in order to get your message across. Otherwise, people won't take you seriously. **3.** To dream of glass objects or ornaments represents someone or something you must treat with special care right now. This is a fragile situation. See also *cup or glass, window.* ☽ **rock** ℂ *caretaking, communication, impediments, inanimate objects, protection, relationships.*

glasses **1.** To dream of wearing glasses means you should look at something more closely. You've missed the fine print. **2.** To dream of breaking or losing your glasses symbolizes your desire *not* to see what's really going on. You'd rather this situation stayed blurry. Are you hiding behind your glasses? ☽ **vision problems** ℂ *communication, inanimate objects, messages, resistance.*

glove **1.** To dream of wearing a glove or a pair of gloves symbolizes something you don't want to touch, or something you want to protect yourself against that involves details and complicated communication. **2.** To dream of taking off your gloves means you are prepared to deal with a complicated or inflammatory situation right now. **3.** To dream of losing your gloves symbolizes your fear that you are unprepared for something that you expect will happen any minute. You feel like you don't have the resources to deal with this. ☽ **hand** ℂ *clothing and accessories, communication, inanimate objects, insecurity, resistance.*

glue **1.** Dreaming of using glue

means you are trying to keep a situation, or a group of people, together. It all wants to fall apart, but you refuse to let it! **2.** If the glue you are using won't stick, you fear a situation or relationship really is falling apart. Maybe it should. ● **breaking free** ℂ *control issues, loss, relationships, solutions and remedies.*

goat   Goats represent sacrifice, blame, rebellion against societal rules, and also destruction. **1.** To dream of an injured or dead goat symbolizes a sacrifice you have made for someone, or that someone has made for you. **2.** To dream of a goat inside your home or workplace or in any other place where a goat wouldn't normally belong means you have shifted the blame for something onto someone else, or someone has decided to blame you for something. **3.** To dream of a person who is part goat, or a goat in the forest, represents your desire to escape society's rules and restrictions and really let go. You are ready for a party. **4.** To see a goat eating or destroying something symbolizes a situation so carelessly managed that you won't be able to repair all the damage. ● **cow** ℂ *animals, celebration, destruction, nature, rebellion, rules and laws, sacrifice.*

goatee   See *beard.*

The goat must be the most sacrificed animal in history. The Bible is filled with people sacrificing goats, and goats were often sacrificed to various gods and goddesses in ancient Greece and Rome as well as elsewhere in Europe. Half-goat people, called satyrs, represented paganism, and those who worshipped goat gods were denounced by the early church as devil worshipers. The word *scapegoat* may have come from the notion that sacrificing a goat would get people off the hook for something they had done to anger the gods.

gods   Dreams of gods symbolize strong masculine energy, authority, or spiritual direction for your life. **1.** To dream God is speaking to you could be a divine message. Better listen up! **2.** Dreams about God could also symbolize your instinct that you have a divine purpose, or that you have strayed from your true path and you need a reminder to return to the straight and narrow. **3.** To dream of a god you don't believe in, such as Zeus, or some god you don't recognize, indicates your own feelings of power and authority. This is your masculine energy speaking. **4.** To dream you are a god means you have strong personal power and a positive self-image right now. ● **goddesses** ℂ *authority, characters, creation, divine power, ethics and morals, image, journeys and quests, listening, masculine, messages, myths and legends, personal power, spirituality.*

goddesses   Goddesses represent the original female principle, the yin to the yang, the moon to the sun. **1.** To dream of a goddess speaking to you signifies a voice from the feminine divine. This is your female energy speaking. Goddesses may appear in dreams to protect you or your children, to deliver messages about your fertility or nurturing skill, or to help ease your transition from one life stage to another. **2.** You may have a goddess dream if you are entering puberty, become pregnant, or are entering menopause. A goddess might also appear to a man or a woman as a reminder to honor the sacred feminine. **3.** Dreams of the goddess could symbolize a direction you should take or the desire for a more spiritual life. **4.** To dream you are a goddess means you are going through a time of intense feminine energy and a positive self-image. You have tapped into goddess power! ☽ **gods** ☾ *authority, caretaking, changing course, characters, communication, creation, divine power, feminine, image, journeys and quests, listening, messages, myths and legends, personal power, spirituality.*

gold   To dream of gold symbolizes wealth and value, not necessarily material. **1.** To dream of gold objects—statues, structures made of gold, regular items suddenly turned gold—suggests that, like King Midas, you overvalue material possessions or money. **2.** To dream of gold jewelry symbolizes a passionate attraction you feel to someone. **3.** To dream of a gold halo over someone or someone who is shimmering or lit up in gold suggests that person, or someone that person represents, can help you to discover something important for your spiritual growth. See also *bling, jewelry, ring.* ☽ **silver** ☾ *abundance, divine power, financial resources, love, relationships, spirituality.*

goldfish   Goldfish represent protection, insulation from the outside world, and untouchable beauty. To dream of a goldfish symbolizes your admiration for something pristine and elevated beyond your reach, or your desire for a quiet, simple, protected life free from the interferences and crass influences of the world. Hmmm, wonder what goldfish dream about us? ☽ **shark** ☾ *animals, beauty, innocence, isolation, protection, water.*

golf   Playing or watching golf in your dream represents a pleasant and satisfying feeling of leisure. You aren't in any hurry, and you plan to enjoy yourself, thank you very much. ☽ **football** ☾ *competition, play, pleasure, sports and games.*

gossip   **1.** Hearing gossip about yourself in your dream suggests that you suspect people are talking about you behind your back or not telling you the whole story. **2.** Listening to gossip about someone else in a dream belies your deep curiosity about the lives of others, or about someone in particular. What are you just dying to know? **3.** Gossiping about others in your dream means you have recently begun to question your own reliability and trustworthiness. Are you being a true friend? ☻ **secret** ℂ *communication, loyalty, relationships, trust issues.*

government Dreams about the government symbolize your feelings about authority figures in general and can reveal whether you trust or distrust the authorities that influence your life. ☻ **child or children** ℂ *authority, rules and laws, trust issues.*

government spying Dreaming that the government is spying on you doesn't mean you are ready to sign up with some conspiracy theory group, but it does mean you feel a certain distrust for an authority figure. You don't think someone or some institution has your best interest in mind, and they might even be trying to bring you down. ☻ **truth** ℂ *authority, dishonesty, loyalty, people, threats, trust issues.*

graduation 1. Dreaming of graduation means you've finished something or look forward to finishing something very soon. You have confidence that you've done a good job and you are recognizing this in your dream. **2.** To dream of being handed a diploma during graduation symbolizes an official move upward in your career or status. **3.** Dreaming of a graduation party or other big celebration surrounding a graduation signifies a major accomplishment. You did it! **4.** Dreaming that you forgot to graduate, missed graduation, or graduated unfairly

and fear someone will figure it out all symbolize your insecurity about your current position or status. You don't really believe you deserve it, or you fear you will make a mistake and lose everything you've worked for. **5.** To dream of watching someone else graduate symbolizes your pride—or jealousy—at the accomplishment of someone else. ☻ **failing** ℂ *celebration, changing course, envy, goal-setting, insecurity, opportunity, personal power.*

grandchildren 1. Dreaming that something bad happens to your grandchildren symbolizes anxious feelings about them—you worry about them a lot! Give them a call. Everything is probably just fine. **2.** Dreaming that your grandchildren accomplish something that makes you proud or show their love for you symbolizes your deep grandparental pride in your offspring's offspring (or grandchildren figures in your life). **3.** Dreaming you have grandchildren when you don't actually have them symbolizes that you feel a strong obligation for someone younger, or someone younger really needs you to be a grandparent figure to them. **4.** On the other hand, you may be concerned about who will take care of you when you are old. Is it too late to adopt? ☻ **grandparents** ℂ *anxiety, caretaking, family, people, protection, relationships.*

grandparents 1. To dream that something frightening or worrisome happens to one or both of your grandparents symbolizes your worry that you will soon lose them. This is a common anxiety in anyone who has a close relationship with someone who is aging. Give your grandparents a call, just in case, to make sure they are okay. **2.** To dream of a grandparent after that person has died means you want to resolve something or say something to them that you didn't have a chance to. It could also symbolize how much you miss them. **3.** If a deceased grandparent visits you in a dream and tells you something, it just might be a visitation! Your grandparent might need to convey something important, or something that will help you come to terms with his or her passing. Take time to review the helpful things your grandparent taught you. ☽ **grandchildren** ☾ *death, family, messages, people, relationships, spirituality.*

grapes   Juicy and bursting on the vine, grapes symbolize abundance. Like the god(dess) of wine, you have unlimited resources and you know how to party. Get ready to reap the amazing harvest you have sown. See also *fruit, wine.* ☽ **sober** ☾ *abundance, celebration, eating, food and drink, fruit.*

grass   **1.** To dream of your lawn represents your external appearance. If your lawn is weedy or yellowing, you fear you look bad or disreputable or incompetent to others. If your lawn is lush and green, you are making a good impression. **2.** To walk barefoot in grass symbolizes your deep feeling of connection with the earth. You can feel the planet under your feet, and the grass makes this communication soft and pleasant. **3.** To dream of a grassy field or a grassy stretch of land in a park symbolizes possibility and opportunity. You have a great chance to move in a new direction right now. **4.** Grass also represents your youth and playfulness. ☽ **dirt** ☾ *image, nature, opportunity, plants, reputation.*

grave   **1.** To dream of looking at a grave symbolizes mourning for something you've lost. **2.** To recognize the name on the headstone symbolizes a warning about that person, or someone or something that person represents. Something is about to change. **3.** To dream you are in a grave suggests you've gotten yourself into a bad situation, but if you make a change, you can get yourself out. It's not over. See also *buried alive, cemetery, coffin.* ☽ **cradle** ☾ *changing course, death, fear, loss, places, transformation.*

graveyard   See *cemetery.*

greedy   **1.** To dream of being greedy signifies your feeling that you've lost control of your behavior. You know you've done something inappropriate, but you just couldn't help it. You were overcome by your desire for more. **2.** To dream someone else is greedy in a dream symbolizes your recognition that someone has been getting more than his or her fair share. It might be someone you know, or it might even be you. **3.** Or you may just need a couple more hours of sleep. ☽ **abstinence** ☾ *abundance, addictions, control issues, desires, feelings, food and drink, greed, hedonism, risky behavior.*

The Green Man, so named in the 1930s but existing for many centuries before, is a man's face surrounded by leaves, sometimes with leaves coming out of his mouth and eyes. This figure has been carved into the poles of churches and in various stone incarnations in many countries around the world for centuries. Some believe the Green Man is a depiction of an early pagan nature deity. Others see the Green Man as an archetypal symbol of man's connection to the natural world. Whatever his origin, or his name—he has sometimes been called Jack-in-the-Green, Leaf Man, or the May King, and linked with such mythical figures as Robin Hood, Puck, John Barleycorn, and even Peter Pan—the Green Man remains a memorable and enduring figure, particularly beloved today by neopagans and Wiccans as an incarnation of Nature's male energy.

---

green   Seeing green in a natural setting or in a home represents nature and the influence of nature in human life and culture. If you dream of being surrounded by green or seeing large areas of green, you feel balanced and healthy, unfettered by cultural restraints. Green objects, found or lost, represent money. Check the pockets of that jacket you haven't worn since last winter. ☽ **orange** ☾ *balance, color, financial resources, health and hygiene, nature.*

Grim Reaper   See *death.*

groom   1. To dream you are the happy groom in a wedding symbolizes your satisfaction regarding a recent commitment. You are glad you did it. **2.** If you are not already planning a wedding but you dream you are an unhappy groom trapped at a wedding or fleeing a wedding, you are feeling anxiety about a commitment you wish you hadn't made or fear you will be coerced into making. This might be related to your job, a relationship, or a family situation. Whatever it is, you don't feel ready for it. **3.** To be engaged and to dream of your wedding represents either your hopes about how it will go or your worries about making such a big life change. **4.** To dream someone you know is a groom and you are marrying him symbolizes a dependency on that person for some physical, financial, or emotional need. You may not want to marry this person at all, but you feel connected or obligated to that person. See also *marriage, ring.* ☽ **divorce** ☾ *burdens, celebration, characters, financial resources, freedom, happiness, people, relationships, responsibilities.*

growing   1. To dream you are growing symbolizes a feeling of awkwardness or a feeling of power, depending on whether the growth in your dream makes you feel

uncomfortable or powerful.
2. To see someone else growing in a dream represents your awe or envy about someone else's progress. ☾ **destruction** ₡ *age, embarrassment, insecurity, personal power.*

grown-up To dream of someone who seems very grown-up, or to dream you are suddenly more grown-up than usual, signifies the need for you to act more mature in a current situation. It's time to step up and take responsibility. What? You're 84? You don't look a day over 83, darling. ☾ **child or children** ₡ *age, authority, people, responsibility.*

guillotine See *decapitation.*

guilty conscience To have a guilty conscience in a dream usually means you have a guilty conscience! But what you feel guilty about will be symbolized by, rather than exactly the same as, what you feel guilty about in your dream. For instance, if you dream you committed a crime, such as stealing, you may actually feel guilty about stealing credit for someone's idea, stealing the attention from someone who could have used a boost, or stealing someone's self-esteem away by insulting or demeaning them. Your dream will hold the clues. It's best to rid yourself of guilt by making things right in your waking life. You'll sleep better afterward. ☾ **saint** ₡ *guilt.*

guitar See *musical instrument.*

gum 1. To dream someone offers you chewing gum means you can be less formal in a current situation. People will appreciate your more casual approach. 2. To dream of spitting out your gum means you should be more formal or mature in a current situation. You are coming across as childish or even rude. 3. To dream of offering someone else gum suggests you would like to be friends with that person, or someone that person represents, but you don't want to be too obvious about it. ☾ **garlic** ₡ *image, inanimate objects, relationships.*

gun Dreaming of guns symbolizes drastic upheaval, change, or forceful disengagement from someone. 1. If you dream you are holding a gun, threatening people with a gun, or shooting a gun, you want to get out of a situation, change it dramatically, or get away from someone, but you aren't sure how to do it. Your dream is busting a cap in this feeling. 2. If you dream of carrying a gun and feeling safe because of it, something or someone is protecting you. 3. If you dream someone is threatening you with a gun or pointing or shooting at you, you feel threatened by and fearful of someone or something. Your dream is telling you to get out of this situation before something bad happens. 4. If you dream of getting shot but it doesn't seem to hurt you, you are handling a current problem with self-confidence. Nobody can bring you down. 5. If you dream of finding a gun and feeling fearful or unsure about what to do with it, or you fear for the safety of others because of the gun's presence, something in your life right now threatens you or others and feels dangerous. Is it something you are doing, or someone else? It bothers you. **6.** If you dream of holding a bullet, you already know the solution to your problem. It's simpler than you think. (And it doesn't involve violence!) **7.** Also, there's the obvious phallic symbol. Is the safety on, or are you trigger-happy? ☯ **nonviolence** ☾ *changing course, danger, inanimate objects, personal power, protection, solutions and remedies, relationships, risky behavior, threats, violence.*

gypsy   To dream of meeting a gypsy symbolizes your wanderlust, rebellious nature, and desire for a free and unfettered lifestyle—even if just for a little while. You feel like doing something out of character, something that would surprise people. Taking off for Europe without notice? Piercing your ear and wearing a big gold hoop? Cooking something exotic? Look into your crystal ball. What do you see? ☯ **homebody** ☾ *changing course, characters, freedom, people, rebellion, travel.*

G

H

hail   1. To dream of hail pounding on your roof means you've been ignoring signs about what direction to take. Nature is trying to get your attention! **2.** To dream of being caught out in a hailstorm symbolizes a difficult challenge you are facing. **3.** To dream your car or roof is damaged by hail symbolizes financial loss. It wasn't your fault, but now you're going to have to deal with it. **4.** To dream of picking up or holding a piece of hail symbolizes your desire to look at a problem close-up. **5.** Don't forget the hell homonym synergy here. Did you wake up in a pool of sweat? ☾ **sun** ☾ *destruction, impediments, nature, solutions and remedies, weather and seasons.*

hair   1. To dream of looking at or styling your own hair symbolizes your recent concern with your appearance or image. You feel pressured to look *just so*, or you wish you projected a different image. **2.** To dream your hair is falling out symbolizes insecurity. You don't feel comfortable about how you look or appear to others. You feel exposed and unattractive or incompetent. **3.** To dream of curling your hair symbolizes your desire to be more social, flirtatious, and outgoing. You'd like to be seen as more free-spirited. **4.** To dream of straightening your hair symbolizes your desire to be taken more seriously. You'd like to be seen as more professional, mature, or elegant. **5.** To dream of brushing, styling, or touching someone else's hair symbolizes admiration or envy for someone else's image or reputation. See also *blond hair, brunette hair, red hair.* ☾ **baldness** ☾ *beauty, envy, image, insecurity, loss, reputation, vulnerability.*

hair loss   See *baldness.*

Halloween   A fun holiday for kids in masks, or an ancient and sacred time of year where ordinary humans get to catch a glimpse of the spirit world? Only your dream knows! **1.** Fun, celebratory dreams about Halloween can symbolize a desire for childhood days when holidays and other rituals seemed so exciting. Your cynical adult mind may long for these times. **2.** Exciting, adventurous

Halloween dreams represent a longing within for excitement beyond the normal possibilities in your life. Putting on costumes and becoming someone else presents an opportunity to stretch the limits of your personal reality. Even if the dream gets suspenseful—people chasing you, monsters jumping out at you— if you feel exhilarated and thrilled by the dream, your dream has given you a chance to try on a different "mask" and live a life with more thrills and danger than your regular life, all from the safety of your bed. **3.** Solemn, serious Halloween dreams symbolize a deep instinctual recognition of the autumn equinox. The season is changing and this is the season of aging, passing on, transformation. That costume you put on in your dream, or that costumed figure you see, might just be signaling you toward a direction of personal growth and maturity. **4.** Frightening Halloween dreams can represent a childhood fear come back to life during the time when the spirits come closest to our earthly realm. These dreams can also represent your fear of change. Being someone else or seeing others in costumes that disguise who they really are makes you uncomfortable. **5.** Weird or supernatural Halloween dreams might be a glimpse into that spirit realm. Have you lifted the metaphorical veil and seen to the beyond? Even if the "beyond" exists only in your own mind, this might be a rare glimpse of something you don't normally get to see: your subconscious mind. The images and symbols you see represent what's going on in the deepest recesses of your soul, and you may only understand them on an intuitive level. You're seeing part of you, and your identity, that you might not normally acknowledge. See also *autumn, costume, disguise.* ☾ **Easter** ☽ *adventure, celebration, clothing and accessories, fear, fun, identity, image, myths and legends, risky behavior, spirituality, weather and seasons.*

The ancient Celts originally began wearing costumes on Halloween because they believed this was the time of year when spirits walked the earth. In their fear of being recognized as vulnerable human beings, they disguised themselves as spirits— to "blend in." In dreams, wearing disguises or costumes may also help us not only become someone else, trying on a new identity, but also let us "sample" a more supernatural or spiritual existence.

hallway   Dreaming of a hallway symbolizes the path you are taking. **1.** If the hallway has many doors, you have many opportunities and possibilities right now. **2.** If the hallway has no doors and ends abruptly, you've taken a path without much room for growth. You might be in a rut, or stagnating. **3.** If the hallway has doors but they are locked, you need to stay on the straight and narrow right now. Don't let yourself get distracted. **4.** If the hallway seems to go on and on forever, you have a long journey ahead, but it may take you into some interesting places. As the poet Robert Frost once wrote, you have "miles to go before [you] sleep." **5.** If the hall is long and has a smooth wooden floor, put some socks on, take a running start, and slide down it as fast as you can. ☽ **dead end** ℭ *buildings and rooms, career, ethics and morals, journeys and quests, opportunities, places.*

halo   1. To have a halo in a dream symbolizes your recent behavior: you've been good—very, very good. You've done something for someone else with no thought to yourself, and now your dream is patting you on the back. **2.** If you see yourself with a halo and some spiritual figure—an angel, saint, or religious person—tells you something or signals to you, you may need to focus more on your spiritual development. Or you might just have a divine mission. Ancient people would take such a dream very seriously, as a message from the higher realm. **3.** To see a halo over someone else symbolizes your reverence and admiration for that person. Halos around people or objects can also portend a significant event surrounding whatever has a halo. Something really big or amazing might be about to happen. **4.** To see a halo around an angel or religious figure means your spiritual life needs attention. Have you been "worshipping" material things? Have you gone astray in your spiritual journey? ☽ **horns** ℭ *divine power, journeys and quests, predictions, spirituality.*

hammer   Hammers represent hard work. Using or seeing a hammer in your dream means you've been working hard, or you should start working hard. A job needs doing. ☽ **hammock** ℭ *inanimate objects, work.*

hammock   1. Slow down. Take a load off. You've been working hard, and dreaming of lying luxuriously in a hammock or seeing a hammock means you deserve a break. Grab a book, or an umbrella drink, and take at least a few hours to yourself. Your body calls out for it. **2.** To be unable to get out of a hammock in your dream, however, means you've been relaxing *too* much. You're bordering on sloth these days, so maybe it's time to get moving and get something accomplished. **3.** To dream of lying in a hammock but feeling guilty about it means you know you need some time to yourself but you don't feel able to take it. You've been giving so much to others lately that you've forgotten how to give time to yourself. Don't get out of your hammock until you've figured this out. ☽ **hammer** ℭ *comfort, solutions and remedies.*

hand   Hands are the "doing" body parts. They get right in there and touch, they direct and lead, they describe and express, they can do remarkably detailed work, and they were your first tools for exploring the world. Hands are the tools of leaders and doers. **1.** Dreaming of your hands symbolizes your involvement in the world, your interaction, skill, and interests. You are hands-on and you want to get even more involved—take the wheel, direct the choir, point something out, give someone the high-five. The metaphors are endless, but you've grasped that by now. **2.** Dreaming you have injured your hands symbolizes your fear of getting involved. You've been hurt by getting too close to something, or you have been so withdrawn from the active, interactive world that you don't know how to reach back in and hold on. **3.** To dream your hands are bound so you can't use them symbolizes your lack of power in a situation. Someone else has taken control. See also *handcuffs.* ☽ **gloves** ☾ *body parts, control issues, injuries, insecurity, personal power, work.*

handcuffs   1. To wear handcuffs in a dream symbolizes insecurity, vulnerability, and subjugation by authority. You aren't in control anymore. Are you unjustly accused or wracked with guilt? You may be unable to act because you know you did something wrong. **2.** To put handcuffs on someone else or see handcuffs on someone else symbolizes your recognition that others are helpless in a situation, or obviously guilty. See also *escape.* ☽ **breaking free** ☾ *anxiety, authority, control issues, ethics and morals, guilt, inanimate objects, insecurity, vulnerability.*

hang-gliding   1. If you hang-glide in your dream, you are feeling particularly daring and free-spirited. **2.** If you hang-glide but you don't want to do it, and/or you feel terrified or you can't control the hang-glider, you've gotten yourself into something you aren't sure you can handle. ☽ **homebody** ☾ *adventure, anxiety, control issues, freedom, personal power, risky behavior, sports and games.*

hanging   1. To see a person being hanged represents a major change in your life. As in the Death major arcana tarot card, this dream doesn't necessarily signal a bad change—just a *big* one. **2.** If you are the one who is being hanged, you are ready to say good-bye to a part of your life or image that isn't working for you and start with a brand new one, as in tarot's Hanged Man card. **3.** If you see objects hanging from trees or other strange places in your dream, someone knows what you are doing, even though you don't consciously realize it. How do they do it? ☽ **falling** ☾ *changing course, death, knowledge, predictions, subterfuge.*

happy   Wake up with a smile. **1.** Dreaming you feel happy probably means you really do feel happy. But feeling happy can also represent self-confidence, or be a sign that you are on the right path or have made the right decision about something. **2.** To dream that someone else is particularly happy suggests that you perceive their good fortune. **3.** If you dream of being annoyed or envious of someone else's happiness in a dream, you aren't seeing a current situation or relationship in a productive way. ☽ **depression** ☾ *decisions, envy, feelings, personal power, relationships.*

harmonica   See *musical instrument.*

hat   **1.** To dream of wearing a formal hat symbolizes finishing something, deciding something, or formalizing something. You've made it happen, and that's that. **2.** To dream of wearing an informal or silly hat (a backward baseball cap, a beanie with a propeller) symbolizes your casual, irreverent attitude. You don't intend to take a current situation very seriously. **3.** To dream of wearing a warm winter hat symbolizes your need to protect yourself. You don't feel safe or in league with anybody, so you are summoning up your inner protective resources. **4.** To dream of someone else wearing a hat signals a change in a situation. Have you noticed the rules have shifted? **5.** To dream of throwing a hat means you are ready to volunteer for something. You want that new job, that audition, that big chance, and you are ready to go for it. ☽ **shoes** ☾ *clothing and accessories, decisions, fun, inanimate objects, opportunities.*

hate   If you feel the strong emotion of hate in a dream, you are repressing strong feelings about someone or something. Your dream is trying to force them out into your consciousness so you can deal with them. Hate dreams can also help you to discover what you really think about a situation you've been

pretending not to care about. ☽ **love** ☾ *anger, anxiety, extremism, feelings, pain, repression.*

haunted house   Houses symbolize your mind, and haunted houses symbolize a mind haunted by memories, repressed feelings, and other things you can't quite let go of that wander around when perhaps they should really be set free. **1.** Exploring a haunted house in your dream symbolizes your desire to explore your inner feelings and thoughts. What lurks inside that you haven't faced? **2.** Being trapped in a haunted house and frightened symbolizes your feeling of being trapped in your head. You think too much or dwell too much on the past and things you can't do anything about now. **3.** Passing or watching a haunted house but refusing to go inside symbolizes your recognition that you've got some issues you haven't dealt with yet, but you'll let them haunt you a little longer. You aren't quite ready to face them or perform an exorcism just yet. See also *house.* ☽ **future** ☾ *buildings and rooms, fear, guilt, memory, places, repression, secrets, subterfuge.*

headache   **1.** Dreaming of your head symbolizes your intellect, and if you dream you have a headache, you may be overthinking a situation. Try listening to your intuition or your heart, or at least let these other elements of you get a word in. **2.** Dreaming of a headache can also signal a health problem, whether you've had an injury or not. If you are worried, have it checked out. **3.**

Headaches can also symbolize guilt, or something you need to say or do that you are holding back or refusing to remember or acknowledge. That thought or those words need to come out so badly that it hurts! ☾ **ecstasy** ☾ *body parts, guilt, health and hygiene, injuries, intelligence, memory, pain, repression, secrets, subterfuge.*

headstone   See *grave.*

healing   **1.** To dream of healing from an illness or injury represents your internal regenerative power. Your body is trying to heal itself from something—a physical ailment or an emotional one. You just have to get out of the way and follow your body's lead. **2.** To dream of healing someone else means you have the power to help someone who needs help right now. **3.** To dream of being healed by someone else or by a divine or spiritual source means you should ask for help. The solution lies within an external source. ☾ **disease** ☾ *caretaking, feelings, healing, health and hygiene, relationships, solutions and remedies, spirituality.*

health   **1.** To dream of your own health may be a signal from your body that you need to take better care of your body before it gives up and turns against you. Are you eating well and getting enough sleep? Are you engaging in some unhealthful habits like smoking or excessive drinking? Your body is wise and it can speak

to you through your dreams, and any health issues in your dreams may symbolize, if not be literally the same, as real health issues you have or might be developing. **2.** To dream of being in excellent health means you are on the right path to success. **3.** To dream of someone else's health means that person, or someone that person represents, needs your attention. ☾ **disease** ☾ *caretaking, feelings, health and hygiene, journeys and quests, risky behavior, transformation.*

heart   To dream of your own heart means you should listen to your heart right now. It is crying out for your attention. To dream something is wrong with your heart means you have spent far too long ignoring your heart's needs— physical or emotional. See also *heart attack.* ☾ **brain** ☾ *body parts, caretaking, feelings, health and hygiene, listening, love, relationships.*

heart attack   **1.** If you dream you are having a heart attack, you might really be worried about your heart health. Your body might be sending you a sign that you should have your heart checked, and/or change your bad habits to better nurture your heart. Do you need to reduce stress? Eat better? Exercise more? (If you are like most people, you could probably benefit from all three!) **2.** Heart attack dreams can also be symbolic. Your heart hurts so badly that you feel you might just drop, at least emotionally. Maybe it's time to acknowledge that pain so your heart can heal. Be gentle with yourself. ◐ **brain** ℂ *body parts, caretaking, feelings, healing, health and hygiene, love, pain, relationships.*

heat   If your dream is getting hot—in any sense of the word—you are warming up to a situation. You might just be getting passionate about it—or him … or her …. See also *fever.* ◐ **cold** ℂ *heat, love, relationships, weather and seasons.*

heaven   **1.** To dream of heaven gives you a glimpse into what you consider the ultimate perfect reality. **2.** Dreams of heaven can also indicate a craving for a more spiritually rewarding existence, or play out the ecstasy of a well-nurtured spiritual existence. **3.** Heaven dreams can help to ease the fear of death, or serve as an incentive for changing the course of your life. **4.** If the heaven you dream about seems familiar, you could be getting a sneak peek into the nature of your own soul in a higher plane of existence, or even a glimpse of a past life. See also *utopia.* ◐ **hell** ℂ *changing course, death, divine power, ethics and morals, happiness, hopes and dreams, love, myths and legends, places, spirituality.*

heavy   If something feels unusually heavy in a dream, you can't lift something, or you can't lift your own feet because they are so heavy, something is holding you back in

your progress. It might be another person, a situation, or your own attitude, but whatever it is, your dream is trying to show it to you by making your burden literal. If you find yourself able to lift something incredibly heavy in a dream, you are emotionally strong right now. ◐ **feather** ℂ *anxiety, burdens, impediments.*

hell   **1.** To dream of glimpsing hell, or being in hell, is a warning. You face the possibility of a very bad situation. What you do next could determine whether you land there. **2.** Dreams of hell can also signify deep-seated guilt and fear about something you've done. You fear punishment. ◐ **heaven** ℂ *changing course, danger, death, decisions, divine power, ethics and morals, fear, guilt, heat, myths and legends, places, punishment, spirituality.*

helping someone   If you dream of helping someone, you are acting out something you feel you should be doing, although the situation in your dream may be only a symbol of the real situation that requires your intervention. Examine your dream for clues. Who needs you? It might even turn out that you are dreaming about helping yourself. ◐ **dropping something** ℂ *caretaking, relationships, solutions and remedies.*

hemorrhage   See *blood.*

hen   See *chicken.*

According to Dante's classic work, *The Inferno,* hell consists of nine levels or circles, and your sins damn you to the appropriate level, depending on what they are. The unrepentant sinners get assigned according to their transgressions, along these lines:

- First level (Limbo): The virtuous but unqualified (the unbaptized)
- Second level: The lustful
- Third level: The gluttonous
- Fourth level: The greedy
- Fifth level: The wrathful
- Sixth level: The heretics
- Seventh level: The violent
- Eight level: The cheaters and liars
- Ninth level: Traitors, including Lucifer himself

Literary scholars find many symbols from Dante's current time in the imagery, such as nasty veiled criticism of political figures and other clever but acerbic commentary on current events. Of course, this sort of thing would send Dante straight to the fifth level of hell.

hero **1.** To be a hero in a dream symbolizes your feelings of personal power. You feel strong enough to help yourself—and everyone else, too. You could take advantage of this period of confidence to make the world better. **2.** If you take an extreme risk to be a hero in your dream, you may be acting out your compulsion to rescue people so you can feel good about yourself. **3.** If you dream you are a superhero with super powers, you might just be enjoying a bit of fantasy, but you also might recognize special talents or gifts you have that really could help others. Are you using them? **4.** If you dream a hero rescues you, you feel stuck in a situation and you don't know how to get out of it yourself. You wish someone would come and save you, and then everything would be okay. See also *rescue.* ☯ **villain** ℭ *caretaking, characters, hopes and dreams, people, personal power, responsibilities, risky behavior, solutions and remedies.*

heterosexuality **1.** If you dream of having a heterosexual experience or relationship even though you are homosexual in your waking life, you probably aren't "secretly straight," but you may be playing out how things would be if you were, or remembering a time when you thought you were. If the dream doesn't upset you, it simply means you have a balanced sexual energy. If the dream does upset you, you may have unresolved sexuality issues. Have you really accepted yourself for who you are? **2.** If you are heterosexual but dream that you live in a society where heterosexuality is abnormal, you may be questioning your own sexual feelings or not admitting to their full range because of social fears or restrictions. ☯ **homosexuality** ℭ *balance, gender issues, love, relationships, sexual activity.*

H

hex See *curse.*

hiccup Dreaming of having the hiccups means you should stop and think before you talk. You might not want to say the things you are thinking about saying. They might be misinterpreted or make you look foolish. Think about it some more first. (And have a glass of water.) ☽ **speaking in public** ℂ *communication.*

hickey Tired of wearing that turtleneck in the middle of summer? If you dream you have a hickey, you're filled with youthful rebellion lately. You want everyone to know you don't follow the rules. If you feel guilty about a hickey in your dream or try to hide it with clothes or makeup, you're ashamed of something you did. Were those self-inflicted? It could be something recent or something from "way back when." ☽ **freezer** ℂ *body parts, guilt, love, memory, rebellion, relationships, rules and laws, subterfuge.*

hiding 1. To dream you are in hiding means you fear something or you don't want to attract any attention to yourself. You may feel guilty or insecure about your image, or you may fear interaction with others in a current situation. 2. To dream of hiding something or someone from others indicates a protective instinct or a jealous one. Either you need to keep someone safe or you don't want others to have what you have. 3. Hiding treasure, jewels, or other valuables symbolizes protection of your financial resources from someone or something you fear could compromise them. 4. Hiding from a spouse or partner because you are cheating with someone else symbolizes your guilty feelings about being attracted to someone or wanting more excitement in your love life. 5. Finding someone who is hiding symbolizes your intuition that somebody isn't being straight with you. They might be afraid of you or intimidated by you. ☽ **exhibitionism** ℂ *fear, financial resources, guilt, image, insecurity, repression, secrets, sexual activity, subterfuge.*

high school See *school.*

highway Highways symbolize your current life path or journey. Where are you going and how are you getting there? 1. Driving or riding in a vehicle down a straight highway suggests good progress and confidence about your direction. 2. A highway full of potholes, construction, or barricades suggests a difficult journey with many obstacles to overcome. You won't get there quickly. 3. Walking down a highway as cars speed by suggests that you've chosen a slower, more methodical approach. You may take longer but you'll catch details others miss. 4. Seeing a highway from far away or from above, or looking at highways on a map suggests you have been looking at the big picture and considering whether this is the path for you. You may be preparing for a decision about changing direction. ☯ **barrier** ☾ *changing course, direction, impediments, journeys and quests, travel, vehicles.*

hijacked plane 1. The all-too-common dream of being a passenger on a hijacked plane reveals your fear that someone with great power will influence your life in a tragic way, and you won't be able to do anything about it. 2. To dream you foil a hijacker symbolizes your resolution to take control of your own life, even though you are facing adversity. 3. To dream you are hijacking a plane symbolizes your powerful need to control a current situation that hasn't been going your way. You want to put a stop to it, and the hijacking represents the strong or even desperate and irrational way you are considering taking action. It might be best to think before you act rashly. ☯ **flying** ☾ *anxiety, control issues, fear, risky behavior, solutions and remedies, vehicles.*

hiking 1. Hiking through the woods symbolizes a journey through a complicated issue. If the hiking is pleasant, you enjoy the process of navigating this problem. If the hiking is unpleasant, difficult, or tiring, or if the environment seems hostile or scary, your current task has turned out to be more challenging than you expected. 2. Hiking through the desert symbolizes the need for isolation (if the dream is pleasant) or frustration

at a project's current monotony (if it isn't). 3. Hiking through the mountains represents a difficult passage you must make. This will take some serious effort; focus and keep going. 4. Hiking with no particular destination in mind, just to enjoy your natural surroundings, suggests you crave interaction with nature. Maybe it's time to take a walk in the fresh air. ☯ **hammock** ☾ *journeys and quests, nature, places, solutions and remedies, travel.*

hill 1. Climbing a hill symbolizes a problem you are trying to solve. 2. Seeing a hill from far away or from above suggests you finally have some perspective on a past problem or situation. 3. Getting to the top of a hill and looking beyond means you probably have a good idea about how something is going to turn out. You've got foresight. ☯ **valley** ☾ *impediments, nature, places, predictions.*

hired 1. To dream you get hired for a new job and you feel excited, happy, or proud means you've accomplished something new, changed your life's direction, or made an important decision, probably involving your work but possibly also involving your social position or relationship with someone. You feel good about the change and you look forward to the future. 2. To dream of getting hired but being filled with anxiety about whether you can do the job also signals a life change, but one about which you aren't quite so confident. You aren't

H

sure you deserve these new opportunities, or you aren't sure you can do what others expect of you.
◐ **fired from a job** ℂ *anxiety, career, changing course, decisions, hopes and dreams, opportunities, personal power, relationships, responsibilities, work.*

hitchhiking   Hitchhiking dreams symbolize a risk you are thinking about taking. **1.** To dream you are hitchhiking but nobody picks you up suggests you are considering something risky but you aren't quite sure about going through with it. **2.** To dream you are hitchhiking and someone friendly picks you up suggests your adventurous nature. You want to do something daring and you just know it will all turn out fine. **3.** To dream you are hitchhiking and someone dangerous or threatening picks you up symbolizes your anxiety about a decision. You aren't sure the course of action you've been considering is safe for you. **4.** To dream you drive by a hitchhiker without stopping symbolizes your decision to pass on a risk. You're not going to go there. **5.** To dream of picking up a person suggests you are leaning toward taking the risk because you think you can learn something new.
◐ **homebody** ℂ *anxiety, control issues, danger, fear, opportunities, risky behavior, solutions and remedies, travel.*

hitting   **1.** Hitting someone in a dream suggests strong feelings you've repressed. You've kept yourself from acting rashly, but the impulse has cropped up in your dream. **2.** Someone hitting you in a dream suggests fear that you've done something to make somebody angry and you are just waiting for that person to get back at you.
◐ **nonviolence** ℂ *anger, anxiety, control issues, fear, risky behavior, violence.*

hole   Holes represent the unknown, deep mystery, secrets, and, yes, in true Freudian spirit, the "center of a woman." **1.** To dream of looking down a hole symbolizes your fascination and desire for exploration of a great mystery or mysterious woman. **2.** To dream of falling down a hole suggests you have been caught up in a passionate quest for the unknown, or you feel consumed by female energy. **3.** To dream of standing back from a hole suggests your fear of the unknown or your anxiety about getting too immersed in female energy.
◐ **tower** ℂ *anxiety, fear, feminine, love, mystery, places, secrets, sexual activity, shapes and symbols.*

home   Your home represents your most basic need for shelter, comfort, and stability. Dreams of your home reflect how safe and comfortable you feel in your life right now. **1.** If you dream of being glad to get home or feeling like a certain place is home to you, you feel comfortable and secure, like you belong somewhere. **2.** If you dream your home is unpleasant or frightening, you feel a basic lack of security in your life right now. See also *house.*
◐ **hotel or motel** ℂ *buildings and*

rooms, comfort, control issues, happiness, home, identity, insecurity, places, protection, stability, vulnerability.

homebody   Staying home all comfy and cozy suits you just fine—at least, in your dream. **1.** To dream you want to stay home may mean you've been spending too much time away from home and/or family, and you crave balance. **2.** To dream you stay home because you fear something outside your home suggests you don't feel in control of external forces and you seek a safer, easier route. **3.** Staying home in a dream and avoiding everyone, wrapping yourself in a cocoon of home and hearth, may also signify your need for healing or replenishment. Listen to your body and take some down time. ☽ **gypsy** ☾ *caretaking, characters, comfort, control issues, family, happiness, healing, home, people, stability.*

If a mysterious but comforting female figure appears in your homebody dreams, it might be Hestia, the Greek goddess of home and hearth, who protects the sanctity and safety of the home and makes all who dwell there feel welcome. She also protects children, and the burning fire in the fireplace is her symbol. Keeping the fire stoked honors Hestia.

---

homeless person   **1.** Seeing a homeless person or being homeless in your dream symbolizes anxiety about your finances and fear of losing your place so that you are without sanctuary or protection. You worry you could lose everything, and the homeless person is a symbol of this loss, warning you to be careful with your resources. **2.** Dreaming of helping a homeless person symbolizes an inner call to share your resources with others who are less fortunate. ☽ **castle** ☾ *anxiety, characters, control issues, fear, financial resources, home, people.*

homosexuality   **1.** Dreams of being homosexual do not indicate you are homosexual, although they can sometimes symbolize curiosity about homosexuality. But just because you dream of homosexual interactions doesn't mean you have any intention of acting them out. Instead, homosexuality dreams usually symbolize a healthy balance between your own male and female energy. **2.** Dreaming of having an excited, giddy crush or lustful feelings about someone of the same sex symbolizes an interest in that person, or something that person represents. You might be "in love" with that person's job or image or societal position. **3.** Dreaming of homosexual interactions with someone you don't like means you envy or covet something that person is or has, and you may feel pressured to be like that person. **4.** Feeling forced to engage in homosexual activity in a dream symbolizes pressure you are feeling in your waking life to be or do something that isn't you. **5.** Dreaming you are thinking "Maybe I'm gay?" or "I must be homosexual," symbolizes a question about your current image or identity. You may be repressing a real side of yourself, and it may have nothing at all to do with sexual preference in waking life. See also *lesbian.* ☯ **heterosexuality** ℂ *balance, envy, feminine, gender issues, identity, image, love, masculine, relationships, sexual activity.*

honesty See *telling the truth.*

hooker See *prostitute.*

hooky See *playing hooky.*

horns **1.** To dream of seeing (or being) an animal with horns symbolizes your need to be assertive in a situation right now. You need to take control. **2.** To dream you have devilish horns suggests you have done something you may feel guilty about, or, as in tarot's Devil card, you may feel imprisoned in a hellish reality. If the horns are awkward and silly looking, you fear someone is cheating on you or making you look foolish. **3.** To dream someone else has horns means you are suspicious or fearful of someone. You think that person, or someone that person represents, may have an evil streak. ☯ **halo** ℂ *animals, control issues, courage, fear, guilt, image, loyalty, people, personal power, threats.*

horse Horses represent personal freedom, instinct, and travel. **1.** If you dream of riding a running horse, you want to escape a situation, a habit, or a rut you're in. You want to break free and feel the wind on your face. **2.** If you dream of seeing a horse, you should listen to your instincts right now. They are trying to tell you something your logical side wouldn't see. If the horse is black, something in your life is about to change. If the horse is white, someone needs your help—you can make a small sacrifice or take a small step that will make a big difference to someone else right now. **3.** If you see someone else riding a horse away from you, someone has slipped out of your control. They need to find their own way now. ☯ **cow** ℂ *adventure, animals, caretaking, changing course, freedom, escapism, relationships, sacrifice.*

hospital **1.** If you dream you are in a hospital, or you dream of thinking you should go to a hospital, you need to pay attention to a health issue you've been ignoring. **2.** If you dream of having surgery or a procedure in a hospital, you need to fix a problem. Use your head. This one requires a rational approach. **3.** If you dream of something going wrong in a hospital, you don't trust an authority figure or institution right now. Deep down, you think you can handle this problem better without formal intervention. Patient, heal thyself. ☯ **self-help** ℂ *authority, healing, health and hygiene, medicine and surgery, places.*

hostage **1.** If you are a hostage in a dream, someone has control of you right now and you don't like it. Or if you enjoy being a hostage in a dream, maybe you do like it. If you dream of escaping a hostage situation, you feel ready to make a change. You're not going to take it anymore. **2.** If you hold someone else hostage in a dream, you have too much control over someone else right now. Did you mean to take on this much responsibility for someone else? If someone escapes from you in a hostage situation, you fear you're losing the control you've had over someone. **3.** If you see or hear about someone being taken hostage in a dream, you may feel you're under someone's influence but it's hard for you to admit it. You recognize the situation in your subconscious only as if it's happening to someone else—but it's probably you. Also, the news media might be affecting your sleep. Do you watch the late news right before going to bed? Try something more relaxing. ☽ **breaking free** ☾ *changing course, characters, control issues, people, personal power, relationships, risky behavior.*

hot See *heat.*

hot air balloon Sailing through the sky, or plummeting disastrously to Earth? **1.** Dreaming you are floating in a hot air balloon and watching beautiful scenery or really enjoying yourself signifies your current ability to see the big picture and be truly objective about your life. You have perspective and you're not all caught up in the details. **2.** Dreaming you are in a hot air balloon that is crashing or falling to Earth symbolizes your fear that your life is going out of control and you might lose something important. **3.** Dreaming you see a hot air balloon in the distance suggests your need to be more objective. **4.** Dreaming you see a hot air balloon crashing but you aren't involved means you see the signs of an impending disaster. ☽ **buried alive** ☾ *control issues, disaster, fear, loss, personal power.*

hot tub See *Jacuzzi.*

hotel or motel Vacancy/no vacancy. To be in a hotel or motel in a dream symbolizes a temporary state of being for you—you don't plan to stay here, keep doing this, or be this person forever, but this state is necessary or enjoyable for now. **1.** If the hotel or motel is dirty, run down, or scary, you aren't comfortable with this temporary situation or persona you've taken on. **2.** If the hotel or motel is luxurious or pleasurable, you're having a great time right now, even though you know that, eventually, you'll have to check out and go home. ☽ **home** ☾ *buildings and rooms, changing course, control issues, identity, places, pleasure.*

house Houses symbolize your mind, with all their levels and secret passageways and dark closets and wide-open rooms with windows, and dreams about houses (or any living space) reflect the current state of your mental life. **1.** Huge

H

spaces mean you have an open mind and lots of potential. **2.** Tiny, cramped spaces mean you have narrowed yourself too much. **3.** Lavish furnishings and opulence show inner richness. **4.** Spare, meager furnishings or a run-down house mean you need to enrich your mind. **5.** Secret rooms and hidden passageways show you still have much to discover about yourself. **6.** If you are only renting, you haven't quite settled into your real way of thinking yet. Some self-examination may be in order. **7.** An empty living space means great potential to take your life in any direction. **8.** If you are looking at homes to buy, you are trying out a big change in attitude and perception. Are you upgrading or downgrading? ☯ **homeless person** ℂ *buildings and rooms, family, home, happiness, identity, journeys and quests, places.*

housekeeper 1. To dream you have a housekeeper suggests that you rely on someone else to keep your life in order. How you treat or interact with the housekeeper will give you clues to who it is and how you see that person in your waking life. **2.** To dream you are working as a housekeeper means someone is relying on you for things that perhaps they ought to be doing for themselves. ☯ **slob** ℂ *career, caretaking, characters, health and hygiene, home, people, responsibilities.*

hugging 1. If you hug someone in your dream, you want to support someone who needs a mood or self-confidence boost, or you feel a strong affection for someone. **2.** If someone hugs you in your dream, you crave basic human touch, and you wish someone understood you better. **3.** To dream of passionate, romantic hugging symbolizes your strong emotional connection with someone. **4.** Hugging or being hugged can also mean you have finally forgiven someone, or someone has finally forgiven you. ☯ **shunning** ℂ *caretaking, desires, feelings, forgiveness, happiness, love, relationships, sexual activity, support.*

Studies show that people experience a drop in stress hormones after hugging or being hugged. Studies also suggest that premature babies do better when touched, and that in adults, hugging raises self-esteem and even decreases appetite. So don't just dream about hugging—go ahead and do it when you are awake!

hunger If you dream of feeling hunger, you crave something. It might be actual food, if you didn't eat much that day, but more likely you crave emotional nourishment. You aren't getting what you need from other people. ☯ **eating** ℂ *desires, feelings, food and drink, relationships, vulnerability.*

hunting Hunting represents your search for something you want or something you desire. **1.** If you dream of hunting, and hunting is something you actually do and enjoy in your waking life, you crave a break or a vacation. You need time out in nature, away from that desk. **2.** If you dream of hunting but you have never hunted or would never actually go hunting, the hunting symbolizes the thing you want most right now. Is it a person, a job, an object? **3.** To dream of hunting and killing an animal and finding this upsetting symbolizes your instinct that winning what you seek might not be as great as you thought it would be. You might prefer to let your desire for that object remain unfulfilled. **4.** If you dream you are being hunted, someone wants you for something. You feel pursued, even stalked, by someone's attentions or needs ☯ **setting something free** ☾ *adventure, animals, desires, journeys and quests, nature, relationships, sports and games, threats, violence.*

hurricane See *storm.*

husband 1. To dream of your own husband in everyday circumstances suggests a feeling of camaraderie and support. **2.** To dream of having romantic or sexual interaction with your husband may signal your desire for closeness, or it might just mean you are in the mood. If the interaction is unusual or experimental, you may be in an adventurous mood. **3.** To dream of fighting with your husband, or to dream he does something that makes you angry or hurt, suggests buried feelings of resentment,

anger, or disappointment in your relationship. These might be caused by something small, but you haven't acknowledged them so they are popping up in your dream. **4.** To dream you have a husband when you aren't actually married, or to dream your boyfriend is your husband, symbolizes your desire for more security and stability in your relationship. You might not necessarily want to get married yet, but you just want to feel like you know someone will be there for you in the long term. **5.** To dream you are married (even if you aren't actually) but it isn't going well suggests that you feel pressured to make some kind of commitment right now. It might not be about a relationship; it could be a commitment to a job or a social obligation. Whatever it is, you have been resistant to doing so because your instinct tells you it might be a mistake. See also *boyfriend, marriage.* ☯ **wife** ☾ *decisions, desires, love, people, relationships, resistance, responsibilities, sexual activity, stability.*

hypnotized 1. To dream of being hypnotized means you don't want to take responsibility for something, or you need help solving a problem. **2.** To dream of hypnotizing someone else suggests that you wish you had effortless control over someone or some situation. ☯ **taking responsibility** ☾ *control issues, responsibility, solutions and remedies.*

hysterectomy 1. If you dream you are getting, or must get, a hysterectomy, please pay attention to your health. Your body might be signaling you about a potential problem. **2.** Hysterectomy dreams can also signal your feeling that you may not want to become pregnant, or that you are ready to move beyond the reproductive years—either as a return to the carefree time of girlhood or as a step beyond motherhood to the freedom of mature womanhood. **3.** If you dream you have a serious medical problem and need an emergency hysterectomy, you may fear that you won't be able to become pregnant or have children. This kind of dream could signal a crisis of creativity and the need to reclaim your creative self. **4.** A hysterectomy dream can also symbolize frustration with your female nature. You want to be rid of some aspect of your femaleness, or you think life would be easier if you were more androgynous or had more male energy. ☽ **pregnancy** ☾ *decisions, family, feminine, gender issues, health and hygiene, loss, medicine and surgery, pain.*

ice See *snow*.

ice cream Creamy, sweet, and sensuous, ice cream represents childish delight in sensual pleasures, innocence, and indulgences of all kinds. Craving ice cream in a dream also symbolizes a craving for more sweetness and pleasure in your life. ☽ **vegetables** ☾ *age, desires, food and drink, happiness, hedonism, innocence, pleasure.*

ice skating 1. Sailing around the ice like an Olympian symbolizes a quest for freedom and a desire to do something really amazing with your life. You have the power. 2. Dreaming you are ice skating but you aren't very good at it or you keep falling symbolizes your courage in a difficult situation. You aren't having an easy time, but you keep trying. ☽ **falling** ☾ *adventure, competition, courage, desires, freedom, impediments, journeys and quests, opportunity, personal power, sports and games.*

iceberg See *glacier*.

illness See *disease*.

immortality 1. Dreaming you will live forever suggests you feel unlimited personal power right now. You have all the time in the world. 2. Finding out you will live forever and being upset, horrified, or fearful about it symbolizes the dread or burden you feel from too much responsibility. You've taken on too much and it has sucked the joy from your life, like a vampire's kiss, and who would want to live forever like that? ☽ **death** ☾ *age, burdens, fear, freedom, personal power, responsibilities, time.*

impotence 1. Dreaming of being impotent symbolizes frustrated feelings of insecurity or being foiled in your goals. The thing you wanted to do didn't work, and this probably has nothing to do with sex. You aren't in control, or your ego or male identity has suffered a humiliation. 2. If you dream of pleasant sexual interaction while remaining impotent or not having an erection, you desire an emotionally intimate relationship with someone, rather than a physical one. 3. If you dream your partner is impotent, you may desire more power in the relationship or feel your partner is withholding vital energy from you. ☽ **erection** ℂ *control issues, ego, failure, fear, frustration, insecurity, masculine, relationships, sexual activity.*

in vitro fertilization **1.** If you dream of success with in vitro fertilization and you are really trying this in your waking life, your dream expresses your desire for this procedure to work. **2.** If you dream the process doesn't work, that doesn't mean it won't work. It means you are expressing your fear that it won't work. **3.** If you dream of trying in vitro fertilization but you aren't actually doing this in real life, you may want to become a parent but you aren't sure you know how to go about it, or you fear you won't be able to do it in the normal way. **4.** If you are getting older and dream of in vitro fertilization, your biological clock is probably ticking. ☽ **infertility** ℂ *age, creation, desires, failure, health and hygiene, hopes and dreams, medicine and surgery.*

inaccessible **1.** If you aren't accessible in your dream, you need some time alone. **2.** If someone else is inaccessible in your dream, you are having communication problems with that person, or someone that person represents. **3.** If an object or information is inaccessible in your dream, you realize that you don't have everything you need or you don't know everything you should. ☽ **overflowing** ℂ *communication, impediments, relationships.*

inanimate objects coming to life Toys moving, furniture springing to action, walls breathing, dishes rattling—dreams that inanimate objects come to life symbolize your fear that you don't understand everything that's going on. You aren't in control in this strange and creepy world. ☽ **dead body** ℂ *anxiety, control issues, crawling creatures, danger, fear, inanimate objects, threats.*

Science fiction sometimes tackles the idea that computers can get so complex that they eventually attain consciousness, or that robots can become conscious and therefore human. This melding of machine with humanity has become such a common theme in modern society that it is bound to show up in our dreams. However, it isn't new. Some ancient cultures believe that animated energy surrounds and penetrates all objects in the world, from humans and animals to trees, rocks, and water. Others believe that spirits reside within all objects, animate and inanimate. These ancient beliefs may also rise up to animate our dreams.

incest Don't be alarmed by incest dreams. Generally, these dreams don't mean you want to commit incest, and they don't mean you are uncovering a buried memory of incest, either. In most cases, these dreams simply reveal a close emotional relationship with a family member or a desire for better communication. Incest dreams can also reveal unresolved conflicts with family members. (If these dreams seriously upset you or they are not clearly metaphorical in nature, we recommend seeking professional advice from a counselor to sort out the dream meaning.) ☾ **setting something free** ℭ *burdens, communication, desires, family, guilt, love, relationships, sexual activity.*

infant   See *baby.*

infection   See *disease.*

infertility   **1.** Dreaming you can't have children symbolizes a fear that you will lose your creativity. This could directly relate to a fear that you won't be able to have children but could symbolize many other creative processes as well: the creation of art, ideas, even relationships. You feel blocked. **2.** Dreaming a medical problem is causing your infertility could be a sign from your body to have something checked. Have you been ignoring subtle physical signs? **3.** To dream your partner is infertile symbolizes a recent dry spell in your relationship. You've lost the spark, or you aren't on the same wavelength lately because something has gotten between you. ☾ **pregnancy** ℭ *creation, creativity, failure, fear, health and hygiene, impediments, loss, relationships.*

infidelity   If you or your partner cheated in your dream, one of you isn't getting what you need from the relationship right now. What, or who, has come between you? These dreams don't mean anybody

actually intends to be unfaithful, but they do signify a problem in communication, trust, or loyalty in your relationship. ☾ **promises** ℭ *communication, competition, desires, impediments, love, loyalty, relationships, sexual activity, threats, trust issues.*

injection or needle   **1.** To dream of seeing a needle or getting an injection symbolizes your fear that something has infected your life. You need protection from a bad influence or morally questionable situation. **2.** Getting an injection can also represent an addiction to something or an obsession with somebody. Something's gotten under your skin. ☾ **healing** ℭ *addictions, desires, ethics and morals, fear, medicine and surgery, risky behavior.*

injuries   Dream injuries represent many things but, in general, symbolize an emotional injury, hurt feelings, or a damaged ego. **1.** To dream of a flesh wound, cuts, or other superficial lacerations symbolizes an insult to you or a scandal involving your reputation. **2.** To dream of getting burned symbolizes someone's betrayal of your trust. **3.** To dream of bruises represents a blow to your ego or an embarrassment. **4.** To dream of broken bones symbolizes an intense emotional injury that threatens your very stability and sense of identity. See also *bandages, blood, bones, bruises, car accident, fire.* ☾ **healing** ℭ *body parts, destruction, ego, embarrassment, failure, feelings, injuries, insecurity,* *loss, love, medicine and surgery, pain, relationships, violence, vulnerability.*

in-laws   Love 'em or can't stand 'em, your in-laws might just mom and pop up unannounced—in your dreams. If they do, you may feel you are suffering from too much family interference in your relationship, or you may feel a comforting sense of support from your extended family. It all depends on how happy you are to see those in-laws in your dream. ☽ **parents** ☾ *characters, comfort, control issues, embarrassment, family, frustration, impediments, people, relationships, stability, support.*

insane   **1.** If you dream you are insane, you've been taking on way too many responsibilities. **2.** If being insane feels comforting, you desire the escape of losing your mind. Nobody can blame you or hold you responsible for anything! This also comes with old age .... **3.** If you feel frightened and confused by feelings of insanity, you fear you really might lose your mind if the pressure doesn't let up. **4.** If you dream of going insane because of eating or drinking something or taking some kind of drug that someone else made you take, you fear that others could control you without your consent. **5.** If you dream of going insane because of something you chose to do, such as taking a drug or doing something very risky, you fear that a bad habit or inclination might really be affecting your mind. **6.** If you

dream someone else has gone insane, you fear for someone's safety or you fear someone won't be able to control their own situation, putting them at risk. See also *insane asylum.* ☽ **brain** ☾ *addictions, anxiety, escapism, fear, feelings, identity, image, insecurity, medicine and surgery, reputation, responsibilities, risky behavior, stability, threats, vulnerability.*

insane asylum   **1.** If you dream you are living in an insane asylum, you need an escape from the rational world of responsibilities and obligations. You want to fade away into mental oblivion for a while. **2.** If you dream you are perfectly sane and trapped in an insane asylum, you feel nobody understands or appreciates your ideas or way of thinking. It's like the whole world is crazy! **3.** If you are stuck in an insane asylum and you get attacked by insane people or feel terrified, you feel drastically out of balance. You harbor anxiety about your security in the world, your place in society, and the life you've built, as if one wrong move could send it all toppling down and you spiraling out of control and into a situation you can't escape. What has got you feeling so off-kilter? **4.** If you dream someone is giving you medication inside an insane asylum, you fear a bad habit has gotten out of control. Are you addicted? **5.** If you dream of visiting someone else in an insane asylum, you fear for someone's safety or stability. See also *insane.* ☽ **castle** ☾ *addictions,* *anxiety, balance, danger, escapism, fear, identity, image, insecurity, medicine and surgery, places, reputation, responsibilities, risky behavior, stability, threats, vulnerability, violence.*

insect   See *bugs.*

insomnia   Dreaming you can't sleep may seem ironic, but it could represent a guilty conscience or anxiety about something you forgot to do or something you know you really should do. Even though your body isn't having any problem sleeping, your mind is.   ☽ **dreaming that you are dreaming and dreaming that you wake up** ☾ *anxiety, burdens, feelings, frustration, guilt.*

instant message   See *chat room.*

insult   **1.** Is that outfit supposed to match, or have you just gained weight? If you dream someone insults you, you are feeling insecure and actually putting yourself down in your own dream. You need an ego-boost. **2.** If you dream of insulting someone else, you recognize that you haven't been very nice to someone, or you have bad feelings toward someone and you are getting out your aggressive energy by verbally assaulting that person, or someone that person represents, in your dream.   ☽ **compliment** ☾ *communication, ego, embarrassment, image, insecurity, relationships.*

intercourse   See *sex.*

Internet dating   Internet dating has become so common that it's not surprising to dream about it, but if the dating stays virtual in your dream, you fear getting too close to someone. You want companionship—just not too much companionship.   ☽ **marriage proposal** ☾ *communication, control issues, electronics, freedom, protection, relationships, technology.*

Internet surfing   **1.** As if you don't surf the Net enough when you are awake? Dreaming about Internet surfing may actually be a sign that you are spending too much time in front of that computer. Maybe you need a break. Take a look at something that isn't on a screen. **2.** Dreaming of surfing for some particular piece of information on the Internet symbolizes your search for an answer or the solution to a problem. If you only had enough information, you could solve it. **3.** Dreaming of looking for potential mates or people to date on the Internet suggests you are ready to increase your social circle or get into a relationship. Disconnect and get out there and connect.   ☽ **nature** ☾ *communication, electronics, journeys and quests, knowledge, relationships, technology.*

interstate   See *highway.*

interview   **1.** Dreams of being interviewed for a job symbolize an upcoming opportunity. You are anxious about whether you will be able to grab it and concerned that you are making a good impression. **2.** Dreams of being interviewed for the media, such as for television or a magazine, symbolize your reputation and image. You feel like you are in the spotlight and you want to make a good impression. **3.** Dreams of interviewing someone else suggest that you want someone to fill a role in your life and you are considering who might fit best. ● **hiding** ℂ *communication, identity, image, opportunity, reputation, relationships.*

intoxicated   See *alcohol.*

intruder   1. Is somebody there? Dreaming an intruder enters your house symbolizes your fear that someone or something threatens you. You feel vulnerable and unprotected. **2.** To dream of catching or killing an intruder suggests you don't trust someone and you feel highly motivated to catch them in the act. **3.** To dream you are the intruder means you have overstepped your boundaries, and you know it. ● **friend** ℂ *danger, insecurity, people, protection, risky behavior, threats, trust issues, violence, vulnerability.*

invisible   1. To dream you are invisible and enjoying the fun suggests that you feel invulnerable right now. You think you can get away with anything. **2.** To dream you are invisible and this makes you uncomfortable or afraid suggests that you don't feel like anyone notices you. You fear that nobody cares about you at all. **3.** If you dream someone else is invisible, you haven't been paying enough attention to someone, or a problem involving that person has escaped your notice. Subtle cues you didn't even recognize have surfaced in your dream, so start paying attention! This might be important. **4.** To dream an object is invisible symbolizes an intuition that there is more going on in a situation than you thought. ● **celebrity** ℂ *anxiety, caretaking, identity, image, inanimate objects, insecurity, intuition, mystery, solutions and remedies.*

invitation   If you dream you get an invitation, you are expecting something. If you dream of sending out invitations, you have a plan to be in the spotlight. ● **not invited** ℂ *celebration, communication, desires, ego, fun, hopes and dreams, image, inanimate objects, messages, opportunity, social life, taking action.*

island   1. If you dream of relaxing on an island and living the island life, you crave a break from your work. You feel ready for a vacation. **2.** If you dream of being stranded on an island, you feel isolated from others. You fear you won't ever escape your role as the loner or as the only one who knows what you mean. **3.** If you dream of escaping from an island, you have a radical plan to change your life, and you are working out ways to make it happen in your dream. You'll need courage and a personal floatation device. ● **bridge** ℂ *changing course, courage, escapism, impediments,* *isolation, nature, places, pleasure, solutions and remedies.*

People sometimes dream of islands when they feel isolated from others, but the English poet and writer John Donne (1572–1631) believed this was not possible and that all human beings were interconnected. Here's what Donne had to say about the proverbial island (you might recognize the last line because the American writer Ernest Hemingway used it as the title of one of his most famous novels):

"No man is an island, entire of itself; every man is a piece of the continent, a part of the main. If a clod be washed away by the sea, Europe is the less, as well as if a promontory were, as well as if a manor of thy friend's or of thine own were. Any man's death diminishes me, because I am involved in mankind; and therefore never send to know for whom the bell tolls; it tolls for thee."

itching Itching in your dream could signal an allergy problem, or it could symbolize a bad reaction to something that has happened. But this is just scratching the surface here, something is really bugging you. ☽ **healing** ☾ *anxiety, feelings, health and hygiene, impediments, resistance, senses.*

I

J

Jacuzzi **1.** To dream of lounging in a Jacuzzi or hot tub symbolizes the desire for some true R&R. You don't just need a mental break; you need some physical pampering, particularly involving water and warmth. **2.** To dream something has gone wrong with a Jacuzzi—a chemical problem, the water's too hot or too cold—symbolizes your guilt about wanting to relax. Are you forgetting that you won't be as productive if you are full of stress? ☯ **stress** ☾ *desires, escapism, guilt, heat, places, water.*

jail **1.** If you dream you are in jail, you feel guilty or trapped … or both. You may be stuck in a situation because, deep down, you think you deserve it. As it is now, someone else holds the power. **2.** If you dream you are in jail but are wrongly accused, you feel unjustly judged by someone. **3.** If you dream you will be going to jail or get sentenced to a jail term, you are having second thoughts about a commitment or promise you've made. Is it too late to back out or think about it a little longer? **4.** If you dream of breaking out of jail, you have a plan to get out of a situation or solve a problem, but it will take some courage. **5.** If you dream of visiting someone else in jail, you are worried about someone. You see them making mistakes or getting in a rut. See also *court, escape.* ☯ **breaking free** ☾ *anxiety, authority, control issues, courage, guilt, image, impediments, personal power, places, punishment, rebellion, regret, reputation, rules and laws, stasis.*

janitor Clean-up in aisle 2! Seeing a janitor in your dream means something unpleasant has to be dealt with. Dreaming you are the janitor symbolizes your recognition that you are the one who will probably have to deal with it. Better get a bucket. ☯ **slob** ☾ *career, characters, people, responsibilities, solutions and remedies.*

jaw **1.** Getting hit in the jaw in your dream symbolizes something you shouldn't have said or done. You stepped over the line. **2.** Jaw pain in a dream symbolizes a recognition that you've said too much. You need to learn to close your mouth and listen better. **3.** Jaw pain can also indicate a problem with your jaw. You might be grinding your teeth or clenching your jaw in sleep. Talk to your doctor or dentist if your jaw really does hurt when you wake up. A splitting earache or headache is also a symptom of nightly teeth grinding. **4.** Dreaming of noticing someone else's jaw means someone has been communicating to you, possibly in a very indirect way, and you haven't been getting it. ☻ **ear** ℂ *body parts, communication, listening, messages.*

jealousy 1. Dreaming of the green-eyed monster can clue you in to waking-life jealousy you hadn't even realized you were feeling. Are you jealous of another person, another person's life, or someone's stuff? Are you being distrustful or materialistic? **2.** Dreaming someone else is jealous of you may actually symbolize your jealousy of that person, or someone or something that person represents. It can also mean you have been feeling a bit superior to others lately. ☻ **giving away possessions** ℂ *competition, desires, envy, feelings, relationships, trust issues.*

jet See *airplane.*

Jet Ski If you dream of zooming over the water on a Jet Ski, you crave freedom from and mastery over your emotions. You don't want to wallow in them anymore. You're ready to start living life again. ☻ **depression** ℂ *control issues, escapism, feelings, freedom, personal power, play, sports and games, vehicles, water.*

jewelry Jewelry symbolizes things you value or desire—including qualities, emotions, and relationships—depending on the piece of jewelry and what you do with it. **1.** To dream of gorgeous, sparkling jewelry symbolizes something you place much value on. If someone gives you the jewelry, you place the value on a relationship with that person, or someone or something that person represents. Or, you wish for a meaningful relationship with that person. **2.** Ugly, tarnished, or broken jewelry, or jewelry that is missing gemstones symbolizes something that you think you should value but that you aren't so sure about. If someone gives you this kind of jewelry, you aren't ready to make a commitment yet. **3.** If you dream of a necklace, you value your own ability to communicate or your communication with someone else. Or you desire better communication with someone. **4.** If you dream of a bracelet, you value something physical that someone does for you or a physical, hands-on ability you have, such as a craft or artistic ability. Bracelets can also symbolize your desire for greater manual skills. **5.** If you dream of earrings, you value the things someone says to you or your own ability to listen. Or, you desire a better ability to listen. **6.** If you dream of a ring, you value a commitment you have with or to someone or something, or you wish for a commitment. Here's bettin' more women dream about jewelry than men. See also *bling, diamond,*

J

gold, ring. ☽ **garbage** ℂ *abundance, beauty, desires, hopes and dreams, inanimate objects, love, pleasure, relationship, wishes.*

jewels   Impossible wealth, indulgence and luxury, diamonds and rubies, sapphires and emeralds …. Jewels signify great wealth, beauty, and power. **1.** If you receive a jewel, someone has recently given you something more valuable than you expected. This could be an object or even a piece of advice. **2.** If you give someone a jewel, you value that person or what that person represents to you. **3.** If you see piles of jewels, look for a great undiscovered treasure in your life, waiting to be noticed. **4.** What color is your jewel? What is the clarity—bright or dull? What is the cut or shape? Color, clarity, and cut may reveal deeper clues to dream meanings. See also *diamond, jewelry, ring, treasure.* ☽ **poverty** ℂ *abundance, beauty, color, desires, financial resources, hopes and dreams, inanimate objects.*

job   **1.** If you dream of working at your job, or being at your job, in much the same way you are in waking life, your job is a big part of how you define yourself. It takes up a lot of space in your mind—which is great if you love your job. **2.** If you dream of starting a new job, you have a new opportunity and you think you might want to go for it. This could open up whole new areas for you. If taking the job in a dream feels burdensome and dreadful, however, your dream may be telling you that this opportunity isn't really what you want. See also *fired from a job, hired.* ☽ **unemployed** ℂ *burdens, career, changing course, hopes and dreams, identity, opportunity, work.*

jogging   See *running.*

judge   See *court.*

juggling   **1.** If you dream you are juggling, you are dealing with a lot of things at once right now and your life seems like a juggling act. The more complicated the juggling is in your dream, the more complicated your life has become. Are you feeling like a three-ring circus? **2.** If you are doing a great job at juggling and feel entertained and even empowered, you thrive on the energy you get from so much activity and so many different interests and engagements. **3.** If you keep dropping balls or feel frustrated about juggling, you've got too much going on. You can't keep track of everything, and some areas are bound to suffer. **4.** If you watch someone else juggling in a dream, you've been living on automatic pilot lately. You don't know how you do everything you do, but you do it because you think you have to. Your dream may be signaling your dissatisfaction with this too-busy situation. ☽ **dropping the ball** ℂ *anxiety, burdens, career, fun, home, play, relationships, responsibilities, sports and games, work.*

jumping   Jumping symbolizes courage, a leap of faith, or a risk.

Are you jumping over something, through something, to something, or away from something? Is it a competition or a survival move? The situation in your dream mirrors the way you've been dealing with a current obstacle or dilemma. ☽ **crawling** ☾ *competition, courage, creativity, decisions, direction, personal power, risky behavior, solutions and remedies, sports and games.*

jungle **1.** To find yourself exploring or traveling through a jungle in your dream signifies an adventure, if the dream is exciting. You crave challenges in exotic locations and maybe even a little danger, or you see a current situation as a thrilling chance to prove yourself. **2.** To dream of being lost and frightened in a jungle or fighting for survival against the elements or wild animals means you have been feeling overwhelmed by a hostile or difficult situation. You feel like you are barely hanging on. **3.** To dream you live in the jungle and feel comfortable and at home there suggests you have a wild, untamed side that isn't fulfilled by technology, society, and culture. If you can communicate with jungle animals in the dream, more contact with nature and animals is a path of spiritual growth for you. ☽ **homebody** ☾ *adventure, animals, control issues, courage, fear, instincts, nature, places, threats, spirituality.*

jury See *court.*

Even before Edgar Rice Burroughs wrote *Tarzan of the Apes* in 1912, people have fantasized about a vine-swinging, free-wheeling life in the bush. But Tarzan, especially in his many movie incarnations, brought this vision into the public imagination like never before. Almost a superhero, Tarzan had super strength, brute charm, and good looks. He could talk to the animals and charm attractive city girls, too. No wonder so many people escape, via their dreams, to a wilder, more exotic life in the jungle.

J

K

karaoke So you like to get up and sing your favorite song in front of a crowd … in your dream? **1.** Dreaming of karaoke symbolizes your desire to let others know your talents without making a big deal about it. Anybody can do karaoke, right? But secretly, you think you really will impress others. **2.** If you dream of doing karaoke badly, you feel insecure about how others view you, or you fear being in the spotlight. ☽ **shy** ☾ *adventure, competition, courage, desires, ego, embarrassment, fear, fun, image, music and sound, peer pressure, personal power, play, social life, sports and games, taking action.*

keg Buying a keg, tapping a keg, and drinking out of a keg of beer or wine all symbolize a Dionysian-like party spirit. You are in the mood to celebrate in a big way with wild revelry and a hedonistic spirit. Yeah! Tap into the inner you. See also *alcohol, beer, wine.* ☽ **abstinence** ☾ *abundance, celebration, desires, food and drink, hedonism, inanimate objects, pleasure.*

key Keys unlock secrets, hidden things, private things, diaries, doors, valuables, and even hearts. Dreaming of a key means you have the chance to unlock or discover something important, possibly privileged, possibly quite valuable to you, possibly just for you. ☽ **lock** ☾ *code, inanimate objects, knowledge, mystery, secrets, shapes and symbols, solutions and remedies, subterfuge.*

keyboard The keyboard on a computer is the level-one communication tool. Type your message, and there it is in front of you. Musical keyboards, too, offer the tool through which you can deliver a musical message. Dreaming of a keyboard means you have a message to send. Compose it carefully. See also *computer.* ☽ **silence** ☾ *code, communication, electronics, messages, music and sound, technology.*

kid See *child or children.*

kidnapping **1.** Dreaming you've been kidnapped suggests that someone else has control.

Do you enjoy the experience or fear it? Are you attracted to your kidnapper, or do you feel fear or resentment that this person is using you for personal gain? Your answer determines how you feel about letting someone else take the reins. **2.** To dream you've kidnapped someone else symbolizes your strong desire to control someone or to use someone to get something you want. See also *escape*. ☽ **breaking free** ☾ *control issues, desires, fear, goal-setting, relationships.*

killing   Killing symbolizes forced change, sometimes under dramatic circumstances. **1.** If you kill someone in your dream, you need to change something about your life. If you respond with strong emotions to the action, you are very motivated or fearful of making this change, even as you feel it is necessary. **2.** If you dream of seeing a killing, you perceive change happening that will affect you, but you aren't the one causing it. **3.** If you dream of killing an animal, you have been suppressing, or feel you should suppress, a natural instinct within you. Are there better ways to deal with this instinct than obliterating it? If the killing upsets you, you are fighting an inner battle. You can't help this instinctual response, but your intellect is telling you that it must be suppressed. **4.** If you dream of seeing someone else killing an animal or seeing an animal killing another animal, you've been overwhelmed by a feeling of the world changing all around you. You aren't neces-

sarily ready for all the changes, but they seem to be happening in spite of you. **5.** If you accidentally kill someone or something in your dream, you feel you've made a big decision without totally thinking it through, and now it's too late to change your mind. You wonder if you might have made a mistake. See also *manslaughter, murder*. ☽ **birth** ☾ *accidents, animal, changing course, death, decisions, fear, instincts, nature, transformation, violence.*

king   **1.** To see a king and be in his kingly presence in a dream signifies your recognition of a solemn and authoritative presence in your life. **2.** If you are the king, you have strong personal power right now and others look to you for guidance. See also *crown*. ☽ **queen** ☾ *authority, career, characters, people, personal power, rules and laws.*

kissing   **1.** Locking lips in your dream signifies your attraction to someone or something. The person you kiss might not actually attract you, but something about that person—such as a personality trait, position in life, appearance, age, or possessions—might attract you. Or, the person could stand for someone else you don't really want to admit attracts you. **2.** To dream someone surprises you with a kiss suggests that you've begun to see someone in a completely different way. **3.** If your dream kiss is particularly passionate or sexually charged, you are feeling passionate and excited about someone or something. The very

K

idea of this influence arouses you. Did it arouse you out of your sleep? ❍ **bite** ℂ *body parts, desires, envy, feelings, love, pleasure, relationships, senses, sexual activity.*

kitchen The kitchen is the heart of the home, where people tend to congregate and where food is prepared and sometimes served. Houses symbolize your current state of mind, and kitchens symbolize your social and nurturing side—the part of you that interacts with and cares for others. **1.** If your dream kitchen is warm, inviting, and comfortable, you have a satisfying group of people to care for and nurture, and you feel supported and bolstered by this important part of your life. **2.** If you dream of a messy, dirty, or dilapidated kitchen, you've been neglecting friends or family, or you feel neglected by them. You aren't getting enough support from others, and people may be taking advantage of you. **3.** A dark, empty kitchen symbolizes loneliness. **4.** Dreaming of a kitchen with no food in the refrigerator or cupboards symbolizes drained inner resources. You have nothing left to give right now. You need to replenish yourself first. **5.** Dreaming of cooking in your kitchen or putting out food for people symbolizes your current social priorities. Are you cooking for a crowd or setting out an intimate dinner for two? See also *cooking.* ❍ **bathroom** ℂ *buildings and rooms, caretaking, family, food and drink, home, love, places, relationships.*

kite Flying a kite in a dream symbolizes your quest for an answer from a higher source. You seek a spiritual resolution to an earthly problem. ❍ **digging** ℂ *divine power, play, solutions and remedies, spirituality, sports and games.*

knee **1.** You know how to compromise … or you'd better learn. A current situation demands some flexibility, if you dream about your knees. **2.** To dream of a skinned knee represents a minor annoyance or embarrassment you've suffered in order to make something happen. **3.** A broken or seriously injured knee symbolizes too much flexibility. You are giving too much and it's not going to help anyone, least of all you. ❍ **elbow** ℂ *body parts, changing course, control issues, injuries.*

knife Dreaming of a knife symbolizes a problem that needs some dissection. You need to really get inside this one to see what's going on, and it might not be pretty. **1.** To dream of cutting food with a knife means you need to break down a problem involving a loved one into small pieces so you can both deal with it together. **2.** To dream of using a knife as a tool to cut something like rope or underbrush signifies a problem at work that will require some heated discussion in order to solve. Or, you might have to solve it yourself, but heads might have to roll. (Not literally, of course!) **3.** To dream of stabbing someone with a knife symbolizes a passionate disagreement in a romantic relationship. You need to cut to the heart of the problem and bare your inner soul to solve this one. **4.** To dream of getting stabbed with a knife suggests that someone has betrayed you, or you fear they might. You've lost your trust. See also *utensils*. ❧ **bandages** ℭ *authority, food and drink, control issues, destruction, inanimate objects, relationships, solutions and remedies, trust issues, violence.*

knitting Knitting in your dream means you are slowly but surely putting something together in your mind—a complex plan, a new vision for your life, even a whole new image. It's coming along slowly, but you are making progress. ❧ **unraveling** ℭ *changing course, journeys and quests, solutions and remedies, work.*

knocking Knocking on a door symbolizes asking a question. It implies pushing boundaries, being vulnerable or brave, and heading into new frontiers. **1.** If you dream of knocking on a door, you have made the first step in establishing a communication with someone. You've said, "Here I am. I'm ready." **2.** If you dream of someone knocking on your door, someone has made the first move toward you. Someone wants to come into your life. **3.** If nobody answers the door when you knock, you fear that your advances will be rejected in a current endeavor. **4.** If you don't answer the door when someone knocks, you have too many things going on right now and you can't possibly take on anything else. ❧ **closed door** ℭ *adventure, communication, courage, goal-setting, messages, relationships.*

A poltergeist is a ghost that makes noises, from the German for "jangling spirit" or "knocking spirit." Dreaming of a ghost that knocks or makes noises could signal an inner disturbance. Something is bothering you, but you don't want to face it.

K

label   Labels carry information, and a label in a dream may have specific information for you. The name or other information on the label symbolizes the thing that requires your attention. **1.** If a label falls off something like a package or box, you've been neglecting something. **2.** If you can feel a label in your clothing and it bothers you, something is bothering you in your waking life. **3.** If you dream of cutting the labels out of your clothes, you want to hide something from others or you want to escape a current image people have of you. ◐ **faceless** ℂ *code, communication, clothing and accessories, identity, image, messages.*

laboratory   Test tubes bubbling, strange experiments brewing—the laboratory symbolizes mystery, experimentation, new territory, and Jekyll-and-Hyde transformations. Whether you dream of seeing a laboratory or working in one, you are cooking up something radical and new. Are you trying out a new persona? A new life plan? A new relationship? A new hairdo? Whatever it is, it is still in the experimental phase. ◐ **museum** ℂ *buildings and rooms, changing course, creation, places, transformation.*

labyrinth   See *maze.*

ladder   **1.** You can advance in your current position, or you can rise above it all and be more objective. Either way, you've taken the high road if you dream about climbing a ladder. **2.** If you see a ladder in front of you, you have the opportunity to take the high road or to take a daring risk that could really take you to the next level. **3.** If you dream of walking under a ladder, falling off a ladder, or being on a ladder when it falls over, you fear that a potential opportunity might not be worth the risk. **4.** If you refuse to climb a ladder in your dream, you have chosen to pass up an opportunity for advancement. Maybe you are perfectly happy right where you are, with your feet firmly on the ground. **5.** If you hold a ladder for someone else, you have the opportunity to boost someone else's chances for success. ◐ **slide** ℂ *career,* *caretaking, changing course, courage, decisions, direction, inanimate objects, opportunity, risky behavior.*

lake   See *water.*

lamp   Let's shed some light on the subject. Lamps illuminate what you need to see. Dreaming of turning on a lamp symbolizes your quest for knowledge or understanding, while turning off or breaking a lamp means you'd really rather stay in the dark. ☽ **dark** ☾ *inanimate objects, journeys and quests, knowledge, subterfuge, transformation.*

landlord or landlady   To dream of the person who holds your lease in his or her hands symbolizes your feelings about where you live and the authority figures that govern this particular stage in your life. Landlords and landladies could symbolize your parents, older siblings, mentors, influential friends, or roommates. **1.** If you dream of a disagreement with your landlord or landlady, you aren't happy in your current situation. You want to move on or make some changes. You don't like being under the thumb of this particular leadership. **2.** If you dream of a kind, friendly, or helpful landlord or landlady, you feel content in your current situation. You feel lucky to have benevolent forces governing your life right now. See also *eviction.* ☽ **tenant** ☾ *authority, career, characters, home, people, relationships, rules and laws.*

landslide   The very earth is sliding out from under your feet ... or from under your whole life. That's how you feel if you dream about a landslide. Everything has shifted and everything has changed. This will be a radical transformation. ☽ **floor** ☾ *changing course, destruction, disaster, nature, transformation.*

late   See *running late.*

laughing   **1.** Good-hearted, happy laughing in your dream, or even being told you have been laughing in your sleep, suggests an inner sense of well-being and a light-hearted approach to life. Sure, you may feel blue now and then or lose your temper, but at the very heart of you, you feel safe in the world. **2.** To dream others are laughing at you symbolizes your self-consciousness and insecurity. You aren't comfortable around someone because that person, or the situation that person represents, makes you feel bad about yourself. **3.** If you laugh at someone else in your dream, you carry a grudge against someone or feel insecure in your position of authority over a situation. ☽ **crying** ☾ *authority, control issues, feelings, fun, happiness, insecurity, pleasure, relationships, senses, stability.*

laundry   **1.** Your laundry represents your personal, private self, and washing your laundry represents personal maintenance, hygiene, and taking care of your own private needs. **2.** Dreaming of doing your laundry in a laundromat suggests that you feel your private self has recently been made public.

3. Doing someone else's laundry means you have been taking care of personal details for someone. Do you enjoy helping out, or do you feel resentment? Perhaps someone ought to be washing his or her own underwear. Prim and modest ladies from days gone by would often hang their undergarments inside pillowcases when drying them on the clothesline so the neighbors wouldn't see them. ☽ **dirt** ☾ *caretaking, clothing and accessories, health and hygiene, inanimate objects, knowledge, secrets.*

lava Lava flowing from a volcano represents an outpouring of instinct. Did you smell something? Your deepest passions, desires, and animal instincts are spouting to the surface. There's that smell again. Get ready! These are instincts you can't ignore any longer, but you've kept them down for so long that they could cause a major upheaval in your life if you don't handle them carefully. Or maybe upheaval is just what you need. See also *volcano*. ☽ **snow** ☾ *changing course, desires, destruction, disaster, heat, instincts, nature.*

lawn See *grass*.

lawsuit If you dream you are involved in a lawsuit, as either the plaintiff or the defendant, you've been embroiled in a battle with someone, even if you don't realize it consciously. You may not want to admit you are wrong, or you may feel unjustly accused, but you take the situation seriously and you

foresee important consequences for your financial situation and/or reputation. ☽ **friends** ☾ *control issues, financial resources, reputation, rules and laws.*

lawyer **1.** If you dream of hiring a lawyer, you are in a situation you feel you aren't quite qualified to deal with. You have your eye out for someone to help you. **2.** If you dream you are a lawyer or are studying to be a lawyer, you have recently taken on more responsibility involving money, legal issues, or rule enforcement. You feel inspired to shoulder this new responsibility with expertise. And the pay's not bad. ☽ **doctor** ☾ *authority, career, characters, financial resources, people, personal power, responsibilities, rules and laws, solutions and remedies.*

lazy **1.** To dream of being lazy in an enjoyable way—lounging in a hammock, staying in bed all day, relaxing in the shade while others work—suggests you recognize that you deserve some you-time, and you might even need a lazy day to feel better. You can take the time to pamper yourself in your dream, so why not do it in your waking life, too? It's good for your physical and mental health to be lazy once in a while, and your dream is trying to tell you that. **2.** Dreaming of laziness with a slight knowing sense of guilt can symbolize your hedonistic side. Maybe you've been indulging yourself too much and you are shirking your responsibilities. Is a life of leisure worth letting go of the things you've worked for? Are you letting someone else shoulder all the responsibility? Do you need a leisure consultant? **3.** If you dream of being lazy and feeling frustrated that you can't get yourself to do anything, you may be unhappy in your current work. Consider what kind of life might make you less prone to feeling so uninspired. **4.** If you dream someone else is being lazy and you really need or want him or her to stop, it symbolizes either your frustration at your lack of ability to control someone else's actions or your frustration at yourself. That lazy person in your dream might represent you. ☽ **working hard** ℂ *burdens, career, control issues, desires, feelings, frustration, hedonism, health and hygiene, responsibilities, work.*

leader **1.** Dreaming you are leading others in any situation or event signifies your personal power at the moment. You have authority and others look to you for guidance. **2.** If you feel insecure in this leadership position, you aren't sure what you think about your recent status as an authority figure. Can you handle it? **3.** To dream someone else is leading you in any situation and you resent that person's authority suggests you don't feel like your own authority is properly recognized or respected by others. **4.** To dream someone else is leading you and you appreciate the guidance and authority suggests you welcome help right now and look to someone else for direction in what you should be doing. You don't mind letting someone else steer just now.

☽ **following** ℂ *authority, burdens, characters, control issues, direction, people, personal power, relationships, responsibilities.*

leak If something springs a leak in your dream, you are losing money through some channel. You could prevent this from happening if you were more careful or observant. ☽ **fixing something** ℂ *accidents, financial resources, loss, water.*

leather **1.** Wear leather in your dream, and you desire a more aggressive, forward, or self-confident persona. You wish you seemed a little more wild or rebellious. You beast! **2.** Seeing or using an object made of leather in your dream symbolizes something you want to do or achieve with your own two hands. You want this to come from you. **3.** If someone else wears leather in your dream, you have a strong instinct about that person—an animal attraction or an instinctual revulsion or mistrust. ☽ **feather** ℂ *changing course, image, instincts, personal power, rebellion.*

leaves **1.** Falling leaves and fall-colored leaves (brown, orange, red, yellow) represent aging or the end of something, like a relationship that has fallen away or a stage of your life you've come out of. **2.** Green leaves on a tree rustling in the breeze symbolize a passionate impulse or brilliant idea stirring within you. **3.** Holding or looking at a single leaf in a dream represents an area of your life you need to examine more closely. An organic,

L

natural approach might work better than what you are doing now. **4.** Strange-looking leaves or trees with artificial leaves symbolize an unnatural environment. You don't feel comfortable about some aspect of your life or environment, almost like you are on some other planet. ☻ **logs** ℂ *age, changing course, desires, intuition, loss, nature, plants, relationships, weather and seasons.*

left hand **1.** If you dream of being left-handed even though you are not, you long for a way to distinguish yourself from others. You want to feel special and different. You don't want to conform. **2.** If you dream of using your left hand for something, you need to look at a problem in an entirely different way than you have been. Consider doing just the opposite. How would that work? **3.** If you dream of injuring your left hand, your nonconformity has been all for show and it's not working for you anymore. Rebellion purely for the sake of rebellion doesn't accomplish much, does it? ☻ **right hand** ℂ *body parts, conformity, image, rebellion.*

> Approximately 10 percent of the population is left-handed. This trait used to be associated with witchcraft and considered a vice to be overcome. Today, however, left-handed people are more likely to consider themselves special and distinct from the masses. August 13 is Left-Handers Day.

legs You stand on your feet, but your legs give you height, movement, flexibility, speed, and stability. Dreaming of your legs symbolizes your place in and interaction with the world. **1.** To dream your legs are stronger, longer, or more gorgeous than you believe them to be in your waking life suggests you have great potential for improving your position or image right now. It's time to move up. **2.** To dream your legs are weaker, shorter, or less attractive than you believe them to be in your waking life suggests you are feeling insecure about your image or position in society right now. You don't feel confident. **3.** If you dream your legs are injured or broken, you are in a weak position to negotiate right now. You don't have good or credible reasons for your position. See also *feet, knee.* ☻ **arms** ℂ *body parts, control issues, decisions, image, reputation, stability.*

lemon and lime The tang of these citrus fruits awakens the taste buds and the senses, and their presence in your dream suggests a recent sensual awakening as well. Something has happened in your life to key up your senses. You feel alive and awake, and you seem to see, hear, smell, taste, and feel more keenly than before. **1.** To suck on a lemon or lime in your dream means you've encountered something unusually sour or initially unpleasant in your life, but your first reaction may give way to a feeling of inner cleansing. Maybe the experience wasn't so bad after all. You actually kind of enjoyed it. **2.** To dream you have a lemon or lime wedge in your drink suggests that something needs jazzing up. What can you do to add excitement or color to a normally dull situation? You are in the right mode to make that decision. **3.** To dream of slicing or peeling lemons or limes suggests enlightenment. Suddenly you understand the pleasure of something that eluded you before. ☽ **arms** ☾ *body parts, control issues, food and drink, fruit, image, reputation, senses.*

leprechaun   Dreaming of a leprechaun symbolizes luck, either good or bad. **1.** If the leprechaun offers you wishes or you find the pot of gold at the end of the rainbow, you've got a rare opportunity, and you feel pretty lucky to get the chance. If your dream is heavy with gold and rainbows, you have a strong feeling that you shouldn't waste your wonderful luck. Chances like this don't come along very often. **2.** If the leprechaun is scary or evil in your dream, you feel like forces beyond your control are causing you bad luck. **3.** To dream someone you know is actually a leprechaun suggests your bafflement at someone's recent behavior. That person has a side you never saw before, and that person's power is greater than it seems. **4.** To dream you are, or have the chance to become, a leprechaun suggests that you've recently realized you are the one who creates your own luck. The power is in you. ☽ **arms**

☾ *abundance, characters, control issues, fear, myths and legends, opportunity, personal power, relationships.*

lesbian   To be a heterosexual woman and dream you are a lesbian does not (necessarily) mean you are secretly a lesbian. It could mean you are questioning or experimenting in your subconscious with a broader approach to sexuality, or it could simply suggest an increasing awareness of both the male and female sides of yourself as they jockey for position and work toward equilibrium. **1.** If you dream you are a lesbian and the dream is interesting, pleasant, or exciting, you still have many mysteries within yourself to discover, and this is an exciting time of exploration. The dream may symbolize self-discovery rather than the desire for discovery of another woman. **2.** If dreaming you are a lesbian disturbs you, you may be struggling with your own perceptions of sexual attraction and your own sexual energies. Do you feel guilty about your feelings or do you repress them? Your dream is helping you work out any repressed feelings about sex you may have. These might have nothing to do with lesbianism—they may symbolize a more difficult issue you are working out. **3.** Many women have lesbian dreams with no intention of doing anything about them, but for a few, you might be discovering part of yourself you didn't want to acknowledge before. Only you can gauge whether your dream is a fun fantasy or an inkling of a path not

L

yet taken. **4.** If you dream about meeting or talking to a lesbian, you may feel out of balance with either your inner male or female energy. **5.** If you are a man and you dream of a lesbian, you may be fulfilling a fantasy, but this dream character may also be a glimpse into your own female energy within. See also *homosexuality*. ☽ **heterosexuality** ☾ *balance, desires, feminine, gender issues, identity, love, masculine, people, relationships, sexual activity.*

letter Anything written in a dream—whether someone else writes it or you write it—has particular power as a message you are sending yourself about something you have noticed in your waking life and need to bring to your own attention. A letter in a dream may convey something very important, so read it carefully and try to remember upon waking what it said. Even if it doesn't make sense, it symbolizes something you need to know. If you dream of a letter of the alphabet, that letter stands for something important: a person's initials, something you must do, a place you must go. Your subconscious mind has called your attention to this code or message in a big way. ☽ **numbers** ☾ *code, communication, inanimate objects, messages, shapes and symbols.*

levitation "Light as a feather, stiff as a board …." Remember that old slumber-party mantra when you and all your friends were sure you could levitate someone? And did!

The concept of levitation thrills and frightens people, perhaps because of its frequent employment in spooky stories and movies, but in dreams, it usually symbolizes handing over control to a higher power—a benevolent one or not. **1.** If you dream that you are levitated above your bed and you enjoy it or feel amazed or enlightened by it, you are experiencing a spiritual awakening. Something has happened to make you see that you aren't the only master of your universe. Something higher guides you. **2.** If you dream you are levitated by an evil force or the dream is scary, you fear that something or someone has too much power over you. Have you opened yourself to bad influences? **3.** If you dream of seeing someone else levitated, you fear for someone's safety or you don't understand the path they've taken. They may have their reasons, but you don't get it. **4.** If you dream of levitating objects, material possessions have become too important to you. You've raised them above more human concerns, and this has sent you down a dangerous path. **5.** If you dream of levitating an elephant, you need to check the spare tire in your trunk to see if it is inflated or not. And if you didn't dream this, it's still a good idea to check your spare. ☽ **falling** ☾ *control issues, divine power, fear, inanimate objects, myths and legends, spirituality.*

library Dreaming of a library symbolizes your quest for knowledge. You want to *know*, and you have the passion to find out. If the library is locked, you fear that the information you want won't be accessible or that someone is hiding it from you. ☯ **secret code** ℭ *code, journeys and quests, knowledge, messages, places.*

life jacket 1. You need saving, and you need it now! If you dream you are wearing a life jacket, you face a dangerous emotional situation, and you need to take some precautions to protect yourself. Can you bring a friend along? 2. If you dream of putting a life jacket on someone else, you feel the need to protect someone from emotional harm. ☯ **drowning** ℭ *caretaking, clothing and accessories, danger, inanimate objects, protection, water.*

lifeguard 1. If a lifeguard flags you down, whistles at you, or berates you for unsafe behavior in your dream, you are exerting a safety check on yourself. You know you've been doing something a little too emotionally risky, and your intellect is giving your risk-taking heart a nudge. 2. If a lifeguard saves you from drowning in your dream, you've gotten yourself into a difficult emotional situation, and you long for someone to save you because you aren't sure how to save yourself. 3. If you dream someone you know is a lifeguard, you rely on that person, or someone that person represents, to keep an eye on you because you don't totally trust yourself in an emotional situation. 4. If you dream you are a lifeguard,

you feel responsible for the safety of others, like it or not. Your eye always scans for signs of danger. ☯ **drowning** ℭ *caretaking, career, characters, feelings, people, protection, risky behavior, support, trust issues.*

light 1. Dreams flooded with light signify understanding, enlightenment, spirituality, and those "aha" creative moments. You can see more clearly right now than usual, so take advantage of this enlightened time. 2. If you feel blinded by intense light in your dream, you aren't quite ready to recognize something obvious. Or is it the morning sun? 3. If bright light accompanied by a disembodied voice tells you something in your dream, this is a message from your higher self or possibly even a higher power than you—your alarm clock! ☯ **darkness** ℭ *creativity, divine power, knowledge, intuition, messages, senses, spirituality, yin-yang.*

light bulb 1. Like the proverbial light bulb blinking on over some cartoon character's head when a brilliant idea strikes, dreaming of a light bulb symbolizes a great idea you have. You've been truly inspired. 2. If you dream of a burnt-out or broken light bulb, you've been going through a creative dry spell, and you just can't think of any good ideas. Life seems dull, and you've slipped into a rut. ☯ **monotony** ℭ *creativity, electronics, inanimate objects, intuition, knowledge, solutions and remedies.*

L

lightning   Lightning can cause destruction in a flash and produce intense heat, a jolting charge of electricity, or even death. It can also symbolize a flash of sudden understanding or an overpowering chemical attraction to someone. **1.** If you dream of watching lightning but aren't threatened by it, you feel detached from some pretty intense activity in your life. You see the situation objectively. **2.** If you dream of being caught in a dangerous lightning storm, your life is in transition and upheaval. If you feel fearful in the dream, the change threatens your sense of security. If you feel excited or adventurous, the transformations going on all around you feel illuminating. **3.** If you dream of being struck by lightning, something has changed in your life, and you are still waiting to feel the after-effects. Was it a tiny buzz of electricity or a major shock? This could be a passionate attraction, a major loss, or a brilliant idea. **4.** If you dream of seeing someone else get struck by lightning, you've just discovered something significant about that person or someone that person represents. See also *storm*. ◕ **thunder** ℂ *accidents, adventure, anxiety, changing course, caretaking, danger, desires, heat, injuries, insecurity, nature, protection, transformation, weather and seasons.*

lily   Lilies represent purity, innocence, and spiritual love. To see a lily in your dream suggests you have these feelings for someone, or you recognize someone has them for you. ◕ **dandelion** ℂ *beauty, divine power, innocence, nature, plants, relationships, spirituality.*

lime   See *lemon and lime.*

limousine   Wealth, abundance, riches—you desire them if you dream of riding in a limousine. If you dream of driving someone else in a limousine, you envy someone else's material wealth. ◕ **motorcycle** ℂ *abundance, envy, financial resources, image, vehicles.*

limping   **1.** Limping suggests an impediment in your movement. Something is keeping you from being your most efficient self if you dream of limping and you aren't making progress at the pace you could. **2.** If you see someone else limping in a dream, someone in your life isn't doing well, physically or emotionally. ◕ **running** ℂ *body parts, impediments.*

line   See *straight line.*

lingerie   **1.** You sexy thing, you! For women, wearing lingerie in a dream can symbolize a celebration of your own sexuality or, if wearing the lingerie makes you uncomfortable, a struggle with how you think you are supposed to be sexually, as opposed to how you really feel. Are you trying to play a role that isn't you, just to match someone else's idea of what makes you sexy? **2.** If you dream of someone else wearing lingerie and being attracted to that person, you are most stimulated by visual cues and openly seductive behavior. But you already knew that. **3.** If you dream of someone else wearing lingerie but do not find it attractive, someone is trying too hard to impress you, and it's not working. This could be the person you dream about, or that person could represent someone else. You might not be sure how to tell this person to stop it, or that you aren't interested, or that she should just be herself. ☾ **blanket** ☾ *body parts, clothing and accessories, conformity, desires, sexual activity.*

lion This ancient symbol represents courage, boldness, leadership, and action. If you dream of a lion, you desire these characteristics, admire them in someone else, or feel the potential to bring them out more strongly in yourself. In any case, the current situation demands bold action. ☾ **deer** ☾ *animals, authority, courage, control issues, decisions, nature, personal power, responsibilities, solutions and remedies.*

The lion is one of the most common symbols in heraldry, which is the study or art of the symbols on coats of arms, family crests, and genealogical lines. In heraldry, the lion represents courage and strength for those individuals or family lines known for displaying or acting according to this quality.

liposuction See *plastic surgery.*

lips Dreaming of your lips represents desire, passion, oral stimulation, and even the female genitalia. **1.** If your lips are soft, full, red, and luscious in your dream, you are feeling passionate and full of desire. **2.** If you dream of putting lipstick or lip gloss on your lips, you want someone to notice you as a passionate or sexual being. **3.** If your lips are thin, dry, and cracked, you are *not* feeling passionate desire—quite the opposite. You don't feel receptive to someone's, or anyone's, advances right now. **4.** If you dream of someone else's lips, you feel a strong physical attraction to someone. See also *makeup.* ☾ **nose** ☾ *body parts, desires, pleasure, sexual activity.*

list **1.** Dreaming of making a to-do list means you need to get organized, and fast. Your brain is over-run by details, and even in your dreams, you are trying to figure out just exactly what you need to do. Plan ahead! **2.** Dreaming of making a top-ten list or list of your favorite somethings or least-favorite somethings symbolizes your need to get your priorities in order. Somewhere along the line, you've forgotten what you really believe to be important or not-so-important. **3.** Dreaming of making a grocery or shopping list means you need to go back to basics. You're getting ahead of yourself and forgetting what you need because you are too focused on what you want. **4.** Making a wish list in your dream symbolizes your desires. What is it

L

you really want? The items on your list may tell you, or they may be symbols for what you truly desire. **5.** Dreaming of using or working off of a list suggests that your best path of action right now ought to come from forethought and planning rather than impulse. **6.** To dream of finding someone else's list suggests that you ought to be focused right now on objectively considering what someone else wants or needs. ◑ **amnesia** ℭ *caretaking, changing course, control issues, decisions, desires, direction, goal-setting, responsibilities.*

litter See *pollution.*

liver The first word in liver is *live,* and you can't live without your liver, so pay attention to it. **1.** To dream of pain or disease in your liver may be a sign from your body of a health imbalance. If you are worried, have it checked out. However, liver problems can also symbolize issues with processing emotions. Are you repressing something you don't want to work through? Keep it inside too long, and it could affect your emotional health. **2.** If you dream of eating liver, you are working on incorporating negative emotions into your vision of your life. They are part of you, and you are acknowledging them. ◑ **heart** ℭ *body parts, food and drink, health and hygiene, pain, repression.*

living room The living room of a house symbolizes the social side of you, the part that interacts with the world and leaves a particular impression. **1.** If you dream of a living room filled with happy, friendly people, you have a satisfying social life and a good reputation. **2.** If you dream of a pristine but empty living room, you may have a reputation for perfection but not warmth. You may wish for more social interaction with others, but you aren't sure how to be more inviting. **3.** If you dream of a dirty, unkempt living room or a room filled with broken or shabby furniture, you fear people see you as irresponsible, unreliable, or of a low social status, or you fear your financial problems may be obvious to others. ◑ **bedroom** ℭ *buildings and rooms, image, places, reputation, relationships, social life.*

lizard See *reptiles and amphibians.*

loaning money Money represents resources, and loaning money represents sharing resources—material or emotional. **1.** If you dream of loaning money to someone, you recognize that someone needs some kind of help from you, and even if you aren't rolling in resources, you are willing to help in whatever way you can. **2.** If you dream of grudgingly loaning money or refusing to loan money, someone has become a drain on your time or financial or emotional resources, and you no longer feel comfortable helping this person. It may be time to help someone learn to help himself or herself. **3.** If you dream someone loans you money, you are hoping for help from an outside source. You don't feel like you can do it on your own. **4.** If you feel guilty or ashamed of asking for a loan of money, your ego has suffered from a feeling that you can't do something on your own. Yet you feel that you really do need to ask for help. **5.** If you dream someone refuses to loan you money, you feel abandoned by the people you thought you could count on in your time of need, or your dream is trying to tell you that you really can find what you need on your own. See also *money*. ☯ **rich** ☾ *caretaking, financial resources, guilt, relationships, responsibilities, solutions and remedies.*

lock A lock symbolizes something you don't want others to have, see, or know about. **1.** The thing you lock up in your dream symbolizes that very thing you want to keep to yourself. You might feel more protected or secure knowing that something—or someone—is for you and you alone. **2.** Dreaming of locking up a valuable item suggests that something extremely personal or valuable to you is better off kept secret. **3.** Dreaming of locking up a person suggests jealousy or a need to control someone. Of course, you know you can't really ever control others entirely, right? Yet in your dream, you are playing out this desire. **4.** Losing the key or forgetting the combination to a lock suggests that you've kept something so secret from others that even you've lost access to it. Sometimes sharing something is the best way to keep

it. **5.** If you dream that someone has something locked away from you, you suspect that something important is going on and you aren't in the loop. See also *locked out*. ☯ **open door** ☾ *control issues, desire, protection, relationships, secrets, subterfuge.*

locked out 1. Dreaming of being locked out of your own house could mean you are having a bit of an identity crisis. You aren't sure who you really are right now. You may be baffled by feelings you are having or surprised by something you did. Whatever the case, you feel in some way locked out of your own inner motivations and emotions. **2.** Dreaming of being locked out of someone else's house suggests you feel a separation from someone. You don't understand them, or you think they don't want you to understand them. **3.** Dreaming of being locked out of a building suggests your feelings of being left out of the circle of knowledge surrounding whatever field the building represents—your job, a social group, or some area that interests you. **4.** Dreaming you have locked out others symbolizes your desire to spend some time alone. You don't want input from others right now. See also *lock*. ☯ **open door** ☾ *control issues, desires, identity, image, protection, relationships, secrets, subterfuge.*

locker 1. Hey, is that your old school locker in your dream? The place you used to keep your backpack, your band instrument or pom-poms, those clippings of your favorite celebrities, and photos of your crew? Dreaming of your locker symbolizes a search back into the past for comfort and the reassuring feeling nostalgia brings. Weren't those just the best times? You might need some reassurance that the person you loved being back then is still somewhere inside you. **2.** Dreaming of locker issues— such as not being able to open yours, getting shoved into one, finding your locker empty or defaced, or frantically searching through your locker for the notes on that test you *totally forgot about* symbolizes a resurfacing of past anxieties from your school days. Nope, those days weren't all fun and frivolity, were they? School can be traumatic, and some of those memories are bound to stick. What has happened recently to bring past anxieties to the surface? See also *locker room, school.* ☽ **grown-up** ☾ *age, anxiety, buildings and rooms, happiness, insecurity, memory, peer pressure.*

locker room   What could make you feel more vulnerable, or more powerful, than the place where you had to take off all your clothes in front of all your peers? **1.** Anxious, embarrassing, or humiliating locker room dreams can recall insecurities from the past. Something has recently made you feel vulnerable in the same way you did back in school, so your dream has sifted through your memories to find an appropriate setting to play out those feelings. **2.** If you dream of disrobing in the locker room to show

everyone your fantastic physique, you are feeling powerful, both in the present and in the context of your past experiences. Others admire you. They might even feel humiliated in your presence. **3.** If your dream locker room is the setting for a sports fantasy—you as the star player or the lucky reporter— then you are enjoying a personal power or brush-with-greatness fantasy in your dream. To dream of fame or great athletic prowess is natural and a great way to boost your mood for the day. **4.** If the locker room becomes a setting for a sexual fantasy dream, this steamy, secret room symbolizes your secret desires. You may never act on them, and there is nothing wrong with indulging yourself in some interesting retelling of the past in your own dream. ☽ **public places** ☾ *age, buildings and rooms, desires, embarrassment, image, insecurity, memory, personal power, places, sexual activity, sports, vulnerability.*

logs   **1.** Seeing a pile of logs in your dream symbolizes hard work you know you must finish. This dream says you can do it. **2.** To dream of chopping logs symbolizes your current efforts. You have to do this in order to get what you need. **3.** To dream of walking on logs, either on land or over water, symbolizes a difficult but instinctual path you know you must take. It may be hard to stay balanced, but this is the best way for you. **4.** If you dream of falling off logs, you have shirked your responsibility or been tempted away from the path you know is right. ☯ **hammock** ℂ *balance, ethics and morals, goal-setting, instincts, responsibilities, work.*

lollipop **1.** If you dream of watching a child lick a lollipop or giving a lollipop to a child, you long for the more innocent pleasures of your past. Life seemed so much simpler then. **2.** If you dream of sucking on a lollipop in front of someone or watching another adult suck on a lollipop, you have a passionate longing for physical contact with the object of your desire. **3.** If you have a memorable dream centered on sucking on a lollipop, you have a generalized hedonistic desire for sensual pleasures, or more sweetness in your life—literally (have you been avoiding all sugar?) or metaphorically (to balance life's bitterness?). ☯ **vegetables** ℂ *age, desires, food and drink, inanimate objects, innocence, love, pleasure, relationships, sexual activity.*

loneliness **1.** To dream of feeling lonely in a dream often brings to the conscious mind feelings of loneliness you haven't been acknowledging consciously. Even if you have people around you, you aren't getting something you need on a deeper emotional level, and your dream is calling out for meaningful human connection. **2.** If you dream of encountering a lonely person in your dream, that person might symbolize you, or it might symbolize someone who isn't getting what they need from you on a

deeper emotional level. ☯ **crowd** ℂ *caretaking, feelings, relationships, repression.*

losing You lose! If that's the case in your dream, you are playing out fears and insecurities, organizational problems, or a fierce competitive spirit. **1.** Losing your car keys or other small but important personal items in your dream symbolizes stress and the fear that you aren't capable of managing your daily life. Maybe it's time to clear your calendar and practice some stress management! **2.** Losing a child or a friend in a crowd or in a strange place signifies the fear that you can't hold on to someone important to you, or you fear you've neglected or let someone down. You might really be shirking your responsibilities, or you might feel so protective over someone that you've become overanxious and fearful about what could happen to that person. **3.** Losing a race or other contest or competition signifies your competitive spirit. Losing is a big deal to you. You feel threatened by losing, and the competition in your dream probably symbolizes a competitive situation in your waking life in which you fear you might not prevail. **4.** Losing your mind in your dream? Your stress level is so high that you just want to escape in any way possible. ☯ **finding something** ℂ *anxiety, competition, control issues, ego, failure, fear, image, inanimate objects, loss, protection, relationships, responsibilities, threats.*

L

lost Getting lost in a dream suggests you've lost your way in your waking life in some larger sense. Have you forgotten where you are going or what you really wanted in the first place? Have you lost track of your values or your goals? Something has distracted you along the way, or you stopped paying attention. See also *asking for directions*. ☾ **compass** ☾ *changing course, direction, ethics and morals, identity, loss, responsibilities, travel.*

lottery See *winning*.

love Ah, the passion, the excitement, the bittersweet torture that is love. Dreaming of being in love can represent a desire for love, a longing for the early days of love when a relationship was new and exciting, or the simple electric thrill of a crush. Love in dreams can be pure and innocent or lusty and carnal—the former usually represents a spiritual desire, while the latter represents a physical desire. People often dream of new love and crushes, flirting, and that wonderful feeling of just meeting someone new and exciting when they initially enter a relationship—the dream is using up some of that excess love energy. Or when they haven't had that thrill in a while, the dream is a desire. Either way, dreams of love can boost your mood all day, so we hope you have lots of them. **1.** If your love dream is about your actual partner, you have a strong foundation and you feel supported by your partner. You might wish for a little more romance. **2.** If you dream of being in love with someone you just met, you are inwardly exploring the potential of that relationship, even if you aren't actually feeling anything strong in your waking life just yet. **3.** If you dream of being in love with someone or having a crush on someone other than your partner, you are looking for something in your relationship or trying to understand something that has happened. Your partner may have recently behaved in an uncharacteristic way, making you see him or her in a new light. Or you may be looking for something you aren't getting right now in your relationship. **4.** If you dream of being in love with or having a crush on someone you aren't attracted to in your waking life, it doesn't mean you secretly harbor any desires for that actual person. More likely, you desire something that person has or represents to you. **5.** If you dream your partner is in love with someone else, you are playing out a separation or emotional gap you have been feeling. You probably don't actually suspect your partner of straying, but something has come between you. See also *lust*. ☾ **hate** ☾ *desires, feelings, happiness, hopes and dreams, innocence, love, pleasure, relationships, sexual activity, spirituality, threats, wishes.*

The Greek goddess of love, Aphrodite, and later, her Roman incarnation, Venus, had one duty alone: to make love. This goddess governs love, dreams of love, crushes, seductions, lust, sex, marriage, and even those products of love: children. One of the most powerful and irresistible of the goddesses, Aphrodite/Venus inspires one of the most powerful emotions humans can feel. If you are in love with love, say a prayer to Aphrodite or Venus before you fall asleep to help you dream of love and to help you manifest love in your waking life, too.

luggage See *suitcase*.

lunch 1. To dream of eating lunch with friends or family symbolizes balance and a happy sociability. **2.** To dream of eating lunch alone symbolizes a project you are working on that involves others but that you must accomplish on your own. You need to draw from your own resources this time instead of relying on others. **3.** To dream of skipping lunch suggests you could use a break from constant consumerism. Can you stop buying and using for a bit and start giving and returning? It's hard to shop with a measly 30-minute lunch break anyway. ◑ **dinner** ℭ *food and drink, family, relationships, social life, work.*

lungs If you dream that something is wrong with your lungs, your body may be signaling that you have a health problem. If you smoke or are exposed to smoke or polluted air frequently, be especially attuned to this kind of dream. Your wise body is sending you an important smoke signal. The effort in waking life to stop smoking may seem overwhelming, but the payoff is precious—a longer life. Do your best to quit. A suffocating feeling in your lungs can also indicate feelings of being trapped or a desire for more freedom. An expansive, free feeling in your lungs represents feelings of freedom and power. See also *breathing problems.* ◑ **suffocating** ℭ *body parts, control issues, freedom, health and hygiene, risky behavior.*

lust 1. To dream of feeling lust for someone in a dream or feeling generally lusty without an actual object of desire symbolizes a physical urge for more human contact. You might just be feeling passionate, or you might actually be feeling desire for someone in particular. **2.** Lusting after someone in a dream, especially someone who doesn't attract you in waking life, usually suggests a strong desire for something that person has or represents to you rather than the actual person. **3.** Lusting after possessions, food, beauty, or other material or sensual pleasures signifies a state of high energy and consumption. You are in a *wanting* mode. You need something to fill you up. It might not be sex that you need, or food, or drink, or anything obvious, but you feel a strong need for *something*. Your dream will give you clues

L

about what it is. **4.** Feeling guilty about lust in a dream suggests that you don't totally trust yourself in a particular situation. ☽ **love** ☾ *beauty, desires, feelings, guilt, happiness, hedonism, instincts, love, pleasure, relationships, risky behavior, sexual activity, trust issues, wishes.*

luxury   If you dream of luxury, there may be a windfall coming your way, but more likely, your dream is helping to release your pent-up frustration at having to do without more than you would like. At least in your dreams, you can live the lush life. ☽ **poverty** ☾ *abundance, comfort, desires, envy, escapism, financial resources, hedonism, hopes and dreams, pleasure.*

lying   Is it hard to lie while lying? **1.** Lie to others in a dream, and you aren't being honest with yourself. You have been justifying a behavior that you know, deep down, is wrong, and your dream is trying to show you what you are doing. **2.** If someone lies to you in a dream, you don't trust somebody, or you aren't getting the whole story and you know it. ☽ **telling the truth** ☾ *dishonesty, ethics and morals, guilt, relationships, risky behavior, subterfuge, trust issues.*

M

machinery **1.** If you dream of watching a machine working and you find it interesting or useful in some way, a logical, mechanistic, or superefficient approach will work best for your current project. **2.** If you dream about highly sophisticated technological machinery, you've been thinking inside the box, and you're zeroing in on complex reasoning. **3.** If you dream of watching a monotonous machine, or the machine is operating slowly or tediously, you feel your life has become too mechanistic. You've been operating on automatic pilot. Can you shake up your routine? **4.** If you dream you are part-machine, you've been so logical and objective that you aren't seeing the human element in a current situation. Maybe you should start listening to the rhythms of your heart.
❧ **garden** ℭ *intelligence, stasis, technology.*

madness See *insane.*

maggots Maggots crawling on food, in your house, or on you symbolize neglect, bad hygiene, bad habits, and moral degrada-

tion. Something is rotten, disintegrating. Is something eating away at yourself or your life? It's time to focus on cleansing and the pursuit of rejuvenation.
❧ **cleaning** ℭ *animals, crawling creatures, ethics and morals, health and hygiene, nature, risky behavior.*

magic Dreams often seem magical anyway, but dreams specifically about performing magic usually mean surprising success or underhanded deceit. **1.** If you dream you are performing magic, you have succeeded at something you once would have thought impossible, using creativity or cleverness. **2.** If you dream of performing black magic or any magic to hurt someone, you've achieved your goals through deceit. **3.** If you dream that someone else is performing magic, someone else's skills are benefiting you, or someone is trying to trick you into believing something that isn't so. **4.** If you dream of magical elements of nature or religion, protecting yourself with magic, or being inspired by magical miracles, you are feeling spiritually open right now to the possibilities of the world beyond the known. If this spiritual magic seems dangerous or evil, you feel vulnerable to outside influences and your dream is telling you to protect your spiritual self. ☽ **science experiment** ☾ *creativity, dishonesty, ethics and morals, mystery, myths and legends, personal power, protection, spirituality, subterfuge, success, transformation, trust issues.*

magnifying glass   Looking at something up close through a magnifying glass symbolizes your need to take a closer look at a problem or situation. This may look like something entirely different if you look closely. Are you glossing over something that requires your attention? You might be missing the crucial details. ☽ **garden** ☾ *inanimate objects, knowledge, transformation.*

maid   See *housekeeper.*

mail   Dreaming of sending or receiving mail suggests you have something to say or something you need to hear. Losing mail suggests you know you should be aware of something, but it has somehow slipped out of your grasp. Ladies, have you lost a boyfriend lately? Check your male box! ☽ **silence** ☾ *communication, inanimate objects, listening, messages.*

mail carrier   **1.** To dream of a mail carrier means someone is trying to tell you something indirectly through someone else. The message might be important. **2.** To dream you are a mail carrier suggests you have been the go-between in a com-munication. Nobody is talking to you, but without you to facilitate the conversation, they wouldn't be talking to each other. ☽ **secret** ☾ *career, caretaking, characters, code, communication, messages, people, relationships.*

mailbox   Seeing a mailbox in your dream symbolizes all the things you need to say or all those things you need to hear. Send those messages, or open the box and take out the letters. You're ready. ☽ **mute** ☾ *communication, inanimate objects, listening, messages.*

makeup   Makeup can improve how you look, or it can cover your natural face with a garish mask. It's all in how you use it … or how you dream about it. **1.** To dream of putting on makeup the way you always do suggests your daily beauty routine makes you feel comfortable and secure. **2.** To dream of putting on makeup more heavily or putting on more dramatic makeup than usual symbolizes your need to be noticed. You feel the need to make a memorable impression. **3.** To dream you are putting on makeup but you can't make it look right symbolizes insecurity. You feel you aren't making the right impression on others—they aren't seeing the real you, and you aren't sure how to show your true self in the right way. This kind of dream can also mean you are seeking beauty and good feelings in the wrong way. Your body wants to feel healthy and good from within, and it is telling you that the external things you've been doing aren't working. **4.** To dream of putting on lipstick symbolizes an emergence of your passion. Something has fired up your desire, and you want to attract it to you. **5.** To dream of putting on eye shadow or mascara symbolizes your need to see something you've been missing. Use your eyes! **6.** If you dream of putting on blush or foundation, you desire beauty, youth, or elegance for yourself or as represented in someone else. **7.** If you dream of putting makeup on somebody else, you've been trying to make, reinvent, or create something or someone through your own efforts. Or you've hurt that person in some way and you want to make up. ☽ **naked in public** ☾ *age, beauty, clothing and accessories, desires, dishonesty, health and hygiene, image, reputation.*

making out See *kissing.*

mall Buy anything and never step outside—that's the appeal, or the lack of appeal, the mall offers. In dreams, malls symbolize insulated consumerism, and the quality and mood of the dream indicates how you feel about being a consumer. **1.** If you dream of happily shopping or wandering through a mall, or if the mall is even more fantastic than in your waking life, with new stores and interesting things to see, you enjoy the material life and/or the social network it involves. Shopping, dining out, and social activities related to buying things are a great source of pleasure for you. **2.** If you dream of buying large amounts of clothing or other items in the mall, you want things right now. Have you been depriving yourself or cutting back due to financial limitations? Your mind is rebelling, or you might be getting addicted to shopping. Your strong desire for material goods or your need for the rush of buying things might also symbolize an emotional need that isn't being fulfilled or an addiction to a feeling rather than stuff. **3.** If you dream of getting lost in a mall or being pursued, or if you feel otherwise overwhelmed or scared, you've let materialism get in the way of more important things. Excessive shopping may be responsible for your current financial difficulties. **4.** If you dream of working in a mall, your current job has taken up a large part of your life. Your friends, your thoughts, and your free time all seem to have something to do with your job. It has become your little universe. Now … where did you park that car? ☽ **nature** ☾ *abundance, addictions, buildings and rooms, career, clothing and accessories, desires, financial resources, places, relationships.*

man **1.** The man in your dream symbolizes the male side of you (even if you are a woman). **1.** If you fear or feel revulsion toward the man in your dream, you fear or feel uncomfortable with your own strong, aggressive, dominant side, and you might be repressing it more than you should to feel healthy and balanced. **2.** If you feel passionate about or admiring of the man in your dream or have sexual interaction with the man, you honor your own male energy. This balancing kind of dream helps you free both sides of yourself. **3.** If you dream of a man you vaguely recognize as someone you know, but you aren't quite sure who it is, this could symbolize someone you know in your waking life who has recently revealed an unfamiliar quality or unexpected behavior. You aren't sure how to define that person anymore, and that can be exciting. ☾ **woman** ☾ *balance, identity, masculine, people, relationships, sexual activity, yin-yang.*

mandala   The beautiful circular art known as the mandala is an object for meditation or contemplation common in many Eastern traditions, particularly in Tibetan Buddhism and Hinduism. To dream of circular designs, particularly with a center focal point, represents a spiritually aware sense of your place in the universe and your ability to focus on the unity common to all creation. These powerful symbols can bring you a centered sense of peace and tranquility in your dreams or may even be a calming and reassuring message to you from a higher power: you belong. ☾ **straight line** ☾ *balance, divine power, myths and legends, relationships, shapes and symbols, spirituality, yin-yang.*

Ancient cultures often used circular symbols to represent the universe; the cycle of life; and the cycle of birth, death, and rebirth. It can even be the female or goddess symbol for the creation of life itself when the circular symbol resembles the yoni, which is the ancient symbol for the female genitals. Some examples of traditional circular symbols include the mandala; the almond-shaped mandorla (a yoni symbol); the Native American medicine wheel symbolizing the lunar cycle; round labyrinths in many ancient churches; wheels representing the chakra or energy centers in the body and the world; spherical shapes representing the planets and the universe; the spiral symbol representing the cycle of life and death and the universal womb; the sun sign, a circle with a dot in the center, also symbolizing the primal womb; and the classic Chinese yin-yang sign symbolizing the balance of male and female energies inherent in all things.

manicure or pedicure   Dreaming of having your fingernails or toenails done signifies your need for some pampering or a hint to yourself to pay attention to the details. See also *fingernails.* ☾ **roughing it** ☾ *beauty, body parts, desires, pleasure, solutions and remedies.*

mannequin   You're just phoning it in, aren't you? Dreams of a mannequin imply that you aren't giving your real self to someone else or to a project. You aren't invested.

Mannequin dreams can also mean that someone else isn't fully invested in you. A mannequin missing body parts implies that you've disengaged parts of yourself—your active participation (arms), your leadership (legs), your intellectual side (head)—from a relationship or activity. ◐ **body** ℭ *body parts, characters, relationships.*

mansion   A mansion represents the whole vast scheme of your life: your history, your current self, your potential. If the mansion is luxurious and beautiful, you have great potential for magnificent success. If the mansion is dilapidated, dirty, or spooky, your life is not going well right now and you fear you've wasted your potential. Visiting someone else's mansion symbolizes your recognition of the successes of others and your desire to achieve something just as great. See also *castle, house.* ◐ **cabin** ℭ *abundance, buildings and rooms, envy, opportunity, personal power, places.*

manslaughter   **1.** To dream of committing manslaughter symbolizes your fear that you've mistakenly hurt others. **2.** To dream of being convicted of manslaughter symbolizes your anxiety that others might think you've been hurtful or might discover something hurtful you've done. See also *killing, murder.* ◐ **murder** ℭ *accidents, anxiety, relationships, violence.*

manuscript   **1.** To dream of writing a manuscript suggests you have a story to tell and you need to get

it out of you. **2.** To dream of delivering a manuscript or mailing a manuscript means others need to hear your story. **3.** To dream of losing a manuscript symbolizes your disregard for the past. If you don't remember what happened before, how will you avoid the same mistakes? **4.** To dream someone gives you a manuscript means someone else's story will affect you in an important way. See also *book.* ◐ **painting** ℭ *communication, creativity, inanimate objects, knowledge, listening, messages.*

map   Find your way with the map in your dreams—it wants to show you where to go and symbolizes the direction you know you should be taking. ◐ **lost** ℭ *changing course, direction, inanimate objects, journeys and quests, messages, travel.*

marching   **1.** If you dream of marching in a parade or with a group of people, you feel swept up by the crowd, peer pressure, or the desire to conform. Is your identity still intact? **2.** To dream of marching in protest against an injustice symbolizes your need to speak up or act in your waking life regarding something you believe is wrong. Your dream is helping you practice taking a stand. ◐ **escape** ℭ *conformity, identity, peer pressure, rebellion.*

marijuana   See *smoking.*

marriage   Ahhh, the dream marriage. No, just the marriage dream. **1.** If you dream you are married when you aren't actually married in your waking life, you have a strong, solid relationship with someone you can depend on. **2.** Dreams of an unsettled or disagreeable marriage symbolize a problem in your current relationship that you haven't voiced. You are holding in your unhappiness regarding some aspect of your relationship, and it is surfacing in your dream. **3.** To dream of proposing marriage signifies your readiness to make a commitment to someone or something. This might have nothing to do with an actual love relationship. It simply signifies your commitment. **4.** Dreams about getting married or preparing to get married mean you are preparing your psyche for a major life change. See also *proposal, wedding.* ☯ **divorce** ℂ *caretaking, changing course, hopes and dreams, love, relationships, repression, subterfuge.*

Mars **1.** Exciting and stimulating dreams about Mars symbolize a yearning for new frontiers, adventure, and strange new experiences. **2.** Frightening dreams about Mars symbolize your fear of new frontiers, adventure, and strange new experiences. **3.** Dreaming of frightening aliens on Mars suggests your fear in an unfamiliar situation. You feel threatened. ☯ **home** ℂ *adventure, anxiety, changing course, fear, journeys and quests, myths and legends, places.*

mask **1.** If you wear a mask in your dream, you are putting on an act for others or maybe even for yourself. This isn't you, but you feel more comfortable being this other person right now. You might be protecting yourself—this disguise is more comfortable. Or maybe you just don't want to admit the truth. **2.** If you dream someone else is wearing a mask, someone is hiding something from you. See also *costume, disguise.* ☯ **naked in public** ℂ *clothing and accessories, comfort, dishonesty, image, identity, mystery, protection, subterfuge, trust issues.*

massage **1.** Dreaming of getting a sensual, sexy massage suggests you are physically "in the mood" and your dream is scratching the itch. You crave physical contact. **2.** Dreaming of giving a sensual massage to someone else plays out your physical desire for someone. **3.** Dreaming of getting a therapeutic massage may be a message from your body that you require stress relief and/or some body therapy. Have you been overworking or using your body in a way that has you achy or sore? ☯ **fight** ℂ *body parts, comfort, desires, healing, health and hygiene, pleasure, relationships, sexual activity, solutions and remedies.*

Massage is more than pleasurable—it really is therapeutic. Humans need physical contact with each other, and massage is a good way to take care of someone, relieve sore muscles, and satisfy the craving for touch. Regular massages can help you sleep better and maybe even dream more sweetly. For more on the benefits of massage and how to give a really good massage, check out *The Complete Idiot's Guide to Massage* (Alpha Books, 1998).

mastectomy Dreaming you've had or must get a mastectomy can symbolize your fear of illness or the loss of feminine mothering or sexual energy. It can also be a clue from your body to get your breasts checked, but more often, mastectomy dreams play out anxieties about aging, beauty, sexuality, and body image. In this way, a woman's dream of mastectomy can be similar to a man's dream of castration—a fear that sexual power will be taken away. If you have had a mastectomy and you dream about it, you may be mourning your loss, working through your acceptance, or coming to terms with your hopes and health as a survivor. ☽ **breasts** ☾ *age, body parts, fear, feminine, health and hygiene, image, loss, medicine and surgery, pain, personal power.*

masturbation Dreaming about masturbation can help burn off excessive sexual energy almost as well as the real thing, but you might dream about masturbation for other reasons, too. **1.** If you dream of taking pleasure in masturbating in front of someone as part of a sexual experience, you may be acting out a fantasy of self-confidence and body confidence. You feel powerful and in control of your own needs. **2.** If you dream of getting caught while masturbating, you feel guilty about your natural urges, or you fear that if people discover the real you, your reputation will suffer. **3.** If you dream of masturbating in public and feeling embarrassed or ashamed about it, you feel insecure about your ability to control your own behavior. **4.** If you see or catch someone else masturbating in a dream, someone has been getting too personal with you. You feel like you've learned more than you wanted to know about someone, and it makes you uncomfortable. ☽ **impotence** ☾ *body parts, comfort, control issues, desires, ethics and morals, guilt, image, personal power, pleasure, reputation, sexual activity.*

matches **1.** Light a match in your dream, and you just may have the beginnings of a great idea. **2.** If someone else lights a match in your dream, you may have recently experienced a spark between you and someone else. There could be great potential here. **3.** To see a book or box of unlit matches in your dream suggests you aren't taking advantage of an opportunity. Are you afraid of success? **4.** If you try to light matches that won't light or you ruin matches by breaking them or getting them wet, something you thought had great potential has turned out to be a disappointment. ☽ **fountain** ☾ *creativity, heat, inanimate objects, love, opportunity, relationships.*

maternal instinct **1.** To feel a welling-up of maternal instinct in a dream suggests that someone or something (even a pet) has recently inspired maternal feelings within you. You may not have acknowledged these feelings for what they are, so they have come up in your dreams. **2.** Maternal instincts in a

M

dream can also signal to your conscious mind that someone needs or wants you to take care of them, and you won't mind playing that role. **3.** Maternal instincts in a dream can also signal your own displaced feelings of need for a parental figure to take care of you. **4.** You are finally beginning to understand how your mother felt. **5.** If you are a man, dreams of feeling a maternal instinct are entirely natural and part of your internal feminine energy. Your dream is helping you to express your nurturing side. ☽ **abandonment** ℭ *caretaking, comfort, desires, feelings, instincts, relationships.*

math Do you play the numbers in your dreams? **1.** Dreaming of math suggests a logical and quantitative mindset that you need to employ right now or that you've been overusing. **2.** Dreaming of being in math class, taking a math test, or doing math homework can all represent your immature analytical side. If you find yourself back in school in your dreams, you need to backtrack and look at a situation starting from the beginning. One plus one …. **3.** Numbers and mathematical formulas or problems appearing in dreams can also be code for real formulas or problems in your waking life. Numbers could stand for important dates, ages, or other symbols representing certain people or situations. Can you solve the code? ☽ **reading** ℭ *code, communication, knowledge, shapes and symbols, solutions and remedies.*

mattress A mattress cushions you and protects you while you sleep or gives you a soft, bouncy surface for intimacy. What could be nicer? **1.** If you dream of lying on a mattress, you feel protected or lazy. **2.** If you dream of having sex on a mattress, you feel comfortable and satisfied. **3.** If you dream of an uncomfortable mattress, something isn't right in your life, and it's bothering you. **4.** If you dream of a dirty, broken, or stained mattress, you've compromised your principles. ☽ **floor** ℭ *comfort, desires, ethics and morals, furniture and appliances, happiness, protection, sexual activity, stability.*

maze **1.** Working your way through a maze or labyrinth in a dream suggests a difficult or convoluted path ahead. You are working your way through, but you aren't sure what direction you are supposed to go. **2.** Helping or leading someone through a maze suggests you are playing an important role in someone else's progress right now. **3.** Watching animals navigate a maze, such as mice in a laboratory setting, means you have good objectivity about a complicated situation. What behavior modifications should you make? ☽ **straight line** ℭ *animals, caretaking, changing course, direction, journeys and quests, responsibilities, shapes and symbols, solutions and remedies.*

measuring—How many inches? If you dream of measuring something, you are taking stock of or quantifying some aspect of your life. Do you measure up? You are trying to find out. Measuring dreams can also indicate a desire for a more precise or exact grasp on a situation. You want to know the facts. ☽ **palm reading** ☾ *competition, control issues, desires, direction, knowledge, solutions and remedies.*

meat **1.** Dreaming of eating meat can symbolize a need for more protein in your diet, but it can also symbolize a need to get your head out of the clouds and ground yourself in the world. Eating meat, especially ground beef, is among the more grounding and worldly experiences, and your body is telling you to *live* a little more, right here, right now. **2.** If you are a vegetarian, it is common to dream about eating meat, just as anyone who gives up anything—smoking, drinking, eating carbs—often dreams about doing that very thing. If you feel guilt about eating meat, you are worried you have compromised your principles, possibly in some way that doesn't involve meat-eating at all. **3.** Dreaming of cooking or serving meat for others signifies your wish to bring others into the present moment with you and to provide earthy and comforting nourishment. **4.** Dreaming of killing an animal for its meat symbolizes a flaring-up of deep survival instincts. (Or maybe your ancestors survived by climbing the nearest tree!) Something has challenged you to use your natural ability to provide for yourself, or you are struggling with a violent instinctual

response to something. ☽ **fruit** ☾ *animals, caretaking, comfort, food and drink, instincts, stability, violence.*

medicine **1.** Taking medicine in a dream means your physical, mental, or emotional self needs some kind of healing or remedy. **2.** Giving medicine to someone else in a dream means you have the remedy someone else needs, or you have the remedy you yourself require for healing. **3.** If you dream of taking the wrong medicine or getting sick from medicine, the thing you thought you were doing to help yourself is actually having a negative effect. See also *drugs, pills.* ☽ **poison** ☾ *caretaking, comfort, healing, medicine and surgery, solutions and remedies.*

meditation Dreaming of meditation can signal a need for waking-life meditation for stress relief or mental centering, but meditation dreams can also signify a search or longing for a more spiritual life. You may have important questions you need to consider about your life's purpose or direction. ☽ **stress** ☾ *changing course, journeys and quests, solutions and remedies, spirituality.*

melons Plump and juicy, round and sensual, big or small, melons symbolize earthly pleasures, sensuality, hedonism, sexuality, and passion. If you eat melons in your dream, you crave pleasure. Holding or touching melons symbolizes your longing for or deep appreciation of

the female form. ☯ **banana**
℃ *desires, feminine, food and drink, fruit, hedonism, pleasure, sexual activity.*

menopause **1.** If you dream you are going through "the change," your body might be experiencing a hormonal fluctuation, or you are worried or preoccupied with aging or the loss of your youthful self. **2.** If you dream that menopause causes relationship problems for you, you fear that changes in your life are making you into a person who may not be as successful in a relationship. You may be feeling like you want to go it alone. **3.** Menopause dreams can also symbolize any major transition from one life stage to another. Menopause dreams could also be triggered by the full moon. **4.** A new sense of independence and adventure signifies the shedding of stereotypical feminine roles for a reexploration of self in menopause. **5.** Hot flashes can signify emotional distress; hot, electric cleansing or flushing; or a state of profound realization or catharsis. ☯ **menstruation** ℃ *age, beauty, changing course, feminine, health and hygiene, nature, pain, relationships, transformation.*

menstruation **1.** Dreaming it's "that time of the month" can be a signal from your body of a change in your hormones, including a sign that you really are getting ready to menstruate. Such dreams can also signal to you that you are not

pregnant. **2.** Menstruation dreams can symbolize a powerful feminine energy, representing the lifecycle and the peak of mothering power in a woman's life. **3.** If you dream you get your period in an embarrassing situation, you feel self-conscious about some aspect of your femininity or uncomfortable with the stronger aspects of feminine energy. **4.** If you dream someone else is menstruating, you feel an instinctual connection to that person. **5.** If you dream that menstruation keeps you from having sex or becomes an issue in a sexual experience, you've recently suffered from bad timing in your life, particularly related to romance. See also *blood*. ☯ **menopause** ℃ *age, body parts, creation, embarrassment, feminine, health and hygiene, pain, personal power, relationships, sexual activity.*

mermaid **1.** To see a mermaid in your dream symbolizes personal power and seduction. You have charisma right now and the power to manipulate the emotions of others. **2.** To dream you are a mermaid means you are ready to spawn your creativity. Being a mermaid in a dream can also symbolize your awareness that someone desires you desperately but you are not ready to be physically intimate. Well … there's that whole tail thing going on. ☯ **servant** ℃ *beauty, characters, creativity, desires, feminine, myths and legends, personal power, sexual activity, water.*

meteors and meteorites   1. Any bodies flying through space in dreams—comets, shooting stars, meteorites—symbolize significant events, memorable moments, or historically important occurrences. They can mark significant life changes or the creation of something influential and meaningful. **2.** Dreaming of a meteor hitting the earth marks an event of more sobering or jarring import. Something that seems small at first will get bigger and bigger. It may not seem like a big thing right now, but it will certainly change everything. ◑ **lava** ℂ *changing course, destruction, disaster, history, nature, transformation.*

microwave   Dreaming of a microwave means you need to change or improve upon something, but you need to do it fast. Speed matters more than quality right now. ◑ **stalling** ℂ *changing course, creativity, furniture and appliances, transformation.*

midwife   1. If you are pregnant and you dream of giving birth with the help of a midwife, your body or feelings may be telling you that natural childbirth is a good option for you. **2.** If you dream of using a midwife and having a problem, your body or feelings may be telling you that you will feel more comfortable giving birth in a more modern way and that natural childbirth isn't necessarily for you. **3.** If you dream of a midwife but you aren't pregnant or don't think you are preg-

nant, this could be a sign from your body that either you are pregnant already or you are ready to become pregnant. Or it could symbolize a longing to become pregnant. **4.** If you dream you are a midwife, you have a strong urge to help women and/or children using your natural intuition and healing abilities. You have a good bedside manner, no matter how you choose to use it. ◑ **doctor** ℂ *career, caretaking, characters, comfort, creation, desires, family, fear, feminine, health and hygiene, hopes and dreams, intuition, medicine and surgery, people, predictions, wishes.*

military   1. If you dream you are in the military and the experience is exciting or interesting to you—in other words, it's a good dream—then you crave more authority and structure in your life, as well as more adventure and the chance to really exercise your skills in extreme situations. **2.** If you dream you are in the military but you don't like it, or the experience is frightening or horrible, you've felt subject to too much structure or authority recently, or you've been exposed to disturbing experiences beyond your control. **3.** If you dream you are subject to military action, or military personnel force you to do something or go somewhere, you are suffering from generalized anxiety about the world, or you feel your life is not your own. **4.** If you dream military action saves you from a bad situation, you feel overwhelmed in your life now or because of something that will happen soon, and you wish some authority figure would come in and relieve the pressure and anxiety by rescuing you. You are tired of taking on all the responsibility. ❍ **rebel** ☾ *adventure, anxiety, authority, career, control issues, fear, peacemaking, protection, risky behavior, rules and laws.*

milk   Dreaming of milk symbolizes the maternal instinct, caretaking, nurturing, and the power of creation. **1.** If you dream you are drinking milk, you crave nurturing and internalize creative power. **2.** If you dream of giving milk to someone else, you feel a strong instinct to nurture and care for others. **3.** If you dream of putting milk or cream into your coffee, you are enjoying a surge of creativity right now.
❍ **lemon and lime** ☾ *caretaking, creativity, family, food and drink, instincts.*

Hindus consider the cow sacred, and although milk is a staple in the Hindu diet, beef is forbidden. For thousands of years, Hindus have considered the cow a sacred symbol, but other cultures esteem the cow, too, as a symbol of abundance and nurturing. The Egyptian goddess, Hathor, sometimes incarnates as a cow and is the goddess who protects mothers, children, and breastfeeding.

minister   See *religious authority figures.*

mirror   Dreaming of looking in a mirror reveals the real you—at least, in your mind, at the present time. How you look or feel about what you see represents your current self-esteem or perception of your own image. ❍ **mask** ☾ *identity, image, inanimate objects, insecurity, personal power.*

missing a class, meeting, or appointment   Oh no, is that the time? Dreams that you have missed your class, a meeting, or an important appointment tap into general anxiety that you aren't fulfilling your obligations or doing everything you are supposed to do. Even for those who haven't been in school for years, dreaming of missing a class—or even all the classes for the entire semester (and it's time for finals!)—is still one of the most common dreams. These dreams usually mean you need to slow down and simplify your life a bit, or just take some time off. Now why didn't they let us do that in school? We wouldn't be having all these nightmares …. ❍ **graduation** ☾ *anxiety, responsibilities, time.*

mob mentality   If you dream of getting caught up in a hysterical or violent mob of people or being coerced to do things you wouldn't normally do (such as committing violence or looting) because of being in a crowd, you fear that forces beyond your control may impact you in a dangerous or frightening way. Mob dreams can also happen when you've been around too many people or when you feel overly influenced to go along with the group against your better judgment. You need some alone time to regroup and recapture your own identity. See also *crowd*. ☯ **alone** ☾ *anxiety, conformity, feelings, identity, peer pressure, risky behavior, rules and laws.*

mobile home   Like any home, a mobile home represents your current self, but because of the moveable aspect, a mobile home represents a temporary self or persona you've taken on. You may move on to another one soon, or dreaming of a mobile home could mean you have the urge or plan to pick up and move your life somewhere entirely new. **1.** If the mobile home is new and shiny, your new identity is working well for you, and you still enjoy the novelty of it. **2.** If the mobile home is old and dilapidated, you feel stuck in a role that isn't you and doesn't work for you. You feel like you are better than what you've become. **3.** If you dream of towing a mobile home somewhere, you are ready to relocate. ☯ **stop signs and stoplights** ☾ *changing course, home, image, identity, journeys and quests, places, vehicles.*

modem   Dreaming of a modem means you are trying to communicate with someone in an indirect way. If the modem isn't working or won't connect, your message isn't getting through. ☯ **alone** ☾ *communication, electronics, failure, inanimate objects, listening, messages, technology.*

modesty   **1.** Dreams of feeling more modest or dressing or acting more modestly than you usually do suggest that you've recently gone a little too far the other way in your waking life. You've been too immodest, perhaps, so your dream is trying to balance out this overstepping by giving you a little advice about what kind of behavior might be prudent right now. **2.** If you dream someone else is displaying modesty, your dream may also be showing you an example of behavior that might be helpful or becoming to you right now. **3.** If the modesty in the dream is inappropriate, you may be acting out your own inclination to be too modest, and your dream is showing you how it looks, in order to help you go the other direction. ☯ **exhibitionism** ☾ *anxiety, embarrassment, ethics and morals, feelings, image, reputation.*

monastery   **1.** Pleasant, restorative dreams of living in or visiting a monastery play out your desire to escape from the decadent world for more spiritual contemplation. **2.** If you dream you are called to go to a monastery, you desire or may feel compelled to lead a less material, more spiritual existence. **3.** If you dream of being trapped in a monastery or being abandoned to a monastery and you don't like it or you find it frightening or dangerous, you aren't prepared for inner contemplation right now. You feel more comforted by living in the world. There may be something within you that you don't want to face right now or unresolved issues from your past having to do with organized religion. **4.** To dream of a monk in a monastery suggests that someone has important spiritual advice for you right now or can serve as your mentor or guide. This person might not even realize that what they say or do is wise and important for you. ☽ **crowd** ☾ *buildings and rooms, comfort, divine power, escapism, isolation, places, spirituality.*

money   Money makes a powerful symbol for all the resources we do or don't have and all the material things we desire. **1.** Dreaming you have a lot of money suggests a desire for more prosperity or the opportunity to become more prosperous. **2.** Dreaming of finding money, from a wallet stuffed with big bills to coins scattered on the sidewalk, suggests a surprise opportunity and good luck. **3.** Dreaming of losing money suggests a mistake you've made that will have a bad effect or recent bad luck. You may also be suffering a financial drain you feel you can't control. **4.** Dreaming of someone else's money means someone has something you want but don't have. See also *loaning money.* ☽ **counterfeiting** ☾ *abundance, desires, financial resources, inanimate objects, loss, opportunity, solutions and remedies.*

monk   See *monastery.*

monotony   **1.** Oh, the boredom. Usually dreams seem to involve something exciting or memorable, but if you dream of monotony, you might be fearful that your life or work has become too staid or regular, or that you could fall into a rut

and become like everyone else. **2.** If you find yourself enjoying a dream of monotony, your waking life might be too stimulating, and you long for an easy and regulated life. ☽ **adventure** ☾ *anxiety, burdens, career, conformity, frustration, responsibilities, stasis.*

monster   **1.** Children have monster dreams all the time, but adults don't have them nearly so often. If you have a nightmare about a monster, something truly frightens you, and it might be a grown-up version of what typically frightens children: starting a new job instead of starting school; a dangerous or undermining colleague instead of a bully; or the universal fears of change, the unknown, or the future. Whatever it is, it has come to life in your dreams to frighten you. **2.** If you dream of defeating or befriending a monster, you are ready to face a new and difficult challenge with confidence. ☽ **friend** ☾ *animals, anxiety, changing course, characters, control issues, danger, fear, myths and legends, threats.*

moon   What could be more ancient, mythical, and mysterious than the moon? Dreams about the moon symbolize all the cycles of change and transformation we experience as humans living on an Earth circled by the changeable moon. Moon dreams also tap into changeable feminine energy, the yin to the sun's yang—dark and mysterious, unpredictable yet cyclical. **1.** Dreaming of a full moon means you are ready to do something daring or change your life in a radical way. Or maybe you are just ready to do something out of the ordinary. The time is right. **2.** Dreaming of a new moon means you are at the very beginning of something. You have made a fresh start or discovered something entirely new, and you look forward to seeing how it will grow. **3.** Dreaming of a half-full moon symbolizes balance. You need more balance in your life now, or you have achieved a good balance and your dream is encouraging you to go forward with your energies, priorities, and relationships in this healthy state of equilibrium. **4.** Dreaming something is wrong with the way the moon looks or moves could be a signal from your body to check your health related to female hormones. **5.** Dreaming of a lunar eclipse symbolizes a feeling of solitude and the necessity for spending some time alone in quiet contemplation. You need a break from the world—even just a short break—to renew your spirit and energy. Your mind is on the mystery that is you. **6.** To dream of the tides influenced by the moon suggests that you are experiencing emotional fluctuations related to hormones, your own inner energy cycles, or a transition between life stages. Tidal dreams can also represent a particularly sensitive emotional time. Overwhelmed by your feelings, you need to protect yourself right now. **7.** If the moon seems to have consciousness or speak to you, you are tapping into divine female energy.

The moon goddess herself may be visiting you in your dreams to tell you something about your feminine journey. See also *tides, werewolf.*
☽ **sun** ☾ *balance, changing course, divine power, feelings, feminine, isolation, mystery, myths and legends, nature, shapes and symbols, spirituality, transformation, water, weather and seasons, yin-yang.*

motel See *hotel or motel.*

mother **1.** If you are a woman and you dream of your own mother, she often symbolizes you—her dream actions, problems, and successes usually symbolize your own actions, problems, and successes. **2.** Dreams about your mother can also symbolize your desire for protection and nurturing. You long for someone to step in and take care of you the way your mother did when you were a child, so you have called her up to nurture you in your dream. Again, however, this could also symbolize you and your impulse to nurture and protect someone else. **3.** If you dream your mother has a health issue, this may be your health issue, but it might also actually be a health problem with your own mother or someone who is a mother figure to you. **4.** If your mother has passed away before you dream of her, she may be sending you a message. Many people claim to receive important messages from their departed parents. Or the dream could be your own memories or thoughts about your mother, stepping in to guide you when she

M

cannot. **5.** If you dream you are a mother, you may feel a maternal responsibility toward someone or something, such as a needy friend, a child, or even a pet. Or dreams that you are a mother could be playing out your longing to become a mother. ◐ **dangerous person** ℭ *caretaking, comfort, family, feminine, health and hygiene, love, messages, people, protection, punishment, relationships, sacrifice, stability.*

motor See *engine.*

motorcycle Get your motor running. **1.** Dreaming you are riding a motorcycle symbolizes your desire for freedom, your rebellious spirit, or your impulse to take risks. You may not actually want to "live fast and die young," but in your dream, it can be a lot of fun to just break free and ride with the wind. **2.** Dreaming of traveling somewhere on a motorcycle symbolizes your desire to see the world close-up rather than through a car or airplane window. You want to experience life rather than just watch it. **3.** If you dream of getting in a wreck on a motorcycle, you may be facing a risk, and you fear that you might get hurt, either physically or emotionally. You may also fear too much freedom or going against the rules. **4.** If you dream of riding on the back of a motorcycle while someone else drives, you have handed over control to someone else right now and have decided to trust that person with a risk involving you—for better or for

worse. **5.** To dream of watching someone else riding a motorcycle symbolizes your worry about someone else's safety or your envy at someone else's freedom. ◐ **jail** ℭ *adventure, control issues, courage, desires, escapism, fear, freedom, rebellion, risky behavior, travel, trust issues, vehicles.*

mountain Mountains symbolize challenges to meet and obstacles to overcome. **1.** Dreaming of looking at or climbing a mountain signifies your contemplation of or readiness for a challenge. **2.** If you can't get around or over a mountain in your dream, a problem you face seems insurmountable. See also *hill.* ◐ **coastline** ℭ *goal-setting, impediments, nature, opportunity, places.*

mountain lion **1.** To dream of being threatened or attacked by a mountain lion means your instinctual sense of danger has been activated. Something threatens you. **2.** To see a mountain lion from far away means you sense danger is lurking, even if it hasn't affected you yet. **3.** To dream of escaping from or killing a mountain lion suggests that you feel ready to meet a dangerous challenge or foil a threat. **4.** To dream of befriending or making a pet of a mountain lion symbolizes your desire to tame something, or someone, that seems wild or out of control. See also *cat.* ◐ **dog** ℭ *animals, danger, instincts, nature, threats.*

mouse   **1.** The answer is in the details if you dream of a mouse. **2.** If you dream of a mouse infestation in your house, you've gotten lazy or irresponsible. You've let things go too far. **3.** If you dream of killing a mouse, your heavy-handed approach may be effective in the short term, but you may also be missing out on the subtle side of the situation. **4.** If you dream of watching a mouse, saving a mouse, or keeping a mouse as a pet, you are curious and courageous. **ele-phant** *animals, control issues, courage, crawling creatures, health and hygiene, nature, responsibilities.*

> In neopaganism, the mouse as a personal symbol can help to teach the art of invisibility: how to move without being heard, the importance of silence, and the skill of stealth.

moustache   To dream you have a moustache symbolizes your desire to change your image. To dream of shaving your moustache symbolizes your desire to tell the truth. **shaving** *body parts, changing course, communication, dishonesty, image.*

mouth   Dreaming of your mouth represents the way you want to talk about how you feel or what feelings you want to take into yourself—the give-and-take of emotions with others. **1.** If you dream of having trouble opening your mouth, you may feel stifled by your inability to tell someone the truth. You don't feel emotionally able to do it, even though you wish you could. **2.** To dream your mouth is full of something—food or anything else—suggests you've been receiving so much emotional support from others that it's time to give back. **3.** To dream your mouth is dry or you are very thirsty and can't find anything to drink, or that drinking doesn't relieve the feeling, symbolizes a lack of emotional fulfillment. You aren't getting the emotional support you need. **4.** To dream you have sores or injuries in your mouth symbolizes your resistance to emotions out of the fear of getting hurt. **5.** To dream your mouth looks particularly beautiful or supple suggests a passionate desire for someone or a brand new crush. You feel emotionally sustained by this ego-boosting feeling. **6.** To dream of sexual activity using your mouth suggests a physical desire for release without emotional entanglement. See also *kissing, lips, oral sex, teeth.* **hand** *body parts, communication, desires, feelings, food and drink, injuries, pleasure, relationships, sexual activity.*

movie   In dreams, movies play out an alternate vision of your life for your viewing pleasure, either the way you wish it was or the way you fear it could become. **1.** If you dream you are in a movie, you are trying out possible scenarios for you to consider before you commit to a change in your life. **2.** If you dream you are in a movie with a celebrity or are filming a movie with a celebrity, you wish for more excitement or status in your real life and your dream has let you experience this. **3.** If you dream of making or directing a movie, you have decided to take control of a situation. ☾ **lost** ℭ *adventure, changing course, control issues, hopes and dreams, journeys and quests, wishes.*

movie star   See *celebrity.*

moving   Dreams you are moving to a new home symbolize an impending life change. How you feel about moving represents how you feel about this life change, which could have nothing to do with physical relocation. ☾ **homebody** ℭ *buildings and rooms, changing course, direction, home, taking action, transformation.*

MP3 player   **1.** If you dream of downloading songs to your MP3 player, you have created a scenario in your life and orchestrated it just the way you want it to go. **2.** If the download doesn't work, your well-laid plans didn't have the effect you thought they would. **3.** If you dream of listening to your MP3 player, you feel comfortable with your current image. **4.** If you dreamed about listening to a particular song on your MP3 player, the song may have a message for you about your current situation or how you really feel about someone. ☾ **silence** ℭ *electronics, goal-setting, image, inanimate objects, listening, messages, music and sound, technology.*

mudslide   See *landslide.*

multiple births   **1.** To dream you are pregnant with twins or triplets can signal hormonal fluctuations, actual pregnancy, or the desire for pregnancy. **2.** Dreaming of giving birth to twins or triplets symbolizes multiple sides of you: you are playing several roles, probably new ones, and you feel split in many directions, but this may be a source of pride and your good reputation. **3.** To dream you are already a parent of twins or triplets is more likely to symbolize your responsibility for a group. ☾ **infertility** ℭ *caretaking, creation, health and hygiene, identity, reputation, responsibilities.*

murder   Dreaming of murder can be frightening or disturbing, but dreams about murder usually have more to do with change inflicted on one person by another rather than any sort of actual evil impulse or prediction of violence. If you have strong recurring or troubling violent dreams, please seek the counsel of a licensed therapist to help you interpret their specific meaning. **1.** If you dream that you witness a murder, you expect something in your life to change dramatically, or you expect—or have recently experienced—some kind of loss. **2.** If you dream someone is trying to murder you, you feel anxious about someone's intentions, or you fear a change in your life and the effect it could have on your own idea of yourself. **3.** If you dream you murder or are trying to murder someone, you feel the need to force a change in your life or to end a friendship or association with someone. You may also be repressing your anger toward someone, and it is coming out violently in your dream. **4.** If the murder is accidental, you fear you may have hurt someone by mistake. See also *killing, manslaughter.* ☻ **nonviolence** ℂ *accidents, anger, anxiety, changing course, danger, death, destruction, ethics and morals, identity, loss, relationships, risky behavior, taking action, violence.*

muscum   1. Dreaming of a museum symbolizes your fascination with or need to explore your own past. Something from your personal history is calling out to you for acknowledgment, and facing or discovering the details will help you with a current situation. **2.** To dream of meeting someone in a museum or seeing someone you know suggests you are ready to face something from the past regarding that person or something that person represents. This dream often means you are ready to forgive someone, or someone is ready to forgive you. **3.** To dream a museum is locked symbolizes your inability or unwillingness to access a past memory. **4.** To dream a museum is frightening, dark, or threatening means something has come up from your past that you fear or don't want to remember. Like … a giant, hairy mammoth is chasing you and your flimsy little fur toga is slip-

ping off your shoulders. Don't you hate when that happens? ☻ **laboratory** ℂ *fear, forgiveness, memory, places, repression, threats.*

music   1. Hearing music in your dream symbolizes something you want to remember or something that has had a strong emotional impact on you. **2.** Playing music in your dream symbolizes your participation in a creative act. You are part of something important. ☻ **silence** ℂ *creativity, feelings, listening, music and sound.*

musical instrument   Seeing musical instruments in your dream represents the creative path to your goal: how will you make it happen? To dream of playing a musical instrument suggests you are already on the creative path. If you dream of playing an instrument you actually play, you may be working on refining your technique in your dream. This can actually improve your playing in your waking life. If you dream of playing an instrument you don't actually play, the meaning depends on the instrument. **1.** To dream you are playing the drums symbolizes your need to set the tone for a group. Everyone depends on you to stay together, and they wait for your ideas before anybody takes action. **2.** To dream you are playing the guitar suggests that you are the "front man" in a current project—you are the visible one with the flashy ideas and the inspiration for others. **3.** If you dream of playing a wind instrument, like a saxophone, flute, clarinet, or oboe, people count on you to fill in the details. Other people might rough out the general idea, but you make it special. **4.** If you dream of playing a brass instrument, like a trumpet, French horn, trombone, or tuba, your role in a current project is to speak for others or to communicate the project's purpose. **5.** If you dream of playing the bass, you provide the basic structure of an idea. **6.** If you dream of playing the violin, viola, or cello, you've added a touch of class to a current creative effort. **7.** If you dream of playing the harmonica, people see you as a rebel. You want to do things your own way, and you don't necessarily work well with a group. ☾ **mute** ℭ *creation, creativity, inanimate objects, music and sound, personal power, relationships, responsibilities.*

mute **1.** If you dream you can't talk, you have something to say but you are afraid of the effect it might have, or you don't want to recognize what you really need to say. **2.** If you dream you refuse to talk even though you could, you are being the stubborn one in a current conflict. **3.** If you dream someone else is mute, you haven't been paying attention to someone's less obvious attempts at communication. ☾ **talking** ℭ *communication, fear, listening, repression, resistance.*

nails **1.** If you dream of grooming your fingernails, you are concerned with appearances right now, and your reputation depends on paying attention to the visible details. **2.** If you dream of broken or dirty fingernails, you have neglected the details, and this oversight has had a negative influence on your reputation. **3.** If you dream of pounding nails with a hammer, you will have to put forth some serious effort to make something work. ☽ **compliment** ☾ *body parts, communication, creation, ego, image, inanimate objects, insecurity, relationships.*

naked in public Do you realize you aren't wearing any pants? This exceptionally common but no less embarrassing dream of being fully or partially naked in public signifies a feeling of vulnerability or, alternately, of self-confidence. **1.** If nobody seems to notice you are naked in your dream, sometimes you feel like a fraud. You feel insecure about your abilities, as if you've fooled everyone into thinking you are capable of more than you really are. You don't feel like you truly deserve the reputation or resources you've gained. You may not feel like this all the time, but recent events may have triggered this insecurity. **2.** If people do notice you are naked in your dream, you feel exposed. Someone has compromised your position or authority, or revealed your weakness to others. **3.** You may just like the freedom of being unencumbered; you're self-confident and happy about your body and unafraid to show it. Shed inhibitions with each stitch of clothing! See also *embarrassment, exhibitionism.* ☽ **blanket** ☾ *body parts, clothing and accessories, embarrassment, image, insecurity, reputation, threats, vulnerability.*

nap **1.** To dream of napping is a sign from your body that you aren't getting enough sleep, or that your sleep hasn't been restful enough. **2.** If you dream you can't seem to wake up from a nap or you keep falling back into a nap, you are having momentum problems. You feel frustrated about being unable to get something done. Something is holding you back. ☽ **insomnia** ☾ *frustration, health and hygiene, impediments.*

natural disaster   See *disaster*.

nature   Dreaming of nature usually symbolizes a call from your instinctual, animal side to get back to the natural world for perspective and balance. **1.** To be lost or scared in nature signifies a separation from the natural world. You've gotten way too civilized, and nature has become a stranger. Your anxiety comes from a loss of balance. **2.** To enjoy being in nature in a dream means you need a retreat where the air is fresh, the sun warm, and the scenery green. ☽ **mall** ☾ *adventure, animals, balance, beauty, changing course, courage, danger, fear, freedom, journeys and quests, nature, weather and seasons*.

nausea   Nausea makes you feel vulnerable, sometimes frightened, certainly not in control. Dreams of nausea can reveal nervousness or predict a big change. **1.** To dream of nausea can signify some kind of stomach problem, pregnancy, or the desire for pregnancy. **2.** Dreaming of nausea can also foretell a long trip or major change. **3.** To feel nauseous for no apparent reason in a dream can signal repressed guilt about something you did that you are ashamed to admit. Admit it, at least to yourself, and you'll feel better. ☽ **health** ☾ *body parts, changing course, feelings, guilt, health and hygiene, repression, travel, vulnerability*.

navel   See *belly button*.

navy   See *military*.

nearsighted   See *vision problems*.

neck   Your neck is among your most vulnerable spots, and dreaming of your neck reveals your vulnerability. **1.** To dream of admiring your own neck or putting jewelry or a scarf around your neck symbolizes the strength in your softer feminine side and an awareness of your own beauty and attraction. **2.** To dream your neck hurts or gets injured symbolizes a recent exposure. You feel vulnerable and unsafe. ☽ **head** ☾ *beauty, body parts, ego, feminine, health and hygiene, image, injuries, reputation, vulnerability*.

necklace   See *jewelry*.

necktie   See *tie*.

needle   See *injection or needle*.

neighbor   **1.** Dreaming of friendly, helpful neighbors symbolizes friendly, helpful people in your life. Either you need them, or you already have and appreciate them. **2.** Dreaming of cruel, vindictive, or evil neighbors symbolizes distrust of someone in your personal life. You suspect treachery. **3.** Dreaming of passionate or sexual relationships with a neighbor suggests you crave more intimacy—not necessarily sexual, but emotional—with the people you already know. It feels safer to you than meeting someone new. ☽ **stranger** ☾ *characters, desires, fear, people, relationships, sexual activity, social life, support, threats, trust issues*.

neighborhood   **1.** Dreaming of your own neighborhood, or that your neighborhood is nicer or fancier than it really is, means you feel like you belong to a satisfying and rewarding social network. **2.** If you dream your neighborhood is dark and scary or altered in some disturbing way, something has changed within your social network or community that has made you feel alienated. Where is Mr. Rogers when you need him? See also *neighbor.* ☽ **foreign language** ☾ *places, relationships, social life, stability.*

nest   **1.** Dreaming of a bird's nest symbolizes the desire to settle down. You want to make a happy home for someone. **2.** Dreaming of finding an abandoned nest or a nest fallen out of a tree symbolizes your fear of losing your caretaker role. You may not feel needed anymore, or you dread your dependents moving on to their own lives. **3.** If you dream of "nesting," or fussing about in your home to make it more comfortable and nurturing, you are ready to take in someone who needs you. If you are pregnant, this can be a sign—just like actual waking-life nesting—that the baby is getting ready to come out into the world. ☽ **homeless person** ☾ *birds, caretaking, comfort, family, home, nature, places, responsibilities, stability.*

net   **1.** Dreaming of using a net to catch something—fish, butterflies, birds, even a falling person—means you need to catch something … or someone. Something teases or eludes you, flirts with you or tempts you, and you've taken tools

in hand to make it yours. **2.** Falling into a net means somebody has your back. You are in a precarious situation, but you feel protected. **3.** To be caught in a net symbolizes something holding you back or trapping you. You aren't free to do things the way you want. See also *Internet surfing.* ☽ **breaking free** ☾ *desires, goal-setting, impediments, inanimate objects, journeys and quests, protection, threats.*

New Year's Eve   Dreaming of New Year's Eve and making New Year's resolutions symbolizes a desire for a fresh start, a new image, or the abandonment of bad habits. You are really committed to making it happen this time! Let's drink to that! Oops, that's your resolution—to stop drinking? ☽ **Thanksgiving** ☾ *celebration, changing course, goal-setting, weather and seasons.*

newborn   See *baby.*

newspaper   **1.** If you read the newspaper in a dream, you work hard to keep up on what's going on so you are on equal footing with everyone else. **2.** If the newspaper in your dream is blank, you suspect you aren't in the loop. **3.** If you dream of ripping, burning, or otherwise destroying newspaper, you are tired of keeping up with others. You want out of the rat race. ☽ **not invited** ☾ *career, communication, conformity, image, inanimate objects, knowledge, messages, reputation, success, taking action.*

nightclub   Move to the beat, baby. Dreaming of being in a nightclub can symbolize your desire for the release of wild social revelry, dancing, drinking, and partying. **1.** If you feel isolated or ignored in a nightclub, you may be feeling neglected or shunned by your friends. **2.** If you dream of an empty or abandoned nightclub, your life has become all work and no play. You long for the days when you used to have more fun. **3.** If you dream of having passionate or sexual contact in a nightclub, your dream has indulged your hedonistic desires. **4.** If you dream of being abused, being mistreated, or fighting in a nightclub, you've been feeling defensive lately. You feel like others are trying to goad you. ☽ **homebody** ☾ *desires, fun, hedonism, places, pleasure, relationships, sexual activity, social life.*

nightgown   See *lingerie.*

nightmare   If you have a nightmare, something is making you anxious or fearful in your waking life. Look up the particular images in the nightmare to see what might be causing your anxiety. If you wake up generally fearful or anxious but can't remember the details of the nightmare, something is bothering you, and you need to face it if you want to have a peaceful sleep. ☽ **dreaming that you are dreaming and dreaming that you are awake** ☾ *anxiety, fear, danger, threats.*

According to the International Association for the Study of Dreams, a nightmare is a distressing dream that usually results in the dreamer waking up. Fear and anxiety are the most common feelings associated with nightmares, and the most common theme is probably being chased. Adults often dream of being chased by an unknown man, while children often dream of being chased by animals or monsters. Night terrors are something completely different. They are not dreams, but panic attacks that occur during non-REM sleep, often accompanied by screaming, thrashing around, and getting out of bed. It can be very hard to awaken someone in the throes of a night terror. If you are plagued with night terrors, talk to your doctor about treatment for this problem.

no   See *saying no.*

noise   Dreaming of any loud or obvious noise symbolizes something you need to hear. Haven't you been listening? ☽ **deafness** ☾ *communication, listening, messages, music and sound.*

nonviolence   Dreaming of purposeful nonviolence or pacifism, or protesting against violence symbolizes your stand against violence, even if you didn't realize you had one. Something has happened to make you feel compelled to act in your dream against what you believe to be wrong, hurtful, or dangerous. Gandhi would be proud. ☽ **aggression** ☾ *caretaking, peacemaking.*

noodles   See *pasta*.

noose   1. Is the noose around your neck? If you dream it is, you feel guilty about something or blamed for something. **2.** If you see a noose around someone else's neck, you are the one casting the blame or the one refusing to step forward and clear someone's name. **3.** If you see an empty noose hanging, you have a sense of foreboding. You expect someone is going to have to pay. Is it you? Ever wonder why men wear ties? ◐ **breaking free** ℂ *anxiety, danger, ethics and morals, fear, guilt, innocence, threats, violence.*

north pole/south pole   1. Dreaming of seeing or visiting either of the earth's poles suggests extremism. You are ready to go all the way to the ends of the earth for a cause or for someone important to you. You'll make the sacrifice. **2.** If you dream of traveling to the poles under extreme weather conditions, you crave adventure or extreme challenges in your life. ◐ **monotony** ℂ *adventure, caretaking, extremism, places, sacrifice, travel, weather and seasons.*

northern lights   See *Aurora Borealis.*

nose   1. What could be more obvious? Dreaming of your nose symbolizes something that is, well ... right under your nose. Something is right there, and you might be missing it. **2.** To dream you break or injure your nose symbolizes an injury to your image or appearance.

What you did or suffered is obvious to everyone. What's that smell? See also *breathing, breathing problems.* ◐ **mouth** ℂ *body parts, image, injuries, reputation.*

not invited   You mean you *didn't* get an invitation? To dream you are not invited to something signifies a feeling of isolation, insecurity, or rejection from a group. Your reaction to not being invited in your dream will clue you in to how you feel about your perceived or expected rejection in your waking life. ◐ **invitation** ℂ *anger, anxiety, ego, embarrassment, envy, failure, frustration, image, impediments, insecurity, isolation, pain, peer pressure, punishment, relationships, reputation, social life, vulnerability.*

nuclear bomb   Dreaming someone has launched a nuclear bomb and you will be in or near the strike zone suggests you are anxious or fearful of a major life-altering change, and you can't imagine what your life will be like after it happens. You feel like the whole world will change. Who is dropping the bomb, where, when, and why? See also *war.* ◐ **monotony** ℂ *changing course, danger, death, destruction, disaster, fear, transformation, violence, war.*

nuclear power   1. If you dream of a nuclear power plant operating smoothly and safely, you trust science and technology. **2.** If you dream of a nuclear accident at a nuclear power plant, you don't trust a recent technological advancement that hasn't been fully proven. You want more evidence before you invest your confidence or genealogical future. See also *nuclear bomb*. ☽ **old-fashioned** ☾ *anxiety, creativity, danger, disaster, fear, health and hygiene, technology, trust issues.*

numb **1.** To dream that you feel numb or that part of your body feels numb suggests you need to separate yourself from an emotional reaction to something right now. You need to *not* feel, for your own protection. **2.** Feeling numb in a dream can also mean you don't feel able to drum up any more emotion in a situation. You don't have anything left to give. **3.** If your extremities (hands, feet) feel numb, your body could be sending you a signal that you have a nerve- or spine-related problem. Maybe it's time to visit the orthopedist or the chiropractor. **4.** If you dream your genitals are numb, you feel emotionally distanced from your romantic partner. Get a grip. ☽ **emotional** ☾ *body parts, feelings, health and hygiene, protection, relationships, sexual activity.*

numbers If numbers appear in your dream, they are usually a code that stands for something, like a significant date, someone's age, an address, or a phone number, relating to something you need to notice or acknowledge. Run out and buy a lottery ticket. ☽ **letter** ☾ *code, messages, shapes and symbols.*

nurse **1.** Nurses symbolize health concerns and caretaking. If you dream a nurse is attending to you, you may need to attend to your own health. Are you ignoring symptoms? Or you may need to attend to your own emotional needs. If you don't take care of yourself, who will? **2.** If you dream you are a nurse, someone needs your gentle care and loving beside manner. **3.** If you dream of a romantic or sexual encounter with a nurse, you are acting out the common fantasy of someone whose gentle caretaking extends to your sexual needs when you are at your most vulnerable. ☽ **doctor** ☾ *career, caretaking, characters, healing, health and hygiene, people, responsibilities, sexual activity, vulnerability.*

nurturing See *maternal instinct*.

obesity   See *fat*.

obituary   **1.** If you dream of reading your own obituary, you face an inner transformation. You are changing—not dying—although some part of you might be metaphorically "dying" in favor of the birth of something new. **2.** If you read an obituary of someone else you know, you may fear someone is slipping out of your control or out of your life. **3.** An obituary can also symbolize your reputation, or someone else's. ☽ **giving birth** ℭ *changing course, death, identity, messages, reputation, transformation*.

occult   See *magic*.

ocean   See *water*.

odor   See *smell*.

office   Dreaming of working in an office usually has something to do with the work you do to make your life happen—either your actual job or things like paying bills or managing paperwork, insurance, school, and everything else that keeps you a working member of society. **1.** If you dream of success within an office, you are enjoying a boost in status or financial resources. **2.** If you dream of betrayal or treachery in an office, you have lost control of some important aspect of your daily functioning, and/or someone at your job can't be trusted. **3.** If you dream of office romance, you are either passionately involved in your work or passionately interested in someone you work with, even if it isn't the person you dream about. That person may represent someone or something else. Either you are getting a lot of work done, or none at all. **4.** If you dream of working on or fixing office equipment, a technological solution will work best for a current problem you are having. Maybe a new software program will straighten everything out. See also *fired from a job, hired*. ☽ **hammock** ℭ *career, control issues, love, places, relationships, technology, work*.

old-fashioned   **1.** To dream of an old-fashioned house symbolizes your desire for history, beautiful and valuable things that have endured from the past, and your wish to incorporate more tradition into your current life and surroundings. **2.** To dream of wearing old-fashioned clothes represents your desire to return to more traditional values in your life. **3.** If you dream that everyone around you is old-fashioned or you are in an old-fashioned time period and you feel frustrated or baffled by this switch in time, you are progressing faster than those around you. You are thinking ahead, and others don't understand. **4.** If you dream of living in an old-fashioned time period and you enjoy it or feel relieved by it, the modern world has become too stressful for you, and you long for a simpler time. ☽ **future** ☾ *age, beauty, changing course, clothing and accessories, escapism, ethics and morals, history, home, stability, time, transformation, wishes.*

old person   1. If you dream about an old person you don't know or someone you do know who is suddenly older than in your waking life, someone has wisdom to offer you. Listen carefully; it could be important. **2.** If you dream you are older than you are in your waking life, you've experienced a recent maturing experience or something has happened to make you feel old. ☽ **child or children** ☾ *age, changing course, characters, death, identity, people, transformation.*

omen   If you dream of any kind of omen—a blood-red moon, a plague of locusts, an eclipse, or anything that seems like a sign of some sort— then chances are, it is a sign from

you to yourself. Something important, serious, and perhaps dangerous is going on or will soon happen, and you can sense it, and you must be ready to face it. Dreams of omens can also happen if you crave excitement in challenges in an otherwise relatively uneventful period of your life. You *wish* something big would happen, so you dream of a sign pointing to something exciting. Wishing and dreaming … isn't that daydreaming? ☽ **monotony** ☾ *adventure, changing course, danger, death, disaster, divine power, messages, mystery, threats, transformation, weather and seasons.*

one-of-a-kind   A dream of a lifetime. To dream of finding something that is truly unique, the only one of its kind, and to be aware of the great value inherent in the object symbolizes your desire to distinguish yourself and achieve success. You want to do something nobody else has done, find something nobody else has found, *discover.* Your dream may also be a clue that you have a unique opportunity in front of you. Don't miss your chance! ☽ **copy machine** ☾ *adventure, desires, inanimate objects, opportunity, success, wishes.*

onion   The many-layered onion has long been a folk remedy for absorbing warts, killing infections, and otherwise slaying evil in its microscopic form. Even in its metaphysical form, onions (and also garlic) absorb or repel evil. **1.** Dreaming of cutting an onion and crying suggests you have decided to turn away from a bad influence, but you nevertheless mourn the loss. **2.** Dreaming of eating onions suggests you feel protected and safe. **3.** Dreaming of cooking onions means you work to keep others safe. ☽ **wine** ☾ *caretaking, food and drink, plants, protection, solutions and remedies.*

Onions have a long and illustrious role in human history. Egyptian mummies were sometimes buried with bandage-wrapped onions, ancient Egyptian leaders took their oaths of office with one hand resting on an onion, and the early Greeks and Romans prized onions so much that Olympic athletes drank onion juice and rubbed onions on their bodies before competing. The Romans also believed onions could cure vision problems, insomnia, dysentery, toothaches, canker sores, and dog bites. In many cultures, the onion's concentric circles represent eternity. Could there be a more enlightening vegetable?

open door **1.** Dreaming of an open door symbolizes an opportunity available to you right now. **2.** If you dream of opening a door, you are curious about something and ready to find the answer. **3.** If you dream of seeing an open door and walking through it, you have already decided to make a change. **4.** If you dream of seeing an open door and not walking through it, you still aren't sure whether something you are considering is the right decision. ☽ **locked out** ☾ *changing course, decisions, opportunity.*

opera Dreaming of opera means your life is full of drama right now. Do you enjoy it, or does all the hoopla bore you to tears? ☽ **monotony** ☾ *adventure, desires, extremism, music and sound.*

operation See *surgery.*

oral sex **1.** Dreaming of pleasurable oral sex suggests the physical urge for intimacy, a passionate need for communication in an intimate relationship, or the simple and straightforward desire for oral sex! **2.** Dreaming of giving someone oral sex suggests an intimate sensual awareness of someone else. **3.** Dreaming of receiving oral sex from someone suggests an intimate sensual awareness of your own needs. **4.** Dreaming of oral sex with someone you know but are not intimately involved with, or even attracted to, can feel embarrassing when you wake up, but it usually just means you need to be more open, honest, and communicative with that person or with someone that person represents. **5.** If an oral sex dream is unpleasant or nonconsensual, you feel unable to communicate important feelings in an intimate relationship. You might feel bullied, manipulated, overly vulnerable, or forcefully silenced. ☽ **impotent** ☾ *body parts, communication, control issues, desires, pleasure, sexual activity, vulnerability.*

O

orange **1.** Dreaming of orange food, orange furniture, orange dishes, or orange bedding, or eating a juicy orange, symbolizes a robust appetite, not only for food, but for other sensual pleasures. **2.** Dreaming of orange rooms or orange clothes symbolizes a passionate and rebellious personality. **3.** Dreaming of looking at or peeling and sectioning an orange (the fruit) symbolizes a complex problem. You may be having a hard time seeing all the different facets because of your strong feelings. ☽ **green** ☾ *feelings, food and drink, fruit, desires, hedonism, pleasure, solutions and remedies.*

orchestra **1.** If you watch an orchestra performing in your dream, a recent project has come together successfully. **2.** If you watch an orchestra rehearsing, you are still trying to pull together all the pieces. **3.** If you play in an orchestra in your dream, your creativity plays an important role in a greater effort. See also *music, musical instrument.* ☽ **silence** ☾ *creativity, goal-setting, music and sound, relationships.*

orgasm **1.** If you dream of having an orgasm, your body may have needed to experience physical release, and you might really have had an orgasm. **2.** If you dream of having an orgasm in a sexual scenario with someone other than your partner, don't worry. You haven't cheated! Your dream has simply provided a context for your physical release that includes someone recently in your nonsexual thoughts, crossing off several subconscious issues with one stroke (so to speak). The person you dreamed about either is relevant to some other aspect of your life or represents something relevant to your current concerns. **3.** If you dream of having an orgasm in response to a totally nonsexual situation, your dream has provided much-needed emotional or mental release in response to a complex and tense issue in your waking life. You can take only so much pressure! ☽ **impotent** ☾ *anxiety, feelings, relationships, sexual activity, solutions and remedies.*

orgy **1.** Orgy dreams can act out a secret fantasy, even if you would never join in on an orgy in your waking life. Remember, fantasy is not the same as true desire. Orgy dreams let you burn off excess sexual energy by imagining indulging in multiple attractions all at once, acting with hedonistic abandon, or experimenting beyond your normal partner. **2.** If orgy dreams make you uncomfortable, they may signal discontent with your current relationship. You may be dreaming of qualities you need in a partner that you aren't getting. Or you might be fearful that you really might stray. **3.** Stressful or disturbing orgy dreams or orgy dreams that make you feel jealous often play out anxieties you might have about the influence of other people in your personal relationships—a "too many cooks spoil the broth" sort of scenario. Do you fear other people lurk emotionally within the intimate boundaries of your relationship? ◔ **loneliness** ℂ *anxiety, creativity, envy, hedonism, pleasure, sexual activity, social life.*

orphan **1.** If you dream of meeting or finding an orphan, you've picked up where someone else left off in a current project or social situation. You've done a good deed that can benefit you as well. **2.** If you dream of adopting an orphan, you feel the need to take care of others, and you need more people or pets to nurture. **3.** If you dream you are an orphan, you feel isolated from or misunderstood by your family. You don't feel like you belong in their circle the way you once did. ◔ **family** ℂ *caretaking, characters, family, isolation, loss, people.*

Ouija board You might have played it at slumber parties back in school, but if you dream about a Ouija board, your recent thoughts about someone who has died or passed out of your life still haven't left you. You wonder if someone is trying to send you a message, or you miss someone so much that you wish that person would send you a message. You are hungry for communication that you believe to be logically impossible. ◔ **death** ℂ *communication, death, inanimate objects, loss, messages, myths and legends, shapes and symbols, wishes.*

oval Ovals symbolize creation, birth, and female energy. In ancient cultures, ovals represented the female genitals or the shape of an egg—the female's contribution to the creation of life. If you dream of oval shapes, you are in an intense creative period right now, possibly even tapped into a divine source of creative energy, and you are exuding strong sexual, fertile, or creative signals. You are ready to make *something* wonderful. So why is there an Oval Office in the White House? ◔ **square** ℂ *body parts, creation, creativity, divine power, goal-setting, sexual activity, shapes and symbols.*

oven **1.** Using an oven in your dream suggests transformation, a maturing of the creative process, and a finishing of a project. Something is coming to an end … and it smells delicious! **2.** If you dream of leaving the oven on and causing a fire or other dangerous situation, you have been so absorbed in a project that you have neglected the basic needs of others or yourself. ◔ **refrigerator** ℂ *caretaking, creation, danger, furniture and appliances, goal-setting, heat, journeys and quests, solutions and remedies, success, transformation, work.*

overflowing **1.** If something wonderful overflows in your dream—bowls of food, cups of wine, pots of gold, beautiful fountains, treasure chests, feelings of joy—you are enjoying abundance right now, an overflowing of resources or emotions. **2.** If something overflows resulting in destruction or disaster—an overflowing toilet or bathtub, a flood,

O

bugs or dirt—you've let a situation go too far, and it's time to rein it in. This dream is a warning. ☯ **empty** ☾ *abundance, destruction, disaster, feelings, financial resources, pleasure.*

owl   The wise old owl, an ancient symbol of both wisdom and darkness, can be an omen of death, change, or loss, as well as a reminder to use your head in an emotional situation. Some cultures believe the owl is the goddess of night or an incarnation of death, or protection from death. Most cultures attribute some spiritual significance to owl dreams, so some important aspect of your spiritual life may be relevant to consider if you dream about an owl. ☯ **dove** ☾ *animals, birds, changing course, death, divine power, knowledge, intuition, loss, nature, predictions, protection, spirituality.*

oysters   An aphrodisiac if you eat them and a symbol of passionate female emotion if you find them, oysters symbolize love and desire in its most feminine incarnation. If you dream of oysters, your own female energy is keyed up, or you are particularly in tune with someone else's female energy. ☯ **bull** ☾ *animals, desires, feelings, feminine, food and drink, nature, pleasure, sexual activity, water.*

package Are you all wrapped up in something, and you can't think outside the box? **1.** If you dream of receiving a package, you are expecting something to happen soon. **2.** If you dream of sending a package, you are expecting to make something happen soon. ☽ **inaccessible** ℭ *goal-setting, inanimate objects, predictions, taking action.*

Many dreams about a mysterious package, unopened envelope, present, treasure chest, safe, or container with unknown contents invoke the myth of Pandora's box and could be interpreted as a test of the dreamer: are you a risk taker, craving intense life experience, or a caretaker, putting safety for yourself and others ahead of the thrill of discovery? In the myth, Pandora's box contained evil, and Pandora was charged not to open it, but her curiosity got the better of her. One peek, and she unleashed evil upon a formerly perfect world. Any unopened container carries with it that risk—does it contain treasure or tragedy?

packing for a trip Dreaming of filling up that suitcase and gathering your travel-size toiletries together? You're planning to make a change, even if it doesn't involve a change of location (although it might). You are getting all your ducks in a row so you can be mentally and emotionally prepared. ☽ **homebody** ℭ *adventure, changing course, clothing and accessories, taking action, transformation, travel.*

pain **1.** Dreaming you are in physical pain could be a sign from your body that something needs attention. Pain is like an internal alarm system, so you may feel threatened or endangered, physically or emotionally. **2.** Dreaming of emotional pain lets you experience a feeling you are afraid to let loose in your waking life. **3.** Dreaming someone else is in pain suggests that you recognize someone needs your help, but you aren't sure what to do about it. ☽ **ecstasy** ℭ *body parts, caretaking, danger, fear, feelings, health and hygiene, injuries, pain, senses, threats.*

painting   **1.** Dreaming of the act of painting means you are visually tuned in to something right now—you notice beauty, color, pattern, texture. Your creativity is manifesting itself in visual ways. **2.** Dreaming of watching someone else painting suggests you envy or appreciate another person's creativity. You might even be getting some good ideas. **3.** Dreaming of looking at a painting suggests you appreciate the beauty in someone or something. In fact, appearance could be this person's or thing's most important quality to you. **4.** Dreaming of an ugly painting suggests that something you made or thought of didn't come out as well as you would have liked. **5.** Have you painted yourself into a corner? ☽ **manuscript** ☾ *beauty, creation, creativity, envy, goal-setting, image, inanimate objects, work.*

pajamas   **1.** Wearing your pajamas in public? This dream means you're sick of responsibility or formality and you just want to take it easy for a while, but nobody seems to be cooperating. **2.** Wearing your pajamas at home? Your body is telling you that you aren't getting enough sleep. How about turning in early tonight? **3.** If you dream of someone else wearing pajamas in an inappropriate situation, you haven't consciously noticed that somebody is having problems coping with something. Maybe you can help relieve some of his or her burden. ☽ **tuxedo** ☾ *caretaking, clothing and accessories, desires, escapism, frustration, health and hygiene, solutions and remedies.*

palm reading   Having your palm read in real life suggests a willingness to explore your inner motivations and tendencies, and dreaming of having your palm read suggests a less conscious, more intuitive desire to discover who you really are and where you are going. The results of your dream palm reading could shed some light on what you really think about your own personal life's journey right now. See also *fortune teller.* ☽ **science experiment** ☾ *body parts, identity, intuition, journeys and quests, predictions.*

palm tree   What you wouldn't give for a vacation in a tropical paradise right now … at least, that's what dreams about palm trees suggest. Exotic, stress-free destinations are calling your name. ☽ **snowman** ☾ *caretaking, escapism, nature, plants, travel.*

pandemic   See *disease.*

panic   Don't panic! Oops, too late. If you dream of feeling panic, you might really be suffering from anxiety, or you might recognize subconsciously that something really does need more urgent attention than you've been giving it. Have you forgotten all about something important? ☽ **relaxation** ☾ *anxiety, burdens, caretaking, danger, fear, feelings, responsibilities, threats.*

panting   1. Can't ... catch ... your ... breath? To dream of panting means you are too hurried or too worn out to be effective. It's time to take a break and cool off. **2.** If you dream of someone else panting, you have exhausted a resource. **3.** If you dream of a dog panting, your inner instinct is to take it easy. You've been a little too overexcited about something. ☯ **relaxation** ☾ *animals, desires, feelings, heat, instincts.*

pantry   The pantry symbolizes your material resources. **1.** If you dream of a full pantry, you have what you need to function and thrive right now. **2.** If you dream of an empty pantry, you aren't getting what you need to survive—at least, not emotionally. Your soul needs nourishment. **3.** If you dream of a pantry filled with rotten, spilled, or stale food, you have compromised your principles. It's time to stock up on the real you. ☯ **starvation** ☾ *abundance, buildings and rooms, caretaking, ethics and morals, food and drink, financial resources, places.*

parachute   1. If you dream of watching someone falling through the air with a parachute or seeing an inflated, billowing parachute, you've got a dream, and you put much emotion and hope into that dream. You just know it will happen. **2.** If you dream you are wearing or using a parachute, you are ready to take action to make your dream a reality. **3.** If you dream of a deflated parachute or a parachute on the ground, you've lost hope in a dream. See also *falling.* ☯ **losing** ☾ *desires, hopes and dreams, predictions.*

parade   1. Are you the leader of a parade in your dream? Others look to you for direction right now in a group effort. **2.** If you are in a parade following a leader, you look to someone else for direction. **3.** If you are in a parade but you can't find the leader and everyone is in chaos, your current project requires a leader so it doesn't fall apart. **4.** If you dream of watching a parade, you have a plan of action in mind regarding a group effort, but you aren't ready to put it into practice yet. ☯ **rebel** ☾ *authority, control issues, relationships, work.*

paradise   See *heaven, utopia.*

paralyzed   To dream you are paralyzed symbolizes inaction or intense fear. You are either unwilling or unable to move right now. **1.** If the dream is pleasant and easy, you are looking for an excuse to get out of your responsibilities. Have you become overextended? **2.** If the dream is scary, something has stalled you, and you aren't sure how to get started again. See also *running problems, spine injuries.* ☯ **running** ☾ *accidents, anxiety, body parts, escapism, fear, feelings, frustration, impediments, injuries, protection, vulnerability.*

P

Sleep paralysis is a relatively rare condition in which the brain activity that normally inhibits your body's movement during dream sleep doesn't switch off right away; as you awaken, you remain completely paralyzed. This can be extremely frightening, but it almost always fades after a minute or two. Sleep paralysis may be hereditary, but nobody knows for sure what causes it. Recent studies estimate that approximately 6 percent of the population has experienced sleep paralysis.

parents 1. Dream of your parents, and you are looking for guidance or direction. You want an authority figure. **2.** If you dream of being a caretaker to your parents, that you are one of your parents, or you are a parent to someone else, you have stepped up into that position of leader and guide to others. You are feeling awfully grown-up. **3.** If you dream of a parent who is dead or estranged, you feel that loss in your life and long for that missing connection because of questions about your own identity. You are seeking for yourself in a dream of your parents. ☪ **orphan** ☾ *authority, caretaking, family, identity, people.*

park 1. Dreaming of a small, pretty, well-manicured park represents an idealistic image you have of the way you want something to be. **2.** Dreaming of a huge, wild, or natural park symbolizes your desire to have adventures and dangerous experiences without getting *too* risky. **3.** Dreaming of getting lost in a park means you don't feel comfortable in your current environment. See also *amusement park.* ☪ **wilderness** ☾ *adventure, goal-setting, nature, places, protection.*

parking lot or garage 1. If you dream of a parking lot or parking garage, you are waiting for something in a protected state. You aren't quite ready to move yet. **2.** If you dream you can't find your car in a parking lot or parking garage, your project is stalled. You can't seem to get going. ☪ **highway** ☾ *impediments, stasis, places, protection, vehicles.*

parking meter 1. If you dream of putting money into a parking meter, you have only so much time to do something important. Don't forget to watch the clock. **2.** If you dream your parking meter runs out, it's time to take action. ☪ **stalling** ☾ *goal-setting, taking action, time.*

parking ticket 1. Dream you get a parking ticket, and you've acted irresponsibly. You took too long to get something done, or you forgot to take care of the details. **2.** Dream of giving someone a parking ticket, and you feel resentful that someone else has shirked their responsibility. **3.** Parking meter ticket dreams are so minute compared to all your other important dreams, just ignore them … like you may be tempted to do with the actual tickets! ☪ **graduation** ☾ *punishment, responsibilities, rules and laws.*

party   Party dreams represent your current social status and outlook regarding socializing. If the party in your dream is wild and crazy, subdued and classy, or mind-numbingly boring, that's exactly how you view your current social life. It's hard to get up and go to work after partying all night in your dreams. ☻ **loneliness** ℂ *celebration, fun, extremism, food and drink, hedonism, people, relationships, social life.*

passenger   To dream you are a passenger in a vehicle someone else drives—a car, a boat, a motorcycle, or whatever it is—symbolizes your recognition that someone else is in charge and controls, at least in some ways, where you are going. If you worry that the driver isn't doing things right or you get irritated or upset about where the vehicle is going, the passenger role makes you uncomfortable. You'd rather be in charge. If you enjoy the ride, you like someone else steering … at least, once in a while. ☻ **driving** ℂ *authority, control issues, people, rebellion, relationships, travel, vehicles.*

passport   You've got wanderlust, and you crave adventure beyond your ordinary life if you dream of a passport. Or you're concerned about being able to get out of the country fast. ☻ **homebody** ℂ *adventure, anxiety, changing course, rules and laws, travel.*

past life   **1.** If you dream of a past life, some people believe you really are remembering an actual past life. This is one way to explain fears, anxieties, or passions with no obvious basis in your current life experience. **2.** Past life dreams can also symbolize things you've left behind. Just because you aren't that person or you aren't in that place in your life anymore doesn't mean those images and feelings don't still exist somewhere deep inside you. **3.** Past life dreams often (ironically) symbolize your desires for the future—what you dream you were is actually what you wish you could become. ☻ **fortune teller** ℂ *history, identity, memory, myths and legends, repression, spirituality, time, wishes.*

pasta   **1.** Dreams of eating pasta symbolize a desire for comfort. You need to feel good and pamper yourself, and a little dream comfort food is just the ticket. **2.** Eating pasta with someone else in a dream means that person or someone that person represents makes you feel comfortable or happy. Have you ever done that thing where you each start eating one end of the spaghetti strand till your lips are together? Now, that's romantic dining! **3.** Cooking pasta or serving it to others means you have created a comforting environment for your friends and/or family. ☻ **vegetables** ℂ *caretaking, comfort, food and drink, home.*

pastry   See *dessert.*

P

path Dreaming of a path symbolizes your life path, not in a long-term, big-picture way, as a dream about an interstate or large street might imply, but where you are going right now in your daily life and where your current thinking and behavior are leading you. If the path is beautiful, pleasant, or interesting, you are on a good path. If the path is scary, dangerous, or ugly, the things you are doing right now in your life may be leading you in a direction you don't really want to go. ☾ **dead end** ☾ *direction, journeys and quests, travel.*

patient **1.** If you dream you are a patient in a hospital, or even in a doctor's office, and you are facing a procedure, surgery, or other treatment, you feel vulnerable because of an inner physical or emotional imbalance. **2.** If you dream you are trying to make doctors or nurses understand something and they aren't listening, or you fear you are getting the wrong surgery or procedure, you feel powerless in the face of some authority figure that doesn't have your best interest, or any interest in you at all, in mind. Do you have health insurance? **3.** If you dream that you are a patient and you feel safe and protected in a hospital, or a doctor or nurse is taking good care of you, you have decided to address an inner imbalance or problem. You are taking action. And you probably have health insurance. **4.** If you dream you are being, or feeling, patient in a dream, you can wait for something you want. Your dream is showing you how. ☾ **doctor** ☾ *authority, caretaking, characters, feelings, healing, health and hygiene, people, protection, solutions and remedies, taking action, vulnerability.*

peace See *nonviolence.*

pear Pears represent the female form, feminine energy, and sensual pleasures. **1.** If you dream of eating a pear, you delight in sensuality, and your sensual energy attracts others. You either project or seek feminine sensuality. **2.** If you dream of giving a pear to someone else, you desire someone. **3.** If you dream of picking a pear off a tree or selecting a pear in a grocery store, you are in the market for a love interest. Sounds like Eve should have chosen a pear to tempt Adam …. See also *fruit.* ☾ **banana** ☾ *desire, feminine, food and drink, fruit, pleasure, sexual activity.*

pedicure See *manicure or pedicure.*

pendulum Pendulums represent balance and the answers to questions. To dream of a pendulum symbolizes your search for balance in your life. If you dream a pendulum stops, you already know the answer to the question you've been asking yourself. ☾ **question** ☾ *balance, predictions, solutions and remedies.*

An ancient divination tool, the pendulum is still used to answer questions or predict the future. Different people use different techniques, but one common method is to hold any kind of pendulum, such as a ring or pendant on a chain or string, in your nondominant hand (left hand for right-handed people). Put your elbow on a table, and hold the pendulum so it dangles over the surface. Concentrate and ask the pendulum which way it will swing for "yes." The pendulum will typically move up and down, side to side, or in a circular motion, clockwise or counter clockwise. When you are sure of the answer, ask the pendulum what it will swing for "no." It should move in a different way. Make note of these, then concentrate, holding your hand very still, and ask your yes-or-no question out loud or clearly in your mind. The pendulum will swing in the "yes" or "no" direction to answer your question.

penis See *sex organs.*

pepper Dreaming of putting pepper on your food or cooking with pepper symbolizes your desire to spice up your life. You wish things would get a little wild. ☽ **salt**
℃ *adventure, desires, food and drink.*

performing Do you love to be in the spotlight, or are you horrified by the idea? **1.** Dreams of performing to wild applause, praise, and worship by adoring fans—whether acting on a stage, jamming with a band, or even singing in church—suggests strong personal power and self-confidence right now. You know you rock, and you wish you had more chances to show the world. **2.** Dreams of messing up a performance or being terrified about performing suggest that you fear too much attention or focus on you, or you aren't confident enough in your abilities. Anxious performing dreams can also arise in response to worry over an impending high-stress event. ☽ **hiding**
℃ *adventure, anxiety, courage, creativity, desires, ego, hopes and dreams, image, music and sound, opportunity, personal power, success.*

perfume One of the most powerful and most overlooked of the senses is the sense of smell. Dreaming of odors and aromas usually signifies a strong emotion, memory, or response to an experience. They are quite diSTINKtive. Perfume dreams can conjure up something from your past, if the scent reminds you of a person or experience. **1.** Smelling a sweet, pleasant, or alluring perfume in a dream suggests desire and the allure of the slow seduction. **2.** Smelling an unpleasant perfume symbolizes an experience, situation, or person that is meant to attract you but is having the exact opposite effect. You are repelled. ☽ **stink**
℃ *desires, feelings, memory, pleasure, senses, sexual activity.*

period See *menstruation, punctuation.*

P

pet Pets you dream about but don't actually have in your waking life usually symbolize one of two things: an instinct you've tamed (or not) or a dependent you care for. **1.** If the pet is sweet and cuddly or interesting and rewarding, you crave the chance to nurture someone or something, or you fully relish your natural urges. **2.** If you mistakenly neglect or forget about a pet and it gets very sick or dies, you have been denying a deep inner urge, or you have been neglecting someone who depends on you. **3.** If the pet is dangerous or annoying, you've had enough of someone who keeps following you around, or you fear your inner instincts and can't seem to control them. **4.** If you are a lucky dog, you will occasionally dream about a pet you loved and lost. It's bittersweet. Also see type of pet, such as *birds, cat, dog, reptiles and amphibians.* ☽ **wildlife** ☾ *animals, caretaking, desires, instincts, nature, relationships.*

phallic symbol Phallic symbols are any objects that resemble the male genitalia: bananas, obelisks, skyscrapers, even swords and guns. To dream of an object that seems to you, upon waking, to be a phallic symbol suggests that you either admire, desire, envy, or fear male sexual energy—it all depends on whether your dream perception of the object is positive and passionate, anxious and jealous, or fearful and threatened. See also *sex organs.* ☽ **goddesses** ☾ *body parts, code, desires, gender issues, inanimate objects, masculine, pleasure, sexual activity.*

pharmacy **1.** Browsing through a pharmacy in your dream suggests you are looking for ways to improve your health or alter your mood, and you hope there is an easy solution. **2.** Dreaming of ordering or picking up a prescription at a pharmacy means you have the solution to a problem all worked out. **3.** If you dream you work in a pharmacy, you rely on conventional, ready-made solutions to your problems. You figure that if something has been proven to work, why get creative? ☽ **disease** ☾ *changing course, conformity, healing, health and hygiene, places, solutions and remedies.*

phobia See *fear.*

phone Dreaming of this most basic form of electronic communication suggests a need for basic communication. **1.** If you dream of answering the phone, you need to listen to what someone is telling you. **2.** If you dream of calling someone on a phone, you are getting ready to talk to someone about something important, and your dream is helping you to prepare for making this connection. **3.** If you dream of not answering a ringing phone, you know perfectly well that someone is trying to get your attention. You're just not willing—or able—to give it right now. **4.** If you dream of calling someone and not getting any answer, someone isn't willing to listen to you. A more direct approach might work better. ☾ **mute** ☾ *communication, electronics, inanimate objects, relationships, social life, technology.*

phone number If you dream of a phone number, you are probably dreaming of an actual number you've seen before that has been stored in your subconscious mind. But what—or whom—does the number represent? It could be an actual phone number, a birthday, another significant date, an address, even a social security number, morphed into phone-number shape for dream purposes. Whatever it is, it signifies a person or an event, a winning lottery number, brought forward in your mind due to some trigger in your waking life. ☾ **letter** ☾ *code, communication, shapes and symbols.*

phone sex **1.** Dreaming of having phone sex is much the same as dreaming of online sex. You desire someone or crave the thrill of sexual stimulation, but you don't want to get *too* involved with the actual flesh-and-blood reality of a relationship. **2.** Dreams of phone sex could symbolize longing for someone you can't actually have because they are too far away or unavailable. **3.** Maybe you find communication sexy! ☾ **marriage** ☾ *communication, desires, love, relationships, sexual activity, social life, technology.*

photograph **1.** To see a photograph in your dream suggests you have taken a mental snapshot of a person or image that you need to remember or notice right now. **2.** If you take a photograph, dream you are a photographer, or meet a photographer in your dream, you should be visually tuning in to your world. Your dream is telling you that there is something in your life right now you need to *see*, especially if it's a digital photograph. ☾ **vision problems** ☾ *beauty, image, memory, senses.*

piano This majestic and complex instrument symbolizes the intricate interplay of subtle communication signals or the expression of multilayered desire—or both. **1.** If you dream of playing the piano, you have something out of the ordinary and artful to express to someone or to the world. **2.** If you dream of listening to someone else play the piano, you appreciate someone's beauty, talent, or complexity. **3.** If you dream of moving a piano, you face a monumental and complicated task. You won't be able to do this alone. ☾ **deafness** ☾ *beauty, communication, creativity, desire, inanimate objects, listening, messages, music and sound, pleasure, senses.*

pickup truck See *trucks and semis.*

picnic **1.** To eat food in the great outdoors symbolizes your desire to make the natural world more a part of you … but in a civilized sort of way. You romanticize nature, and you picture an idyllic view of you in the natural world unbothered by dangers or lacking in resources.

P

2. If you dream of having a picnic with others, you have, or crave, a rewarding relationship with family and friends, and you may even romanticize those relationships. You long for perfection. 3. To dream of a picnic gone awry—ants, rain, spoiled food—suggests that your vision of the perfect family or perfect romance has recently been disappointed (as dreams of perfection usually are). ☽ **restaurant** ℭ *abundance, family, food and drink, hopes and dreams, love, nature, relationships.*

pier Stretching out into the water, piers represent the efforts we make to reach out emotionally to others. **1.** If you dream of standing on a pier, you are trying to make a connection with someone. **2.** If you resist going out on a pier, you resist making that connection. **3.** If you stand on a pier with someone else, you have an emotional bond with that person or someone that person represents. ☽ **camel** ℭ *feelings, places, relationships, water.*

piercing **1.** Getting something pierced in your dream? Piercing dreams symbolize a longing for life experience—or, at least, the reputation for having had life experience. You want to feel strong emotions, have adventures, rebel, even be seen as a dangerous character. **2.** Piercing dreams can also represent a strong desire to feel when your emotions seem dull and your life seems uninteresting. **3.** If you dream of giving a piercing to someone else, you play a significant role

in someone else's emotional growth. **4.** An infection after a piercing may mean you've not thought through your plan of action, or there is some dishonesty—something is not clean or pure, as you'd hoped it might be. See also *belly button, ear.* ☽ **healing** ℭ *adventure, body parts, danger, desires, rebellion, relationships, reputation, senses.*

pig **1.** Pigs represent slovenly habits and greed, hedonistic behavior, excessive consumption, and decadence, or good luck and financial prosperity, depending on whether the pig or pigs in your dream seem dirty and gluttonous or clean and well cared for. **2.** If you actually touch, talk to, or have a pig as a pet in your dream, you have used your intelligence to overcome your bad habits. **3.** If you dream of cooking or eating pork, you put pleasure before conformity, so pig out. ☽ **bread** ℭ *abundance, addictions, animals, financial resources, food and drink, greed, health and hygiene, hedonism, intelligence, nature, pleasure.*

pigeon **1.** If they act as pests, appear in large groups, or steal food in your dream, pigeons represent your own or other people's greed, mob mentality, bad hygiene, or mental instability. Sound like an Alfred Hitchcock film? **2.** If you dream of sending or receiving a message via carrier pigeon, a current communication is working. **3.** If you dream of keeping pigeons as pets or finding a tame pigeon, your gentle way has charmed someone. ☽ **dove** ℭ *animals, anxiety,* communication, conformity, greed, health and hygiene, messages, nature, relationships.

> New Yorkers may call pigeons "rats with wings," but the pigeons so common in cities are actually feral rock doves. Pigeons have a reputation for being messy, greedy, pushy, and pests, while doves have a reputation for beauty and peace, and are seen as messengers from God. Witness the power of good PR!

pillow Lie down and relax. You don't need to take action right now if you dream about your pillow. You just need to relax or get some more sleep. Pillows encourage thought before action. Then your course of action will be clear. ◐ **moving** ℂ *inanimate objects, solutions and remedies, stasis.*

pills Pills represent solutions, quick-fixes, panaceas in a tiny package. You long for an easy answer or cure to your problem if you dream of taking a pill. See also *drugs, medicine.* ◐ **fight** ℂ *addictions, health and hygiene, medicine and surgery, solutions and remedies.*

pilot 1. To dream of a pilot suggests you have a plan to go somewhere, either literally or metaphorically, in your life. You are ready to soar within the structure of your plan. 2. To dream you are a pilot symbolizes your controlling role in your own destiny. You know

what you want, and you know how to make it happen. 3. To dream something happens to the pilot to put an aircraft in danger symbolizes your lack of confidence in the authority figures that control your life or current situation. ◐ **passenger** ℂ *authority, career, changing course, characters, control issues, goal-setting, journeys and quests, people, travel.*

pimp 1. Dreaming of a pimp suggests someone is taking advantage of you or someone you care about. 2. Dreaming you are a pimp suggests the person taking advantage of someone is *you* and/or that you are getting a bad reputation as someone who takes advantage of others for personal gain. 3. Are you overaccessorized? Is your bling at the expense of someone else or more show than substance? ◐ **prostitute** ℂ *career, characters, control issues, financial resources, people, relationships, reputation, risky behavior.*

pimples See *acne.*

pink Noticing the color pink in a dream symbolizes optimism, cheerfulness, innocence, and youth. Pink can also represent female sexuality. The brighter or deeper the shade of pink, the less innocent and more passionate and sexual the symbolism. ◐ **green** ℂ *age, color, feminine, innocence, sexual activity.*

pirate 1. Aargh! If you dream of pirates—calling Captain Jack Sparrow—you crave adventure,

P

travel, and a life of rebellion outside of the norms of society. You get a thrill from the thought of such an extreme existence, especially if you are one of the pirates. **2.** If you get attacked by pirates in a dream, you fear those very forces that encourage some to live beyond rules or those that use violence to take things from others. ☽ **homebody** ☾ *adventure, career, characters, courage, danger, desires, escapism, extremism, fear, freedom, greed, people, rebellion, risky behavior, rules and laws, travel, violence.*

planets other than Earth **1.** To dream of seeing other planets suggests a willingness to go beyond typical thinking to uncover a truly creative, even revolutionary, solution. **2.** If you dream of actually being on another planet and the dream is interesting or exciting, you crave adventure beyond your normal experience. You really want to push the atmospheric envelope. **3.** If you dream of being on another planet and being afraid or in danger, you aren't comfortable with a recent change in your life. You don't relate to this new situation at all, you even feel ... alienated. See also *Mars.* ☽ **homebody** ☾ *adventure, creativity, escapism, fear, places, solutions and remedies, travel.*

plastic surgery A dream of getting plastic surgery suggests you aren't happy with yourself and you feel the need to make a drastic change. **1.** Dreaming of a nose job suggests you feel insecure about the way you appear to others. You

don't like your image. **2.** Dreaming of a facelift suggests you have issues with aging. **3.** Dreaming of liposuction suggests you have body image problems, or you feel you are carrying too many emotional burdens and you wish someone could take them away. **4.** Dreaming of a tummy tuck suggests you feel emotionally vulnerable and you aren't sure how to express your feelings to others without help. **5.** Dreaming of breast reduction surgery suggests you feel self-conscious about your sexuality or feminine energy. You aren't comfortable being an object of desire. **6.** Dreaming of breast augmentation surgery suggests you feel like you don't have enough sexual or feminine sensuality and you don't know how to increase this quality on your own. You wish it was easy to make you feel more womanly. **7.** If you dream you are performing plastic surgery on someone else, you have been judging someone on appearances or putting pressure on someone to change. ☽ **nature** ☾ *age, anxiety, beauty, body parts, burdens, control issues, desire, feminine, image, insecurity, relationships.*

play acting To dream you are acting in a play means you want to be the center of attention but under the guise of an identity that isn't quite you. You have a role that works, and you want to try it out. Will you bring down the house or bring down the curtains? See also *audition.* ☽ **naked in public** ☾ *image, personal power, play.*

playground   **1.** Dreaming of watching a playground filled with children symbolizes contentment with the current state of your life. **2.** Dreaming of playing on a playground symbolizes a desire to return to a more carefree, youthful existence. Haven't you been letting yourself play very much lately? **3.** Dreaming of an empty or dilapidated playground suggests you mourn for your lost youth, or you feel like you can never recapture the innocence and fun you used to have. **4.** Dreaming of a threat to a playground—strangers, drug dealers, predators—suggests your fear or instinct that a child you are responsible for might be in danger or that your own innocence and youthful spirit might be endangered by external monsters on the playground of life. ◑ **office** ℂ *age, caretaking, escapism, fun, happiness, innocence, places, play, threats.*

playing hooky   Aren't you supposed to be in school … or at the office, acting like a grown-up? If you dream of playing hooky, you feel oppressed by your adult responsibilities and you wish you could just ditch it all and go have some fun. Maybe it's time for a day off. ◑ **working hard** ℂ *age, career, fun, play, rebellion, responsibilities, risky behavior, rules and laws, work.*

playing it safe   If you dream of playing it safe in a situation rather than taking a risk, you are playing out your inclination regarding how you want to handle a situation in your waking life. Your dream is suggesting to you that maybe this isn't a risk you want to take. ◑ **extreme sports** ℂ *caretaking, protection, responsibilities, risky behavior, stability.*

plumbing   The plumbing delivers water to all the right places, and because water usually symbolizes emotion, dreams about plumbing usually symbolize the way you are channeling and expressing your emotion. **1.** If you dream your plumbing is clogged, you are repressing an important emotion. You aren't even letting yourself feel it. If you don't release it, you might cause some damage to the whole system (the system being you). Use it or lose it. **2.** If you dream the faucets don't work, you haven't been able to express a feeling to someone else. Is it hot or cold? You might have tried to say something, but nothing comes out. **3.** If you dream your plumbing is leaking, you are feeling so much emotion lately that it is leaking into other areas of your life and affecting things it really shouldn't affect. Whether sadness, passion, or anger, your emotions could be hurting you. Let your head have a say in this discussion, too. See also *bathroom*. ◑ **construction** ℂ *feelings, buildings and rooms, repression, water.*

pocket knife   See *knife.*

poison   To dream of poison suggests something has gone horribly wrong. You've lost your trust or

P

confidence in someone, a situation is no longer safe for you, or a relationship or job has become toxic to your emotional health. **1.** To dream someone is trying to poison you suggests that you don't trust someone or suspect you've been betrayed. **2.** To dream of poisoning someone else suggests extreme anger at someone. **3.** To dream of finding poison where children or pets could have gotten it suggests your current environment is no longer safe for you or others. **4.** To dream of food poisoning is a message from your body to closely examine the effect your dietary habits are having on your health. **5.** To dream of environmental poisons like pesticides, herbicides, rat or insect poison, or other chemicals suggests you feel poisoned by the advances of the modern world, and you wish you could get back to a simpler, more basic, more natural life. **6.** To dream of getting bitten or stung by a poisonous animal like a bee, rattlesnake, or tarantula and injected with venom suggests distrust in your current work environment. You've been stung, and you don't feel comfortable as part of the team anymore. **7.** To dream of a poison plant like poison ivy suggests that a recent brush with nature has left you feeling frightened or anxious. You would feel much better safe inside your house. See also *bait, food poisoning.* ☯ **medicine** ☯ *anger, animals, caretaking, danger, fear, food and drink, health and hygiene, instincts, plants, threats, trust issues.*

poison ivy   See *poison.*

poker   Ante up. Poker dreams symbolize risks you are willing to take, often in the realm of your career. Are you a gambler at heart? **1.** To dream of playing and winning at poker suggests that you believe a risk you are considering will be worth it, or it has already paid off. **2.** To dream of losing at poker suggests that risk won't be worth it or already has resulted in a loss. **3.** To dream of bluffing at poker shows your inner courage … or rashness. You love the thrill of risk. **4.** To dream of cheating at poker symbolizes a lack of confidence in your own luck or a fear of loss. **5.** To dream of watching others play poker but not to play yourself suggests an unwillingness to take a risk. You'd rather wait and see what happens to others first. **6.** To dream of playing poker with someone you know suggests a personal contest or joint venture. You are both vying for top position or the most gain. Whoever wins in the dream suggests how you think this all might turn out. ☯ **playing it safe** ☯ *adventure, career, competition, dishonesty, ego, fun, loss, play, risky behavior, sports and games.*

police officer   **1.** Dream of getting stopped, interrogated, or arrested by a police officer, and you are probably feeling pretty guilty about something—or unjustly accused. What has got the dream police hunting you down? **2.** Dream that you are a police officer, and your sense of righteous indignation seeks a symbol or uniform. You feel responsible for making sure others behave as well and as responsibly as you do. ◑ **convict** ℂ *authority, career, characters, guilt, people, punishment, responsibilities, rules and laws.*

pollution   Dream pollution represents pollution in your own body or mind. **1.** If you see litter in a dream, your mind is littered with extraneous details, distracting thoughts, or addictions. You could be feeling and behaving much better. **2.** If you dream of smog, your health may be at risk. Bad habits—overeating, smoking, drinking too much alcohol, not getting enough sleep—may be having a tangible effect now. You might want to get your health checked and consider how to clean up your act. **3.** Dirty, polluted water symbolizes emotions clouded by anger or hate. You are having trouble forgiving someone, and it is hurting your progress in your own life. ◑ **cleaning** ℂ *addictions, anger, feelings, forgiveness, health and hygiene, nature, risky behavior.*

poltergeist   See *ghost.*

pomegranates   This ultimately sexy fruit is just bursting with seeds, and pomegranates, appropriately, represent fertility as well as desire and the transition from innocence to sensual experience. Dreaming of eating a pomegranate suggests you have a strong physical desire for someone or something. This isn't a childish whim; this is more akin to lust. Adam should have held out for a pomegranate. See also *fruit.* ◑ **vegetables** ℂ *desires, food and drink, fruit, hedonism, pleasure, sexual activity.*

The pomegranate's most famous appearance in mythology is in the story of Persephone and Hades. Hades, god of the underworld, admired Persephone's beauty and stole her away from her mother, casting the earth into cold, barren winter. Her mother, Demeter, god of the harvest and fertility, looked everywhere for her and finally found out from a water nymph what had happened. She traveled to hell to beg for Persephone's return, and Hades said Demeter could take her daughter back if she hadn't yet eaten a single bite of food in the underworld. Alas, Persephone had eaten a pomegranate seed—symbolic of a sexual awakening. She could never again be the symbol for pure, innocent spring. And yet Demeter struck a deal. Half the year, Persephone could come up to the surface, and the other half, she would live with Hades. When Persephone lives below, the world experiences fall and winter. When she returns, spring arrives, and the world wakes up and blossoms again. So if you don't like winter, you can blame that sexy little pomegranate seed.

pond   See *water.*

pornography   **1.** If your dream could put a porn flick to shame, don't be embarrassed. Dreams are the places where we can let go of our deep, inner, sometimes socially inappropriate instincts, and one of those very human instincts is the instinct to have sex. Even if the subjects of your adult film are not of romantic interest to you, dreams that seem pornographic simply release sexual energy using whatever images they can pluck from the top levels of your subconscious awareness. **2.** If your pornographic dream feels degrading or wrong to you, you may be working through some personal issues regarding sex. Do you feel objectified or mistreated by others? Do you fear intimacy and play a role in your sexual life to protect yourself rather than being yourself? Your dream is trying to coax the negative feelings into your conscious mind so you can work through them. **3.** If you dream of watching pornography, you may seek more adventure in your sex life, but you are still researching the subject. You aren't quite ready for …. Now just how did they *do* that move? **4.** If you dream of filming pornography, your sexual energy has begun to seep into other areas of your life. This could, of course, be a bad thing or a good thing, depending on who you are and what you do. ☻ **impotence** ℂ *addictions, desires, fear, guilt, pleasure, risky behavior, sexual activity.*

porpoise   See *dolphin.*

portal   Either you watch a lot of science fiction, or you want an easy way to escape to far away places if you dream of a portal (or a wormhole or other mode for time-space travel). See you last year. ☻ **home-**

body ℂ *adventure, escapism, time, travel.*

possessed by demons   Possession horrifies and fascinates us, maybe because so many movies have illustrated, in scary and gory detail, what it might be like. But rather than signifying some communication with evil forces, dreams of possession signify your awareness of the negative influences right here in the world that can change, corrupt, influence, or subtly sway people to do things they wouldn't normally do—addictive substances, peer pressure, excessive spending or eating or drinking, or whatever it is that has you in its evil clutches. **1.** If you dream of seeing someone possessed by demons, you suspect someone you care about is being negatively influenced by others, or the person in your dream could symbolize you. **2.** If you dream you are possessed by demons, you know, deep down, that something other than your own good sense and pure spirit has begun to take over what you do and who you are, but your fear and feelings of vulnerability keep you from knowing exactly how to stop it from happening. Your dream is trying to make sure you know what you are up against. It might be time for some reassessment, outside help, or a new group of friends. **3.** If your dream of possession truly scares you, your subconscious mind is urging you to take a close look at who you want to be and where you want to go. If these disturbing dreams recur and are troubling to you, consider seeking the guidance of a licensed psychologist to help you work through their meaning. ☽ **angel** ℂ *addictions, control issues, changing course, divine power, fear, insecurity, peer pressure, personal power, risky behavior, spirituality, threats, transformation, violence, vulnerability.*

possum   Dreaming of possums, which are nocturnal animals, suggests that you don't want anyone to see you. You feel like hiding out and being by yourself, and if anybody tries to get too close, you'll attack and they'll be sorry. ☽ **dog** ℂ *anger, animals, isolation, nature, secrets.*

postman   See *mail carrier.*

pottery   Traditionally, pottery represents your virtue, and chipped pottery represents broken resolve, moral degradation, and a loss of virtue. **1.** If you dream of beautiful, whole, artistic pottery, you have a strong, solid vision of your own values. **2.** If you dream of broken, chipped, or cracked pottery, you've strayed from that vision, or you never established it in the first place. See also *dishes.* ☽ **glass** ℂ *ethics and morals, inanimate objects, reputation.*

poverty   Millionaires … even billionaires … (yes!) dream of poverty. But this doesn't necessarily signify actual loss of wealth or even the fear of poverty itself. More likely, these dreams indicate poverty in some other area: are you lacking true friends, meaningful

connections, love, or passion for your work? (Who cares? You're rich!) Poverty dreams ask you to enrich some aspect of your life. See also *bankruptcy.* ☽ **rich** ℂ *changing course, failure, health and hygiene, financial resources, insecurity, loss.*

power failure   Dreaming of a power failure suggests literal low energy because of a health or emotional issue, a lag of energy in your career or a relationship, or a sexual low point. In any of these cases, the power failure is happening within. ☽ **power lines** ℂ *career, changing course, electronics, failure, health and hygiene, image, impediments, loss, personal power, sexual activity.*

power lines   **1.** Dreaming of standing under power lines suggests you have strong high energy right now. You can do big things … or accidentally hurt someone. Channel your crackling electricity wisely. **2.** Dreaming of downed power lines indicates a dangerous situation. Don't touch anything. Ground yourself. See also *electrocution.* ☽ **lazy** ℂ *accidents, danger, personal power.*

power tools   **1.** If you dream of using power tools—power saws, nail guns, electric drills—you are serious about getting something done. You have taken action. **2.** If you dream of someone else using power tools, somebody is taking over a project, whether you want that person to or not. **3.** If you dream of an accident with power tools, your harsh, fast, and sweeping efforts might result in someone getting hurt. Can you tone it down? See also *tools*. ☾ **lazy** ☾ *accidents, changing course, control issues, danger, electronics, inanimate objects, personal power, taking action, technology.*

praying   If you pray in a dream, does it count as actual praying? Maybe it does, but dreams of praying usually suggest your desire for the intervention of a higher power. You've recognized you can't do something alone. Dreams of prayer can also be a signal that you need to nurture your spiritual life a little more. You might be neglecting this important part of yourself. ☾ **curse** ☾ *communication, divine power, protection, spirituality, support.*

Many studies have been conducted to determine whether prayer affects health and healing, such as specific studies measuring the effects of prayer on fertility and recovery after surgery. While some studies show obvious health benefits in people recovering from surgery who are being prayed for by others, these studies have been linked to bad and sometimes even falsified research methods. Perhaps the studies, however, aren't the point. Praying does seem to have benefits for the person doing the praying, and a well-balanced spiritual life has been linked to greater happiness and health. In other words, it may or may not help others if you pray for them, but it will probably help *you*.

pregnancy   **1.** Dreaming you are pregnant can mean that you really are pregnant! Many women claim to have dreamed about their pregnancy before they knew for sure. This dream can also symbolize a strong desire for pregnancy, especially if you are currently trying to become pregnant. **2.** Dreaming you are pregnant doesn't have to mean you are *literally* pregnant. Often dreaming you are pregnant symbolizes the birth of an idea or some creative inspiration gestating within you. You are full of the creative force. **3.** If you dream your mother or sister is pregnant, this could represent your own pregnancy or desire for pregnancy. Or you could be predicting—that is, seeing—their coming pregnancy. **4.** If you dream of taking a pregnancy test, you are questioning the viability of an idea or artistic venture. The result of the test, if you dream of a result, signals your inner intuition about how fruitful the idea really is. **5.** Of course, dreaming of the results of a pregnancy test could also signal your actual status as pregnant or not pregnant. ☾ **contraception** ☾ *creativity, creation, desires, family, hopes and dreams, sexual activity.*

present   See *gift*.

president   **1.** Dream you see the president, and you've either recently experienced some brush with greatness or you are worried about some political issue. **2.** Dream you *are* the president, and you are planning to do something that will have a significant impact on people beyond your immediate family and friends. You want to make a difference, or you crave power and influence and plan to move up in the world. ☽ **servant** ☾ *authority, career, changing course, people, personal power, taking action.*

pride To feel pride in a dream suggests a period of high self-confidence, or an excess of ego. ☽ **embarrassment** ☾ *ego, feelings, personal power.*

priest See *religious authority figures.*

prison See *jail.*

prisoner 1. Dreaming you are a prisoner suggests you really do feel trapped in some way in your waking life. Someone or something—a situation, a job, even an attitude—has got you feeling trapped. 2. If you dream you are holding someone prisoner, you are aware of, and perhaps not entirely comfortable with, your power over someone else. 3. If you dream you are a prisoner of war, you feel fearful about your general life situation, or you feel guilty about something you've done. See also *jail.* ☽ **breaking free** ☾ *anxiety, authority, characters, control issues, fear, freedom, guilt, impediments, isolation, people, punishment, rules and laws, war.*

privacy 1. If you dream of enjoying privacy in your dream, you probably don't get enough privacy in your waking life. Your dream is trying to show you what you need. 2. If you dream of privacy but feel ashamed of it, you are hiding something from others or yourself, and privacy is your excuse for getting away with it. ☽ **crowd** ☾ *control issues, desires, isolation.*

prom 1. Could you really be back at your prom again? Would you fit into that dress or tux again? If you dream of a prom similar to one you once attended, you are reliving old memories in a new way to incorporate them into your current view of reality or your own identity. Or you are working through issues from your school days you still haven't resolved, like you weren't asked to the prom. 2. If you dream of the prom but all your current friends are there, some part of you feels stuck in adolescence. Are your current friends or social pursuits too young for you? Or maybe that's just the way you like it—your friends now give you the same support and pleasure your high school friends once did. 3. If you dream of a prom entirely unlike any you ever attended (or you never actually attended the prom), how you feel about this prom experience in your dream symbolizes your view of your social or dating life right now. ☽ **not invited** ☾ *age, memory, identity, relationships, social life.*

promise 1. If you dream of making a promise, this promise symbolizes some commitment or resolve you've made in your waking life or a commitment or promise you intend to make. You are testing out how it feels first, in your dream. Look for clues surrounding the dream promise, which may, on the surface, seem totally unrelated to the promise it represents. **2.** If you dream of breaking a promise, you regret a commitment you've made, or you made a commitment but don't intend to follow through with it. See also *breaking something.* ☽ **infidelity** ℂ *decisions, ethics and morals, relationships, trust issues.*

proposal 1. If you dream of proposing marriage, you are considering a commitment or reflecting on a commitment you've already made. This could have to do with a relationship or something entirely different—an offer on a house, a promotion, an idea. How you feel about proposing in your dream reflects how you feel about this commitment. Does it feel good, wonderful, exciting? Or does it fill you with dread? **2.** If you dream of accepting a marriage proposal, you expect an offer—it might have nothing to do with marriage—and you plan to accept it, or you hope for an offer for something you want very much. It could be a relationship commitment, but it could also be something regarding your life or work. **3.** If you dream of turning down a marriage proposal, you aren't ready for a commitment to something or someone. You need more time. Possibly forever. **4.** If you dream of proposing an idea, a project, or an activity to others and everyone loves the proposal, you feel confident about your current direction. **5.** If you propose something and nobody likes the idea in your dream, you are rethinking a recent decision. The idea isn't working as well as it did in your head. See also *marriage.* ☽ **saying no** ℂ *decisions, desires, hopes and dreams, personal power, relationships, taking action.*

prostitute 1. Dreaming of seeing a prostitute may mean you are considering doing something you aren't sure is morally right. **2.** Dreaming of being with a prostitute suggests you've done something you feel guilty about or you are planning on doing something you could potentially feel guilty about. You are battling temptation, and you haven't quite decided which way you will choose to go yet. **3.** Dreaming you are a prostitute suggests you feel like people are taking advantage of you or appreciate you only for qualities you don't consider to be a reflection of the real you, such as your appearance or sex appeal. **4.** Dreaming you enjoy being a prostitute suggests that you have been romanticizing or obsessing over sex. ☽ **pimp** ℂ *career, characters, decisions, desires, ethics and morals, guilt, people, relationships, risky behavior, sexual activity, vulnerability.*

psychiatrist See *therapist.*

psychic 1. Dream of visiting a psychic, and you are eager to know what your future holds—you desire knowledge of what you can't know. **2.** Dream that you have psychic powers, and your dream may be nudging you to pay closer attention to your own natural intuition … and to your dreams. ☾ **past lives** ☾ *career, characters, intuition, people, predictions, spirituality.*

psychologist   See *therapist.*

public speaking   See *speaking in public.*

punctuation   Like a sign or a written message, noticing punctuation in your dream means you are receiving a clear code from your subconscious to your conscious mind. **1.** A period means you've said or done enough; it's time to stop. **2.** A comma means wait a moment before you continue; you might miss something. **3.** A colon means the answer is coming and you're ready for it. **4.** Quotation marks mean someone is telling you something memorable and you ought to listen. **5.** A question mark means you need to ask. **6.** An exclamation mark means speak up! What you have to say is important! ☾ **paint-ing** ☾ *changing course, code, messages, shapes and symbols, solutions and remedies.*

punishment   **1.** If you dream of being punished, you already feel guilty about something. **2.** If you dream of being unjustly punished, you think others are judging you unfairly. **3.** If you dream of punish-ing someone else and feeling justi-fied, your righteous indignation at the behavior of someone else is frustrated, and your dream is giv-ing you satisfaction. **4.** If you dream of punishing someone else and feel guilty, you've treated someone too harshly, or fear that you have. Some nights it's just hard to sleep. ☾ **reward** ☾ *ethics and morals, guilt, punishment, relationships, rules and laws, solutions and remedies.*

puppet   **1.** Puppets symbolize manipulation of you by others or of others by you, depending on who is the puppet and who is operating the puppet. **2.** Evil puppets symbolize fear of the unknown or supernatu-ral. **3.** Children's puppets represent innocence and play. ☾ **painting** ☾ *age, characters, control issues, fear, fun, inanimate objects, innocence, play.*

purple   Purple represents cha-risma, power, prestige, and spiri-tual enlightenment. And what was your favorite crayon? Favorite ice pop? Favorite eggplant? Favorite dinosaur? Purple. **1.** If you dream you are wearing purple, you have charisma right now. You can con-vince people of anything. **2.** If you dream of a purple room, you have an opportunity for a prestigious advancement. **3.** If you dream part of your body is purple or you have purple rays or halos around your body, you are on the brink of a spiritual leap. You will understand things in a way you never did before. **4.** If you dream someone else is wearing or emanating purple,

P

you are aware of—and admiring or jealous of—someone else's material or spiritual power. If the person is your parent or sibling, he or she might represent you. ☽ **yellow** ☾ *color, personal power, spirituality.*

purse   Your purse represents your personal life. In the 1950s, Art Linkletter was the first live show host to go out and interact with his audience, mainly women. They would let him look through their purses and pull things out that he couldn't believe anyone would carry around. It was hilarious! **1.** If you dream your purse is filled with money or treasures, you feel fulfilled and emotionally wealthy and/ or secure in your personal material resources. **2.** If you dream of losing your purse, you feel like you've lost someone or something very important to your inner sense of yourself. This loss has compromised your well-being. **3.** If you dream someone steals your purse, something has happened to make you feel unsafe or question who you really are. Your identity is threatened. **4.** If you dream someone looks into your purse and sees embarrassing personal items, you feel exposed. Someone has let out personal information. ☽ **hat** ☾ *clothing and accessories, feelings, financial resources, identity, inanimate objects, insecurity, personal power.*

In the Middle Ages, the purse—often worn attached to the waistband or belt—was a status symbol. The wealthy and privileged had fancy purses in expensive fabrics, like silk and fur, adorned with jewels. The less wealthy had less fancy and more utilitarian purses. Apparently, some things never change!

Q

quarry Dreaming of a quarry, where rock or other products are mined out of a huge hole in the earth, symbolizes the deep soul-searching or discovery process you are undergoing right now. You have been digging to discover the many layers and hidden treasures within you. **1.** If the quarry is dark or frightening in your dream, your journey of self-discovery may be frightening, too, as journeys of self-discovery often are. **2.** If the quarry is full of interesting things to see, amazing scenery, or great recreational opportunities—cliff diving, anyone?—then your journey into the fascinating universe of you has kept you vastly fascinated and wonderfully entertained. Did you realize you were so interesting? Fascinating, darling. Just fascinating. ☽ **sky** ℂ *adventure, fear, identity, journeys and quests, personal power, places.*

queen Dream queen. **1.** To see a queen in a dream signifies your admiration for and respect of a female figure in your life. You look to this person for guidance and as an authority figure. **2.** If you dream you are a queen, you have strong personal power right now and others look to you for guidance. They respect you even if they don't always like what you say. See also *crown.* ☽ **king** ℂ *authority, career, characters, people, personal power, rules and laws.*

question If you see a written question or hear a spoken question in your dream, this symbolizes an important question you have been asking yourself, something you really need to know. The dream question may not be worded like the real question you've been asking yourself, but it will contain symbols or represent the substance of your true question. ☽ **billboard** ℂ *code, communication, knowledge, listening, mystery, personal power.*

quicksand **1.** If you dream of sinking in quicksand, the stress is really getting to you. You feel overwhelmed, like you'll never get out of this fine mess you've gotten yourself into. **2.** If you dream of escaping from quicksand, you have a plan to solve a big problem of your own making. You might just come out of this one clean. **3.** If you dream

someone else is sinking in quicksand, you recognize someone else's
dilemma. Do you try to save that
person in your dream or watch him
or her sink? The answer suggests
how you'll react to this person's distress signals. ☯ **flying** ℂ *anxiety,
caretaking, danger, decisions, health and
hygiene, solutions and remedies.*

quitting If you throw in the towel
in your dream—quitting a job,
quitting a relationship, quitting an
idea—you are trying out quitting
to see what it feels like before you
give up on something in your waking life. How you react to quitting
in your dream suggests how you will
feel if you really go through with it.
☯ **contest** ℂ *changing course, solutions and remedies.*

rabbi See *religious authority figures.*

rabbit Rabbits symbolize timidity, intimacy, nurturing, and yes, of course, fertility. **1.** If you see a rabbit in your dream, you might be fertile right now. **2.** If the rabbit runs away or seems scared, you might need protection, or someone else might need your protection. **3.** If you dream you have a rabbit for a pet, you have a warm and fuzzy intimate connection with someone. ☯ **lion** ☾ *animals, caretaking, creation, desires, fear, nature, protection, relationships, sexual activity.*

rabies **1.** If you dream of a rabid animal, someone is dangerous to you right now and can't be reasoned with. Best to back off. **2.** If you dream of killing a rabid animal, you've made the best of a bad situation. **3.** If you dream a rabid animal bites you or you have rabies, you've been influenced by something that has led you down a wrong path. You need to escape the bad influence and spend some time healing before you can go

on with your life again. ☯ **lifeguard** ☾ *animals, danger, ethics and morals, healing, health and hygiene, threats, violence.*

race On your mark, get set .... If you dream you are in a race, you are feeling particularly competitive right now and pressured to succeed. **1.** If you are in a running race, you need all your wits about you, and your physical condition counts. Is your poor health putting you at a disadvantage? **2.** If you dream of racing in a vehicle, like a car or a bicycle, seconds count. You need to make something happen, and make it happen fast. **3.** If you dream of riding a horse or some other animal in a race, you can succeed if you use your natural instincts and enlist the help of trusted allies. **4.** If you dream of watching a race, you can succeed by examining the strategies of others before you. See also *contest, losing, winning.* ☯ **depression** ☾ *career, competition, control issues, ego, image, journeys and quests, personal power, sports and games, success, time, vehicles.*

raft   You're floating, and you don't seem to have much control over where you are going. Will you float forever? Rafts can symbolize a loss of control, putting you at the mercy of circumstance, or they can symbolize protection from the raging waters of emotional upheaval. **1.** To dream you are floating on a raft symbolizes your inability to affect your situation. **2.** If you feel safe on the raft, you are protected from the problems of others. **3.** If you feel helpless or struggle to survive on the raft, you are at the mercy of the metaphorical wind and tides. **4.** To see a raft floating without anyone on it symbolizes something or someone you've allowed to drift away. Have you been neglecting something? ❧ **coffin** ☾ *caretaking, control issues, inanimate objects, protection, responsibilities, water.*

rage   **1.** Dreaming of rage is usually a release of anger or high energy that you don't feel you can release in your waking life in a socially appropriate way. **2.** If you dream of someone else flying into a rage, you may fear someone's volatile or unpredictable behavior. **3.** If you dream of rage resulting in violence, you fear that a situation has gotten out of control because of extreme emotions. Someone might really get hurt if people don't start using their heads. **4.** If you dream of road rage, someone has blocked your advancement in your career or life and you feel angry about it, or you are impeding someone else's progress.

Take a deep breath, and approach the situation rationally. See also *temper tantrum.* ❧ **kissing** ☾ *anger, anxiety, danger, fear, feelings, threats, violence.*

railroad tracks   **1.** Gaze down a long set of railroad tracks in your dream, and you've got wanderlust. You are ready to set out for adventure. You want to travel. **2.** If you dream of getting stuck on railroad tracks when a train is coming, you feel trapped by a situation and you see no way out. If you narrowly escape in time, you already know the way out; you just haven't realized it yet. ❧ **dead end** ☾ *adventure, danger, escapism, impediments, places, travel, vehicles.*

rain   Rain symbolizes an outpouring of emotion. It might be grief or it might be joy, but most often, dreams about dreary rainy days signal sadness or depression. If you stand out in the rain, however, this means you are letting your emotions wash over you, and in feeling them, you can deal with them. That must feel good. If you watch rain through a window from inside, you recognize your sadness but you aren't really ready to deal with it yet, so you are still keeping it inside, staying dry. ❧ **umbrella** ☾ *feelings, water, weather and seasons.*

rape   **1.** If you have a frightening or traumatic dream of being raped, you may be transposing some past traumatic experience into this new context to help you deal with it, or you may feel seri-ously threatened by or distrustful of someone who has power over you. **2.** If you dream of being raped but the dream is romanticized and the dream excites you (don't be embar-rassed, this is a common dream), you have physical desires, but you don't want to take responsibility for them or you don't want to have to do anything about it. You want someone to sweep in and take all the power, and therefore all the blame for any "sinful" actions. Rape dreams can also be triggered by your waking-life attraction to someone you shouldn't be attracted to, such as someone who is married. **3.** Rape dreams can also be trig-gered by attraction to power or a desire to take a break from running everything and let someone else take control for a while. **4.** If you dream of raping someone, you have overstepped your boundaries and are taking advantage of a situation. **5.** If you are a rape victim in wak-ing life, recurring dreams may be a sign of post-traumatic stress; please consider consulting a licensed psy-chologist to help you. ◑ **rescue** ℂ *control issues, desires, fear, responsi-bilities, risky behavior, sexual activity, threats, trust issues, violence, vulner-ability.*

rash   1. Dreaming you have a rash suggests an internal imbalance. You may need to take better care of yourself, or you might be allergic to something in your environment. **2.** Rashes can also symbolize some-thing that has metaphorically gotten under your skin. Something

is bothering you, and you are trying to ignore it, but your dream is try-ing to get you to scratch that itch—or at least get some ointment for it. ◑ **health** ℂ *body parts, desires, health and hygiene.*

rat   1. If you dream of a rat, some-one in your life can't be trusted. That person will do anything to survive, even if it means you will have to go down. **2.** If you dream you have a pet rat, you are han-dling a current difficult situation with cleverness and skill. ◑ **dog** ℂ *animals, dishonesty, intelligence, nature, relationships, trust issues.*

rattlesnake   See *snake.*

reading   If you dream of reading, you are looking for an escape, or you seek information. What are you reading? The title might tell you something you really need to know. ◑ **math** ℂ *escapism, knowledge, mes-sages.*

reality show   Are you the new-est Survivor or American Idol? If you dream you are on a reality show, you might be watching too many reality shows, but, ironically, you also might desire an escape from your own reality. Whether you dream you are stranded on a desert island with attractive and competitive strangers, or you are doing your time on *Wife Swap* or *The Bachelor*, or chowing down on insects on *Fear Factor*, your reality TV dreams aren't reality at all, and that's why they make such good escapism. These dreams can also

R

reveal your inner exhibitionist and competitive spirit. If you find yourself thinking, "I could do better on this show than *that* girl or *that* guy," your dream might just give you the opportunity to prove it. ☽ **hiding** ☾ *adventure, competition, escapism, personal power, risky behavior, sports and games.*

rebel   If you dream of being a rebel, you want to break out of the mold or the monotony of your current life. You are tired of being part of the herd. ☽ **parade** ☾ *adventure, characters, conformity, people, personal power, rebellion, resistance.*

red   Passion, sex, fear, rage, violence ... red is the color of our deepest instincts, our strongest passions, our most outrageous desires, and our greatest fears. Pay attention to anything red in your dreams. This will be the thing you desire, hate, or fear the most—or maybe all three. See also *blood.* ☽ **green** ☾ *color, desires, fear, instincts, sexual activity, violence.*

Arguably the most powerful color, red symbolizes blood, instinct, inner urges, power, violence, and passion—all the really strong emotions. Many cultures believe red has a protective effect, repels evil, and imbues the wearer with power. Red is the color you really can't ignore.

---

red hair   Red hair represents nonconformity, rebellion, independence, strength, and sensuality. **1.** To dream you have red hair when you don't actually have red hair suggests that a rebellious and free-spirited part of you wants to come out (of the bottle) and play. You feel like breaking some rules. **2.** To dream of someone with red hair means you are attracted to someone who you believe can help you stretch the limits, push the envelope, and see life in a new and more exciting way. ☽ **brunette hair** ☾ *beauty, body parts, color, conformity, desires, personal power, rebellion, risky behavior, sexual activity.*

refrigerator   If you dream of looking into a refrigerator, you have been thinking about your personal assets lately. What do you have, and what do you need? **1.** Dreaming of a fully stocked refrigerator means you are enjoying a period of abundance right now, material or emotional. **2.** Dreaming of an empty, dirty, or broken-down refrigerator symbolizes a lack of resources. You don't have what you need to feel comfortable. **3.** Dreaming of standing in a refrigerator or in front of a refrigerator feeling the cold air means you need to cool off regarding a particularly emotional issue, or you are feeling an uncharacteristic lack of emotion. **4.** Refrigerators can also signal a sexual dry spell. ☽ **oven** ☾ *abundance, cold, feelings, financial resources, furniture and appliances, sexual activity.*

rehearsal   Dreaming you are in rehearsal for a performance symbolizes something you really are practicing or preparing for. **1.** If you keep forgetting your part, you are feeling insecure about your readiness for this upcoming event. **2.** If you sail through rehearsal, your confidence is high. **3.** If you realize you have missed rehearsal and it's already time for the performance, you are anxious about an important responsibility. ◐ **performing** ℂ *anxiety, courage, goal-setting, insecurity, personal power, responsibilities, success.*

reincarnation   If you dream you are reincarnated, you are ready to start something entirely new. You feel like a new person. Reincarnation dreams can also mean you have discovered a different side of yourself or evolved to see life, or just a particular situation, in a new way. See also *past life.* ◐ **death** ℂ *changing course, spirituality, transformation.*

rejection   **1.** Dreaming of being rejected expresses your fear of actual rejection by a person or in some area of your life, and it also helps you prepare mentally for the possibility of rejection. **2.** If you dream of rejecting someone else, you are practicing what to say in an upcoming situation when you already know the answer will be "Sorry, but no." ◐ **proposal** ℂ *anxiety, decisions, embarrassment, failure, fear, feelings, relationships.*

relaxation   Ahhh, it's time to relax—at least, in your dream. Dreams of relaxation are like a mental tonic for your stress level: they let you relax even if you aren't relaxing much during your waking hours. Dreams of lying in hammocks or on beaches, or nestled into cushy furniture really can be refurbishing. See also *hammock, island, vacation.* ◐ **panic** ℂ *escapism, feelings, healing, solutions and remedies.*

religious authority figures   For those raised in a religious environment, religious authority figures often pop up in dreams, sometimes as guides in times of spiritual or ethical confusion and sometimes as fearsome or even cruel authority figures, depending on your personal experience with religion. **1.** If you dream of a minister, priest, rabbi, or nun treating you kindly and giving you advice and guidance, inspiring you, forgiving your sins, or making you feel better, your spiritual side has stepped into your dream in the guise of a trusted figure to help you make a decision about your life. **2.** If the religious authority figure is cruel, frightening, or punitive, you may feel guilty about something you've done, or you might feel you deserve punishment. **3.** The religious authority figure can also symbolize other authority figures in your life: a parent, an older sibling, a mentor, or even the government. Your dream reaction to this authority symbolizes your feelings about authority in your waking life. **4.** If

R

you dream you have disappointed or neglected a religious authority figure, you haven't been giving your own spiritual life enough attention and respect. Your soul is giving you a little nudge so you don't forget about it. **5.** If you dream that a religious authority figure is acting inappropriately toward you, in a seductive or coercing manner, it could mean that you are afraid you are being taken advantage of by someone who should be more trustworthy. Are intentions pure of heart and soul? See also *church or synagogue, religious ceremonies.* ☺ **devil** ℭ *authority, career, characters, comfort, decisions, direction, divine power, ethics and morals, forgiveness, people, punishment, rebellion, spirituality, support.*

religious ceremonies If you dream of engaging in a religious ceremony, you need to have some kind of spiritual or ethical structure in your life. **1.** If you dream of taking communion, you crave direct experience with divinity. **2.** If you dream of getting baptized, you need to feel cleansed or forgiven for something you did. You want a second chance. **3.** If you dream of going to confession, you need to admit something to someone so you can get past it. **4.** If you dream of any religious ceremonies related to holidays, your life would be more fulfilling if you incorporated some ritual into it. You want this more than you might realize. ☺ **revolution** ℭ *divine power, ethics and morals, forgiveness, direction, solutions and remedies, spirituality.*

remembering So *that's* where you left your keys! If you remember something in your dream that you forgot about in your waking life, you might really be remembering the answer! Many claim to remember where they put things or important information in a dream. If you dream of remembering something that doesn't seem to bear any relation to your waking life, the dream symbolizes something you have forgotten and need to remember but haven't quite recalled. Like the string around your finger, your dream is reminding you that you need to remember *something*. Look for clues in the dream to figure out what it is. ☺ **amnesia** ℭ *intuition, memory, messages, secrets, solutions and remedies.*

remodeling your house Houses represent your life, and remodeling your house in a dream symbolizes your efforts to remodel your life, your image, your body, your attitude, or anything else intimately related to *you*. **1.** If the remodel goes smoothly in your dream, your plan for the new you is moving along nicely. **2.** If the remodel is a disaster, you may not be quite sure what you want to change about your life. Get a plan before taking action. Heck, get a lawyer. ☺ **homebody** ℭ *changing course, home, identity, image, taking action, transformation.*

reptiles and amphibians Dreaming of reptiles or amphibians, whether snakes, lizards, frogs, or newts, symbolizes deep instincts for survival unrelated to social propriety or responsibility to others. **1.** If you see a reptile or amphibian in your dream, some deep instinct urges you to take action for your own sake. You have to preserve yourself first if you are going to help anyone else. **2.** If you dream of catching or holding a reptile or amphibian, your explorations into your own deepest urges or your indulgence of temptation could result in health or relationship problems. Don't lose all sense of decorum; you still need to bathe and maintain your job and relationships. **3.** If you dream of a lizard's tail coming off or a snake shedding its skin, you are undergoing a transformation. **4.** If you dream a reptile or amphibian leaps away from you, you have a good opportunity, but you have to act fast or you will miss it. See also *snake, turtle.* ❧ **pet** ℭ *animals, crawling creatures, desires, health and hygiene, instincts, nature, opportunity, risky behavior, sexual activity.*

rescue 1. If you dream of being rescued, you feel trapped or unable to help yourself and you wish someone would get you out of the situation, or you don't want to take responsibility and you wish someone would sweep in and make it all better. **2.** If you dream of rescuing someone, you have a strong protective urge and you feel responsible for others. See also *hero.* ❧ **abandonment** ℭ *caretaking, responsibilities, risky behavior, solutions and remedies, taking action.*

responsibility See *taking responsibility.*

restaurant 1. If you dream of eating in a restaurant, you need a break from responsibility. You want someone else to serve you for a change. **2.** If you have a bad meal in a restaurant, others aren't meeting your emotional needs. **3.** If you dream you are working in a restaurant, you feel obligated to serve others. **4.** If you dream you own a restaurant, your existence nourishes many people, and they wouldn't know what to do without you. ❧ **picnic** ℭ *buildings and rooms, caretaking, feelings, food and drink, places, relationships, responsibilities.*

revolution 1. Forget the old regime; you're ready for an entirely new order! If you dream of participating in or leading a revolution, you are ready for a major change in your life or are ready to help change the world. You are feeling strong, powerful, and ready to take chances. **2.** If you dream you are the victim of violence due to a revolution, you fear the changes you are seeing in the world around you or in yourself or your own life. These changes feel threatening to you. ❧ **old-fashioned** ℭ *authority, changing course, danger, fear, personal power, rebellion, resistance, rules and laws, threats, transformation, violence.*

reward 1. If you dream you get a reward, you have done something that you personally feel deserves a little recognition. If you aren't

R

getting it in your waking life, your dream is giving it to you—an ego boost from your subconscious. **2.** If you dream of bestowing a reward upon someone else, you are trying to figure out how to express your appreciation to someone. ☯ **punishment** ℭ *celebration, ego, relationships, solutions and remedies.*

rich Dreaming you are rich symbolizes a desire for more material wealth or a recent feeling of prosperity. If you enjoy being rich in the dream, prosperity is headed your way—or you hope it is! If you don't enjoy being rich, your dream is nudging you to put your emphasis on securing less material wealth. Other things are more important. ☯ **poverty** ℭ *abundance, desires, financial resources, hopes and dreams, wishes.*

ring Will you marry me? Or are we just going around in circles? **1.** Putting a finger through a ring symbolizes sexual intercourse. **2.** Putting a ring on someone's finger means you are expressing your availability or desire for commitment in any form (not necessarily sexually). **3.** If someone puts a ring on your finger, that person—or somebody like that person—wants something from you. **4.** A ring of fire means passion burns inside you. Be cautious! Or write a great song, like June Carter Cash did. **5.** Walking or moving in a ring means you are going in circles. It might be time to approach the problem in a new way. See also *circle, jewelry.* ☯ **straight line** ℭ *control issues, desires, happiness, inanimate objects, love, relationships, sexual activity, shapes and symbols, wishes.*

> The wedding ring probably originated in ancient Egypt and was first made out of reeds and grasses. Metal rings with jewels were originally used not for marriage, but as a status symbol. Some people believe that we wear a wedding ring on the third finger because a vein in that finger leads directly to the heart.

ringtone Someone wants to tell you something. It's time to listen. A familiar ringtone means friends or family need you. An unfamiliar ringtone? Look for hidden messages. See also *cell phone, phone.* ☯ **silence** ℭ *caretaking, code, communication, listening, messages, music and sound.*

rip tide If you dream of swimming and being caught up in a rip tide, you are feeling an exceptionally strong emotion that you fear might carry you away, out of your rational mind and into some uncharacteristic behavior. Wall Street exec to surfer dude? Don't do anything rash! You aren't in control right now and your dream is warning you to be careful. ☯ **surfing** ℭ *anxiety, control issues, feelings, nature, risky behavior, water.*

river See *water.*

roach See *cockroach.*

road See *street.*

road rage See *rage*.

road sign See *sign*.

roadblock See *barrier*.

robbery See *crime, stealing*.

rock 1. If you dream of seeing a large rock, something is done and you can't change it. **2.** If you dream of holding a rock, you have the power to change something right now, but be careful: you also have the power to destroy. **3.** If you dream of standing on a rock, you are well prepared for a coming upheaval. ❧ **feather** ℭ *changing course, nature, personal power, stability*.

roller coaster Your life is full of ups and downs right now, so you hardly know how to feel. The roller coaster in your dreams symbolizes this time of emotional upheaval. Are you enjoying it with your hands in the air, or are you clinging to the bar for dear life? If it's the latter, it might be time to make some changes. ❧ **monotony** ℭ *adventure, anxiety, changing course, extremism, feelings, fun, personal power, risky behavior, stability, vehicles*.

roller skates or inline skates 1. If you dream of skating effortlessly on roller skates or inline skates, you are making swift and satisfactory progress at something you need to do. **2.** If you dream of falling or having trouble moving on roller skates or inline skates in your dream, you've made yourself out to have greater skills or knowledge than you really

do, and now it's beginning to show. Maybe it's time to do more research or practice more in your spare time. ❧ **stalling** ℭ *direction, fun, impediments, insecurity, journeys and quests, play, sports and games, vehicles*.

roof 1. If you dream your roof is leaking, the defense mechanisms you've erected to guard yourself from strong feelings are caving in, and your feelings are coming through. Best to deal with them now before the whole thing collapses. **2.** If you dream of standing on a roof and surveying a magnificent view, you have a strong sense of security and power right now, and people are looking to you for your vision and leadership. **3.** If you dream you are fixing or building a roof, you have taken on a new responsibility in your life, and it has given you structure and a feeling of maturity. ❧ **floor** ℭ *buildings and rooms, personal power, protection, responsibilities, risky behavior, stability*.

roots 1. If you dream of seeing tree or plant roots, you need to look at the cause of a current problem rather than the obvious symptoms. This goes deeper than you thought. **2.** Sitting amongst or on roots suggests great stability. You are in touch with your origins and it gives you a deep inner sense of stability and comfort. **3.** If you dream of tripping over tree roots, you won't feel comfortable until you understand how a situation began. ❧ **leaves** ℭ *comfort, knowledge, nature, plants, solutions and remedies, stability*.

R

rose An ancient symbol of the female, roses symbolize romantic love, passion, sex, and the female genitalia. Dreaming of a rose can symbolize romantic interest in someone, passion about a pursuit, or the desire for strong feminine energy. **1.** If you dream of giving a rose to someone else, you are expressing your desire for someone. **2.** If you dream someone gives you a rose, you have an admirer. Could you use a dozen? **3.** If you dream of pulling the petals off the rose, you are ready for physical intimacy. See also *flowers*. ☽ **dandelion** ℭ *desires, feminine, love, nature, plants, relationships, sexual activity.*

In Dan Brown's popular novel *The Da Vinci Code*, the rose symbolizes the sacred feminine, which was held in secret reverence after being repressed by patriarchal Christianity. The five-petalled rose, or cinquefoil, mentioned in the book really is a popular adornment in medieval churches. This five-petalled rose really was called the Rose of Venus because it imitates the shape of the perfect pentacle the planet Venus follows in the night sky (as described in the book). However, whether this was some heretical symbol of feminine power blatantly adorning the male-dominated medieval church is a matter of debate.

roughing it **1.** If you dream of roughing it and loving it, you need to simplify your life. Technology isn't making you happy. **2.** If you

dream of roughing it and hating it, you need to pamper yourself a bit. Fancy a pedicure? ☽ **luxury** ℭ *adventure, burdens, instincts, nature, sacrifice.*

running This is no time to sit around and dream of tomorrow. You need to get moving! **1.** If you dream you are running, you need to keep going with what you are doing. Don't stop now. **2.** If you dream you are jogging at a relaxed pace, you might need more exercise to help you feel better. **3.** If you dream you are running away from something, you really aren't ready to face a problem or situation right now. **4.** If you dream you are running to get to something, your goal is within reach. You can do it! **5.** If you dream of running in a race, you feel competitive with somebody. You want to win. See also *race, running late, running out of gas, running problems.* ☽ **stalling** ℭ *competition, control issues, escapism, goal-setting, health and hygiene, journeys and quests, solutions and remedies, sports and games.*

running late **1.** To dream you are running late suggests you feel pressure to get something done and anxiety about not fulfilling your responsibility. **2.** If you dream someone else is running late, you feel insecure about your importance to someone, or you feel frustrated about your inability to control someone. ☽ **taking responsibility** ℭ *anxiety, control issues, frustration, insecurity, responsibilities, time.*

running out of gas   If you dream your car runs out of gas, you don't have the energy left to help anyone until you replenish yourself. ❧ **full** ℭ *health and hygiene, vehicles.*

running problems   One of the more common dreams people report is of being unable to run or feeling like you can run only very slowly, as if something is holding you back. Any dream in which you are having running problems symbolizes anxiety about progress, inability to reach a goal, or frustration about circumstances beyond your control that are holding you back. You need to relax and consider a different approach if you want to get anywhere. Remember the fable of the tortoise and the hare? ❧ **running** ℭ *anxiety, competition, control issues, failure, frustration, goal-setting, impediments, peer pressure, success.*

rust   Rust symbolizes neglect and degradation, disease and aging. If you dream of rust, something is falling apart. It might be your health, your body, your feelings, your relationship, or even your personal possessions. What are you neglecting? ❧ **shiny** ℭ *age, caretaking, health and hygiene, relationships.*

R

S

sadness Dreams of feeling sadness suggest you are mourning something you don't consciously acknowledge in your waking life. Symbols or situations in your dreams can clue you in to what exactly has prompted this feeling. See also *depression*. ☯ **ecstasy** ℭ *feelings, loss.*

saint **1.** If you dream you meet a saint or a saint visits you and speaks to you, you have something very important to do that will help others, and you take it seriously. It might even be a divine mission. **2.** If you dream a saint scolds you, you know perfectly well that you haven't been behaving like you should, and you feel guilty about it. You might even think you deserve to be punished. **3.** If you dream you are a saint, you've done something above and beyond the call of duty, and you are giving yourself a little pat on the back. You really made a difference. ☯ **devil** ℭ *character, divine power, goal-setting, guilt, myths and legends, people, punishment, sacrifice, spirituality.*

salad If you dream of eating a salad, you need more vegetables in your diet. Or you, like Caesar, need to cleanse yourself, physically or emotionally, of past bad behavior. ☯ **dessert** ℭ *food and drink, health and hygiene, solutions and remedies.*

salon **1.** Dreaming of a luxurious day at the salon means you need to pamper yourself or pay more attention to your personal needs. Are you neglecting your body because you've been so busy or mentally involved with something? You need a little TLC. **2.** Salon dreams can also relate to your personal self-confidence and feelings of beauty. **3.** If you dream of being poorly treated in a salon, like when they rip your eyebrows off (hey, you ask and even pay for this), you may feel insecure or unattractive, and it is making you self-conscious. **4.** If you dream you get the royal treatment in a salon, your confidence is high. You feel pretty. ☯ **deprivation** ℭ *beauty, caretaking, health and hygiene, insecurity, personal power, places, solutions and remedies.*

salt Salt symbolizes basic survival needs and also flavor and interest in life. **1.** If you dream of putting salt on your food or adding it to food you are cooking, you have been taking steps to make your life more interesting. **2.** If you dream that you can't find the salt, you are missing an essential element in your life that is keeping you from functioning at your best. If you spill salt, it's still good luck to throw some over your shoulder. ☻ **pepper** ℂ *food and drink, health and hygiene, solutions and remedies.*

sand   1. Picking up sand or sifting it through your fingers in a dream symbolizes your preoccupation with time. You might feel your life is slipping through your fingers. You are concerned with aging, and you fear you don't have enough time to get something accomplished. **2.** If you dream of lying on a sandy beach or in the desert, you feel mastery over time. It has been temporarily suspended for you so you can relax. **3.** If you dream of getting buried in sand or struggling to get out of sand, you are panicked about being unable to get something done. You feel like it's too late and you've missed your chance, or something is holding you back so you can't do what you need to do. **4.** If you dream of building a castle or other sculpture out of sand, time is your plaything. You don't worry about it. You spend your time enjoying yourself, not worrying. **5.** If you dream you built something out of sand and it gets destroyed or washed away, you are mourning the days when you used to enjoy yourself. Now you feel too stressed out to spend your time the way you really would like to spend it. See also *beach, desert, quicksand.* ☻ **time travel** ℂ *age, anxiety, fun, impediments, time.*

Satan   See *devil.*

satellite dish   1. If you dream of a satellite dish, someone either physically or emotionally distant from you is trying to contact you or make an impression on you. **2.** If you dream the weather is interfering with your satellite dish reception, your bad mood or someone else's strong emotions are interfering with your communication in a relationship. ☻ **blackout** ℂ *communication, inanimate objects, relationships, technology.*

sauna   Sweating it out in a dream sauna? Your body needs deep inner cleansing because of a poor diet or other bad health habits, or you need to get out a feeling you've been holding in. Express yourself, and you'll feel like a new person. ☻ **freezer** ℂ *communication, feelings, health and hygiene, heat, places, solutions and remedies.*

saying no   "No!" Such a small word, so difficult for some people to say. **1.** If you dream of saying no, you might be practicing for real life. Your subconscious mind recognizes your need to take control of your own life, and that can all start with that one little word. **2.** If you dream of saying no to something you thought you wanted, reexamine your motives. Are you sure you

S

want this? Your dream is encouraging you to consider other options. **3.** Saying no in a dream to something you know is wrong, or wrong for you, suggests inner courage and the will to build up your own moral defenses against bad influences. You have integrity. **4.** If you dream of saying no to something you really do want, you fear getting what you want. What is holding you back from success? ☾ **proposal** ℂ *authority, changing course, communication, control issues, courage, decisions, desires, direction, ethics and morals, fear, impediments, opportunity, peer pressure, personal power, rebellion, resistance, sexual activity, social life, solutions and remedies, success, taking action.*

scars and scabs 1. If you dream you have a scar or scab you don't have in your waking life, something has hurt you or left a strong impression on you. You may have forgiven, but you haven't forgotten. **2.** If you dream that a scar or scab you really do have in your waking life is gone, you really have forgiven someone for something. You've healed. **3.** If you dream of seeing a scar or scab on someone else, you worry that you might have done something to hurt someone physically or emotionally, or you might be concerned that someone you care about has been hurt. See also *injuries.* ☾ **skin** ℂ *caretaking, forgiveness, healing, injuries, pain.*

school Could you really be in school *again?* We have all spent so many years in school that it's hardly surprising school crops up in our dreams. School dreams typically involve anxiety—being late for class, dealing with bullies, forgetting about a test—or nostalgia—old friends, good times, youth. **1.** If you dream of being in an old classroom or seeing old school friends you haven't seen in years, something has recently happened to make you feel like the person you felt like back in school. An old, unresolved issue or memory from those days has come to the surface recently in some other context, triggering a trip back in time. **2.** If you dream you are late for class, forgot a test, can't open your locker, or have some other school-related anxiety, some current situation in your waking life is making you feel like a nervous teenager. It might be a daunting new responsibility at work you aren't sure you can handle, a relationship that seems too mature or is moving too fast, or a deadline you can't imagine how you'll meet. This anxiety and feeling of insecurity has popped you right back to that angst-ridden teenager state of mind. **3.** If you dream of grade school, kindergarten, or school experiences from before the teen years, a recent experience with a child has triggered a sympathetic memory. ☾ **grown-up** ℂ *age, anxiety, buildings and rooms, memory, places, repression, relationships, responsibilities, time.*

school bus See *bus*.

science experiment **1.** If you dream you are conducting a science experiment, you have been thinking about trying something new in your life and wondering what the effects might be. You are looking at the prospect analytically (or with four eyeballs?). **2.** If you dream a science experiment goes horribly wrong— exploding beakers or laboratories, Frankenstein monsters coming to life and attacking you, Jekylls and Hydes, mutant creatures, or poisonous gases—you fear something new in your life isn't working at all the way you thought and has gotten out of your control. Now, that might be worth the dream! **3.** If you dream you are part of a frightening or intimidating science experiment, someone is treating you with analytical precision rather than warmth and caring, and you don't like it. **4.** If you dream you are part of an interesting science experiment that gives you some new power or positive feature, the future is your friend. You are constantly working to improve yourself in the newest and most cutting-edge ways (ouch!), whether through the latest diet or exercise craze, supplement regimen, or self-help approach. ❂ **magic** ℭ *changing course, control issues, fear, intelligence, relationships, solutions and remedies, risky behavior, technology.*

So many books and movies in our culture portray science experiments gone awry—from Mary Shelley's *Frankenstein* to *Spider-man's* Green Goblin—that it's no wonder these mutant creatures and frightening scenarios enter our dreams as sources of fear, invoking the mad scientist archetype and the fear of scientific progress superseding ethics and morality. We fear what we don't understand, and science often provides us with a context for those fears within our dream lives.

scooter **1.** If you dream of riding a scooter, your approach to a project is whimsical and youthful. **2.** If you dream of falling off a scooter or injuring yourself while riding a scooter, you haven't been acting your age, and you wonder if it is making you look silly. **3.** If you dream of seeing someone else riding a scooter, you admire someone's free spirit and wish you could be more like that person. **4.** If you see a scooter and nobody is riding it, you have an opportunity to do something fun. ❂ **walking** ℭ *age, fun, image, injuries, opportunity, play, sports and games, vehicles.*

scorpion Dream of a scorpion, and you don't trust someone, or you are in a dangerous situation. Watch your back. ❂ **rabbit** ℭ *animals, crawling creatures, danger, nature, threats.*

S

screaming   If you scream in a dream or wake up screaming, something has triggered severe anxiety or fear. See also *yelling*. ☽ **silence** ℭ *anxiety, communication, danger, extremism, fear, feelings, threats.*

scuba diving   See *snorkeling and scuba diving.*

sculpture   1. If you see a sculpture in your dream, it symbolizes and likely resembles—at least, metaphorically—something or someone in your waking life that you want to hold on to. 2. If you dream of creating a sculpture, you are using your creativity to add something wonderful to your current life. 3. If you dream of seeing a sculpture that is cracked or damaged, some important part of your life, something that adds to your enjoyment, is falling apart or changing. ☽ **painting** ℭ *beauty, changing course, creativity, inanimate objects, taking action, transformation.*

sea   See *water*.

séance   If you dream of being part of a séance in which you are trying to contact the dead, you have unresolved issues or something you want to say to someone who is no longer in your life (even if that person is still alive). In your dream, you are trying to conjure a way to express that unresolved matter. ☽ **darkness** ℭ *communication, death, repression, solutions and remedies, spirituality.*

secret   1. Whispering secrets to someone in your dream? You want to have a more intimate and private relationship with someone. 2. Hearing a secret in a dream suggests that you've recently gotten some privileged or private information. 3. Giving away a secret in your dream symbolizes your own distrust of yourself. 4. If someone gives away your secret in a dream, you don't trust someone to keep something private. You are playing out your worst fears. ☽ **gossip** ℭ *communication, embarrassment, listening, relationships, secrets.*

secret code   1. If you dream of seeing or trying to figure out a secret code, you may have a waking-life mystery on your hands. You don't know the answer yet, but you enjoy the quest. 2. Secret codes can also symbolize communication you don't understand. It's like someone is speaking a different language, and you just don't get it. 3. If you dream of cracking a secret code, you have figured out the solution to a problem using your own ingenuity. ☽ **billboard** ℭ *code, communication, intelligence, messages, journeys and quests, shapes and symbols, solutions and remedies.*

secretary   1. If you dream you are someone's secretary, somebody orders you around a lot or needs you to take care of many aspects of their life. If you enjoy the job in your dream, you don't mind this waking-life scenario one bit. If you resent or dislike the job, you've had enough of this treatment, and you are ready to quit. **2.** If you dream you are a secretary and you have a romantic or sexual encounter with your boss, you are attracted to people who have authority over you, or you are attracted to the idea of authority figures. **3.** If you dream you have a secretary, you feel important and authoritative. **4.** If you dream of a romantic relationship with a secretary, you feel attracted to someone who you consider to be beneath you in social or financial status, or you are simply attracted to the idea that people are below you in social or financial status. You are turned on by your own power. See also *sexual harassment*. ☻ **boss** ℂ *authority, career, caretaking, characters, financial resources, people, personal power, sexual activity, work.*

seduction **1.** Dream of seducing someone, and you desire or recognize that you have power over others, and this gives you a rush. **2.** Dream of seducing someone forbidden, such as someone who is married, and you feel like taking a risk for the sake of pleasure, even though you know you might have to pay the price later. This risk might have nothing to do with a romantic relationship. **3.** Dream of being seduced, and you desire a pleasurable release from responsibility. It wasn't your fault! You couldn't help it! You were seduced! ☻ **self-control** ℂ *personal power, pleasure, responsibilities, risky behavior, sexual activity.*

self-control **1.** If you dream of maintaining your self-control in the face of temptation, you are rehearsing for a temptation you know you will face. You want to stay strong, and your dream is helping you figure out how. **2.** If you dream of losing your self-control and doing something risky or uncharacteristically crazy, you feel so buttoned-up lately that your dream is giving you a taste of release, just to let off some of that pressure. ☻ **bingeing** ℂ *control issues, ethics and morals, risky behavior, threats.*

semi tractor-trailer See *trucks and semis.*

senile **1.** If you dream someone you care about has become senile, you may be worried about subtle signs that person has a health problem, or you may be fearful about facing the reality of someone's aging or their dependence on you. **2.** If you dream of a senile person you don't know, you are fearful about your own aging, how you might appear to others as you get old, or whether you will become a burden on others. **3.** If you dream you are getting senile, you may be playing out your own fear of aging or being too dependent on others, the common fear of getting Alzheimer's disease, or a desire to be released from the responsibilities of adulthood. If you grow old and senile, you won't have to deal with all this pressure or remember these dreams! See also *insane, old person.* ☻ **child or children** ℂ *age,*

S

burdens, caretaking, fear, health and hygiene, image, responsibilities, solutions and remedies.

serpent   See *snake.*

servant   If you dream you have a servant, you feel powerful and socially elevated or superior to others. If you dream you are a servant, you feel like someone or something has power over you, and you must do what that person says. The situation makes you feel socially inferior or insecure.   ☯ **boss** ☾ *authority, career, characters, control issues, insecurity, people, personal power.*

setting something free   A butterfly or a tiger or a person you love—whatever you set free in your dream symbolizes the part of you that desires freedom from repression, oppression, or control. **1.** Setting butterflies and birds free symbolizes your own free spirit that wants to soar beyond the boundaries of societal constraints. **2.** Setting a wild animal free symbolizes your deepest urges and instincts. You are tired of repressing them, and you just want to let them roar. **3.** If you dream of setting free someone you love, you wish someone would set you free from the obligations of a relationship. Or you fear you might really be constraining someone in your waking life and your dream is trying to tell you not to hold on so tightly. You know what they say about setting free the things you love—they just might come back to

you on their own. See also *breaking free.*   ☯ **trapped** ☾ *animals, control issues, freedom, relationships, repression, solutions and remedies, taking action, trust issues.*

sex   Just about everyone who has ever had sex, wants to have sex, is nervous about having sex, or decides not to have sex has had a dream about sex. This natural human urge naturally surfaces in our very natural dreams, and while people often feel startled or guilty about sex dreams, they are often purely physical responses to our bodies and interactions with other people. The context and content of your sex dream can tell you something about your body's feelings as well as your relationships. **1.** Dreaming of having sex with your waking-life sex partner can give you clues into the dynamics of your intimate relationship. What? You haven't had any dreams about your actual sex partner? Or it can just mean your body needs sexual release, and you are choosing the most logical context in which to dream about it. These dreams can also give you ideas about how to relate to your partner better, courtesy of your subconscious. **2.** If you dream of having sex with someone you are not attracted to, but you are attracted to the person in your dream, you are actually attracted to something this person has or represents to you—beauty, experience, power, material possessions, even some personal trait you admire, like

really great hair or killer biceps.
3. If you dream of having sex with
a fantasy person like a movie star
or that hottie in the next cubicle
who never gives you a second
glance, you are acting out a fantasy,
and why not? That's part of what
makes dreams so much fun. **4.** If
you dream of having sex with a
stranger, you crave adventure and
you feel like taking a risk. Or you
are indulging the idea of pleasure
without any strings attached, even
if you would never actually do what
you did in your dream. **5.** If you
have a sex dream that feels degrading, humiliating, or abusive, you are
probably still working through a
negative past experience or an issue
about sex that you've been trying
to ignore. Your dream is pushing it
to the surface so you can deal with
it. **6.** If you dream of having sex in
public, you feel vulnerable or daring. You fear too much exposure, or
you feel like taking a risk. **7.** If you
dream of doing things during sex
you would normally be too shy or
embarrassed to do, you are thinking
about taking a risk or broadening
your horizons in some area of your
life. You want to be more daring.
8. If you dream of very romantic,
passionate, movie-worthy sex, you
crave more care and special treatment in your personal life. Someone
isn't giving you the attention you
deserve. **9.** If you dream of having
sex with someone of the same sex,
and you aren't homosexual, you
are getting in touch with your own
inner male-female balance. ☽ **impotence** ☾ *balance, body parts, envy,*

gender issues, happiness, health and
hygiene, love, pleasure, relationships,
risky behavior, senses, sexual activity,
social life, solutions and remedies, tak-
ing action, trust issues, vulnerability,
yin-yang.

sex change   So you're a boy but
you dream you're a girl, or you're
a girl but you dream you're a boy?
Or you find yourself as some sort
of mixed-up version of both? Not
to worry, this normal dream signals
your own ability to balance the
male and female energies within
you. **1.** Dreaming of being the
opposite sex from what you really
are suggests an exploration of your
opposite side. We all have both
male and female energies within.
You may be recalibrating yours.
2. Dreaming of having a sex change
may mean you are questioning your
own identity in terms of how you
act, behave, or appear to others in
response to cultural expectations
of your gender. ☽ **man, woman**
☾ *balance, body parts, changing course,*
feminine, gender issues, identity,
image, masculine, transformation, yin-
yang.

sex organs   Dreaming about your
own sex organs can be a sign from
your body to have a doctor check
out a medical problem in that area.
However, more often, dreams fea-
turing genitalia represent female
and male energy and power. **1.** If
you dream of looking at, touching,
or exploring your own genitalia,
you are curious about your own
masculine or feminine energy and

S

how to expand it and make it more powerful. **2.** If you dream of exploring your partner's genitalia, you are seeking balance in your relationship between your energy and your partner's energy. **3.** If you dream of a vagina, you are tapping into ancient female goddess energy, the source of all creation. You may be experiencing a particularly creative or fertile period in your life. Vagina dreams can also symbolize a desire for a stronger, more confident female energy, either in yourself or in your partner. **4.** If you dream of a penis, you are tapping into ancient male god energy, the source of exploration and discovery. You may be experiencing a particularly bold or adventurous time in your life. Penis dreams can also symbolize your desire for a stronger, more potent male energy, either in yourself or in your partner. **5.** If you dream you have sex organs you don't normally have—a penis on a woman, a vagina or breasts on a man—you are balancing out your own male-female energy system. You haven't been giving both sides of yourself enough room to grow and be who you really are. ◐ **androgyny** ℭ *balance, body parts, feminine, gender issues, identity, masculine, sexual activity, yin-yang.*

sexual harassment If you are sexually harassed in your dream, you may resent authority figures and you assume they objectify or look down on you in a threatening way. Or you may feel pushed to the extreme in an intimately personal

way—is someone demanding more of you than you feel comfortable giving? ◐ **rebellion** ℭ *anger, anxiety, authority, control issues, ethics and morals, sexual harassment, personal power, resistance, sexual activity, threats, trust issues, vulnerability.*

Many ancient cultures considered the female and male sex organs to be sacred, and symbolic representations of those organs put together, often without any people attached, represented divine balance in the universe. Sex between a man and a woman was a sacred act and the only way for humans to ever truly experience divine bliss. In India, the vagina is symbolized by the yoni symbol and the penis by the lingam symbol. The ultimate female and male principles were represented by the deities Shiva (male energy) and Shakti (female energy), and symbols of Shiva's lingam and Shakti's yoni in divine union are common in Hindu art, as are paintings and drawings of the god and goddess in various interesting positions of sexual union.

shadow Seeing your own shadow in a dream means you are carrying something with you. **1.** If your shadow is huge, you feel powerful. **2.** If your shadow is small or faint, you feel insecure or weak. **3.** If your shadow looks like you have extra parts or is a different shape than you are, you feel burdened by someone else's problems, or you have been acting like someone other than who you really are. **4.** If you notice shadows from other people or other objects in a dream, you suspect people are hiding from you, or you don't have all the information you need. ☽ **sun** ℂ *authority, burdens, image, insecurity, personal power, secrets.*

shame Feeling shame in a dream usually means you feel shame about something in your waking life, but because you have been repressing the feeling, it has popped up when you aren't consciously able to control it. The context of your dream can help you figure out what has made you feel ashamed. Is it something you did or said, or something you really had no control over at all? ☽ **pride** ℂ *anxiety, burdens, embarrassment, feelings, guilt, image, reputation.*

shark Sharks symbolize threats, danger, or dangerous people who may try to take financial or emotional advantage of you. If you dream of a shark, be careful. You don't want to lose an arm and a leg. ☽ **goldfish** ℂ *animals, danger, financial issues, nature, threats, water.*

shaving **1.** If you dream of shaving a moustache or beard off your face, you want to be honest. You are tired of hiding something, or you need to show someone who you really are. **2.** If you dream of shaving your head, you are ready to become vulnerable in a relationship. You might even be ready to commit! **3.** If you dream someone else forces you to shave your hair, you feel like someone has stolen

your power from you, leaving you vulnerable and insecure. **4.** If you dream of shaving your legs or underarms, you are worried about your image, or you are trying to make a good impression. ☽ **hair** ℂ *beauty, body parts, control issues, image, insecurity, love, personal power, relationships, trust issues, vulnerability.*

sheep If you see sheep in your dream, you feel like one in a crowd. Nobody notices you. Or you haven't been thinking for yourself. Or both. ☽ **tiger** ℂ *animals, conformity, nature, identity.*

shelves See *storage.*

shiny Dreaming of shiny things means you've been given an opportunity, a fresh start, or something valuable. Whatever it is, it's special and rare. ☽ **rust** ℂ *beauty, changing course, financial resources, opportunity.*

shipwreck **1.** If you dream you are in a shipwreck, whether small scale or reminiscent of the *Titanic,* you feel so consumed by your emotions that you are losing track of your responsibilities. You are letting your heart—or your fear or other strong emotions—take over your head, and you are neglecting your responsibilities and the people who depend on you. Ask someone for help so you don't go down with the ship. **2.** If you dream you survive a shipwreck, you've come through a difficult experience, and you are working through the flotsam and

S

jetsam. **3.** If you dream you are in a shipwreck but the dream is exciting, challenging, and full of swashbuckling adventure, you crave more excitement and emotional drama in your life. Aargh! **4.** If a shipwreck lands you on a deserted island, you feel stranded after a traumatic emotional incident, and you feel like you don't have anyone to help you. ☽ **boat** ☾ *accidents, adventure, anxiety, disaster, desires, escapism, fear, feelings, isolation, journeys and quests, personal power, responsibilities, vehicles.*

shoes Shoes represent your image and the way you choose to get through life. **1.** If you dream of wearing beautiful, expensive shoes, status and reputation really matter to you right now. **2.** If you dream of wearing high heels, appearance matters more than function in a current situation. If the high heels hurt or you can't walk very well in them, you feel like someone is judging you on your looks and not for your skills. Comedian Steve Martin would call those cruel shoes. **3.** If you dream of wearing tennis shoes, you might need more exercise, or you might be exercising too much. Are you getting obsessive about it? **4.** If you dream of tattered, old, dirty, or falling-apart shoes, you don't like your current image. You wish people had a higher opinion of you. **5.** If you can't understand why you are wearing a pair of shoes you've never seen before, you are trying to be someone you aren't. It's just not you. **6.** If you dream you can't find your shoes, something is getting in the way of your progress.

You can't go any further until you fix this problem. You'll need your keys too … now where did you put those? ☽ **hat** ☾ *beauty, body parts, clothing and accessories, financial resources, identity, image, impediments, inanimate objects, reputation.*

shooting See *gun.*

shooting star See *meteors and meteorites.*

shoplifting See *stealing.*

shopping Dreaming of shopping can be a reaction to too much deprivation. If you can't afford to shop much, you may crave excessive shopping and dream about it. Shopping dreams can also symbolize a preoccupation with materialism or an addiction to the rush of buying stuff. **1.** If you dream of spending huge amounts of money on shopping and then feeling guilty about it, you are worried about your ability to control your urges, or you are aware that you have been too focused on material things. **2.** If you dream of spending huge amounts of money on shopping and not feeling satisfied, your emotional needs aren't getting met. **3.** If you dream of buying clothes and shoes, you are trying to change your image or reputation. **4.** If you dream of spending large amounts of money on electronics or other technological gadgets, you feel more comfortable with things you can figure out than with people whose feelings are a mystery to you. Plus, you can't buy friends.

5. If you dream of having a great time buying wonderful things you really want, you are having a wish-fulfillment dream. **6.** If you dream of being made to go shopping with someone else, material possessions feel like a burden to you. You'd rather live a simpler life. See also *mall*. ◐ **giving away possessions** ℭ *abundance, addictions, burdens, clothing and accessories, comfort, desires, financial resources, pleasure, risky behavior, solutions and remedies, sports and games, technology.*

shortcut 1. Taking a dream shortcut symbolizes your desire to find the easy way out or to avoid the more traveled path. You don't like to follow the crowds. **2.** Dreaming that a shortcut turns out to be a "long cut" or that you get lost attempting a shortcut suggests you probably shouldn't cut any corners this time. ◐ **detour** ℭ *adventure, changing course, direction, journeys and quests, rebellion, risky behavior, travel.*

showers and baths 1. Dreaming of taking a shower or a bath can be a sign that you need to cleanse or start fresh. Maybe you need to eat cleaner food, exercise and sweat more, or avoid those negative influences. **2.** Showers and baths also represent forgiveness. That thing you did can be washed away. **3.** A shower or bath that leaks or overflows represents a welling-up of emotion into your regular life. Find an emotional drain to help you manage those feelings, or you could suffer structural damage. And keep some emotional drain cleaner handy. **4.** Remember the famous shower scene at the Bates Motel in the movie *Psycho?* Feeling vulnerable? ◐ **dirt** ℭ *buildings and rooms, changing course, feelings, forgiveness, health and hygiene, transformation, water.*

shunning 1. If you dream of shunning someone else, you haven't forgiven someone. **2.** If you dream of being shunned, someone hasn't forgiven you—or you haven't forgiven yourself. **3.** Dreams of shunning can also be advice to yourself about influences you should avoid for your own health and happiness. ◐ **forgiving** ℭ *communication, forgiveness, health and hygiene, isolation, relationships, social life.*

shy 1. If you feel painfully shy in a dream, you are afraid to face something or someone, or you are in a situation where you don't feel like you can really be yourself. Your shyness is a safety mechanism and your dream is alerting you to take care of yourself, or just wait and see. A cautious approach is best now. **2.** If someone else acts shy in a dream, you are intimidating someone. ◐ **naked in public** ℭ *anxiety, fear, feelings, identity, insecurity, social life.*

sibling Dreams about your sister or brother often represent fears or hopes for yourself. For example, if you dream your brother has an accident, you may fear being alone in the world, or you might recognize subconsciously that you have been

S

engaging in too-risky behavior. If you dream your sister is pregnant, you may be pregnant or wish you were. Our siblings are so close to us genetically and emotionally—even if we don't stay close with them in adulthood—that it is easy to transfer our own feelings onto them symbolically in dreams. Sibling dreams can also be warnings, however. Dreams of accidents or illness could be a sign that something is wrong with your sibling. Many people report having dreams about family members' health problems or injuries that turn out to be close to the truth. Give your sibling a call, if you can, just to be sure. If everything is fine, turn that interpretive mirror on yourself. That dream was probably about you. ☯ **stranger** ℭ *desires, family, people, relationships.*

sickness See *disease.*

sign Signs in dreams give us messages, literal or metaphorical, about something we should be paying closer attention to. If you see a *stop* sign, for example, your subconscious recognizes that you should *stop* doing something you've been doing. A *yield* sign means you should probably give in or admit you are wrong. A speed limit or *slow* sign may suggest you are moving too fast in a relationship or project. *No parking* signs suggest you need to keep moving. This isn't the place you want to be. Signs for businesses, billboards, and especially flashing or neon signs all signal you from the subconscious: *this is what you should do.* That is what marketing is all about. See also *billboard.* ☯ **vision problems** ℭ *changing course, code, messages, shapes and symbols.*

silence Dreams of silence can be lovely, finally-I-have-peace-and-quiet wish-fulfillment dreams, or they can be terrifying dreams of isolation and abandonment. It all depends on how you feel about the silence in your dream. **1.** If you dream of peacefully enjoying silence, you need more time to yourself. You've been answering everyone's needs and depleting your own energies. **2.** If you dream of terrifying silence, you fear being alone. You need people around you to support you right now. **3.** If you dream that you purposefully stay silent, you are reluctant to communicate about something right now. ☯ **echo** ℭ *balance, comfort, communication, desires, escapism, fear, health and hygiene, isolation, listening, music and sound, senses, solutions and remedies.*

silver **1.** Dreaming of antique or tarnished silver symbolizes your current attraction to or interest in the past—historical past or your own past. You want to know how things used to be. This knowledge can shed light on how things are now. **2.** Dreaming of shiny, bright silver objects—jewelry, tea services, trays, silverware—suggests stability and comfort. You can count on a situation or person to maintain quality over the long haul, like a treasured heirloom. ☯ **gold** ℭ *comfort, history, stability.*

singing **1.** If you hear singing in a dream but you can't find the source, you are chasing something that you believe will make you happy. **2.** If you see someone singing beautifully in a dream, someone in your life already makes you happy. **3.** If you see a choir or large group of people singing, or you are singing in a choir, your family life or social life is satisfying and fulfilling to you. **4.** If you hear angelic singing and you can't place the source, you feel called to a more spiritual way or quest, or you have a divine mission that takes precedence over your everyday concerns. **5.** If you dream you are singing and you sound great, you can do the thing you've been considering attempting. **6.** If you dream you are singing but you don't sound so great, you lack confidence in a current endeavor. You aren't sure you can do it. ☽ **mute** ☾ *divine power, family, happiness, hopes and dreams, insecurity, music and sound, relationships, social life, spirituality.*

According to angelology, or the study of angels, angels are divided into different groups or levels called *choirs,* probably because one of the primary tasks of angels is to praise and proclaim the glory of God through singing. Although not all organizational systems agree, many group angels into nine different choirs divided into three hierarchies. These include seraphim, cherubim, thrones, dominions, principalities, powers, virtues, archangels, and angels.

single **1.** If you are married but you dream you are single, you crave a little taste of the single life or have a little nostalgia for the single life, even if you love being married. Your dream does not necessarily mean you don't want to be married anymore, although if your marriage is unhappy, dreams of being single could be wish-fulfillment dreams. **2.** If you dream you are single but you don't like it, your dream is confirming to you how much you appreciate the benefits of marriage. See also *bachelor, divorce.* ☽ **marriage** ☾ *adventure, changing course, desires, freedom, relationships, social life.*

sink Sinks symbolize the ability to control emotions. Turn the cold or hot water on and off, and you are turning on and off your most chilling or steamiest feelings. **1.** If you dream of a leaking or overflowing sink, your emotions are getting out of control. **2.** If you dream no water comes out of the sink, you are repressing your feelings. **3.** If you dream a sink is clogged, you can't seem to experience your feelings and let them go. You are obsessing over them. **4.** A sink unconnected to the plumbing suggests you feel emotionally removed from a situation. ☽ **stove** ☾ *control issues, feelings, furniture and appliances, inanimate objects, repression, water.*

siren **1.** If you hear a siren in your dream, you are worried about someone, or you are taking unnecessary risks and you could get hurt. **2.** If

S

you dream of the mythical sirens who lured sailors to their death with their beautiful singing, something tempts you and you don't feel quite able to resist, but you are fighting the urge. ❧ **caution** ℂ *caretaking, characters, danger, music and sound, myths and legends, risky behavior.*

sister See *sibling.*

skateboarding **1.** If you dream of skateboarding and you have never skateboarded, or haven't for years, you want to take more chances or change your image to be more daring and free-spirited. **2.** If you dream of skateboarding and you do skateboard, you are mentally refining your physical technique. Some studies suggest this really can improve your performance. **3.** If you dream of crashing, getting injured on your skateboard, or getting hit by a vehicle while on a skateboard, a current endeavor poses a serious risk. You have to decide if it's worth the thrill. ❧ **caution** ℂ *changing course, fun, image, injuries, play, risky behavior, sports and games, vehicles.*

skeleton **1.** If you dream of finding a skeleton, you've uncovered a secret. If you find a skeleton in your own home, the secret has to do with you or someone in your family. This isn't something you'll want to spread around. **2.** If you get chased or attacked by a skeleton, you fear your motives are too transparent and everyone sees right through

you. This isn't the image you hoped for. See also *bones.* ❧ **hiding** ℂ *body parts, characters, family, fear, image, myths and legends, secrets.*

skiing **1.** If you dream of skiing, your mind rules your heart. You won't be swayed by emotions when logic tells you otherwise. **2.** If you dream of crashing, falling, or getting injured while skiing, you might be too logical in this situation. It could be your downfall. **3.** If you are a frequent skier, dreams of skiing may be a method of refining your technique. The next time you ski, you might actually be even better at it, but colder. ❧ **swimming** ℂ *competition, feelings, injuries, intelligence, personal power, play, risky behavior, sports and games.*

skin **1.** Dreaming about your skin symbolizes the state of your health. The skin shows health imbalances first, so if you dream that you notice how great your skin looks, your body is reporting that you are in excellent physical or emotional health. **2.** If you dream of skin problems like rashes, acne, moles, boils, or other skin irregularities, your body could be signaling a health problem. **3.** Skin changes in dreams can also symbolize changes in your image or reputation. People see you differently than they did before, or you think they do. ❧ **scars and scabs** ℂ *body parts, health and hygiene, image, insecurity, reputation.*

skinny See *thin.*

skinny dipping You wild and crazy kid! If you dream of skinny dipping, you are testing your own bravery, freedom, and sense of fun. Skinny-dipping dreams can also indicate a desire for a more direct and intimate sensory experience of the world. ❂ **blanket** ℂ *adventure, body parts, desires, freedom, fun, nature, play, pleasure, water.*

sky The sky symbolizes your future course. **1.** If you dream of a clear, bright, sunny sky, then full speed ahead. Things look favorable. **2.** If you dream of a cloudy or stormy sky, prepare for problems and delays. **3.** A sky that looks strange and unnatural symbolizes something unexpected. See also *clouds, sun.* ❂ **earthquake** ℂ *impediments, nature, predictions, taking action, weather and seasons.*

slide **1.** If you dream of sliding down a slide, the progress you've recently made has been lost. You're going to have to start over. **2.** If you dream of having fun sliding down a slide, you wish you could go back to feeling younger and more carefree, or a recent experience has made you feel young and playful. **3.** If you dream of falling off a slide, your plan isn't working. ❂ **ladder** ℂ *age, failure, freedom, fun, loss, play.*

slob **1.** If you dream that you have become a slob, you may be getting lax in your personal or work habits and your subconscious is giving you a nudge. **2.** If you dream of cleaning up after a slob, you feel responsible for someone else who isn't doing their part. You carry an unfair share of the work. ❂ **housekeeper** ℂ *burdens, caretaking, characters, health and hygiene, people, responsibilities.*

slot machine See *gambling.*

smell **1.** If you notice a distinct smell in a dream, this usually signifies a potent memory and the feeling associated with that memory. Something has triggered this feeling from the past. **2.** Good smells can also be a sign of something you need, while bad smells can be a sign of something you need to stop. For instance, if you smell oranges, you may need more vitamin C. If you smell roasting meat, you may need more protein. If you smell perfume, you may need to spend more time with someone. If you smell a bad chemical odor, you may be exposing yourself to something physically or emotionally toxic. **3.** Sometimes smelling something in your immediate environment while sleeping will translate into your dream, such as the smell of coffee or breakfast, or smoke from a fire. Sometimes you just need to lift the sheet and fan it out. ❂ **taste** ℂ *danger, food and drink, health and hygiene, memory, senses, threats.*

S

Humans can distinguish approximately 10,000 different odors, and about 80 percent of the sensation of taste is really the sensation of smell. Also, your sense of smell becomes more acute when you are hungry.

smoking **1.** If you dream you are smoking cigarettes but you don't actually smoke, something you are doing is bad for your health or is drawing you toward an overwhelming addiction or desire to escape. **2.** If you dream you are smoking and you used to smoke but you quit, your body is reliving the memory of indulging your addiction. **3.** If you dream of smoking a pipe or a cigar, you want to stand out from others and crave intense experiences. **4.** If you dream of smoking marijuana, you feel rebellious, or you may have the desire to escape to an altered, more pleasant reality or to relieve pain. **5.** If you dream of someone else smoking and you find it irritating or invasive, someone's behavior offends you. **6.** If you dream of someone pressuring you to smoke, you feel peer pressure to do something you think is bad for you. **7.** If you dream of quitting smoking, you are reclaiming health and confidence. ☽ **breathing** ☾ *addictions, health and hygiene, peer pressure, risky behavior, threats.*

snake The quintessential symbol for evil and the sacred symbol for healing, the snake has many archetypal meanings for modern society. Snakes are among the most feared of all animals and one of the most fascinating. **1.** If you dream a snake threatens you, such as a rattling rattlesnake or a lunging cobra, or if you dream a snake bites you, you feel unsafe or in danger on a deep instinctual level. You are sensing a real threat. **2.** If you dream of see-ing a snake but you aren't scared of it, having a snake as a pet, or seeing a shed snakeskin, you are preparing for a transformation in your life. Like a snake shedding its skin, you have outgrown the old and you are ready for the new. **3.** If you dream of killing a snake, you resist change and will go to great lengths to avoid it. **4.** If you dream of the snake in the Garden of Eden tempting you, you are facing real temptation in your life and are trying to decide how you will handle it. You may also be facing a spiritual crisis. **5.** If you dream of holding a snake and not being afraid, you have the power to heal someone. See also *reptiles and amphibians.* ☽ **mouse** ☾ *animals, crawling creatures, danger, fear, healing, myths and legends, nature, resistance, solutions and remedies, threats, transformation.*

snorkeling and scuba diving You want to explore the depths of your own feelings so you really understand what's down there. You are feeling analytical and courageous enough to do this now, so go ahead. Dive in. ☽ **surfing** ☾ *adventure, courage, feelings, knowledge, play, sports and games, water.*

snow Pure and white, icy and sparkling, snow blankets the landscape and transforms reality into something colder, slicker, more beautiful … and safer? Or more treacherous? Snow dreams can indicate impotence or power, isolation or bonding. **1.** If snow starts to fall in your dream, you have a chance for a fresh start. Act now. **2.** If you must walk through heavy, deep snow, something difficult holds you back in your life. Whatever it is, you're going to need a shovel. **3.** Getting caught in a blizzard means you've been blindsided by a big problem and you can't seem to find your way through it. Watching a blizzard from inside means you've managed to avoid a big problem. **4.** If you touch, stand, lie, or walk on ice, your fluid, passionate side has frozen. You may be feeling asexual or even impotent, as if the chill has stifled your desires. You might be doing this to protect yourself or just because nobody has lit your fire for a while. **5.** Slipping and falling on ice or snow means you are ready to warm up and get back in touch with your passionate side. This cold weather isn't working for you anymore. **6.** Standing alone in the snow indicates your feeling of isolation and perhaps superiority. Lie down and make a snow angel, and maybe somebody will want to play with you. **7.** Walking through snow with somebody else means you feel supported in adversity. Let others help you, and you can achieve anything. **8.** If you are buried in snow, you need help now. If you rescue someone else buried in snow, someone needs your help. See also *glacier, storm.* ☽ **fire** ℂ *cold, impediments, innocence, isolation, nature, transformation, water, weather and seasons.*

snowboarding **1.** You like to take risks, and you want everyone to know it if you dream of snowboarding. **2.** Snowboarding also symbolizes mastery over your emotions and strong self-confidence. **3.** If you dream of crashing on a snowboard, you aren't sure you are up to the image you are trying to project, or a risk might not be worth it. **4.** If you really do snowboard, dreams of snowboarding can actually help improve your technique. ☽ **swimming** ℂ *feelings, fun, image, reputation, personal power, play, risky behavior, sports and games.*

snowman That snowman in your dream may be you, and you aren't feeling any emotion, either because you can't or because you refuse to. Just remember what happens to snowmen (and women) when things heat up. ☽ **palm tree** ℂ *characters, cold, feelings, repression, weather and seasons.*

snowstorm See *storm.*

sofa See *couch.*

soil See *dirt.*

soldier **1.** If you dream of a soldier, some authority figure is influencing your life, making things happen or keeping things in order. **2.** If you dream a soldier takes you prisoner or forces you to do something against your will, you fear or distrust an authority figure or force relevant to your current life. **3.** If you dream of soldiers marching into a city, you have a foreboding feeling that things are going to change for the worse. Does this mean war? **4.** If you dream you are a soldier, you want to change things, or you crave more structure in your life. ☾ **prisoner** ☾ *authority, career, changing course, characters, danger, fear, people, predictions, solutions and remedies, violence, war.*

son **1.** If you dream of your son, you may be dreaming of your younger self or are reliving a past feeling or experience through the symbol of your offspring. **2.** If you dream something is wrong with your son, he may really need your attention, or something might be wrong. You might need to be a guiding force right now. ☾ **father** ☾ *age, caretaking, family, memory, people, relationships.*

south pole See *north pole/south pole.*

space **1.** Dreaming you are in space means you have a great sense of adventure and daring, but you lack direction. **2.** Dreaming you are in a spaceship symbolizes a current courageous plan and a sense of limitless possibility. You want to do something you've never done before, breaking new ground for yourself and/or for others. See also *stars.* ☾ **claustrophobia** ☾ *adventure, courage, direction, desires, freedom, journeys and quests, opportunity.*

speaking in public **1.** Dreaming of speaking in public or knowing you will have to speak in public and being terrified about it or totally

unprepared represents anxiety about an upcoming high-pressure responsibility. **2.** If you dream of speaking in public and loving it, doing a great job, and getting applause and praise, you have high confidence and strong personal power right now. You can influence others effectively now. ☾ **hiding** ☾ *anxiety, communication, courage, embarrassment, fear, insecurity, personal power, taking action.*

speeding **1.** If you dream you are speeding, you are taking a risk and moving too fast. **2.** If you dream of getting stopped for speeding, you fear the risk will result in trouble. **3.** If you speed but enjoy it and don't get caught, you think the risk will be worth it. **4.** If you dream someone else is speeding, you think others are getting ahead of you in unethical ways. ☾ **stalling** ☾ *ethics and morals, risky behavior, rules and laws, vehicles.*

spider See *bugs.*

spine injuries Your spine, or backbone, holds you up and channels all your nerve impulses. Dreams of a broken or injured spine mean the basic structures holding up your life or belief system have suffered a blow. What are you questioning? Is it time to make some major life changes? See also *back, paralyzed.* ☾ **flexibility** ☾ *body parts, changing course, destruction, health and hygiene, injuries, stability, transformation.*

spirit   See *ghost.*

spoon   See *utensils.*

spring   Dreaming of spring symbolizes a new beginning, a fresh start, a new relationship, birth, and the creative impulse. You feel new again. ☽ **autumn** ☾ *age, creation, nature, transformation, weather and seasons.*

The vernal equinox, or first day of spring, is an ancient and sacred time symbolizing new beginnings and the end of winter; it occurs around March 21. The days start to get longer starting on the vernal equinox. It's no coincidence that eggs and rabbits represent Easter because eggs symbolize birth and rabbits symbolize fertility, both ancient associations with spring.

square   Squares symbolize equality, balance, the four corners of the earth, and the four seasons. If you notice square shapes in your dream, you are in an organized and orderly period of your life, and you like everything to come out evenly. It makes you feel stable and safe. ☽ **circle** ☾ *balance, shapes and symbols, stability.*

stage   **1.** If you dream you are standing on a stage, you feel like all eyes are on you right now. People expect something, or you feel like they do. **2.** If you dream of being on stage in a play and forgetting your lines, you are feeling anxious about something. You aren't sure how well you will perform. **3.** If you dream of an empty stage, your life is full of possibility right now. You could go in any direction, but you feel like you'll have to do it alone. See also *applause, audience, audition, booing, speaking in public.* ☽ **invisible** ☾ *anxiety, buildings and rooms, changing course, courage, direction, embarrassment, personal power, places.*

stairs   **1.** Dreaming of going up stairs or looking up a flight of stairs symbolizes an opportunity to advance. **2.** Dreaming of going down stairs or looking down a flight of stairs symbolizes an opportunity to discover something that has been hidden from you or to delve more deeply into a subject. **3.** Dreaming of falling down the stairs suggests that all the progress you've made has been lost because of a mistake or bad judgment. ☽ **slide** ☾ *buildings and rooms, direction, knowledge, loss, opportunity, secrets.*

stalling   **1.** Stalling for time in your dream? You probably need the time to think something over. Don't be in a rush. **2.** If you dream your car stalls, it might not be time to move on just yet, or something is keeping you from progressing. **3.** If you dream someone else is stalling and you can't seem to get things moving because of it, someone is frustrating you by holding back a project and controlling everyone else with delays. ☽ **running** ☾ *frustration, impediments, taking action, time.*

S

stars **1.** If you dream of looking at the stars, you have big ambitions. You can't see any limits to how far you can go. **2.** If you dream of looking at constellations, you are trying to find greater meaning in your life, and you are watching for signs to guide you. See also *space*. ☽ **digging** ☾ *creativity, direction, goalsetting, hopes and dreams, journeys and quests, messages, nature, personal power, shapes and symbols.*

starvation **1.** If you dream you are starving, you aren't getting enough nourishment in your waking life, either physically or emotionally. Your basic needs are not being met. **2.** If you dream someone else is starving or an animal is starving, you feel a responsibility for others in need, or you fear you've neglected others in need. ☽ **bingeing** ☾ *anxiety, caretaking, feelings, food and drink, health and hygiene, pain, responsibilities.*

STD See *disease*.

stealing **1.** If you dream you are stealing something, you feel guilty about something you took from someone. Was it pride, the spotlight, credit for someone's work? **2.** If you dream of committing armed robbery, you aren't getting what you need from someone, and you feel driven by desperation to take it by force. **3.** If you dream of shoplifting, you are concerned with material possessions or you envy what others have. **4.** If you get caught stealing, you secretly feel you deserve to be punished for something you did. **5.** If you dream of seeing someone else steal something, someone in your life can't be trusted or isn't being honest with you. See also *crime*. ☽ **citizen's arrest** ☾ *dishonesty, envy, ethics and morals, feelings, financial resources, guilt, punishment, rules and laws, trust issues.*

stiff **1.** If you feel stiff in your dream, you aren't being flexible enough in your relationships with others. Why does it always have to be your way? Don't you trust others to do anything right? **2.** If someone else appears stiff and inflexible in a dream, you may not be able to change somebody's mind about something. **3.** Dreams that you have stiff joints could signal a health problem. ☽ **yoga** ☾ *control issues, feelings, health and hygiene, relationships, trust issues.*

stink If something really stinks in your dream, your subconscious is using one of your most inSTINKual survival mechanisms to warn you to avoid something. ☽ **perfume** ☾ *danger, senses, threats.*

stomach **1.** If you notice your stomach in your dream, you feel vulnerable. **2.** If you dream someone touches your stomach, you are feeling ready to be intimate with someone. **3.** If you dream your stomach hurts, someone has hurt you emotionally, or you could have a health problem. See also *abdomen*. ☽ **spine** ☾ *body parts, feelings,* *health and hygiene, love, pain, trust issues, vulnerability.*

stop signs and stoplights If you see a stop sign or stoplight, your subconscious is telling you to stop what you've been doing. You might need to rethink this course of action. See also *sign*. ☺ **street** ☾ *changing course, code, color, impediments, messages.*

storage Cabinets, drawers, shelves, cupboards, pantries, closets—household storage presents a powerful metaphor in dreams for all the thoughts and emotions we keep inside us, organized for our own perusal or thrown in haphazardly. These objects symbolize our brains, our hearts, and our bodies. They show what we keep hidden, what we keep orderly, what we choose to display to the world. **1.** If you dream of putting things into storage, you want to keep something to yourself or leave it for later. You aren't ready to think about it or share it right now. **2.** If you dream of opening a cabinet, drawer, or cupboard, you are ready to explore something in more depth. **3.** If you dream your cabinets, drawers, or cupboards are full of junk, you have too much on your mind and in your life. Can you purge some of that excess stuff? **4.** If you dream of empty cabinets, drawers, and cupboards, you feel unfulfilled, or you feel like you need more in your life. **5.** If you dream of open shelves filled with display items, you are

open about who you are and proud of what you've made of yourself. **6.** Broken or nonworking storage suggests you've neglected your own internal needs. Are you too busy organizing everybody else's closet? Hey, they have pros for that. ☺ **naked in public** ☾ *caretaking, feelings, furniture and appliances, image, repression, secrets, subterfuge, vulnerability.*

storm Storms symbolize strong emotions, conflicts, and upheaval. People often dream of storms in response to a fight or a major life change. **1.** If you dream of a thunderstorm, you are angry about something. If the storm includes lightning, you may be anxious or fearful about something you perceive as a threat. Thunderstorms can also symbolize verbal arguments. **2.** If you dream about a hurricane, strong emotions have caused people to act in ways they would not normally act. You may feel like everything is changing for the worse or that you aren't safe. Hurricane dreams can also symbolize anxiety about a life change. **3.** If you dream about a blizzard, you have repressed your feelings for so long that they are all coming out at once, and you don't know what direction you are going. Blizzards can also symbolize loneliness and loss. **4.** If you dream of a storm but you think it is exciting and exhilarating, you embrace the changes happening in your life. You see them as a great adventure. Yeah,

S

do that! See also *lightning, thunder, tidal wave, tornado.* ☻ **evacuation** ℂ *adventure, changing course, communication, confusion, control issues, courage, danger, destruction, disaster, fear, loss, nature, repression, threats, transformation, vulnerability, weather and seasons.*

stove **1.** Dreaming of a stove or cooking on a stove means you are caring for someone or changing your situation to be safer and more comfortable. **2.** Dreaming of burning yourself on a stove means something in your domestic or social life has become threatening or unsafe. ☻ **refrigerator** ℂ *caretaking, changing course, comfort, danger, family, food and drink, furniture and appliances, heat, social life, threats.*

straight line If you dream of a straight line, you know exactly where you are going, and you are taking the most direct route. You are taking action and proceeding with a purpose. ☻ **circle** ℂ *direction, goal-setting, shapes and symbols, taking action.*

stranger **1.** Dreaming of a threatening stranger suggests that someone isn't who he or she seems, or a situation is more dangerous than you thought it would be. You may also be anxious about a new situation. **2.** Dreaming of a kind stranger suggests you trust people, and you feel safe. **3.** Dreaming of romantic or sexual interaction with a stranger means you want to take a risk in the name of adventure or pleasure. See also *intruder.* ☻ **neighbor** ℂ *anxiety, changing course, characters, danger, people, pleasure, risky behavior, sexual activity, threats, trust issues.*

street Streets go somewhere, and dreams about streets want to take you somewhere. **1.** Long, wide-open streets or roads with no end signify endless possibilities. **2.** Dead ends ask you to reconsider your current direction. **3.** Cul-de-sacs suggest you've gotten into a rut, a French one at that. **4.** Narrow streets mean you need to open your mind and expand your horizons. **5.** Crowded streets suggest you are going with the status quo. Have you considered the road not taken? See also *car, straight line.* ☻ **stasis** ℂ *direction, goal-setting, journeys and quests, places, transformation, travel, vehicles.*

street sign See *sign.*

stress Feeling stressed in your dream? Maybe you didn't realize how stressed you are in your waking life. Your body is pointing this out. ☻ **hammock** ℂ *anxiety, feelings, health and hygiene.*

student **1.** If you dream you are a student, you still have something to learn, and you know it. Who or what has a lesson for you? **2.** If you dream of something that actually happened in the past when you were still a student, something in your current life reflects that past memory. **3.** If you dream you become a student again at your current age, you have the ambition to go in a new direction in your life. ❧ **teacher** ☾ *age, anxiety, changing course, characters, direction, journeys and quests, knowledge, memory, people, success, taking action.*

success You did it! Dreaming of success symbolizes your confidence that you can do what you are thinking about doing or be who you want to be. ❧ **disappointment** ☾ *goal-setting, personal power, success, taking action.*

sued See *lawsuit.*

suffocating **1.** Dreams of suffocating often symbolize anxiety about a lack of freedom in your life. You feel restrained or controlled, and you can't reach your full potential like this. **2.** Dreams of suffocating can also symbolize a health problem with your lungs or throat. ❧ **breathing** ☾ *anxiety, control issues, feelings, freedom, health and hygiene, repression.*

suitcase Are you really carrying all that baggage? Suitcases symbolize the baggage you or someone else carries. Do you know what's making that suitcase so heavy? Whatever it is, maybe you can finally leave it behind. ❧ **homebody** ☾ *burdens, inanimate objects, travel.*

summer Summer symbolizes the height of youth, energy, and power. Dreams of summer can symbolize your own feelings of strength and personal power or your longing for

a vacation from your responsibilities. ❧ **winter** ☾ *age, heat, nature, personal power, transformation, weather and seasons.*

> The summer solstice begins around June 21, the longest day of the year and the shortest night. After this date, the days get progressively shorter. The summer solstice is also associated with Midsummer's Eve on June 23, which some consider to be the most magical time to gather healing herbs.

sun The quintessential symbol of male energy and the opposite of the moon, which radiates female energy, the sun is an ancient symbol of light, warmth, and God, or the energy of the gods. The sun also symbolizes optimism, power, and male energy, as well as clarity and logical thought. It is the yang in the yin-yang. **1.** Dreams of the sun usually symbolize strength, optimism, and male energy. **2.** Dreams of the sunrise or sunset symbolize a perfect balance between male and female energies, that transition time when both day and night seem to exist together. **3.** Dreams of an overly glaring sun or wearing sunglasses can mean you feel you need to protect yourself from an overabundance of strong male energy in your life. **4.** If you dream of tanning in the sun, you relish the attention of men—or you just really need to take a vacation in a warm climate! ❧ **moon** ☾ *balance,*

S

divine power, heat, masculine, nature, weather and seasons, yin-yang.

superhero See *hero.*

surfing 1. To dream of surfing means you are skimming right over the top of all those emotions, not letting them get to you. You'd rather have fun than dwell on things that are uncomfortable or difficult. **2.** If you are an actual surfer, surfing dreams may help you improve your skill. ☻ **riptide** ℭ *feelings, fun, play, sports and games, water.*

surgery 1. Dreaming of undergoing surgery means you need to get deep inside a problem before you can figure out what is causing your reaction. **2.** Dreaming of performing surgery suggests that you are motivated to understand someone on a deep level or get to the root of a problem. ☻ **bandages** ℭ *journeys and quests, medicine and surgery, relationships, taking action.*

SUV 1. If you dream of driving an SUV, you want to make a strong impression on others, and your reputation as a leader or authority figure is important to you. **2.** If you dream of seeing or riding in an SUV, you envy someone else's power, or you dislike someone else's overbearing personality. ☻ **convertible** ℭ *authority, envy, image, personal power, reputation, vehicles.*

swimming Dreams of swimming symbolize a willingness to immerse yourself in an emotion. You can move through your feelings and feel them without letting them overwhelm or drown you. If you dream of having trouble swimming, getting carried away by a current, or being caught up in something under the water, your feelings may be drowning you. ☻ **flying** ℭ *feelings, sports and games, water.*

sword The sword represents male energy, power, violence, authority, and the male genitalia. **1.** If you dream of wielding a sword, you have control over your own male energy (even if you are a woman) and use this to enhance your personal power. **2.** If you dream of being threatened or injured by a sword, you feel threatened or injured by strong, dominant energy. **3.** If you watch a swordfight, two strong figures in your life are in a battle for dominance or leadership. ☻ **circle** ℭ *authority, body parts, masculine, personal power, threats, violence, war.*

synagogue See *church or synagogue.*

table **1.** Dreaming of a table means you want to tell the truth, and the whole truth. You have nothing to hide anymore. **2.** Dreaming of sitting at a table with family or friends suggests balance and satisfaction with your home or social life. **3.** Dreaming of sticking chewing gum under the table means you have no table manners. ☽ **chair** ℂ *communication, family, furniture and appliances, home, inanimate objects, social life.*

taking responsibility **1.** If you dream of taking responsibility for something you did wrong, your dream may be helping you practice taking responsibility in your waking life. **2.** Taking responsibility for something someone else did in a dream symbolizes a sacrifice you have made, or plan to make, for someone else. **3.** Dreaming that someone else takes responsibility for something you have done suggests you feel guilty for failing to take responsibility for something you did. ☽ **blaming others** ℂ *burdens, failure, guilt, relationships, responsibilities, sacrifice.*

tarot cards See *fortune teller.*

taste **1.** If you dream of tasting something delicious, your body may need the nutrients in that particular food, or you may have deprived yourself of something you think is bad for you, and your body is craving it. Yummmmm, chocolate nutrients! **2.** If you dream of tasting something bad, you may be getting too much of some particular nutrient, or something you have been eating isn't good for you, and your body is telling you to stop eating it. Yummmmm, chocolate nutrients! ☽ **smell** ℂ *food and drink, health and hygiene, pleasure, senses.*

tattoo **1.** If you dream of getting a tattoo, you feel like doing something to make yourself stand out from others, or you want to have a particular image. Where do you want this tattoo? **2.** If you dream you already have a tattoo you don't actually have, you feel like people have a particular idea about you. **3.** If you dream you don't have a tattoo you actually have in your waking life, you want to start over and erase something you've done, or you worry that you might be giving people the wrong impression about you. **4.** If you dream of getting a tattoo and regretting it, you are questioning the wisdom of a recent decision. **5.** If you dream of giving someone else a tattoo, you have the desire to mark that person with your own image of who they are. ☯ **faceless** ☾ *body parts, decisions, image, regret, reputation, shapes and symbols, social life.*

taxi **1.** Dream of hailing a taxi, and you are ready to move on with your life. **2.** Dream of riding in a taxi, and you are in transition but you aren't sure where you will end up. **3.** Dream of driving a taxi, and you are influencing other people's course in life. **4.** Dream that no taxi will stop for you, and you are facing an obstacle to your progress. ☯ **running out of gas** ☾ *changing course, goal-setting, impediments, journeys and quests, relationships, travel, vehicles.*

tea **1.** Dreams of drinking tea suggest calm self-possession and a certain decorum or earthiness. **2.** Serving tea to others suggests diplomatic communication skills or a spiritual nature. ☯ **coffee** ☾ *comfort, communication, food and drink, spirituality, travel.*

teacher **1.** To dream you have a teacher or any kind of coach, guide, or mentor means you seek guidance in your waking life. You want someone to show you the way or help you make a big decision. You aren't sure you have enough experience to do this alone. **2.** If you dream you are

a teacher, you have the power to guide or direct others right now. ☯ **student** ☾ *authority, career, characters, direction, knowledge, people, responsibilities, support.*

> The Japanese art form of the tea ceremony is a carefully rehearsed and respected ritual in which a host offers tea to a guest. The purpose of the tea ceremony, called *chaji,* is to acknowledge, with Zen-like clarity, that every meeting between two humans is sacred and unique and will never recur, so the participants should live fully in the present moment of the tea ceremony, making it as beautiful, real, and full of awareness as possible.

teasing **1.** Teasing someone in a dream symbolizes a playful and lighthearted, even flirtatious relationship to others. **2.** Teasing someone in a mean way symbolizes your anger at or jealousy of someone. **3.** Dreaming someone is teasing you suggests you are feeling insecure in a relationship. You may not be sure whether someone else is serious. ☯ **insult** ☾ *anger, communication, envy, fun, insecurity, relationships, trust issues.*

teenager See *adolescence.*

teeth Your teeth allow you to talk more clearly and eat more easily. Teeth may not be necessary for survival, but they give you more power. **1.** The very common dream of losing your teeth or having your teeth fall out symbolizes a feeling of powerlessness or lack of control. **2.** Dreaming your teeth are stronger and/or whiter than usual symbolizes a strong sense of power and skill. ☯ **lips** ℭ *body parts, control issues, personal power.*

television   See *TV.*

telling the truth   **1.** If you cannot tell a lie in your dream, you have been lying about something in your waking life, and you can't take it anymore. Maybe it's time to fess up, for real. **2.** If you dream someone else tells you the truth, you've recently begun to trust someone more than you did before. ☯ **lying** ℭ *communication, dishonesty, ethics and morals, taking action, trust issues.*

temper tantrum   **1.** If you dream of seeing a child throwing a temper tantrum, you may be projecting. You are angry or frustrated about something, and you are dreaming of someone else throwing the tantrum you wish *you* could throw (which is also childish, huh?). **2.** If you dream that you are throwing a temper tantrum, you are feeling out of control and childish. At least in your dream, nobody has to watch. See also *breaking something.* ☯ **happy** ℭ *age, anger, anxiety, control issues, feelings, frustration, repression.*

temperature   See *thermometer.*

tenant   If you dream you are a tenant, you feel like a guest in your own life. Your current situation isn't permanent, and you don't have a strong sense of stability. **1.** If you dream you are having a problem with your lease, you are considering a change in your life. You aren't satisfied with the current situation. **2.** If you dream of being a tenant in a great apartment with a good lease and friendly landlord or landlady, you like your current temporary situation in life. This is just fine for now, and who needs the hassle of commitment anyway? See also *eviction.* ☯ **landlord, landlady** ℭ *changing course, characters, home, journeys and quests, people, relationships.*

tennis   **1.** Dream of playing tennis, and you aspire to a more aristocratic or opulent way of life. **2.** If you play doubles in your dream, you are working well in partnership with someone. **3.** If you dream of a fiercely competitive tennis game, you want to one-up somebody who thinks he or she can beat you. Play fair. **4.** If you are actually a tennis player, dreaming of playing tennis can literally improve your tennis game. ☯ **baseball** ℭ *abundance, competition, financial resources, play, relationships, sports and games.*

tent   **1.** Dreaming of being inside a tent means you want adventure, but you also want protection. **2.** Dreaming of setting up a tent suggests you know how to solve a problem yourself. **3.** Dreaming of trying to set up a tent but being unsuccessful, or having a hard time at setting up a tent means you don't

T

feel like you can protect yourself. **4.** Dreaming of being inside a tent during a rainstorm means you want to reach out to someone, but you don't feel fully prepared to deal with his or her emotions—or your own. If the tent is leaking, those emotions are going to come out anyway, ready or not. **5.** Dreaming of being inside a tent with a threat—an intruder or bear— lurking outside suggests that your protective mechanisms don't feel sufficient enough to keep you safe. Maybe if you don't make any noise, the problem will just go away. See also *camping*. ☯ **sky** ℭ *adventure, anxiety, buildings and rooms, danger, feelings, inanimate objects, nature, protection, solutions and remedies, taking action, threats.*

terrorism **1.** Dreams of being a victim of terrorism symbolize your anxiety about your own safety. You fear danger beyond your control and the seemingly random threats that lurk. **2.** Dreams of being a terrorist suggest you are angry about some authority figure or institution. You have the urge to instill terror in others to achieve a goal. **3.** If you dream you are duped into a terrorist act against your will, you fear that someone or something is influencing you in a negative way. ☯ **lifeguard** ℭ *anxiety, authority, danger, fear, frustration, peer pressure, personal power, rebellion, resistance, risky behavior, rules and laws, taking action, threats, violence.*

test A test? *Today?* Test anxiety dreams are among the most common, even for those long out of school. **1.** If you dream you have to take a test and you didn't study, you are anxious about an upcoming challenge, and you feel unprepared. **2.** If you dream of acing a test, you feel ready for anything. **3.** If you dream of failing a test, you fear you are out of your league in a current situation. Know how to end this kind of recurring dream? Go back and study and learn whatever that class taught. Really, this works. ☯ **cheating** ℭ *anxiety, competition, failure, fear, insecurity, knowledge, personal power, success.*

text message Gypsy folklorists are at a complete loss on this one. This is new dream territory. You are a dream pioneer or astronaut. **1.** Send text messages in your dream, and you can't get enough of someone. You have a crush or one of those friendships that makes you feel really good about yourself. **2.** Receive a text message in your dream, and you feel like you belong to something. Your social network supports you and makes you feel happy and comfortable. ☯ **blank screen** ℭ *comfort, communication, love, messages, relationships, support, technology.*

Thanksgiving Thanksgiving, that classic family gathering holiday, brings even the most mature adults back to a feeling that they are still children playing the role they once played in the family, and dreams of Thanksgiving often symbolize your own feeling of being cast back into some earlier role or version of yourself. **1.** Dreams of a wonderful, warm, idealized Thanksgiving mean you are feeling nostalgia or a longing for close family relationships. **2.** Dreaming of a luscious Thanksgiving dinner suggests you are getting strong emotional support from your family. **3.** Dreaming of a horrible, nasty, or argument-fraught Thanksgiving suggests anxiety about an upcoming family communication or gathering. You fear slipping into old patterns you thought you had escaped. **4.** Dreaming of terrible or ruined Thanksgiving food suggests you aren't getting enough emotional support from your family. ☽ **New Year's Eve** ☾ *abundance, celebration, comfort, desires, family, feelings, food and drink, identity, memory, relationships, support, weather and seasons.*

theater 1. Dreaming you are in the audience at a theater symbolizes your expectations about something that is going to happen. Did you bring the tomatoes? **2.** Dreaming you are in an empty theater means you feel abandoned by your friends. **3.** Dreaming you are on stage in a theater suggests you feel pressured to make a good impression on others or play a role that isn't you. See also *audience, movie, stage.* ☽ **audience** ☾ *buildings and rooms, creativity, image, isolation, peer pressure, play, relationships.*

therapist 1. If you dream you are seeing a therapist, you need help figuring something out. Your subconscious is playing a role for you in your dream to help you work through something. If the therapist in your dream is your actual therapist, your subconscious has cast itself into that role so you will listen. **2.** If you dream you are a therapist, you think you know what someone else needs to feel better. **3.** If you dream a therapist treats you unethically or badly, someone you trusted has betrayed your confidence. ☽ **patient** ☾ *authority, career, caretaking, characters, ethics and morals, feelings, healing, health and hygiene, listening, people, solutions and remedies, support, trust issues.*

thermometer 1. If you see or read a thermometer in your dream and the temperature is hot, a situation is heating up. Are you ready for some passionate feelings? **2.** If the thermometer says it's cold, a situation has cooled off. It's not so exciting or unstable anymore. **3.** If the thermometer says your own temperature is high, you are passionate about something or someone. **4.** If the thermometer says your temperature is normal, you are handling a situation with more skill and confidence than you thought you would. **5.** If you dream a thermometer breaks, the regular rules won't work in a current situation. Try looking at things from an entirely different perspective. ☽ **weather changes** ☾ *cold, health and hygiene, heat, inanimate objects, love, personal power, rules and laws, sexual activity, weather and seasons.*

T

thin   **1.** If you dream you look thinner than you do in your waking life and you like the way it looks, you feel strong and confident. The recent changes you've made in your life are working. **2.** If you dream you look too thin, gaunt, and unhealthy, you aren't taking care of yourself or getting the emotional support and attention you need. **3.** If you dream someone else looks thin, you feel envious or worried about someone's health or habits. **4.** If you dream of a very thin person you've never seen before, you've suffered a loss, or you are considering leaving someone or something behind. ☻ **fat** ℭ *body parts, changing course, control issues, feelings, health and hygiene, image, loss, personal power, transformation.*

thirst   Thirst symbolizes something you need but aren't getting. If you dream of feeling very thirsty, your body might literally need more water. You could be dehydrated. Dreaming of feeling thirsty can also mean you are feeling frustrated that someone is emotionally unavailable to you. See also *drinking.* ☻ **hunger** ℭ *desires, feelings, food and drink, health and hygiene, relationships, senses.*

throat   **1.** If you dream your throat is sore, tight, or dry, you aren't saying what you need to say to someone. **2.** Dreams of throat pain or problems could also be a sign from your body that you have a health problem, like a throat infection. If you are worried, have it checked out. **3.** If you dream you keep clearing your throat, you are trying to tell somebody something, but you are having trouble finding the right words or getting up the courage to say it. ☻ **stomach** ℭ *body parts, communication, health and hygiene, impediments.*

According to Eastern thought, the body contains many chakras, or energy centers, each governing different areas of our lives and bodies. The fifth chakra is located in the throat and controls communication. When it is blocked, we have trouble communicating what we need to say. When it is too open, we say too much. The color of this chakra is light blue, and wearing light blue stones or scarves around your throat can, some believe, help free up communication blockages in the fifth chakra.

throwing up   See *vomiting.*

thunder   Thunder symbolizes anger, loud words, outbursts of emotion, and aggression. If you dream of rumbling thunder in the distance, someone's anger or aggressive feelings are building. If you dream of loud cracking thunder or a big thunderstorm, you are angrier than you realize. You haven't been letting it come out in your waking life, so it is exploding in a storm inside your dream. See also *storm.* ☻ **lightning** ℭ *anger, communication, feelings, music and sound, repression, violence, weather and seasons.*

ticket **1.** If you dream of having or holding a ticket, you have a great opportunity or a way into something you couldn't get into before, such as a higher social position or a better job. **2.** If you dream you lost a ticket, you missed an opportunity. It might be too late. **3.** If you dream of giving a ticket to someone else, someone else would appreciate something you have more than you do. ☽ **barrier** ☾ *inanimate objects, loss, opportunity, sacrifice.*

tickling **1.** If you dream of being tickled and enjoying it or tickling as part of foreplay, you have a strong sense of your own physicality and the ability to really enjoy physical intimacy. **2.** If you dream of being tickled and hating it or getting angry or upset because someone won't stop tickling you, you have been faking it. Someone has physical and/or emotional power over you, and you feel vulnerable and frustrated, but you have been pretending you are happy with the situation. **3.** If you dream of tickling a child in fun, you feel happy and secure in your life. **4.** If you dream of tickling someone and the person doesn't like it or gets angry with you, you've overstepped your boundaries with someone. It's probably time to back off. ☽ **crying** ☾ *body parts, control issues, feelings, fun, happiness, love, relationships, sexual activity, trust issues.*

tidal wave Tidal wave dreams are common dreams that symbolize anxiety and other strong emotions associated with a major life change.

Sometimes tidal wave dreams also represent powerful emotions you've been holding back. Your dream is telling you that if you keep sucking them in, they will inevitably come at you like a giant wall of water. **1.** If you dream of the signs a tidal wave is coming, such as water being sucked off the beach, and you are mostly worried about getting others to safety, you are feeling worried about someone you feel responsible for. You aren't sure that person can handle an upcoming emotional upheaval or situation. **2.** If you dream you see a giant wave coming toward you and you have no way to get to safety, you feel anxious and fearful about a change in your life you know is inevitable, or your emotions seem too intense to bear. **3.** If you dream a tidal wave is coming but, once it gets to shore, it isn't nearly as big as you thought it would be, you can handle an upcoming change just fine. You aren't nearly as upset as you thought you would be. **4.** If you dream a tidal wave has caused your house or buildings and streets to flood but you aren't hurt, you've accepted some changes in your life and are making the best of them, even though it has been an emotionally turbulent experience. See also *beach, flood, tides, water, waves.* ☽ **drought** ☾ *anxiety, caretaking, changing course, danger, disaster, fear, feelings, nature, responsibilities, threats, water, weather and seasons.*

tides If you dream of the tides, you are dreaming about your own cyclical energies. You may be

T

undergoing a hormonal change or a transformation from one life stage to the next, or simply experiencing a transition in your ordinary life. **1.** If you dream the tide is coming in and flooding things or trapping you, you feel trapped by an excess of emotion or mood swings. **2.** If you dream the tide is going out and leaving sea animals stranded, you feel like your own lack of emotion has hurt or disappointed someone. **3.** If you dream of watching the tides moving in or out and enjoying the experience, you are in harmony with your own emotional and hormonal fluctuations. See also *moon, waves.* ☾ **drought** ☾ *anxiety, changing course, danger, feelings, feminine, health and hygiene, nature, transformation, water.*

tie **1.** Dreaming of tying your tie symbolizes readiness for a big event or the desire to make a good impression. **2.** Dreaming someone else is tying your tie symbolizes emotional intimacy and support. **3.** Dreaming of wearing a bowtie means you have a good sense of humor or you like to stand out in a crowd. **4.** Dreaming of having trouble tying your tie suggests you are nervous about something or worried about your image. ☾ **T-shirt** ☾ *clothing and accessories, image, inanimate objects, relationships, reputation.*

tiger Tigers symbolize power, nonconformity, and standing out from the crowd. **1.** If you see a tiger in your dream, you can make a strong impression right now or strike out on your own and do just fine. **2.** If you are threatened or attacked by a tiger in your dream, you regret a bold move you made. It has come back to bite you. **3.** If you dream that you ride or pet a tiger or have a tiger for a pet, you have power over others. Your strong personality and charisma can rule the show. ☾ **mouse** ☾ *animals, conformity, danger, nature, personal power, risky behavior, threats.*

tightrope Walking on a tightrope in a dream or seeing someone else walk on a tightrope suggests that you are taking a risk, or thinking about it. You know it won't be easy, but it will certainly make a big impression. If you or someone else falls off the rope, you are doubting whether you should take the risk. If the tightrope walk is successful, you are leaning toward going for it. But don't lean too far, or you know what! ☾ **homebody** ☾ *adventure, anxiety, balance, courage, danger, decisions, risky behavior.*

time travel Are you headed back to the future in your dream? Time travel dreams have to do with memory, regrets, nostalgia, and hope for the future. **1.** If you dream of traveling back in time, you want to understand something about the past that has eluded you. **2.** If you dream of traveling into the future, you are enthusiastic about your life's path and just can't wait to see what's going to happen next, or you wish you could be assured that a decision is the right one. **3.** If you dream your time travel goes horribly wrong and turns into a nightmare, you fear knowing too much about something, and your dream is acting out your fear. You'd feel much more comfortable staying right where you are, knowing just what you already know … at least, for now. **4.** If you travel through time in a cool high-tech machine, you not only enjoy technology gadgets, but you think they really will solve society's problems. Beam me up, Scotty. ◐ **homebody** ℭ *adventure, changing course, decisions, history, hopes and dreams, knowledge, memory, places, predictions, regret, technology, time, travel, vehicles.*

tires Tires represent how easily and quickly you can get to where you are going. **1.** If your tires are bald, your methods are haphazard or careless, and your progress is inefficient and even dangerous. **2.** If you dream of brand new tires, you have everything you need to proceed safely and quickly. **3.** If you dream of getting a flat tire and being stranded, you are facing an unexpected obstacle to your progress. **4.** If you dream of getting a flat tire but changing it and moving on, your resourcefulness will help you overcome any problems. ◐ **car accident** ℭ *accidents, creativity, danger, impediments, inanimate objects, journeys and quests, taking action, travel, vehicles.*

toes **1.** To dream of looking at or cleaning your toes or toenails

means you pay attention to detail, and your appearance and hygiene matter a lot to you. **2.** To dream of smashing or breaking a toe symbolizes big pain that will pass quickly or a minor problem that has caused major inconvenience. **3.** To dream that you have beautiful, perfectly manicured toenails means you have a good reputation, and people find you attractive. ◐ **fingers** ℭ *body parts, health and hygiene, image, impediments, injuries, reputation.*

toilet See *bathroom.*

toll booth **1.** If you dream you have to stop at a toll booth, you know how to jump through the necessary hoops. **2.** If you dream you don't have the right change when you pull up to a toll booth, you expect delays in a current endeavor. **3.** If you pull up to an empty or nonworking toll booth, the usual channels aren't an option this time. You'll have to be creative. **4.** If you dream you work in a toll booth and you enjoy it or accept it as normal, you wish your life was simpler. You don't need much excitement to keep you content. **5.** If you dream of working in a toll booth and disliking it, you aren't getting enough excitement in your life. You need more challenges. ◐ **breaking free** ℭ *buildings and rooms, impediments, journeys and quests, places, rules and laws, travel, work.*

tongue **1.** Your tongue represents what you say or don't say. If you dream of looking at your tongue

T

or noticing something wrong with your tongue, you've been holding something back or you've said too much. **2.** If you dream of noticing someone else's tongue, you wish someone else would say more to you … or less. **3.** If you dream your tongue is missing or has been cut out, you don't feel able to speak about something. **4.** If you dream of kissing with tongues, you have a strong physical desire for someone. Less talk, more action. ☽ **teeth** ☾ *body parts, communication, impediments, injuries, relationships, sexual activity.*

tonsils If you dream of getting your tonsils taken out, either you are reliving a childhood experience of illness or hospitalization or you need to reboot your health habits to reinvigorate your immune system. You've been abusing your body, and it's time to start fresh. You will crave ice cream for several days. ☽ **lungs** ☾ *body parts, health and hygiene, memory, taking action.*

tools **1.** Dreaming of working with tools symbolizes your ability to make things happen. You are a self-starter. **2.** Dreaming of losing or breaking your tools means you don't feel you can live up to the image you've created of yourself. **3.** Injuring yourself while using tools symbolizes your frustration or anxiety about a current project. You aren't sure you can do this. **4.** Getting new tools represents personal power and resourcefulness. Getting *big* tools represents sexual

confidence. See also *power tools.* ☽ **hand** ☾ *accidents, control issues, creativity, image, inanimate objects, injuries, personal power, sexual activity, taking action, technology, work.*

tornado Tornadoes represent control issues and volatile situations. **1.** If you dream of seeing a tornado far away and knowing you will be able to elude it, you have control over a potentially explosive situation. **2.** If a tornado is heading straight toward you in your dream, you are involved in a major life change that will cause a lot of upheaval, or you are feeling particularly strong emotions about something. **3.** If you dream of seeing tornadoes and feeling thrilled or excited about it rather than scared, or you dream of chasing tornadoes to get a closer look, you aren't getting enough excitement in your life or you feel like taking a risk. Your courage is high right now. **4.** If you dream that you seek shelter from a tornado and it passes, you feel confident you can get through a difficult situation. **5.** If you get sucked into the tornado or injured by a tornado in your dream, you fear you won't escape a current difficult situation without getting hurt, and your dream is preparing you for the worst. **6.** If you see multiple tornadoes around you, you are dealing with difficult, extremist, or dangerous people. **7.** If you dream of surveying major destruction from a tornado, recent events have changed everything. You'll have to start over or start fresh. See also *storm, wind.* ☽ **rock**

ℭ *adventure, anxiety, changing course, control issues, courage, danger, destruction, disaster, extremism, injuries, weather and seasons.*

torture If you have recurring or strongly violent dreams, please consider seeking the help of a licensed therapist to help you understand their meaning. Torturous dreams, however, may not signify literal bloody deeds or evil, abusive, and cruel behavior, but rather extreme frustration and issues surrounding power. **1.** If you dream of being tortured, you are in an unacceptable situation and you may not realize just how unhappy it is making you. Your dream is showing you that it really is torture. **2.** If you dream of torturing someone, you feel extremely angry or frustrated with someone, and your dream is giving you a way to release these strong feelings. **3.** If you dream of seeing someone else being tortured, you recognize that someone is in trouble and can't help him- or herself. Are you going to do something about it? ☯ **tickling** ℭ *anger, anxiety, control issues, danger, decisions, fear, feelings, frustration, pain, taking action, violence, vulnerability.*

tower Towers are potent symbols of masculine energy and symbolize the male genitalia. If you dream of seeing or climbing a tower, you are getting comfortable with your own masculine power, or you have recently been exposed to someone else's. ☯ **tunnel** ℭ *buildings and rooms, masculine, personal power, places, shapes and symbols.*

toys You would rather not have the responsibility, thanks. Dreams about toys represent your carefree, childish side, the part of you that just wants to play. Dreams of broken toys represent your anger or sadness that you have lost that playful side of yourself. ☯ **tools** ℭ *age, fun, inanimate objects, play, sports and games.*

traffic **1.** If you dream you are stuck in traffic, you are frustrated by barriers to progress. You aren't getting somewhere as fast as you would like. **2.** Dreams of driving through smooth, quick-moving traffic suggest you are making good progress and reaching your goals. **3.** Dreams of a traffic accident symbolize a major delay in a project. See also *car, car accident, rage, sign.* ☯ **street** ℭ *accidents, changing course, control issues, frustration, goal-setting, impediments, travel, vehicles.*

trailer See *mobile home.*

train **1.** Traveling by train and enjoying the scenery means you are on the right path, and life is good. **2.** If you dream you are in a train crash or the train stops and can't get started again, you might be headed in the wrong direction, or you are experiencing a major barrier to progress. **3.** If you dream of missing a train, you have missed an opportunity or narrowly escaped a dangerous situation. **4.** If you dream you are driving a train, you are master of your own destiny. You know just where to go and what to do to create your life the way you want it to be. **5.** If you dream of train tracks or walking on train tracks, you are thinking about your life's direction and where you want to go. You might be ready to set out on a new path. ☽ **airplane** ☾ *accidents, adventure, changing course, control issues, direction, goal-setting, impediments, journeys and quests, opportunity, personal power, travel, vehicles.*

> One of the best-known children's stories is *The Little Engine That Could,* which has stamped the train in many people's minds as a symbol of determination and success in spite of obstacles. Driving a train has come to mean mastering one's own destiny just by effort and the power of positive thinking. It never hurts to keep repeating that beloved mantra: "I think I can, I think I can, I think I can."

train tracks See *train.*

trampoline **1.** You're up, you're down, you're up again, you're down again. If you dream of jumping on a trampoline, you can handle life's changes with a good sense of humor and a strong presence. **2.** If you dream of watching someone else jump on a trampoline, you recognize that life changes, and you don't mind. You can handle it. You find it interesting. **3.** If you dream of injuring yourself on a trampoline, you are taking some risks you aren't quite comfortable about. Or you may need a new mattress. ☽ **chair** ☾ *accidents, changing course, fun,*

inanimate objects, injuries, personal power, play, risky behavior, sports and games.

transsexual See *sex change.*

trapped Dreams of being trapped symbolize trapped feelings in your waking life. You may not literally be stuck inside a well, locked in a basement, shoved in a locker, or tied up in a closet, but you feel trapped in a relationship or a dead-end job or you feel locked into your current situation by your responsibilities and obligations. ☽ **breaking free** ☾ *anger, anxiety, burdens, control issues, fear, frustration, impediments, responsibilities.*

traveling See *trip.*

treasure **1.** Dreams of searching for treasure symbolize your life's quest for meaning. **2.** Finding treasure symbolizes a success or great opportunity. **3.** Failing to find treasure or having treasure stolen from you and giving up the search suggests that your dreams have been foiled or disappointed. ☽ **poverty** ☾ *abundance, hopes and dreams, journeys and quests, opportunity, success.*

trees Trees represent strength, commitment, stability, and the wisdom of the natural world. **1.** If you walk through a forest of trees enjoying yourself, nature replenishes you. **2.** If you walk through a dark, frightening forest, you feel isolated from the natural world or unstable and without roots. **3.** If you dream of chopping down a tree, you are wasting valuable resources or you have disappointed someone. **4.** If you dream of touching tree bark, you know something is going on below the surface of a situation. **5.** If you dream of climbing a tree or building a tree house, you can find greater happiness if you develop your relationship with the natural world, or you still have a childlike energy and you know how to have fun in a healthy way. **6.** If you dream of tree branches or twigs, don't overlook the details. **7.** If you dream of a tree stump or sitting on a tree stump, you have learned an important lesson. **8.** If you dream of tree roots, you need more meaningful connections in your life. Can you quit moving and put down some roots of your own? ◐ **building** ℂ *age, changing course, ethics and morals, family, fear, fun, happiness, health and hygiene, instincts, knowledge, nature, personal power, plants, stability.*

trespassing 1. Hey, get off my property! If you dream of someone trespassing on your property, someone has overstepped his or her boundaries and invaded your personal life. **2.** If the trespasser seems dangerous or threatens you, someone's actions are making you feel unsafe or vulnerable, or someone has betrayed your trust. **3.** If you dream you are trespassing on someone's property and you get caught, you feel guilty about something you've done, or you've learned something you shouldn't know. **4.** If you dream of trespassing but not getting caught, you've done something naughty, but it was fun and you don't feel *too* guilty. ◐ **fence** ℂ *adventure, control issues, ethics and morals, fun, guilt, places, punishment, risky behavior, rules and laws, threats, trust issues, vulnerability.*

triangle Triangles represent female energy and symbolize female genitalia. They represent the three stages of womanhood: virgin, mother, and crone. Many ancient goddesses also had three different forms representing each of these three stages. If you notice a triangle shape in your dream, you are tapping into your own ancient goddess energy, or you are attracted to the strong female energy in someone else. ◐ **square** ℂ *feminine, shapes and symbols.*

trip If you dream you are going on a trip, you expect a change or transition in your life, or you may actually be going on a trip, and your dream is testing out potential scenarios for the experience. Trip dreams also symbolize your journey through life: where you are going and the style in which you are getting there. **1.** If you dream of a relaxing or fun trip, you look forward to the future and future changes. **2.** If you dream of a disastrous or unpleasant trip, you are worried about an upcoming change—you fear it won't be for the better—or you don't like the way your life is going right now. ◐ **homebody** ℂ *anxiety, changing course, hopes and dreams, journeys and quests, travel.*

T

triplets See *multiple births.*

tropical island See *island.*

trucks and semis **1.** Dream of driving a truck, and you feel powerful in your journey through life. **2.** If you are hauling cargo in a pickup truck or a semi, you carry many burdens or responsibilities with you. **3.** If you dream of four-wheeling off-road in a truck, you like to take risks and you know how to have a good time, but you also like to stand out or rebel against the mainstream. ☻ **car** ℂ *burdens, fun, journeys and quests, rebellion, responsibilities, travel, vehicles.*

truth See *telling the truth.*

T-shirt **1.** Is it casual Friday? Dreaming of wearing a T-shirt or noticing someone else wearing a T-shirt suggests a fun and casual approach. Why be so formal? **2.** If you dream you feel uncomfortable wearing a T-shirt, the whole casual Friday concept still eludes you. Can't people make a little effort? **3.** If a T-shirt says something in a dream, this might be a message to you about something you should be paying closer attention to—everyone else is—or it might just highlight your sense of humor. ☻ **tuxedo** ℂ *clothing and accessories, fun, image, inanimate objects, messages.*

tsunami See *tidal wave.*

tulip You have everything you need within you if you dream of tulips. Your life may be simple, but it is also beautiful. See also *flowers.* ☻ **rose** ℂ *beauty, nature, plants, stability.*

tunnel Tunnels symbolize mysteries, secrets, and feminine power. They represent female sexual power and journeys into the unknown. **1.** If you dream of traveling through a tunnel, you have uncovered a mystery or you are attracted to the power of a woman. **2.** Dream of digging a tunnel, and you will work hard to solve a mystery. ☻ **tower** ℂ *feminine, journeys and quests, mystery, personal power, secrets, shapes and symbols, subterfuge.*

turtle If you dream of a turtle, you are patient and steady in your approach. You will get there eventually. If you dream you have a turtle as a pet, other people describe you as patient and persistent. See also *reptiles and amphibians.* ☻ **bird** ℂ *animals, crawling creatures, goal-setting, journeys and quests, nature.*

Aesop's famous fable about the tortoise and the hare has fixed the turtle, in many people's minds and subconscious, with the reputation of determination and a stick-to-it-iveness. The moral of that fable, "Slow and steady wins the race," raises the turtle above the quick-and-dirty hare as a symbol of success.

tuxedo **1.** Dream of wearing a tuxedo, and you have decided to take a formal approach, or you will soon be involved in a formal event and you want to make a good impression. **2.** If you dream of a man in a tuxedo, someone has something very important to tell you or ask you. It could impact your future. ◐ **T-shirt** ℂ *clothing and accessories, communication, goal-setting, image, predictions.*

TV **1.** If you dream of watching TV, you might be watching too much TV, but you might also be getting an electronic message through your dream about something you should pay attention to. Just what are you watching that is so important you have to do it while you sleep? It may symbolize something you need to know or notice. **2.** If you dream your TV is broken, you are missing something important that everyone else knows about. **3.** If you dream someone else is watching TV and won't listen to you, you are having problems communicating with someone. You might have better luck if you use technology. Send an e-mail or a text message. ◐ **talking** ℂ *communication, electronics, inanimate objects, knowledge, listening, messages, technology.*

twins See *multiple births.*

T

U

UFO Dreaming of UFOs can be frightening or fascinating, and how you dream about those unidentified flying objects shows how you feel about the unknown. Something new has happened or will happen, and you are trying to figure out, via your dream, how to deal with it. Are you terrified or curious? **1.** If you dream you see a UFO flying by fast in the sky and then disappearing, you feel that things are moving or changing too quickly, or things are happening that you don't know about. You may not be getting all the information. **2.** If you dream you see a UFO hovering or moving very slowly, you are waiting for something to happen, and you don't know how it's going to turn out. You are filled with anticipation—or dread. **3.** If you dream the sky is filled with many UFOs and you have a sense of impending doom, you expect a major change in your life. You are afraid everything is going to be different soon. See also *aliens*. ☽ **friends** ☾ *adventure, changing course, danger, fear, myths and legends, threats, transformation, vehicles.*

ugliness 1. If you dream of looking at yourself and seeing ugliness, you have done something that has made you feel bad about yourself or caught a glimpse of your own inner ugly side. You may not want to admit it consciously. Have you been abusing your body with bad habits? Have you said something ugly to a friend? **2.** If you dream of seeing an ugly person, someone has done something to disgust or offend you. ☽ **beauty contest** ☾ *beauty, body parts, ego, fear, health and hygiene, image, insecurity, relationships.*

umbrella 1. If you dream of having a pleasant walk through the rain holding an umbrella, you are having good luck and financial abundance. **2.** If you dream of struggling with an umbrella in a storm or wind to keep yourself dry, you are not open to your own strong emotions about something. You want to shield yourself, but it isn't working; those feelings want to come out. **3.** If you dream of walking through the rain with a closed umbrella, you've finally let out some strong feelings, and even though it may be difficult, you've faced something. Good for you! **4.** If you dream of using a leaky umbrella, you are having trouble keeping something inside. You may already have spoken bitter or hurtful words to someone because of strong emotions you aren't sure how to manage. You'll understand your own feelings better if you just let yourself feel them. **5.** If you dream of seeing someone else with an umbrella, someone is hiding his or her own strong feelings from you ☕ **rain** ℂ *abundance, clothing and accessories, control issues, feelings, financial resources, inanimate objects, protection, repression, weather and seasons.*

underground Underground dreams symbolize thoughts, actions, and behaviors different than the societal norm. **1.** If you dream you are underground, you have been doing or thinking something that you don't feel is quite normal. You may feel perfectly comfortable with this and it may be the way you are, but you also recognize that it sets you apart from most people in some way. **2.** If you dream you live underground, you don't like to conform or be a part of the mainstream. **3.** If you dream of traveling or moving underground through tunnels, you don't want someone to know what you are up to. **4.** If you dream of going underground to look for something or someone, you will have to go about getting something you want in an unexpected way. ☕ **mountain** ℂ *changing course, conformity, personal power, taking action.*

undertow See *rip tide.*

underwater **1.** Dream of floating or swimming underwater, and you are so wrapped up in your own emotions that you can't communicate with anyone very well. You may need to really immerse yourself in these feelings for now, but don't forget to come up and take a breath or ask for help if you can't seem to get back up to the surface. **2.** To dream of seeing someone else underwater suggests that you feel separated from someone else because that person is too emotionally engrossed in his or her own problem. See also *drowning.* ☕ **surfing** ℂ *communication, feelings, water.*

underwear **1.** Nice tightywhities. If you dream of being in public in your underwear, you feel exposed. Someone, possibly you, has revealed something personal about you to others in an inappropriate way. **2.** If nobody but you notices you are in your underwear, you've been feeling insecure, but it hasn't had any negative effect on you or your image yet. Still you aren't quite comfortable. **3.** If you dream your underwear is nicer or sexier than usual, or you are showing off your body to someone while in your underwear, you are in the mood to attract someone. **4.** If you dream your underwear is ragged, full of holes, or dirty, you feel ashamed of something you've done, and you hope nobody finds out. If you throw away the underwear, you wish to destroy the evidence.

U

5. If you dream of seeing someone else in his or her underwear, you've received an insight or private information about someone. See also *naked in public*. ☾ **coat** ☾ *clothing and accessories, desires, guilt, image, insecurity, sexual activity, vulnerability*.

unemployed   1. Dreaming you are unemployed and feeling bad or nervous about it means you don't feel like you are holding up your end of the deal with someone, or you don't feel like you are taking responsibility for something that you should. **2.** Dreaming you are unemployed and enjoying it suggests you need a break from too much responsibility. Your dream is giving you the chance to experience a little taste of freedom. **3.** To dream someone in your family is unemployed and more of the burden falls on you or will cause your family to suffer suggests that you worry about financial security or reputation, or you don't trust someone else with your own security or reputation. ☾ **job** ☾ *anxiety, career, control issues, escapism, failure, family, fear, financial resources, freedom, reputation, trust issues, work*.

unicorn   An ancient symbol of innocence and purity, the mythical unicorn symbolizes these same qualities when it appears in a dream. **1.** If you see a unicorn in your dream, you've recently come into contact with someone or something pure and innocent. **2.** If you

ride a unicorn in your dream, you feel cleansed and renewed physically or emotionally. **3.** If you dream a unicorn approaches you and you touch it, someone has forgiven you. **4.** If you encounter an injured or dead unicorn, some innocent part of you has died. You feel older, wiser, and less pure. ☾ **possessed by demons** ☾ *animals, forgiveness, health and hygiene, innocence, myths and legends, transformation*.

uniform   1. Dream you are in uniform, and you've just been given a new important responsibility, or your reputation has recently improved. You feel ready to shoulder this new weight. **2.** Dream someone else is in uniform, and you've gained new respect for the status or maturity of someone in your life. **3.** To dream of a uniform on a hanger suggests your awareness of something you should be doing but haven't started doing yet. **4.** To dream of a uniform crumpled up or dirty suggests you or someone else is shirking an important responsibility, or your reputation has suffered because of something you've failed to do. ☾ **naked in public** ☾ *authority, clothing and accessories, image, reputation, responsibilities*.

unique   See *one-of-a-kind*.

university   See *college*.

unmarried   See *divorce, single*.

unraveling 1. To dream your own clothing is unraveling suggests people are beginning to see what you are really doing rather than what you've been letting everyone think you are doing. Your image is changing, and you can't hide it anymore. **2.** To dream someone else's clothing is unraveling suggests you are beginning to see through someone else's false front. **3.** To dream something you own or something you made, such as a blanket or a knit scarf, is unraveling in your hands means something you've been working hard on is coming apart. All your work seems to have been for nothing. ☻ **knitting** ℂ *changing course, clothing and accessories, failure, image, reputation, work.*

upside-down 1. If you dream you are upside-down, such as hanging from a tree or playground equipment, or standing on your head or hands, you've recently seen your life in a whole new way. Everything looks different, and you are still getting used to this new view, but you are the one who has actually changed. **2.** If you dream someone else is upside-down, someone you thought you knew well has proved to be a complete mystery. Everything you thought you believed about this person is turning out to be wrong. **3.** If you dream things in your environment are upside-down, such as furniture, rooms, trees, and so on, something beyond your control has happened to change your life in a big way. ☻ **backwards** ℂ *direction, changing course, transformation.*

utensils Your tools for the meal, utensils symbolize your personal style and the way you relate to others. **1.** If you dream of eating with a fork, you like to think about what you say before you say it, and you communicate with deliberate and well-chosen words. **2.** Seeing but not using a fork in a dream symbolizes a moral choice or decision you must make. **3.** If you dream of eating with a spoon, you like to gush, and your enthusiasm is contagious. **4.** If you dream of seeing but not using a spoon, money or good luck is coming to you very soon. You might get that check in the mail today. **5.** If you dream of cutting your food with a dinner knife, you like to get to the bottom of things by asking lots of questions and using your analytical skills. **6.** If you dream of seeing but not using a dinner knife, you are going to have to choose between two people or two things you want. ☻ **dishes** ℂ *abundance, changing course, communication, decisions, ethics and morals, financial resources, food and drink, inanimate objects, knowledge.*

utopia To dream of utopia—a perfect society—or any other heaven, paradise, or perfect world or existence suggests a keen optimism and belief in the possibility of perfection, whether via some higher divine power or the ultimate potential of humanity. **1.** If you are a happy and prosperous part of your dream utopia, you have hope or faith that your current situation will improve dramatically, perhaps with the help of a higher power. This

U

really *can* work. **2.** If you feel dis-
satisfied in your dream utopia, your
rebellious spirit is acting up, or the
thing everyone seems to agree on
or enjoy right now isn't for you. You
want something else, and you think
everyone else is deluded. **3.** If you
dream of a utopia that exists but
you aren't a part of it, your dream is
urging you to focus more closely on
your spiritual life or your own personal needs. You've been neglecting this important part of you, and
it is keeping you out of balance.
You won't find happiness without
it. See also *heaven.* ☯ **hell** ☾ *balance, desires, divine power, happiness,
hopes and dreams, myths and legends,
personal power, places, spirituality, yin-
yang.*

In the sixteenth century, a writer, poli-
tician, and devout Roman Catholic
named Sir Thomas More, who was
later canonized and became Saint
Thomas More, invented the term
utopia, from the Greek words *ou-
topos,* which means "no place," and
eu-topos, which means "good place."
In his book, titled *Utopia,* More
described an imaginary island where
people lived in perfect social and
political harmony.

U-turn   If you dream of making
a U-turn or seeing someone else
make a U-turn, you've changed
your mind. You've been heading
in the wrong direction, so you're
going to turn around and do exactly
the opposite of what you were
doing. ☯ **straight line** ☾ *changing
course, decisions, direction, travel.*

V

vacation Dreaming you are on vacation can mean you are looking forward to an upcoming vacation or you desperately need a vacation. However, vacation dreams can also symbolize a vacation you are taking from something in your life or in your mind. You might be taking a mental break from work or a break from a relationship, worrying, working out at the gym, or responsibility in general. How you enjoy the vacation in your dream suggests how much you need or can handle taking a break from whatever you need to get away from in your waking life. See also *trip.* ☯ **working hard** ℭ *responsibilities, solutions and remedies, travel, work.*

vaccination **1.** If you dream you are getting a vaccination, you fear how something might influence you, and you want to protect yourself. You are taking action to be sure you remain strong. **2.** If you dream of giving someone a vaccination, you have the urge to protect someone else. **3.** Vaccinations can also symbolize concerns about your health. Are you doing all you should to prevent health problems? See also *disease, epidemic.* ☯ **disease** ℭ *caretaking, health and hygiene, protection, taking action.*

vacuum cleaner What kind of mess do you need to clean up? Vacuum cleaners symbolize your efforts to keep your life and particularly your health in order. **1.** If you dream of vacuuming your home, you have recently done something to improve your health, financial situation, or status. **2.** If you dream your vacuum cleaner breaks or gets clogged, your bad health habits are putting you at risk. Your body is telling you to take better care of yourself before you get sick. **3.** If you dream of someone else vacuuming your house, someone is trying to take care of you. Are you doing your part to take care of yourself? ☯ **dirt** ℭ *caretaking, financial resources, furniture and appliances, health and hygiene, inanimate objects, reputation.*

vagina See *sex organs.*

valentine **1.** Dream of getting a valentine, and you suspect someone has a crush on you. **2.** Dream of giving a valentine, and you are trying to reach out to someone for attention. ❧ **insult** ℭ *communication, desires, love, relationships.*

valley Valleys symbolize protection, safety, and stability. **1.** If you dream you are in a valley, you feel safe and protected. **2.** If you dream you are trying to climb out of a valley, you crave more excitement in your life. ❧ **mountain** ℭ *nature, places, protection, stability, stasis.*

vampire The ultimate symbol of evil, lust, and power, the vampire also represents a rebellion against society's stuffy rules and decorum. **1.** If you dream you are bitten by a vampire, you've been feeling the urge to break the rules lately, and your resolve is weakening. Or you've already made the leap and done that deed, even though you know it's not the right thing to do—at least, not in the eyes of society. **2.** If you dream of seeing a vampire, you face temptation but you are trying to behave yourself. **3.** If you dream you are a vampire, you've already rejected certain conventions in favor of a more decadent and unrestricted lifestyle— or you like to have that reputation even if you aren't quite as decadent as you want people to think you are. See also *bite*. ❧ **angel** ℭ *characters, ethics and morals, fear, freedom, hedonism, image, myths and legends, personal power, rebellion, reputation, risky behavior, sexual activity.*

vegetables Sure, they have a lot of vitamins, and sure, you might even love to eat them, but vegetables symbolize austerity, frugality, and the straight-and-narrow path to righteousness. The opposite of luxurious indulgences like desserts or purely beautiful things like flowers, vegetables also symbolize utilitarian efforts, which have nothing to do with pleasure and beauty. **1.** If you dream of eating vegetables, you are staying strong in your resolve to do the right thing, and/or you put spiritual pleasures ahead of earthly pleasures. **2.** If you dream of eating vegetables even though you don't like them, you feel resentful that your life is so devoid of pleasures compared to others. **3.** If you dream of cooking vegetables, your creativity takes a useful form. **4.** If you dream of serving vegetables to others, you have the knack for dispensing wisdom to others about the right and healthful way to live. ❧ **cake** ℭ *creativity, ethics and morals, food and drink, health and hygiene, plants, responsibilities, spirituality.*

veil Veils symbolize innocence and mystery. **1.** If you dream you are wearing a veil, you don't want people to know something about you, or you want to preserve your own innocence or lack of knowledge about the world. **2.** If you dream of someone else wearing a veil, someone is hiding something from you. **3.** If you put a veil over someone, you want to protect someone's innocence. **4.** If you lift someone's veil off, you want a deeper, more intimate emotional or physical connection with someone. See also *marriage*. ❧ **underwear** ℭ *caretaking, clothing and accessories,* inanimate objects, innocence, mystery, protection, relationships, secrets, sexual activity, subterfuge.

> According to traditional wedding lore, the wedding veil serves as a protective shield to ward off evil spirits and also hides the bride's potentially blinding beauty from others who might be tempted to steal her away.

venom   See *poison.*

video camera   See *camcorder.*

video game   Dreaming of playing a video game might mean you've been spending too much time playing video games! But video game dreams can also symbolize a longing for a different life, whether you dream of playing the game or actually being inside the game. Maybe you wish you were someone stronger or more powerful, or had a life with more excitement and adventure and the chance to defeat villains. Or you might just wish for a world where good is good and bad is bad; everyone is gorgeous and powerful; and there isn't any gray area, moral confusion, or complicated human relationships. Whatever video game you dream about will suggest what vision of the world you long for. ❂ **reality show** ℭ *adventure, competition, electronics, fun, identity, inanimate objects, personal power, play, solutions and remedies, sports and games, technology.*

villain   1. If you dream of a villain, someone in your waking life is playing that role for you—your nemesis or arch enemy—and your dream is making this easier for you to see by simplifying matters into black and white: good (you) vs. evil (the villain). 2. If you dream you are the villain, you've done something that has given you an unfavorable reputation, or you feel guilty about something you did and now you feel like a bad person. 3. If you dream someone rescues you from a villain, you feel victimized in your life, and you long for someone to save you because you don't feel able or inclined to save yourself from a force so menacing. ❂ **hero** ℭ *characters, guilt, people, protection, relationships, social life, violence.*

virus   See *disease, epidemic.*

vision problems   1. If you dream of going blind, you've seen something in your waking life you wish you hadn't seen or don't want to admit you saw. You are so disturbed by this vision that, in your dream, you have turned off your power of sight entirely. 2. If you dream your vision is getting blurry or you have some kind of eye disease like cataracts or glaucoma, you might need to have your eyes checked. Your body may be signaling a problem. 3. Dreams of blurred vision can also indicate something you don't want to see clearly in your waking life. The blurred version seems so much easier to deal with. ❂ **eyes** ℭ *body parts, health and hygiene, repression, senses.*

V

voice, disembodied If you dream of hearing a voice without anybody attached to it, you are getting a loud-and-clear message from your subconscious mind. Whatever it says, you should listen. It's probably important, although it may be in code. You might have to figure out the meaning. ☽ **mute** ℂ *code, listening, messages, senses.*

The Polynesian goddess of volcanoes, fire, lightning, and violence is Pele, who is said to live on the island of Kilauea and control lava flows. Pele has a violent temper and is a seductress who often appears as a beautiful woman with a white dog at her side.

volcano A volcano symbolizes an eruption of temper or a build-up of stress so intense that you really feel you are going to explode. The dream is helping you release some of these pent-up feelings through imagery. **1.** If you dream of watching a volcano explode and feeling scared or panicked, a situation is about to come to a head. Be ready to deal with it … or run for your life! **2.** If you dream of a volcano exploding and you feel intense excitement or interest, you might be feeling so passionate or physically excited by someone that your body craves sexual release. That volcano is *you!* **3.** If you dream of running from hot lava coming out of a volcano, you are in trouble, and you know it. How are you going to get out of this one? **4.** If you dream a volcano is steaming but not erupting, you are seething, and you need stress release now. Or you are just waiting for someone else to lose it. Can you do something to vent some of that pressure? See also *lava.* ☽ **canyon** ℂ *anger, anxiety, danger, desires, disaster, nature, places, relationships, risky behavior, threats, sexual activity.*

vomiting **1.** To dream of vomiting could mean you really are feeling nauseated; some people have actually vomited in their sleep while dreaming about it. You might just have a stomach bug. **2.** Dreams of vomiting can also mean you need to rid yourself of something in your life that is bad for you. Your dream is telling you that you must expel this metaphorical virus from your body and your life. **3.** If vomiting in a dream is accompanied by a feeling of anxiety, you have mixed feelings about a bad influence in your life. You are still attached even though you know you should move on. **4.** Anxiety related to vomiting can also indicate extreme guilt about something. **5.** If vomiting in a dream is followed by a calm, peaceful, healthy feeling, you are ready to make the change. **6.** Vomiting related to eating in a dream is a message that you need to change your health habits, or anything else you are putting into your body that is making your body rebel. Take a closer look at how you treat yourself. ☽ **eating** ℂ *addictions, anger, anxiety, body parts, changing course, fear, feelings, food and drink, guilt, health and hygiene, solutions and remedies.*

voting See *election.*

waiting   **1.** What are you wait-ing for? It must be something, if you dream of waiting. You might not be ready for action yet. Do you need to prepare more or give something more thought? **2.** If you dream of waiting *for* some-body and feeling impatient about it, someone else is controlling the situation. **3.** If you dream everybody is waiting for you, you are—purposefully or not—controlling a situation in a way that frustrates others. 🌜 **run-ning** ℂ *control issues, frustration, stasis, time.*

waking up   **1.** If you dream of waking up, but you don't really wake up, something you thought was over isn't over yet. **2.** Dream-ing you wake up can also mean you are missing the irony in a situation, or you are missing out on the situation altogether. See also *dreaming that you are dream-ing and dreaming that you wake up.* 🌜 **coma** ℂ *confusion, goal-setting, humor.*

walking   If you dream of walking, you may need more exercise, or you may need to be somewhere other than you are. Either way, it's time to get moving. 🌜 **backward** ℂ *changing course, health and hygiene, taking action, travel.*

wall   If you dream of a wall, something is standing in your way. You can't go any farther in this direction, and you can't even see what's out there. It's time to use your creativity to go another way. See also *barrier.* 🌜 **window** ℂ *buildings and rooms, impediments.*

wallet   **1.** What's in your wal-let? If your dream wallet is full of cash, you feel powerful and confident or well-cushioned with financial resources. If it's empty, you feel insecure or anx-ious about the future, or you feel you have failed others. **2.** If you dream you lose your wal-let, you are questioning your financial security or your iden-tity. You aren't sure who you are anymore. **3.** If you dream of finding your wallet, you have new hope, after thinking all was lost. **4.** If you dream of finding someone else's wallet, someone needs your help, and it's up to you whether you are going to take advantage of the situation or go out of your way to give someone a helping hand. ☽ **poverty** ☾ *caretaking, clothing and accessories, financial resources, hopes and dreams, identity, insecurity, personal power.*

wandering You have no idea where you are going, do you? Maybe that's good! Dreams of wandering mean you are open to discovering new ideas without dictating a strict direction for your life. Let a more instinctive or intuitive method rule you for a while and see what turns up. You might make a fantastic discovery. ☽ **asking for directions** ☾ *direction, freedom, instincts, intuition.*

war **1.** If you dream of war, you feel anxious about the future and fear that it holds instability and anger, even violence, either in your personal life or in the world. **2.** If you dream of nuclear war, you are terrified that an upcoming change will make your situation worse, or you feel fundamentally unstable in your life, like everything could fall apart. **3.** If you dream you are called to fight in a war, you have a big responsibility you know will be difficult. **4.** If you dream you are fighting in a war, a conflict with someone has gotten out of control. ☽ **nonviolence** ☾ *anger, anxiety, changing course, control issues, courage, danger, destruction, disaster, fear, insecurity, loss, violence, war.*

wart See *skin.*

water Water symbolizes emotion in its many forms, and dreams about water usually symbolize dreams about your own strong emotions.

The form the water takes symbolizes how your emotions are going, or flowing, and how well you are managing them. Floods and overflows symbolize excess or uncontrolled emotion, while dry or draught conditions symbolize a lack of emotion. Interaction with water, from scuba diving to surfing to drinking a tall refreshing glass, symbolizes how well you handle your emotions. Do you dive right in, or skim over the top so you don't get all wet? **1.** If you dream of a small body of water, like a small lake, pond, or even a puddle, you have your feelings well contained. If you dream of fishing in the pond or puddle, you stay in tune with what's going on within you. If the water is murky, you don't like to explore the depths of your feelings. It makes you uncomfortable. **2.** If you dream of a large body of water, like a large lake, sea, gulf, or ocean, your emotions seem limitless to you. Stormy seas symbolize anger and out-of-control emotions, while calm, balmy seas symbolize happy contentment. Raging seas can also symbolize excessive passion and desire and sexual energy. Are you rocking the boat? **3.** Waterfalls symbolize changing emotions, mood swings, or the healthful outpouring of emotion to someone else. **4.** Rivers, streams, and creeks symbolize communication of emotions. A river blocked by a dam suggests you aren't telling someone how you really feel. An overflowing or flooding river or streambed suggests you are sharing too much. This may be more emotion than some people can handle. **5.** Drinking water in your dream could indicate actual physical need for water, but it also means you are ready to take a measured and controlled approach to your feelings. See also *aquarium, bathroom, boat, coastline, diving into water, drinking, flood, glacier, plumbing, rain, rip tide, showers and baths, snow, swimming, tidal wave, tides, underwater, waves.* ❧ **thirst** ☾ *changing course, communication, control issues, desires, fear, feelings, food and drink, happiness, nature, repression, sexual activity, subterfuge, water.*

waterfall   See *water.*

water skiing   **1.** You don't let your feelings get to you if you dream of water skiing. You sail over them because you'd rather have fun than get all bogged down. **2.** If you dream of crashing or falling on water skis, your feelings have gotten the better of you, despite your efforts. **3.** If you really do water ski, dreams of water skiing can actually improve your performance. ❧ **snorkeling and scuba diving** ☾ *feelings, fun, play, sports and games, water.*

waves   **1.** Dreams of waves lapping gently at the shore symbolize a calm and peaceful balance with your emotions. You like the way you feel. **2.** Dreams of violent, stormy waves symbolize strong feelings. You are angry and frustrated, and you're not going to take it anymore. See also *tidal wave, tides.* ❧ **desert** ☾ *anger, anxiety, balance,*

feelings, frustration, happiness, taking action, water.

wealthy   See *rich.*

weasel   If you dream of a weasel or a ferret, someone is being sneaky, and you don't trust this person. You think he or she is planning to cause trouble, or is a bad influence. ❧ **dog** ☾ *animals, dishonesty, ethics and morals, nature, trust issues.*

weather changes   If the weather changes in your dream, your feelings about something are changing. If the weather gets stormy, something is making you angrier than you want to admit. If the weather suddenly turns beautiful, things are going better than you expected, and you suddenly feel optimistic. Are you tuned into your dream weather channel? ❧ **turtle** ☾ *changing course, feelings, transformation, weather and seasons.*

website   **1.** If you dream of a website, pay attention to what the website is about. It is a message regarding something you should notice or somewhere you are supposed to go. **2.** Website dreams can also symbolize an image you want to project to others that may or may not be anything like the real you. ❧ **vision problems** ☾ *image, messages, technology.*

wedding   **1.** If you dream of your own wedding, you are ready, even eager, to go to the next level of commitment in a relationship or at your job. **2.** If you dream of

W

your wedding but you feel upset or you want to escape, you regret a recent decision you've made. **3.** If you dream you are at someone else's wedding, you are wondering whether you should be doing what others in your life are doing. Are you getting left behind at the altar? See also *marriage, proposal.* ☽ **divorce** ℭ *career, changing course, conformity, goal-setting, journeys and quests, love, peer pressure, regret, relationships.*

weightless **1.** If you dream you are weightless, you have let go of a burden or forgiven someone, and now you feel free. **2.** If the feeling of weightlessness is upsetting to you, you feel like you aren't doing anything substantial with your life, or you don't have any influence over others. ☽ **heavy** ℭ *burdens, control issues, forgiveness, freedom, insecurity, responsibilities, vulnerability.*

werewolf **1.** If you dream a werewolf is chasing you or attacks you, you fear your own inner urges and instincts. You feel like you might lose control of them and you might do something you shouldn't. **2.** If you dream of escaping from or killing a werewolf, you've mastered your urges ... for now. **3.** If you dream you turn into a werewolf, you aren't acknowledging the darker side of yourself and it is trying to come out in protest. See also *moon.* ☽ **dog** ℭ *anger, animals, anxiety, control issues, danger, desires, fear, instincts, myths and legends, risky behavior, threats, transformation, violence.*

wet dream See *orgasm.*

whale **1.** If you dream you see a whale, something significant has happened, and you feel changed forever. **2.** If you dream of hearing a whale singing, you've had a spiritual experience. **3.** If you dream of getting attacked or swallowed by a whale, a problem you are facing is too big to handle alone. ☽ **fish** ℭ *animals, changing course, divine power, music and sound, nature, spirituality, threats, transformation, water.*

wheel Wheels symbolize the cycle of life and death and, in some cultures, the karmic cycle—what goes around comes around. Wheels also symbolize inner balance. **1.** If you dream of spinning wheels, everything is in balance and will come back around to the way it was. **2.** If you dream of a wheel on a vehicle, you are ready to move on to the next stage of life. **3.** If you dream of holding the steering wheel, you are in charge of your own karma. Put good in the world, and it will come back to you. Do wrong, and that will come back, too. ☽ **square** ℭ *balance, changing course, journeys and quests, karma, shapes and symbols, vehicles, yin-yang.*

wheelchair **1.** If you dream you are in a wheelchair, you face an obstacle, but you've also figured out a way around it. **2.** If you dream of someone else in a wheelchair, someone has overcome a weakness. That person is stronger than you guessed. ☽ **running problems** ℭ *impediments, personal power, vehicles.*

whispering If you dream of whispering, you have the chance to find out a secret, or you need to be more quiet. This situation calls for discretion. ◑ **explosion** ℂ *communication, music and sound, secrets, subterfuge.*

white White symbolizes innocence, purity, cleansing, and forgiveness. **1.** A white animal, like a dog, horse, or bird, symbolizes forgiveness. You have forgiven yourself, or you are ready to forgive someone else. **2.** White clothes symbolize your own innocent, pure side or a longing to find that part of you again. **3.** White clouds, sky, or light symbolize spirituality. You feel luminous and enlightened by something. **4.** White objects and white food represent cleansing. You need to improve your health habits. **5.** White put together with black symbolizes balance and equality, the yin and the yang intertwined in perfect harmony. And the forgiveness and cleansing balances the virtues. You can't be *that* innocent and pure! ◑ **black** ℂ *balance, beauty, clothing and accessories, color, divine power, forgiveness, health and hygiene, innocence, spirituality, yin-yang.*

wife 1. To have pleasant or perfectly ordinary dreams of your own wife suggests a feeling of stability and support. **2.** To dream of having romantic or sexual interaction with your wife means you feel physically and emotionally close in this relationship, or you might just feel like having sex during that particular

dream and your wife is the logical image to dream about. If the dream is unusual or experimental, you may be in an adventurous mood or looking for more excitement or variety in your relationship. **3.** To dream of fighting with your wife or to dream she does something that makes you angry or hurt suggests buried feelings of resentment, anger, or disappointment in your relationship. These might be caused by something small, but you haven't acknowledged them, so they are popping up in your dream. **4.** To dream you have a wife when you aren't actually married, or to dream your girlfriend is your wife, suggests you desire more security and stability in your relationship. You might be ready to take things to the next level, or you might just want to know someone will be there for you over the long haul. **5.** If you dream you have a wife when you aren't actually married, but things are not going well and you feel regret in your dream that you got married, this suggests you aren't ready to make that commitment you were thinking about. This might have nothing to do with a relationship; it is simply a warning sign that you might regret agreeing to something just yet. See also *girlfriend, marriage.* ◑ **husband** ℂ *comfort, decisions, desires, love, people, relationships, resistance, responsibilities, sexual activity, support, stability.*

wilderness 1. Dreaming you are lost, frightened, or threatened out in the wilderness suggests you feel

W

lost or confused about what direction your life is going. **2.** Dreaming you are hiking, camping, or otherwise enjoying the wilderness suggests you feel the urge to escape responsibilities and technology to spend some time in nature. You feel more comfortable in the natural world than in front of the computer … at least, right now. ☽ **city** ℂ *adventure, anxiety, confusion, escapism, fear, happiness, impediments, journeys and quests, nature, places, threats, travel.*

wildlife Dreaming of encounters with wildlife symbolizes encounters with your own natural instincts. **1.** If you feel threatened or fearful of wild animals, you are intimidated or fearful of your own instincts and your ability to control them. **2.** If you feel excited or positively challenged by wildlife encounters in a dream, your own instincts and natural urges interest and thrill you, and you like to make the most of them. ☽ **zoo** ℂ *adventure, animals, control issues, crawling creatures, fear, instincts, nature, risky behavior, threats, violence.*

wind 1. Dreaming of a pleasant, gentle wind suggests you are feeling happiness and optimism. **2.** A strong, blustery wind symbolizes a change in your situation you can't control. **3.** Damaging winds symbolize troublesome people, tempers out of control, or destructive forces in your life. See also *tornado.* ☽ **breathing** ℂ *anger, control issues,*

destruction, happiness, nature, threats, weather and seasons.

window Are you living your life or just watching it through the window? Windows keep the outside from getting in. They keep the weather and bugs out, but they also shield us from experience. Dreams of windows show you in no uncertain terms exactly what you should be looking at: windows frame what your mind wants you to notice. Take a good hard look. Only you can decide whether you need to stay safely inside or open that window and climb out. See also *glass.* ☽ **curtains** ℂ *buildings and rooms, decisions, home, impediments, opportunity.*

wine Dreams of wine invoke the Greek god Dionysus, the god of wine, and symbolize abundance, celebration, fun, hedonism, loosened morals, sexual activity, desires, and natural urges. **1.** If you dream of drinking wine with friends and having a good time, you feel the freedom to celebrate, and you enjoy socializing and parties. Your happiness feels abundant. **2.** If you dream of drinking too much wine and doing something you shouldn't do, you fear your own hedonistic impulses and your ability to control them. See also *alcohol.* ☽ **water** ℂ *abundance, addictions, celebration, desires, ethics and morals, food and drink, fun, happiness, hedonism, pleasure, risky behavior, sexual activity, social life.*

In ancient Greece, people believed that the drunkenness caused by wine meant the drinker was possessed by the spirit of Dionysus (Bacchus in Rome). The god's festival, Oschophoria, meant "Carrying of the Grape Clusters." According to a Gnostic gospel, the forbidden fruit in the Garden of Eden was a cluster of white grapes, and some scholars interpret the snake in the garden, which tempted Eve to taste the fruit, as an incarnation of Dionysus.

winning Everybody wants to be a winner, and if you dream of winning, you are fulfilling that inner desire and boosting your own self-confidence. **1.** If you dream of winning a large sum of money, such as winning the lottery, you've been feeling financial pressure lately, and you wish your problems could all disappear the easy way. **2.** If you dream of winning a trophy or other symbolic prize, you desire recognition for your efforts. **3.** If you dream of winning a race or a contest of skill, you feel confident and capable right now, and your competitive spirit is fired up. ☽ **losing** ℂ *competition, desires, financial resources, hopes and dreams, image, peer pressure, personal power, reputation, success.*

winter Winter symbolizes death and endings, but also hibernation, home, comfort, and family. **1.** If you have a pleasant dream of being cozy inside during the winter or having fun playing with family and friends outside in the winter, you feel stable and secure in your home life. **2.** If you dream of being cold and uncomfortable in the winter, you feel isolated from others. You aren't getting the support you need. **3.** If you dream of feeling frightened or unprepared by the approach of winter, you fear change or aging, or you don't want something to end. See also *snow.* ☽ **summer** ℂ *age, changing course, cold, comfort, death, family, fun, home, relationships, stability, threats, transformation, weather and seasons.*

wolf The wolf symbolizes strength and independence and instincts that seem dangerous. **1.** If you see a wolf in your dream, you may fear the power of the natural world. A recent unpleasant brush with nature could trigger this. You may also fear something within yourself, such as your own anger or violence, that you can't control—the wild part of you. **2.** If you dream a wolf chases or attacks you, you feel threatened by something. **3.** If you dream of petting a wolf or having a wolf as a pet, you tend to be a loner, or you feel like being one recently. You also feel comfortable with your own natural instincts and your place in the natural world—more so than in society. ☽ **dog** ℂ *anger, animals, danger, instincts, isolation, nature, threats, violence.*

woman **1.** The woman in your dream symbolizes the female side of you (even if you are a man). **1.**

W

If you fear or dislike the woman in your dream, you fear or feel uncomfortable with your own receptive, softer side. You might be repressing this part of you more than you should to feel healthy and balanced. Do you fear your feminine side will make you seem weak? **2.** If you feel passionate about or admiring of the woman in your dream, or you have sexual interaction with the woman, you honor your own female energy. This balancing kind of dream helps you free both sides of yourself. **3.** If you dream of a woman you vaguely recognize as someone you know, but you aren't quite sure who it is, this could symbolize someone you know in your waking life who has recently revealed an unfamiliar quality or unexpected behavior. You aren't sure how to define that person anymore. ☽ **man** ℂ *balance, identity, feminine, people, relationships, sexual activity, yin-yang.*

working hard   1. If you dream you are working hard and everyone else is hardly working, you have too many responsibilities. They have become a burden. **2.** If you dream of working hard and loving it, you have found your calling. You are headed in a productive direction. **3.** If you dream someone else is working hard, you feel guilty that others have taken on your fair share. But do you feel guilty enough to do anything about it? ☽ **lazy** ℂ *burdens, career, goal-setting, guilt, responsibilities, work.*

working out   **If you dream of working out, your body may be urging you to get more exercise, or urging you to get less exercise if you've been obsessing about exercise or overtraining. ☽ **hammock ℂ *body parts, health and hygiene, work.*

worm   1. If you dream of finding or seeing a worm, you have a secret, or you've accidentally discovered someone else's secret. **2.** If you dream of keeping a worm as a pet, you have a great but undeveloped potential. **3.** If you find a worm in your food, something you hoped for has been spoiled. See also *bugs.* ☽ **firefly** ℂ *animals, crawling creatures, failure, hopes and dreams, nature, opportunity, secrets, transformation.*

**wounds   **See *injuries.*

wrist   1. If you dream about your wrist, you can be flexible in a current situation. It will help communication. **2.** If you dream of injuring your wrist or wrist pain or numbness, you might actually have a health problem such as carpal tunnel syndrome or an injury. Or you might be inflexible right now. You just don't want to bend. ☽ **ankle** ℂ *body parts, communication, health and hygiene, pain.*

writing   **If you write something in your dream, you are writing a message to yourself or working out what you want to say to someone else. If you can see what you write, take a close look. This is probably important. ☯ **painting ☾ *communication, messages, shapes and symbols.*

wrong size Oh no, it doesn't fit! To dream of clothes that are the wrong size indicates image issues. **1.** Dreaming that you are wearing the wrong size means you are facing a self-image problem. You aren't sure who you want to be. Find the right size, and you'll feel more comfortable. Maybe you should try on a completely different outfit or persona. Or why not try being yourself? **2.** To dream of trying on clothes that are all the wrong sizes indicates that what you are doing now isn't working, like pushing a square peg into a round hole. Why could this be? Explore what action is needed to restore a good fit. ☯ **ballerina** ☾ *clothing and accessories, conformity, confusion, frustration, image, identity.*

W

XYZ

X marks the spot Are you hunting for treasure? If you dream of finding an *X* that marks a particular spot, you really are engaged in a search for something you desire, and your dream symbolizes your real desire. Treasure could symbolize money, a person could symbolize a relationship, a building or piece of furniture could symbolize a new home or a new job. Whatever the case, that *X* means something important to you. Otherwise, your dream wouldn't be so obvious. ☽ **lost** ℂ *adventure, desires, direction, financial resources, goal-setting, hopes and dreams, journeys and quests, wishes.*

Xerox machine See *copy machine.*

yard sale 1. If you dream of having a yard sale, you are in the process of clearing out your life of all the stuff—physical, mental, emotional—that you just don't need anymore. **2.** If you dream of attending a yard sale, you seek undiscovered treasure, or you envy someone else's resources—money, possessions, even

personality—and you want to be a part of them. ☽ **mall** ℂ *desires, envy, financial resources.*

yelling 1. If you dream you are yelling, you feel frustrated that you aren't getting through to someone, or you are letting out your anger in your dream because you don't feel it is possible or appropriate to let out your anger in your waking life. **2.** If you dream someone else is yelling at you, you are punishing yourself for something you feel guilty about or something you know you shouldn't have done. **3.** If you dream of someone else yelling in general but not at you, you are particularly sensitive right now. Maybe you need some quiet time. ☽ **whispering** ℂ *anger, anxiety, communication, feelings, frustration, listening, relationships, senses.*

yellow The color of the sun and the color of cowardice, yellow means many things, depending on the context. Yellow objects might offer you much-needed direction, like the bright sun leading the way to where you should go. Frightening yellow objects could tell you what you fear and suggest you ought to suck it up and face it down—or run away, as the case may be. ☽ **purple** ☾ *color, courage, direction, fear, threats.*

yoga Did you know you were that bendy? If you dream of doing yoga or watching someone else do yoga, you need to be more flexible about something. Is it really worth getting all tense about? Just go with the flow. ☽ **stiff** ☾ *changing course, sports and games.*

zombie **1.** If you dream of seeing a zombie, you feel like you aren't involved in your own life. Are you sleepwalking through your day on automatic pilot? You are frustrated with your inability to be engaged. **2.** If you dream you are being chased or attacked by a zombie, you feel threatened by monotony, boredom, and habit. You want to break the mold and do something crazy and different. Maybe it's time for a life change. **3.** If you dream you are a zombie, you feel you have no power in your life. You might fear the influence of others but don't feel you can do anything about it. ☽ **crowds, public places** ☾ *anxiety, characters, fear, feelings, myths and legends, relationships.*

zoo **1.** If you dream of visiting a zoo and looking at animals in pens or cages, you have reined in your own natural instincts so they don't get out of control. **2.** If you dream

of animals escaping from a zoo, you've let your natural urges get out of control. You may have already behaved inappropriately, or you are about to. **3.** If you dream you are in a zoo, you feel trapped in some area of your life and unable to move on or be appreciated for who you are or what you can do. You are being treated like an inferior, even a prisoner. ☽ **wilderness** ☾ *animals, control issues, desires, instincts, places, repression.*

X
Y
Z

Dream Words

For your convenience, we've included this appendix listing all of the more than 1,400 A to Z dream dictionary entries in alphabetical order. Use this list to help you search and discover Dream Words that may be a part of *your* personal dream vocabulary. Remember, Dream Words often have unique meanings for different dreamers, and you'll want to use our suggested meanings as a springboard for dream interpretations that feel right for you.

abandonment

abdomen

abduction

abnormal

abortion

abstinence

accelerator

accident

acid

acne

ad: see *advertisement*

addiction: see *bad habits*

adolescence

adoption

adultery

adventure

advertisement

advice

affair: see *infidelity*

Africa

aggression

AIDs

air conditioner

air force: see *military*

airplane

airplane crash

alcohol

aliens

alligator or crocodile

alone

Alzheimer's disease: see *senile*

ambulance

amnesia

amputation

amusement park

ancestors

androgyny

anesthesia

angel

anger

animals

ankle

anorexia: see *starvation*

answering machine

antidote

antiques

ants

apartment: see *house*

apocalypse: see *end of the world*

applause

apple

aquarium

archaeologist

archery

argument

Armageddon: see *end of the world*

arms

army: see *military*

arrested

arson

arthritis

artist

ashes

Asia

asking for directions

assassin

asteroid: see *meteors and meteorites*

astronaut

asylum: see *insane asylum*

atomic bomb: see *nuclear bomb*

attacked

attic

audience

audition

Aurora Borealis

Australia

author

autopsy

autumn

avalanche

award

axe

baby

baby animal

bachelor

back

backpack

backward

bacteria: see *disease, food poisoning*

bad behavior

bad habits

baggage: see *suitcase*

bait

bakery

baking

balcony

baldness

ball

ballerina

ballet

balloon

banana

band

bandages

bank

bankruptcy

baptism

bar

bar fight

Barbie doll: see *doll*

barefoot

barricade: see *barrier*

barrier

baseball

baseball bat

basement

basketball

bath: see *showers and baths*

bathing suit: see *bikini*

bathroom

bats

battery

beach

bear

beard

beauty contest

beauty pageant: see *beauty contest*

beauty parlor: see *salon*

bed: see *bedroom, furniture*

bedroom

beer

bees

beggar: see *homeless person*

belly button

berries

best friend

betrayal

bicycle: see *bike*

Big Foot

bike

bikini

billboard

bills and debts

bingeing

bird flu: see *disease*

birds

birth

birth control:
see *contraception*

birthmark

bisexuality

bite

black

black horse: see *horse*

blackout

blaming others

blank screen

blanket

blender or food
processor

blindness: see
vision problems

bling

blister

blizzard: see *snow,
storm*

blond hair

blood

blue

boat

body

body piercing: see
piercing

bomb: see *explosion*

bones

booing

book

boots

border

boredom: see *monotony*

boss

bowling

box

boy

boyfriend

bra

bracelet

braces

brain

brakes not working

branches: see *trees*

bread

breakfast

breaking free

breaking something

breaking up

breasts

breathing

breathing problems

bribing someone

brick wall: see *barrier*

bride

bridge

brother: see *sibling*

bruises

brunette hair

bugs

building

bull

bullet: see *gun*

bully

bungee jumping

buried alive

burns: see *fire, injuries*

bus

butterfly

cabin

cabinet: see *storage*

cactus

cage

cake

camcorder

camel

camera

camouflage

camping

cancer

candle

candy

cane

canyon

car

car accident

cards

carnation

carnival

carpal tunnel syndrome: see *wrist*

carpenter

carry

cartoon

cartwheels

cash register

casino: see *gambling, poker*

casket: see *coffin*

castle

castration: see *amputation*

cat

caterpillar

caution

cave

CDs and DVDs

ceiling

celebrity

celibacy

cell phone

cemetery

chain

chainsaw: see *power tools*

chair

chalk

chameleon

champagne

chasing

chat room

cheating

cheerleader

cherry

chess

chest

chewing gum: see *gum*

chicken

child or children

China: see *Asia*

chiropractor

chocolate: see *candy*

choir: see *singing*

choking

christening: see *baptism, religious ceremonies*

Christmas

church or synagogue

cigar: see *smoking*

cigarette: see *smoking*

cinema: see *theater*

circle

circumcision

circus

citizen's arrest

city

clapping: see *applause*

claustrophobia

claws

cleaning

cliff

climbing

clock

closed door

closet

clothes

clouds

clown

club

coastline

coat

cobwebs

cockroach

coffee

coffin

coins: see *money*

cold

collapse

college

coma

comet: see *meteors and meteorites*

commercial: see *advertisement*

communion: see *religious ceremonies*

compact disc: see *CDs and DVDs*

compass

competition: see *contest*

compliment

computer

concentration camp

concert

condom: see *contraception*

confession

confetti

constellation: see *stars*

construction

contact lens

contest

contraception

contract

convertible

convict

cooking

cop: see *police officer*

copy machine

corner

corpse: see *dead body*

corsage

cosmetics: see *makeup*

costume

cotton candy

couch

coughing

counselor: see *therapist*

counterfeiting

court

cousins

cow

cowboy

co-worker

coyote

crab

cradle

crawling

crazy: see *insane*

cream: see *milk*

credit card

cremation

crib: see *cradle*

crickets

crime

criminal: see *crime*

crocodile: see *alligator or crocodile*

cross

cross-dressing

crossroads

crossword puzzle

crowd

crown

crucifix: see *cross*

cruise

crutches

crying

crystal ball

cult

cup or glass

cupboard: see *storage*

curling iron: see *hair*

curse

curtains

cut

cybersex

daffodil

daisy

dancing

dandelion

dandruff

danger

dangerous person

darkness

darts and dartboards

dating

daughter

dead animal

dead body

dead end

deafness

death

debit card: see *credit card*

debts: see *bills and debts*

decadence

decapitation

deer

deformity

deity: see *gods, goddesses*

dementia: see *senile*

demons: see *devil*

dentist

depression

deprivation

desert

desk

dessert

destruction

detective

detour

devil

diamond

diet

digging

digital camera: see *camera*

dinner

diploma: see *graduation*

dirt

disappearing

disappointment

disaster

disease

disguise

dishes

diving into water

divorce

doctor

dog

doll

dollhouse: see *doll*

dolphin

door: see *closed door, open door*

dorm room

doughnuts

dove

drafted

dragon

drain

drawers: see *storage*

drawing

dreaming that you are dreaming and dreaming that you wake up

drinking

driver's license or ID card

driving

dropping something

dropping the ball

drought

drowning

drug store: see *pharmacy*

drugs

drum

drunk: see *alcohol*

duck

DVDs: see *CDs and DVDs*

dynamite: see *explosion*

ear

earrings: see *ear, jewelry*

earthquake

earwig

Easter

eating

echo

eclipse

ecstasy

egg

elbow

election

electric guitar: see *musical instrument*

electrocution

elephant

elevator

eloping

e-mail

embarrassment

emotional

empty

end of the world

enemy

engine

enter here

epidemic

erection

escalator

escape

espresso: see *coffee*

evacuation

eviction

evil

ex

ex-boyfriend/girl-friend: see *ex*

ex-husband/wife: see *ex*

excrement: see *bathroom*

exercise: see *working out*

exhibitionism

exit sign

explosion

extreme sports

eyeglasses: see *glasses*

eyes

face

face lift: see *plastic surgery*

faceless

failure

fainting

fairy

fall: see *autumn*

falling

family

famous person: see *celebrity*

farm

farsighted: see *vision problems*

fast food

fat

father

faucet: see *plumbing*

fax machine

fear

feather

feet

fence

ferret: see *weasel*

Ferris wheel

ferry

fetus

fever

fight

film

finding something

finger

fingernails

fire

fire engine

firecrackers: see *fireworks*

fired from a job

firefighter

firefly

fireman: see *firefighter*

fireplace

fireworks

fish

fishing

fixing something

flag

flat tire: see *tires*

fleas

flexibility

flies

flirting

floating: see *flying*

flood

floor

flowers

flying

flying saucer: see *UFO*

fog

following

food

food poisoning

food processor: see *blender or food processor*

football

foreign language

foreigner

forest

forgetting: see *amnesia*

forgiving

fork: see *utensils*

fork in the road: see *crossroads*

fortune teller

fossil

fountain

four-leaf clover

free stuff

freedom: see *breaking free*

freezer

friends

frog: see *reptiles and amphibians*

fruit

full

full moon: see *moon*

funeral

furnace

furniture

future

galaxy: see *space*

gambling

gaming system: see *video game*

gang

garbage

garden

garlic

gas

gate

gay: see *homosexuality*

genitals: see *sex organs*

germs

ghost

gift

girl

girlfriend

giving away possessions

giving up: see *quitting*

glacier

glass

glasses

glove

glue

goat

goatee: see *beard*

gods

goddesses

gold

goldfish

golf

gossip

government

government spying

graduation

grandchildren

grandparents

grapes

grass

grave

graveyard: see *cemetery*

greedy

green

Grim Reaper: see *death*

groom

growing

grown-up

guillotine: see *decapitation*

guilty conscience

guitar: see *musical instrument*

gum

gun

gypsy

hail

hair

hair loss: see *baldness*

Halloween

hallway

halo

hammer

hammock

hand

handcuffs

hang-gliding

hanging

happy

harmonica: see *musical instrument*

hat

hate

haunted house

headache

headstone: see *grave*

healing

health

heart

heart attack

heat

heaven

heavy

hell

helping someone

hemorrhage: see *blood*

hen: see *chicken*

hero

heterosexuality

hex: see *curse*

hiccup

hickey

hiding

high school: see *school*

highway

hijacked plane

hiking

hill

hired

hitchhiking

hitting

hole

home

homebody

homeless person

homosexuality

honesty: see *telling the truth*

hooker: see *prostitute*

hooky: see *playing hooky*

horns

horse

hospital

hostage

hot: see *heat*

hot air balloon

hot tub: see *Jacuzzi*

hotel or motel

house

housekeeper

hugging

hunger

hunting

hurricane: see *storm*

husband

hypnotized

hysterectomy

ice: see *snow*

ice cream

ice skating

iceberg: see *glacier*

illness: see *disease*

immortality

impotence

in vitro fertilization

inaccessible

inanimate objects coming to life

incest

infant: see *baby*

infection: see *disease*

infertility

infidelity

injection or needle

injuries

in-laws

insane

insane asylum

insect: see *bugs*

insomnia

instant message: see *chat room*

insult

intercourse: see *sex*

Internet dating

Internet surfing

interstate: see *highway*

interview

intoxicated: see *alcohol*

intruder

invisible

invitation

island

itching

Jacuzzi

jail

janitor

jaw

jealousy

jet: see *airplane*

Jet Ski

jewelry

jewels

job

jogging: see *running*

judge: see *court*

juggling

jumping

jungle

jury: see *court*

karaoke

keg

key

keyboard

kid: see *child or children*

kidnapping

killing

king

kissing

kitchen

kite

knee

knife

knitting

knocking

label

laboratory

labyrinth: see *maze*

ladder

lake: see *water*

lamp

landlord or landlady

landslide

late: see *running late*

laughing

laundry

lava

lawn: see *grass*

lawsuit

lawyer

lazy

leader

leak

leather

leaves

left hand

legs

lemon and lime

leprechaun

lesbian

letter

levitation

library

life jacket

lifeguard

light

light bulb

lightning

lily

lime: see *lemon and lime*

limousine

limping

line: see *straight line*

lingerie

lion

liposuction: see *plastic surgery*

lips

list

litter: see *pollution*

liver

living room

lizard: see *reptiles and amphibians*

loaning money

lock

locked out

locker

locker room

logs

lollipop

loneliness

losing

lost

lottery: see *winning*

love

luggage: see *suitcase*

lunch

lungs

lust

luxury

lying

machinery

madness: see *insane*

maggots

magic

magnifying glass

maid: see *housekeeper*

mail

mail carrier

mailbox

makeup

making out: see *kissing*

mall

man

mandala

manicure or pedicure

mannequin

mansion

manslaughter

manuscript

map

marching

marijuana: see *smoking*

marriage

Mars

mask

massage

mastectomy

masturbation

matches

maternal instinct

math

mattress

maze

measuring

meat

medicine

meditation

melons

menopause

menstruation

mermaid

meteors and mete-
orites

microwave

midwife

military

milk

minister: see *religious
authority figures*

mirror

missing a class, meet-
ing, or appointment

mob mentality

mobile home

modem

modesty

monastery

money

monk: see *monastery*

monotony

monster

moon

motel: see *hotel or
motel*

mother

motor: see *engine*

motorcycle

mountain

mountain lion

mouse

moustache

mouth

movie

movie star: see *celeb-
rity*

moving

MP3 player

mudslide: see *land-
slide*

multiple births

murder

museum

music

musical instrument

mute

nails

naked in public

nap

natural disaster: see
disaster

nature

nausea

navel: see *belly button*

navy: see *military*

nearsighted: see *vision
problems*

neck

necklace: see *jewelry*

necktie: see *tie*

needle: see *injection or
needle*

neighbor

neighborhood

nest

net

New Year's Eve

newborn: see *baby*

newspaper

nightclub

nightgown: see *lin-
gerie*

nightmare

no: see *saying no*

noise

nonviolence

noodles: see *pasta*

noose

north pole/south pole

northern lights: see
Aurora Borealis

nose

not invited

nuclear bomb

nuclear power

numb

numbers

nurse

nurturing

obesity: see *fat*

obituary

occult: see *magic*

ocean: see *water*

odor: see *smell*

office

old-fashioned

old person

omen

one-of-a-kind

onion

open door

opera

operation: see *surgery*

oral sex

orange

orchestra

orgasm

orgy

orphan

Ouija board

oval

oven

overflowing

owl

oysters

package

packing for a trip

pain

painting

pajamas

palm reading

palm tree

pandemic: see *disease*

panic

panting

pantry

parachute

parade

paradise: see *heaven,
utopia*

paralyzed

parents

park

parking lot or garage

parking meter

parking ticket

party

passenger

passport

past life

pasta

pastry: see *dessert*

path

patient

peace: see *nonviolence*

pear

pedicure: see *mani-
cure or pedicure*

pendulum

penis: see *sex organs*

pepper

performing

perfume

period: see *menstrua-
tion, punctuation*

pet

phallic symbol

pharmacy

phobia: see *fear*

phone

phone number

phone sex

photograph

piano

pickup truck: see
trucks and semis

picnic

pier

piercing

pig

pigeon

pillow

pills

pilot

pimp

pimples: see *acne*

pink

pirate

planets other than Earth

plastic surgery

play acting

playground

playing hooky

playing it safe

plumbing

pocket knife: see *knife*

poison

poison ivy: see *poison*

poker

police officer

pollution

poltergeist: see *ghost*

pomegranates

pond: see *water*

pornography

porpoise: see *dolphin*

portal

possessed by demons

possum

postman: see *mail carrier*

pottery

poverty

power failure

power lines

power tools

praying

pregnancy

present: see *gift*

president

pride

priest: see *religious authority figures*

prison: see *jail*

prisoner

privacy

prom

promise

proposal

prostitute

psychiatrist: see *therapist*

psychic

psychologist: see *therapist*

public speaking: see *speaking in public*

punctuation

punishment

puppet

purple

purse

quarry

queen

question

quicksand

quitting

rabbi: see *religious authority figures*

rabbit

rabies

race

raft

rage

railroad tracks

rain

rape

rash

rat

rattlesnake: see *snake*

reading

reality show

rebel

red

red hair

refrigerator

rehearsal

reincarnation

rejection

relaxation

religious authority figures

religious ceremonies

remembering

remodeling your house

reptiles and amphibians

rescue

responsibility: see *taking responsibility*

restaurant

revolution

reward

rich

ring

ringtone

rip tide

river: see *water*

roach: see *cockroach*

road: see *street*

road rage: see *rage*

road sign: see *sign*

roadblock: see *barrier*

robbery: see *crime, stealing*

rock

roller coaster

roller skates or inline skates

roof

roots

rose

roughing it

running

running late

running out of gas

running problems

rust

sadness

saint

salad

salon

salt

sand

Satan: see *devil*

satellite dish

sauna

saying no

scars and scabs

school

school bus: see *bus*

science experiment

scooter

scorpion

screaming

scuba diving: see *snorkeling and scuba diving*

sculpture

sea: see *water*

séance

secret

secret code

secretary

seduction

self-control

semi tractor-trailer: see *trucks and semis*

senile

serpent: see *snake*

servant

getting something free

sex

sex change

sex organs

sexual harassment

shadow

shame

shark

shaving

sheep

shelves: see *storage*

shiny

shipwreck

shoes

shooting: see *gun*

shooting star: see *meteors and meteorites*

shoplifting: see *stealing*

shopping

shortcut

showers and baths

shunning

shy

sibling

sickness: see *disease*

sign

silence

silver

singing

single

sink

siren

sister: see *sibling*

skateboarding

skeleton

skiing

skin

skinny: see *thin*

skinny dipping

sky

slide

slob

slot machine: see *gambling*

smell

smoking

snake

snorkeling and scuba diving

snow

snowboarding

snowman

snowstorm: see *storm*

sofa: see *couch*

soil: see *dirt*

soldier

son

south pole: see *north pole/south pole*

space

speaking in public

speeding

spider: see *bugs*

spine injuries

spirit: see *ghost*

spoon: see *utensils*

spring

square

stage

stairs

stalling

stars

starvation

STD: see *disease*

stealing

stiff

stink

stomach

stoplight: see *stop signs and stoplights*

stop signs and stoplights

storage

storm

stove

straight line

stranger

street

street sign: see *sign*

stress

student

success

sued: see *lawsuit*

suffocating

suitcase

summer

sun

superhero: see *hero*

surfing

surgery

SUV

swimming

sword

synagogue: see *church or synagogue*

table

taking responsibility

tarot cards: see *fortune teller*

taste

tattoo

taxi

tea

teacher

teasing

teenager: see *adolescence*

teeth

television: see *TV*

telling the truth

temper tantrum

temperature: see *thermometer*

tenant

tennis

tent

terrorism

test

text message

Thanksgiving

theater

therapist

thermometer

thin

thirst

throat

throwing up: see *vomiting*

thunder

ticket

tickling

tidal wave

tides

tie

tiger

tightrope

time travel

tires

toes

toilet: see *bathroom*

toll both

tongue

tonsils

tools

tornado

torture

tower

toys

traffic

trailer: see *mobile home*

train

train tracks: see *train*

trampoline

transsexual: see *sex change*

trapped

traveling: see *trip*

treasure

trees

trespassing

triangle

trip

triplets: see *multiple births*

tropical island: see *island*

trucks and semis

truth: see *telling the truth*

T-shirt

tsunami: see *tidal wave*

tulip

tunnel

turtle

tuxedo

TV

twins: see *multiple births*

UFO

ugliness

umbrella

underground

undertow: see *rip tide*

underwater

underwear

unemployed

unicorn

uniform

unique: see *one-of-a-kind*

university: see *college*

unmarried: see *divorce, single*

unraveling

upside-down

utensils

utopia

U-turn

vacation

vaccination

vacuum cleaner

vagina: see *sex organs*

valentine

valley

vampire

vegetables

veil

venom: see *poison*

video camera: see *camcorder*

video game

villain

virus: see *disease, epidemic*

vision problems

voice, disembodied

volcano

vomiting

voting: see *election*

waiting

waking up

walking

wall

wallet

wandering

war

wart: see *skin*

water

waterfall: see *water*

water skiing

waves

wealthy: see *rich*

weasel

weather changes

website

wedding

weightless

werewolf

wet dream: see *orgasm*

whale

wheel

wheelchair

whispering

white

wife

wilderness

wildlife

wind

window

wine

winning

winter

wolf

woman

working hard

working out

worm

wounds: see *injuries*

wrist

writing

wrong size

X marks the spot

Xerox machine: see *copy machine*

yard sale

yelling

yellow

yoga

zombie

zoo

Dream Themes

Intriguing how we dream in themes, isn't it? Every entry in *The Complete Idiot's Guide Dream Dictionary* includes a list of Dream Theme topics that categorize that particular dream or dream symbol according to theme. You'll see this list at the very end of each dictionary entry, beginning with this Moon icon: ☾. Every time you see the Moon, get ready to gain deeper and perhaps unexpected insights into your dreams. For example, using Dream Themes will allow you to see if you tend to dream a lot about things that fit into a single theme (such as **Adventure** or **Relationships**).

How to Use the Dream Themes

Looking at your Dream Themes also lets you see more easily what other themes your dreams might fall into—themes not as readily obvious to you upon first recall of your dreams—so you can interpret your dreams in the most ways possible. For instance, if you dream about a dog, you could look under Dream Themes for **Animals, Communication** (if you talk to the dog), **Injuries** (if the dog attacks you), and **Loyalty.** This can lead you on an interesting search for other symbols that might have occurred in that dog dream or in other dreams you've had recently ... or long ago.

Here's a handy list of all the Dream Theme categories:

Dream Themes

Abundance

Accidents

Addictions

Adventure

Age

Anger

Animals

Anxiety

Authority

Balance

Beauty

Birds

Body Parts

Buildings and
Rooms

Burdens

Career

Caretaking

Celebration

Changing Course

Characters

Clothing and
Accessories

Code

Cold

Color

Comfort

Communication

Competition

Conformity

Confusion

Control Issues

Courage

Crawling Creatures

Creation

Creativity

Danger

Death

Decisions

Desires

Destruction

Direction

Disaster

Dishonesty

Divine Power

Ego

Electronics

Embarrassment

Envy

Escapism

Ethics and Morals

Extremism

Failure

Family

Fear

Feelings

Feminine

Financial
Resources

Food and Drink

Forgiveness

Freedom

Fruit

Frustration

Fun

Furniture and
Appliances

Gender Issues

Goal-Setting

Greed

Guilt

Happiness

Healing

Health and Hygiene

Heat

Hedonism

History

Home

Hopes and Dreams

Identity

Image

Impediments

Inanimate Objects

Injuries

Innocence

Insecurity

Instincts

Intelligence

Intuition

Isolation

Journeys and
   Quests

Karma

Knowledge

Listening

Loss

Love

Loyalty

Masculine

Medicine and
   Surgery

Memory

Messages

Music and Sound

Mystery

Myths and Legends

Nature

Numbers

Opportunity

Pain

Peacemaking

Peer Pressure

People

Personal Power

Places

Plants

Play

Pleasure

Predictions

Protection

Punishment

Rebellion

Regret

Relationships

Repression

Reputation

Resistance

Responsibilities

Risky Behavior

Rules and Laws

Sacrifice

Secrets

Senses

Sexual Activity

Shapes and Symbols

Social Life

Solutions and
   Remedies

Spirituality

Sports and Games

Stability

Stasis

Subterfuge

Success

Support

Taking Action

Technology

Threats

Time

Transformation

Travel

Trust Issues

Vehicles

Violence

Vulnerability

War

Water

Weather and
   Seasons

Wishes

Work

Yin-Yang

Exploring Your Dream Themes

For each Dream Theme, you'll see a list of every entry in this dictionary that cross-references that Dream Theme. Have fun exploring your Dream Themes!

Abundance: bingeing, bling, bull, candy, cash register, champagne, cow, decadence, dessert, diamond, eating, free stuff, freezer, full, giving away possessions, gold, grapes, greedy, jewelry, jewels, keg, leprechaun, limousine, luxury, mall, mansion, money, overflowing, pantry, picnic, pig, refrigerator, rich, shopping, tennis, Thanksgiving, treasure, umbrella, utensils, wine.

Accidents: accident, airplane crash, ambulance, amputation, bandages, blender or food processor, blood, brakes not working, breaking something, bus, cell phone, cut, danger, decapitation, deformity, destruction, drowning, electrocution, elevator, embarrassment, falling, killing, leak, lightning, manslaughter, murder, paralyzed, power lines, power tools, shipwreck, tires, tools, traffic, train, trampoline.

Addictions: alcohol, back, bad habits, bakery, beer, bingeing, bugs, cockroach, drugs, food, full, gambling, greedy, injection or needle, insane, insane asylum, mall, pig, pills, pollution, pornography, possessed by demons, shopping, smoking, vomiting, wine.

Adventure: adventure, aliens, amusement park, Australia, bear, book, boots, border, bungee jumping, camping, canyon, car accident, carnival, castle, cave, cliff, climbing, cowboy, cruise, danger, dangerous person, darkness, dating, desert, dirt, disaster, drafted, dragon, earthquake, eloping, end of the world, extreme sports, football, foreign language, foreigner, forest, future, gambling, garlic, Halloween, hang-gliding, horse, hunting, ice skating, jungle, karaoke, knocking, lightning, Mars, military, motorcycle, movie, nature, North Pole/South Pole, omen, one-of-a-kind, opera, packing for a trip, park, passport, pepper, performing, piercing, pirate, planets other than Earth, poker, portal, quarry, railroad tracks, reality show, rebel, roller coaster, roughing it, shipwreck, shortcut, single, skinny dipping, snorkeling and scuba diving, space, storm, tent, tightrope, time travel, tornado, train, trespassing, UFO, video game, wilderness, wildlife, X marks the spot.

Age: arthritis, autumn, baby, beard, boy, cane, cartwheels, child or children, clock, cradle, daughter, doll, flowers, growing, grown-up, ice cream, immortality, in vitro fertilization, leaves, locker, locker room, lollipop, makeup, mastectomy, menopause, menstruation, old-fashioned, old person, pink, plastic surgery, playground, playing hooky, prom, puppet, rust, sand, school, scooter, senile, slide, son, spring, student, summer, temper tantrum, toys, trees, winter.

Anger: abandonment, aggression, air conditioner, anger, argument, breaking something, breaking up, cockroach, curse, dishes, fight, finger, hate, hitting, murder, not invited, poison, pollution, possum, rage, sexual harassment, teasing, temper tantrum, thunder, torture, trapped, volcano, vomiting, war, waves, werewolf, wind, wolf, yelling.

Animals: alligator or crocodile, animals, ants, aquarium, bats, bear, bees, Big Foot, bite, bugs, bull, cage, camel, camping, cat, caterpillar, chameleon, chicken, claws, cow, coyote, crab, crickets, dead animal, deer, dog, dolphin, dove, dragon, duck, earwig, elephant, farm, feather, firefly, fish, flies, flying, forest, goat, goldfish, horns, horse, hunting, jungle, lion, maggots, maze, meat, monster, mountain lion, mouse, nature, owl, oysters, panting, pet, pig, pigeon, poison, possum, rabbit, rabies, rat, reptiles and amphibians, scorpion, setting something

free, shark, sheep, snake, tiger, turtle, unicorn, weasel, werewolf, whale, wildlife, wolf, worm, zoo.

Anxiety: abandonment; abduction; abnormal; accident; airplane crash; alligator or crocodile; arrested; attacked; avalanche; beauty contest; betrayal; bite; black; blackout; booing; breathing problems; bugs; bully; bungee jumping; buried alive; cancer; car; car accident; cartoon; chasing; cheating; chicken; claustrophobia; cockroach; coffee; collapse; concentration camp; crime; crowd; crystal ball; cult; curse; danger; dangerous person; darkness; dating; deer; destruction; devil; dirt; disappearing; disaster; disease; drafted; earthquake; eclipse; electrocution; elephant; elevator; embarrassment; end of the world; enemy; epidemic; escape; eviction; evil; explosion; failure; falling; fat; fear; fired from a job; fish; flood; forest; grandchildren; handcuffs; hang-gliding; hate; heavy; hijacked plane; hired; hitchhiking; hitting; hole; homeless person; inanimate objects coming to life; insane; insane asylum; insomnia; invisible; itching; jail; juggling; lightning; locker; losing; manslaughter; Mars; military; missing a class, meeting, or appointment; mob mentality; modesty; monotony; monster; murder; nightmare; noose; not invited; nuclear power; orgasm; orgy; panic; paralyzed;

passport; performing; pigeon; plastic surgery; prisoner; quicksand; rage; rehearsal; rejection; rip tide; roller coaster; running late; running problems; sand; school; screaming; sexual harassment; shame; shipwreck; shy; speaking in public; stage; starvation; stranger; stress; student; suffocating; temper tantrum; tent; terrorism; test; tidal wave; tides; tightrope; tornado; torture; trapped; trip; unemployed; volcano; vomiting; war; waves; werewolf; wilderness; yelling; zombie.

Authority: arrested, bad behavior, boss, breathing problems, bus, camouflage, citizen's arrest, claustrophobia, concentration camp, convict, court, crown, drafted, dragon, drugs, election, erection, escape, father, flag, gods, goddesses, government, government spying, grown-up, handcuffs, hospital, jail, king, knife, landlord or landlady, laughing, lawyer, leader, lion, military, parade, parents, passenger, patient, pilot, police officer, president, prisoner, queen, religious authority figures, revolution, saying no, secretary, servant, sexual harassment, shadow, soldier, SUV, sword, teacher, terrorism, therapist, uniform.

Balance: androgyny, bisexuality, black, cane, coastline, crossdressing, food, garden, green, heterosexuality, homosexuality, insane asylum, lesbian, logs, man, mandala, moon, nature, pendulum, sex, sex change, sex organs, silence, square, sun, tightrope, utopia, waves, wheel, white, woman.

Beauty: artist, ballerina, beauty contest, bling, blond hair, bride, brunette hair, butterfly, carnation, celebrity, clothes, corsage, daffodil, daisy, diving into water, flowers, fruit, garden, girl, goldfish, hair, jewelry, jewels, lily, lust, makeup, manicure or pedicure, menopause, mermaid, nature, neck, old-fashioned, painting, photograph, piano, plastic surgery, red hair, salon, sculpture, shaving, shiny, shoes, tulip, ugliness, white.

Birds: animals, birds, chicken, dead animal, dove, duck, feather, flying, nest, owl.

Body Parts: abdomen, abnormal, acne, amputation, ankle, arthritis, autopsy, baldness, bandages, barefoot, belly button, birthmark, blister, blond hair, body, bones, boy, braces, breasts, brunette hair, cancer, chest, circumcision, claws, cut, dandruff, decapitation, deformity, dentist, disease, elbow, eyes, face, faceless, fat, feet, finger, fingernails, flexibility, flowers, hand, headache, heart, heart attack, hickey, injuries, jaw, kissing, knee, left hand, legs, lemon and lime, limping, lingerie, lips, liver, lungs, manicure or pedicure, mannequin, massage, mastectomy, masturbation, menstruation, moustache, mouth, nails, naked in public, nausea, neck, nose, numb, oral sex, oval, pain, palm reading, paralyzed, phallic symbol, piercing, plastic surgery, rash, red hair, sex, sex change, sex organs, shaving, shoes, skeleton, skin, skinny dipping, spine injuries, stomach, sword, tattoo, teeth, thin, throat, tickling, toes, tongue, tonsils, ugliness, vision problems, vomiting, working out, wrist.

Buildings and Rooms: attic, balcony, bank, bar, basement, bathroom, bedroom, building, cabin, carpenter, ceiling, church or synagogue, city, closet, club, collapse, college, construction, corner, curtains, destruction, dorm room, elevator, fire, floor, furniture, hallway, haunted house, home, hotel or motel, house, kitchen, laboratory, living room, locker, locker room, mall, mansion, monastery, moving, pantry, plumbing, restaurant, roof, school, showers and baths, stage, stairs, tent, theater, toll booth, tower, wall, window.

Burdens: back, bills and debts, bra, bride, cage, camel, carry, celibacy, chain, depression, disappointment, dropping something, evil, flood, ghost, groom, heavy, immortality, incest, insomnia, job,

juggling, lazy, leader, monotony, panic, plastic surgery, roughing it, senile, shadow, shame, shopping, slob, suitcase, taking responsibility, trapped, trucks and semis, weightless, working hard.

Career: adventure, archaeologist, artist, assassin, astronaut, author, ballerina, basketball, boss, bowling, carpenter, ceiling, chess, circus, clown, co-worker, cruise, darts and dartboards, dentist, desk, detective, doctor, election, elevator, farm, fingernails, fired from a job, firefighter, football, fortune teller, hallway, hired, housekeeper, janitor, job, juggling, king, ladder, landlord or landlady, lawyer, lazy, lifeguard, mail carrier, mall, midwife, military, monotony, newspaper, nurse, office, pilot, pimp, pirate, playing hooky, poker, police officer, power failure, president, prostitute, psychic, queen, race, religious authority figures, secretary, servant, soldier, teacher, therapist, unemployed, wedding, working hard.

Caretaking: abduction, adoption, AIDs, arms, award, baby, baby animals, belly button, best friend, birth, blanket, blue, box, bra, breasts, bride, cane, carry, caution, child or children, Christmas, cleaning, coat, collapse, cow, cradle, cult, danger, dangerous person, daughter, depression, dinner, disease, egg, family, fever, fixing something, flexibility, flood, glass, goddesses, grandchildren, healing, health, heart, heart attack, helping someone, hero, homebody, horse, housekeeper, hugging, invisible, kitchen, ladder, laundry, life jacket, lifeguard, lightning, list, loaning money, loneliness, mail carrier, marriage, maternal instinct, maze, meat, medicine, midwife, milk, mother, multiple births, nest, nonviolence, North Pole/South Pole, nurse, onion, orphan, oven, pain, pajamas, palm tree, panic, pantry, parents, pasta, patient, pet, playground, playing it safe, poison, quicksand, rabbit, raft, rescue, restaurant, ringtone, rust, salon, scars and scabs, secretary, senile, siren, slob, son, starvation, storage, stove, therapist, tidal wave, vaccination, vacuum cleaner, veil, wallet.

Celebration: alcohol, applause, award, bride, cake, candle, champagne, Christmas, club, confetti, costume, dancing, disguise, Easter, goat, graduation, grapes, groom, Halloween, invitation, keg, New Year's Eve, party, reward, Thanksgiving, wine.

Changing Course: abortion, adventure, aliens, arson, asking for directions, audition, autumn, band, baptism, beard, birth, black, book, border, breaking up, bungee jumping, buried alive, cage, cancer, canyon, car, car accident, carpenter, ceiling, circumcision, cliff, climbing, closed door, coastline, cockroach, coffin, collapse, college, corner, crawling, cremation, crickets, crossroads, dating, dead end, death, destruction, detour, dirt, disaster, disease, divorce, driving, earthquake, eclipse, elbow, election, electrocution, elephant, elevator, empty, end of the world, epidemic, escape, eviction, exit sign, explosion, feet, ferry, fetus, fire, fired from a job, floor, forest, forgiving, fortune teller, freezer, funeral, future, gate, girl, giving away possessions, goddesses, graduation, grave, gun, gypsy, hanging, heaven, hell, highway, hired, horse, hostage, hotel or motel, island, job, killing, knee, knitting, laboratory, ladder, landslide, lava, leather, leaves, lightning, list, lost, map, marriage, Mars, maze, meditation, menopause, meteors and meteorites, microwave, mobile home, monster, moon, moustache, movie, moving, murder, nature, nausea, New Year's Eve, nuclear bomb, obituary, old-fashioned, old person, omen, open door, owl, packing for a trip, passport, pharmacy, pilot, possessed by demons, poverty, power failure, power tools, president, punctuation, quitting, reincarnation, remodeling your house, revolution, rock, roller coaster, saying no, science experiment, sculpture, sex change, shiny, shortcut, showers and baths, sign, single, skateboarding, soldier, spine injuries, stage, stop signs and stoplights, storm, stove, stranger, student, taxi, tenant, thin, tidal wave, tides, time travel, tornado, traffic, train, trampoline, trees, trip, UFO, underground, unraveling, upside-down, utensils, U-turn, vomiting, walking, war, water, weather changes, wedding, whale, wheel, winter, yoga.

Characters: aliens, ancestors, angel, archaeologist, artist, assassin, astronaut, audition, author, bachelor, ballerina, best friend, Big Foot, book, boss, boyfriend, bride, bully, carpenter, cartoon, castle, celebrity, cheerleader, circus, clown, convict, costume, cowboy, co-worker, cross-dressing, dangerous person, dead body, death, dentist, detective, devil, disguise, doctor, doll, enemy, fairy, family, firefighter, foreigner, fortune teller, ghost, girlfriend, gods, goddesses, groom, gypsy, hero, homebody, homeless person, hostage, housekeeper, in-laws, janitor, king, landlord or landlady, lawyer, leader, leprechaun, lifeguard, mail carrier, mannequin, mermaid, midwife, monster, neighbor, nurse, old person, orphan, patient, pilot, pimp, pirate, police officer, prisoner, prostitute, psychic, puppet, queen, rebel, religious authority figures, secretary, servant, siren, skeleton, slob, snowman, soldier, stranger, student, teacher, tenant, therapist, vampire, villain, zombie.

Clothing and Accessories: bikini, black, boots, bra, bracelet, braces, camouflage, clothes, coat, contact lens, corsage, costume, cross-dressing, crown, disguise, doll, glove, Halloween, hat, label, laundry, life jacket, lingerie, makeup, mall, mask, naked in public, old-fashioned, packing for a trip, pajamas, purse, shoes, shopping, tie, T-shirt, tuxedo, umbrella, underwear, uniform, unraveling, veil, wallet, white, wrong size.

Code: cards; cross; crossword puzzle; crystal ball; drawing; key; keyboard; label; letter; library; mail carrier; math; numbers; phallic symbol; phone number; punctuation; question; ringtone; secret code; sign; stop signs and stoplights; voice, disembodied.

Cold: coat, cold, freezer, refrigerator, snow, snowman, thermometer, winter.

Color: artist, black, blond hair, blue, brunette hair, green, jewels, pink, purple, red, red hair, stop signs and stoplights, white, yellow.

Comfort: baby, bakery, baking, baseball, bedroom, best friend, blanket, boyfriend, bra, candy, child or children, Christmas, coat, coffee, dessert, dog, doll, dove, family, father, food, forgiving, friends, furnace, furniture, girlfriend, hammock, home, homebody, in-laws, luxury, mask, massage, masturbation, maternal instinct, mattress, meat, medicine, midwife, monastery, mother, nest, pasta, religious authority figures, roots, shopping, silence, silver, stove, tea, text message, Thanksgiving, wife, winter.

Communication: adultery, advertisement, advice, anger, answering machine, argument, author, bar, billboard, blank screen, CDs and DVDs, cell phone, chalk, chat room, choking, coma, computer, concert, coughing, cup or glass, curse, cybersex, deafness, dentist, dog, drawing, ear, echo, e-mail, family, fax machine, fear, feather, fight, firefly, flirting, foreign language, forgiving, fountain, friends, glass, glasses, glove, goddesses, gossip, hiccup, inaccessible, incest, infidelity, insult, Internet dating, Internet surfing, interview, invitation, jaw, keyboard, knocking, label, letter, mail, mail carrier, mailbox, manuscript, math, modem, moustache, mouth, mute, nails, newspaper, noise, oral sex, Ouija board, phone, phone number, phone sex, piano, pigeon, praying, question, ringtone, satellite dish, sauna, saying no, screaming, séance, secret,

secret code, shunning, silence, speaking in public, storm, table, tea, teasing, telling the truth, text message, throat, thunder, tongue, tuxedo, TV, underwater, utensils, valentine, water, whispering, wrist, writing, yelling.

Competition: archery, ball, baseball, basketball, bike, bowling, cards, chess, contest, darts and dartboards, diving into water, extreme sports, football, golf, ice skating, infidelity, jealousy, jumping, karaoke, losing, measuring, poker, race, reality show, running, running problems, tennis, test, video game, winning.

Conformity: club, cow, crowd, disappearing, left hand, lingerie, marching, mob mentality, monotony, newspaper, pharmacy, pigeon, rebel, red hair, sheep, tiger, underground, wedding, wrong size.

Confusion: abnormal, blackout, blank screen, dreaming that you are dreaming and dreaming that you wake up, fear, storm, waking up, wilderness, wrong size.

Control Issues: abduction, accelerator, airplane crash, assassin, audience, bad habits, bait, bakery, baldness, bar fight, bike, birds, blender or food processor, blister, boss, bracelet, braces, brakes not working, breathing problems, bully, buried alive, bus, cage, candy, car, caution, cave, citizen's arrest, claustrophobia, clown, coma, concentration camp, contraception, cowboy, crime, danger, dangerous person, dead animal, deer, devil, disappearing, driving, elbow, election, elevator, emotional, escape, falling, family, fat, father, Ferris wheel, flood, flying, germs, glue, greedy, hand, handcuffs, hang-gliding, hijacked plane, hitchhiking, hitting, home, homebody, homeless person, horns, hostage, hot air balloon, hotel or motel, hypnotized, impotence, inanimate objects coming to life, in-laws, Internet dating, jail, Jet Ski, jungle, kidnapping, knee, knife, laughing, lawsuit, lazy, leader, legs, lemon and lime, leprechaun, levitation, lion, list, lock, locked out, losing, lungs, masturbation, measuring, military, monster, motorcycle, mouse, movie, office, oral sex, parade, passenger, pilot, pimp, plastic surgery, possessed by demons, power tools, prisoner, privacy, puppet, race, raft, rape, ring, rip tide, running, running late, running problems, saying no, science experiment, self-control, servant, setting something free, sexual harassment, shaving, sink, stiff, storm, suffocating, teeth, temper tantrum, thin, tickling, tools, tornado, torture, traffic, train, trapped, trespassing, umbrella, unemployed, waiting, war, water, weightless, werewolf, wildlife, wind, zoo.

Courage: adventure, astronaut, audience, breaking free, camping, cave, chest, darkness, death, disaster, dragon, earthquake, end of the world, extreme sports, fire engine, firefighter, forgiving, horns, ice skating, island, jail, jumping, jungle, karaoke, knocking, ladder, lion, motorcycle, mouse, nature, performing, pirate, rehearsal, saying no, snorkeling and scuba diving, space, speaking in public, stage, storm, tightrope, tornado, war, yellow.

Crawling Creatures: alligator or crocodile, animals, ants, bats, bees, bugs, butterfly, caterpillar, chameleon, cockroach, crawling, crickets, dead animal, earwig, firefly, fleas, flies, germs, inanimate objects coming to life, maggots, mouse, reptiles and amphibians, scorpion, snake, turtle, wildlife, worm.

Creation: bedroom, birth, blood, breakfast, building, carpenter, castle, caterpillar, circle, construction, cooking, cross, daffodil, earthquake, Easter, eclipse, egg, electrocution, explosion, fetus, future, garden, gods, goddesses, in vitro fertilization, infertility, laboratory, menstruation, midwife, multiple births, musical instrument, nails, oval, oven, painting, pregnancy, rabbit, spring.

Creativity: artist, ballet, birth, camel, carpenter, cat, CDs and DVDs, concert, construction, cooking, costume, counterfeiting, dandelion, dead body, death, disguise, drawing, dreaming that you are dreaming and dreaming that you wake up, egg, fixing something, infertility, jumping, light, light bulb, magic, manuscript, matches, mermaid, microwave, milk, music, musical instrument, nuclear power, orchestra, orgy, oval, painting, performing, piano, planets other than Earth, pregnancy, sculpture, stars, theater, tires, tools, vegetables.

Danger: alligator or crocodile, bear, bite, blackout, buried alive, camping, cave, claws, cockroach, coffin, concentration camp, convict, crime, danger, dangerous person, darkness, deer, desert, devil, disaster, disease, dragon, electrocution, evil, fear, fire, flood, following, food poisoning, forest, gun, hell, hitchhiking, inanimate objects coming to life, insane asylum, intruder, life jacket, lightning, monster, mountain lion, murder, nature, nightmare, noose, nuclear bomb, nuclear power, omen, oven, pain, panic, piercing, pirate, poison, power lines, power tools, quick-

sand, rabies, rage, railroad tracks, revolution, scorpion, screaming, shark, siren, smell, snake, soldier, stink, storm, stove, stranger, tent, terrorism, tidal wave, tides, tiger, tightrope, tires, tornado, torture, UFO, volcano, war, werewolf, wolf.

Death: accident, ashes, assassin, autopsy, buried alive, coffin, cold, concentration camp, cremation, danger, dead animal, death, destruction, devil, end of the world, fear, fire, funeral, grandparents, grave, hanging, heaven, hell, killing, murder, nuclear bomb, obituary, old person, omen, Ouija board, owl, séance, winter.

Decisions: book, border, breaking up, bungee jumping, coastline, coffee, coffin, compass, contract, corner, crossroads, divorce, election, eloping, eviction, explosion, forest, forgiving, gang, happy, hat, hell, hired, husband, hysterectomy, jumping, killing, ladder, legs, lion, list, open door, promise, proposal, prostitute, quicksand, rejection, religious authority figures, saying no, tattoo, tightrope, time travel, torture, utensils, U-turn, wife, window.

Desires: adultery, alcohol, apple, award, baby, beer, birth, breaking free, cake, candy, castle, celebrity, chasing, cheating, coffee, compliment, contest, co-worker, crime, cross-dressing, depression, diamond, diving into water, divorce, eating, evil, exhibitionism, fainting, fever, fight, fired from a job, fish, flirting, flowers, following, food, forgiving, free stuff, garlic, gift, girl, greedy, hugging, hunger, hunting, husband, ice cream, ice skating, in vitro fertilization, incest, infidelity, injection or needle, invitation, Jacuzzi, jealousy, jewelry, jewels, karaoke, keg, kidnapping, kissing, lava, lazy, leaves, lesbian, lightning, lingerie, lips, list, locked out, locker room, lollipop, love, lust, luxury, makeup, mall, manicure or pedicure, massage, masturbation, maternal instinct, mattress, measuring, melons, mermaid, midwife, money, motorcycle, mouth, neighbor, net, nightclub, one-of-a-kind, opera, oral sex, orange, oysters, pajamas, panting, parachute, pepper, performing, perfume, pet, phallic symbol, phone sex, piercing, pirates, pomegranates, pornography, pregnancy, privacy, proposal, prostitute, rabbit, rape, rash, red, red hair, reptiles and amphibians, rich, ring, rose, saying no, shipwreck, shopping, sibling, silence, single, skinny dipping, space, Thanksgiving, thirst, underwear, utopia, valentine, volcano, water, werewolf, wife, wine, winning, *X* marks the spot, yard sale, zoo.

Destruction: arson, axe, bugs, circle, city, coffin, collapse, cremation, cut, destruction, disaster, divorce, earthquake, eclipse, end of the world, explosion, fire, flood, goat, hail, injuries, knife, landslide, lava, meteors and meteorites, murder, nuclear bomb, overflowing, spine injuries, storm, tornado, war, wind.

Direction: archery, asking for directions, backward, barrier, bike, ceiling, circle, climbing, compass, darts and dartboards, dead end, desert, detour, driving, elevator, escalator, feet, finger, following, forest, highway, jumping, ladder, leader, list, lost, map, maze, measuring, moving, path, religious authority figures, religious ceremonies, roller skates or inline skates, saying no, shortcut, space, stage, stairs, stars, straight line, street, student, teacher, train, upside-down, U-turn, wandering, *X* marks the spot, yellow.

Disaster: accident, airplane crash, avalanche, blackout, collapse, cruise, danger, destruction, disaster, dragon, earthquake, end of the world, epidemic, evacuation, falling, fear, fire, flood, glacier, hot air balloon, landslide, lava, meteors and meteorites, nuclear bomb, nuclear power, omen, overflowing, shipwreck, storm, tidal wave, tornado, volcano, war.

Dishonesty: blaming others, cheating, cross-dressing, government spying, lying, magic, makeup, mask, moustache, poker, rat, stealing, telling the truth, weasel.

Divine Power: angel, candle, church or synagogue, cross, dove, ecstasy, evil, firefly, gods, goddesses, gold, halo, heaven, hell, kite, levitation, light, lily, mandala, monastery, moon, omen, oval, owl, possessed by demons, praying, religious authority figures, religious ceremonies, saint, singing, sun, utopia, whale, white.

Ego: audience, baldness, beauty contest, booing, boss, brain, celebrity, cheerleader, evil, exhibitionism, face, fat, girlfriend, impotence, injuries, insult, invitation, karaoke, losing, nails, neck, not invited, performing, poker, pride, race, reward, ugliness.

Electronics: battery, beach, camcorder, camera, CDs and DVDs, cell phone, computer, copy machine, fax machine, Internet dating, Internet surfing, keyboard, light bulb, modem, MP3 player, phone, power failure, power tools, TV, video game.

Embarrassment: barefoot, booing, dandruff, disappointment, embarrassment, exhibitionism, failure, fainting, family, fat, growing, injuries, in-laws, insult, karaoke, locker room, menstruation, modesty, naked in public, not invited, rejection, secret, shame, speaking in public, stage.

Envy: bling, deprivation, graduation, hair, happy, homosexuality, jealousy, kissing, limousine, luxury, mansion, not invited, orgy, painting, sex, stealing, SUV, teasing, yard sale.

Escapism: carnival, eloping, evacuation, feather, fired from a job, horse, insane, insane asylum, island, Jacuzzi, Jet Ski, luxury, monastery, motorcycle, old-fashioned, pajamas, palm tree, paralyzed, pirate, planets other than Earth, playground, portal, railroad tracks, reading, reality show, relaxation, running, shipwreck, silence, unemployed, wilderness.

Ethics and Morals: bankruptcy, baseball, bathroom, beer, betrayal, blaming others, braces, breaking something, bribing someone, cancer, candy, citizen's arrest, claustrophobia, cleaning, club, cockroach, court, coyote, crab, crawling, credit card, crime, crowd, deprivation, devil, disease, eating, flag, flies, forest, garbage, garlic, germs, gods, hallway, handcuffs, heaven, hell, injection or needle, logs, lost, lying, maggots, magic, masturbation, mattress, modesty, murder, noose, old-fashioned, pantry, pottery, promise, prostitute, punishment, rabies, religious authority figures, religious ceremonies, saying no, self-control, sexual harassment, speeding, stealing, telling the truth, therapist, trees, trespassing, utensils, vampire, vegetables, weasel, wine.

Extremism: bingeing, blood, candy, cartoon, food, garbage, hate, North Pole/South Pole, opera, party, pirate, roller coaster, screaming, tornado.

Failure: booing, cancer, climbing, dead end, disappointment, disease, divorce, dropping something, dropping the ball, failure, falling, fired from a job, garbage, impotence, in vitro fertilization, infertility, injuries, losing, modem, not invited, poverty, power failure, rejection, running problems, slide, taking responsibility, test, unemployed, unraveling, worm.

Family: abduction, adoption, ancestors, baby, bachelor, baking, birth, child or children, Christmas, circus, cleaning, cousins, cult, daughter, dinner, divorce, dropping the ball, family, father, fetus, fireplace, flies, furnace, gang, grandchildren, grandparents, homebody, house, hysterectomy, incest, in-laws, kitchen, lunch, midwife, milk, mother, nest, orphan, parents, picnic, pregnancy, sibling, singing, skeleton, son, stove, table, Thanksgiving, trees, unemployed, winter.

Fear: abandonment, abduction, accident, AIDs, airplane crash, aliens, basement, bats, bear, betrayal, Big Foot, birds, birth, bite, blackout, box, brakes not working, breaking up, breathing problems, bugs, bully, bungee jumping, buried alive, camouflage, camping, cancer, carnival, cemetery, chasing, cheating, chicken, claustrophobia, claws, clown, cockroach, coffin, concentration camp, convict, corner, crime, cult, curse, danger, dangerous person, darkness, decadence, deer, devil, disaster, disease, divorce, earwig, elephant, elevator, end of the world, enemy, epidemic, evacuation, evil, falling, fear, fish, flying, gang, garbage, germs, ghost, grave, Halloween, haunted house, hell, hiding, hijacked plane, hitchhiking, hitting, hole, homeless person, horns, hot air balloon, immortality, impotence, inanimate objects coming to life, infertility, injection or needle, insane, insane asylum, jungle, karaoke, kidnapping, killing, leprechaun, levitation, losing, Mars, mastectomy, midwife, military, monster, motorcycle, museum, mute, nature, neighbor, nightmare, noose, nuclear bomb, nuclear power, pain, panic, paralyzed, pirate, planets other than Earth, poison, pornography, possessed by demons, prisoner, puppet, quarry, rabbit, rage, rape, red, rejection, revolution, saying no, science experiment, screaming, senile, shipwreck, shy, silence, skeleton, snake, soldier, speaking in public, storm, terrorism, test, tidal wave, torture, trapped, trees, UFO, ugliness, unemployed, vampire, vomiting, war, water, werewolf, wilderness, wildlife, yellow, zombie.

Feelings: abandonment, adolescence, aggression, anesthesia, anger, baby animal, clouds, coastline, crying, depression, desert, disappointment, diving into water, drought, drowning, ecstasy, embarrassment, emotional, empty, fear, fish, flood, forgiving, fountain, freezer, glacier, greedy, happy, hate, healing, health, heart, heart attack, hugging, hunger, injuries, insane, insomnia, itching, jealousy, Jet Ski, kissing, laughing, lazy, lifeguard, loneliness, love, lust, maternal instinct, mob mentality, modesty, moon, mouth, music, nausea, numb, orange, orgasm, overflowing, oysters, pain, panic, panting, paralyzed, patient, perfume, pier, plumbing, pollution, pride, purse, rage, rain, refrigerator, rejection, relaxation, restaurant, rip tide, roller coaster, sadness, sauna, screaming, shame, shipwreck, showers and baths, shy,

sink, skiing, snorkeling and scuba diving, snowboarding, snowman, starvation, stealing, stiff, stomach, storage, stress, suffocating, surfing, swimming, temper tantrum, tent, Thanksgiving, therapist, thin, thirst, thunder, tickling, tidal wave, tides, torture, umbrella, underwater, vomiting, water, water skiing, waves, weather changes, yelling, zombie.

Feminine: bisexuality, bra, breasts, bride, circle, cow, cross-dressing, daisy, doll, doughnuts, eclipse, egg, girl, girlfriend, goddesses, hole, homosexuality, hysterectomy, lesbian, mastectomy, melons, menopause, menstruation, mermaid, midwife, moon, mother, neck, oysters, pear, pink, plastic surgery, rose, sex change, sex organs, tides, triangle, tunnel, woman.

Financial Resources: bull, chicken, copy machine, counterfeiting, cow, crab, credit card, deprivation, desk, diamond, dishes, fired from a job, flies, free stuff, gambling, gold, green, groom, hiding, homeless person, jewels, lawsuit, lawyer, leak, limousine, loaning money, luxury, mall, money, overflowing, pantry, pig, pimp, poverty, purse, refrigerator, rich, secretary, shiny, shoes, shopping, stealing, tennis, umbrella, unemployed, utensils, vacuum cleaner, wallet, winning, X marks the spot, yard sale.

Food and Drink: abstinence, alcohol, apple, bakery, baking, beer, berries, bingeing, blender or food processor, bread, breakfast, cake, candy, champagne, cherry, chicken, choking, coffee, cooking, cotton candy, cup or glass, decadence, dessert, diet, dinner, dishes, doughnuts, drinking, eating, empty, fast food, food, food poisoning, freezer, fruit, full, garlic, grapes, greedy, hunger, ice cream, keg, kitchen, knife, lemon and lime, liver, lollipop, lunch, meat, melons, milk, mouth, onion, orange, oysters, pantry, party, pasta, pear, pepper, picnic, pig, poison, pomegranates, restaurant, salad, salt, smell, starvation, stove, taste, tea, Thanksgiving, thirst, utensils, vegetables, vomiting, water, wine.

Forgiveness: adultery, baptism, blond hair, cross, Easter, family, forgiving, hugging, museum, pollution, religious authority figures, religious ceremonies, scars and scabs, showers and baths, shunning, unicorn, weightless, white.

Freedom: adolescence, adultery, adventure, airplane, alone, amputation, amusement park, animals, aquarium, ashes, bachelor, birds, boots, breaking free, breaking up, breathing problems, bride, buried alive, butterfly, canyon, car accident, celibacy, chain, claustrophobia, cliff, convertible, couch, dancing, decadence, dolphin, dove, ecstasy, flying, forgiving, groom, gypsy, hang-gliding, horse, ice skating, immortality, Internet dating, Jet Ski, lungs, motorcycle, nature, pirate, prisoner, setting something free, single, skinny dipping, slide, space, suffocating, unemployed, vampire, wandering, weightless.

Fruit: apple, banana, cherry, eating, fruit, grapes, lemon and lime, melons, orange, pear, pomegranates.

Frustration: aggression, backward, barrier, breaking something, buried alive, circle, crime, crutches, dead end, detour, fairy, fight, impotence, in-laws, insomnia, lazy, monotony, nap, not invited, pajamas, paralyzed, running late, running problems, stalling, temper tantrum, terrorism, torture, traffic, trapped, waiting, waves, wrong size, yelling.

Fun: amusement park, beer, carnival, cartoon, cartwheels, cheerleader, circus, clown, club, confetti, costume, cotton candy, crowd, cruise, decadence, disguise, doll, ecstasy, flirting, friends, Halloween, hat, invitation, juggling, karaoke, laughing, nightclub, party, playground, playing hooky, poker, puppet, roller coaster, roller skates or inline skates, sand, scooter, skateboarding, skinny dipping, slide, snowboarding, surfing, teasing, tickling, toys, trampoline, trees, trespassing, trucks and semis, T-shirt, video game, water skiing, wine, winter.

Furniture and Appliances: bedroom, blender or food processor, chair, chest, couch, cradle, desk, freezer, furnace, furniture, mattress, microwave, oven, refrigerator, sink, storage, stove, table, vacuum cleaner.

Gender Issues: androgyny, boy, boyfriend, cross-dressing, girl, girlfriend, heterosexuality, homosexuality, hysterectomy, lesbian, phallic symbol, sex, sex change, sex organs.

Goal-Setting: balcony, balloon, baseball, basketball, bike, bowling, breakfast, car, castle, caterpillar, ceiling, chess, chiropractor, climbing, clock, contest, crystal ball, dandelion, darts and dartboards, dead body, desk, finger, graduation, kidnapping, knocking, list, logs, mountain, MP3 player, net, New Year's Eve, orchestra, oval, oven, package, painting, park, parking meter, pilot, rehearsal, running, running problems, saint, stars, straight line, street, success, taxi, traffic, train, turtle, tuxedo, waking up, wedding, working hard, X marks the spot.

Greed: bingeing, decadence, eating, greedy, pig, pigeon, pirate.

Guilt: adultery, arrested, bad behavior, bad habits, blaming others, blood, boyfriend, bribing someone, cake, chasing, cheating, confession, contraception, convict, costume, court, crime, curse, decadence, dessert, detective, disguise, drugs, eating, finger, flies, garbage, ghost, girlfriend, guilty conscience, handcuffs, haunted house, headache, hell, hickey, hiding, horns, incest, insomnia, Jacuzzi, jail, loaning money, lust, lying, masturbation, nausea, noose, police officer, pornography, prisoner, prostitute, punishment, saint, shame, stealing, taking responsibility, trespassing, underwear, villain, vomiting, working hard.

Happiness: birds, bling, blond hair, blue, bride, cake, camping, candy, carnation, chicken, convertible, crickets, daffodil, dancing, dessert, dinner, drum, duck, Easter, eating, ecstasy, family, farm, fireplace, flying, food, forgiving, friends, full, groom, heaven, home, homebody, house, hugging, ice cream, laughing, locker, love, lust, mattress, playground, ring, sex, singing, tickling, trees, utopia, water, waves, wilderness, wind, wine.

Healing: bandages, breathing, bruises, cancer, cane, chiropractor, couch, doctor, fever, fixing something, healing, heart attack, homebody, hospital, massage, medicine, nurse, patient, pharmacy, rabies, relaxation, scars and scabs, snake, therapist.

Health and Hygiene: AIDs, bathroom, battery, beach, birthmark, braces, bread, breathing, cancer, cane, chiropractor, choking, circumcision, cleaning, cobwebs, cockroach, coughing, crutches, cut, diet, disease, doctor, drinking, drugs, ear, eating, eclipse, enemy, engine, epidemic, fainting, fat, fever, fire, fleas, flies, food, food poisoning, garbage, garden, gas, germs, green, headache, healing, health, heart, heart attack, hospital, housekeeper, hysterectomy, in vitro fertilization, infertility, itching, laundry, lazy, liver, lungs, maggots, makeup, massage, mastectomy, menopause, menstruation, midwife, mother, mouse, multiple births, nap, nausea, neck, nuclear power, numb, nurse, pain, pajamas, patient, pharmacy, pig, pigeon, pills, poison, pollution, poverty, power failure, quicksand, rabies, rash, reptiles and amphibians, running, running out of gas, rust, salad, salon, salt, sauna, senile, sex, showers and baths, shunning, silence, skin, slob, smell, smoking, spine injuries, starvation, stiff, stomach, stress, suffocating, taste, therapist, thermometer, thin, thirst, throat, tides, toes, tonsils, trees, ugliness, unicorn, vaccination, vacuum cleaner, vegetables, vision problems, vomiting, walking, white, working out, wrist.

Heat: candle, desert, fever, furnace, heat, hell, Jacuzzi, lava, lightning, matches, oven, panting, sauna, stove, summer, sun, thermometer.

Hedonism: alcohol, berries, bingeing, cake, candy, champagne, club, cooking, crowd, cruise, cybersex, decadence, dessert, eating, ecstasy, fast food, food, fruit, greedy, ice cream, keg, lazy, lust, luxury, melons, nightclub, orange, orgy, party, pig, pomegranates, vampire, wine.

History: ancestors, antiques, archaeologist, camcorder, camera, fossil, meteors and meteorites, old-fashioned, past life, silver, time travel.

Home: attic, baking, basement, bathroom, bedroom, cleaning, closet, couch, curtains, dinner, dorm room, duck, eviction, fireplace, flies, furnace, furniture, home, homebody, homeless person, house, housekeeper, juggling, kitchen, landlord or landlady, mobile home, moving, nest, old-fashioned, pasta, remodeling your house, table, tenant, window, winter.

Hopes and Dreams: baby, balloon, birth, fetus, flying, heaven, hero, hired, in vitro fertilization, invitation, jewelry, jewels, job, love, luxury, marriage, midwife, movie, parachute, performing, picnic, pregnancy, proposal, rich, singing, stars, time travel, treasure, trip, utopia, wallet, winning, worm, *X* marks the spot.

Identity: amnesia, backward, ballet, boyfriend, breathing problems, camouflage, carnival, carpenter, castle, caterpillar, celebrity, chameleon, clothes, costume, cross-dressing, detective, disguise, doll, dorm room, dreaming that you are dreaming and dreaming that you wake up, driver's license or ID card, face, faceless, family, gang, garden, girlfriend, Halloween, home, homosexuality, hotel or motel, house, insane, insane asylum, interview, invisible, job, label, lesbian, locked out, lost, man, marching, mask, mirror, mob mentality, mobile home, multiple births, murder, obituary, old person, palm reading, parents, past life, prom, purse, quarry, remodeling your house, sex change, sex organs, sheep, shoes, shy, Thanksgiving, video game, wallet, woman, wrong size.

Image: audience, clothes, club, compliment, contact lens, contest, costume, co-worker, crown, dandruff, deformity, diet, disappointment, disguise, doll, ear, embarrassment, exhibitionism,

face, faceless, failure, fat, fingernails, gods, goddesses, grass, gum, hair, Halloween, hiding, homosexuality, horns, insane, insane asylum, insult, interview, invisible, invitation, jail, karaoke, label, leather, left hand, legs, lemon and lime, limousine, living room, locked out, locker room, losing, makeup, mask, mastectomy, masturbation, mirror, mobile home, modesty, moustache, MP3 player, nails, naked in public, neck, newspaper, nose, not invited, painting, performing, photograph, plastic surgery, play acting, power failure, race, remodeling your house, scooter, senile, sex change, shadow, shame, shaving, shoes, skateboarding, skeleton, skin, snowboarding, storage, SUV, tattoo, theater, thin, tie, toes, tools, T-shirt, tuxedo, ugliness, underwear, uniform, unraveling, vampire, website, winning, wrong size.

Impediments: barrier, bear, breathing problems, buried alive, cancer, ceiling, chain, claustrophobia, closed door, clouds, cockroach, contact lens, crutches, curtains, dead end, decadence, detour, disappointment, disease, failure, fear, fence, fog, forest, gate, glass, hail, heavy, highway, hill, ice skating, inaccessible, infertility, infidelity, in-laws, island, itching, jail, limping, mountain, nap, net, not invited, paralyzed, parking lot or garage, power failure, prisoner, railroad tracks, roller skates or inline skates, running problems, sand, saying no, shoes, sky, snow, stalling, stop signs or stoplights, taxi, throat, tires, toes, toll booth, tongue, traffic, train, trapped, wall, wheelchair, wilderness, window.

Inanimate Objects: answering machine, antiques, aquarium, axe, backpack, ball, balloon, bandages, baseball, baseball bat, basketball, battery, bike, billboard, blank screen, blanket, blender or food processor, bling, boat, book, boots, box, bra, bracelet, braces, cake, camcorder, camera, candle, cane, car, cards, cash register, CDs and DVDs, cell phone, chain, chair, chalk, chest, clock, closed door, clothes, coat, coffin, compass, computer, contact lens, copy machine, credit card, cross, crown, crutches, crystal ball, cup or glass, darts and dartboards, diamond, dishes, driver's license or ID card, drum, engine, fax machine, feather, finding something, football, garbage, glass, glasses, glove, gum, gun, hammer, handcuffs, hat, inanimate objects coming to life, invisible, invitation, jewelry, jewels, keg, key, knife, ladder, lamp, laundry, letter, levitation, life jacket, light bulb, lollipop, losing, magnifying glass, mail, mailbox, manuscript, map, matches, mirror, modem, money, MP3 player, musical instruments, nails, net, newspaper, one-of-a-kind, Ouija board, package, painting, phallic symbol, phone, piano, pillow, pottery, power tools, puppet, purse, raft, ring, satellite dish, sculpture, shoes, sink, suitcase, table, tent, thermometer, ticket, tie, tires, tools, toys, trampoline, T-shirt, TV, umbrella, utensils, vacuum cleaner, veil, video game.

Injuries: abdomen, accident, back, bandages, blender or food processor, blister, blood, bones, breaking something, bruises, cane, car accident, crutches, cut, dog, elbow, electrocution, fight, finger, fire, hand, headache, injuries, knee, lightning, mouth, neck, nose, pain, paralyzed, scars and scabs, scooter, skateboarding, skiing, spine injuries, toes, tongue, tools, tornado, trampoline.

Innocence: baby, baby animal, blond hair, bride, candy, carnival, cotton candy, court, cradle, daffodil, daisy, doll, Easter, flowers, goldfish, ice cream, lily, lollipop, love, noose, pink, playground, puppet, snow, unicorn, veil, white.

Insecurity: ankle, assassin, attacked, audience, baldness, blanket, booing, brain, bully, camouflage, claws, disappearing, disappointment, face, failure, fainting, foreigner, glove, graduation, growing, hair, hand, handcuffs, hiding, home, impotence, injuries, insane, insane asylum, insult, intruder, invisible, laughing, lightning, locker, locker room, mirror, nails, naked in public, not invited, plastic surgery, possessed by demons, poverty, purse, rehearsal, roller skates or inline skates, running late, salon, servant, shadow, shaving, shy, singing, skin, speaking in public, teasing, test, ugliness, underwear, wallet, war, weightless.

Instincts: Africa, animals, baby animals, bad behavior, basement, bite, camping, coyote, crab, crawling, dead animal, decadence, deer, dragon, drum, evil, fairy, farm, fish, forest, future, jungle, killing, lava, leather, logs, lust, maternal instinct, meat, milk, mountain lion, panting, pet, poison, red, reptiles and amphibians, roughing it, trees, wandering, werewolf, wildlife, wolf, zoo.

Intelligence: brain, chair, coastline, college, crossword puzzle, decapitation, headache, machinery, pig, rat, science experiment, secret code, skiing.

Intuition: archery, attic, candle, cards, child or children, danger, deer, doctor, dreaming that you are dreaming and dreaming that you wake up, electrocution, elephant, eyes, firefighter, fireworks, invisible, leaves, light, light bulb, midwife, owl, palm reading, psychic, remembering, wandering.

Isolation: abandonment, alone, camping, city, cold, coma, coyote, crowd, echo, eviction, fence, goldfish, island, monastery, moon, not invited, orphan, possum, prisoner, privacy, shipwreck, shunning, silence, snow, theater, wolf.

Journeys and Quests: barrier, baseball bat, bike, boat, body, book, border, camel, canyon, car, car accident, castle, ceiling, circle, cliff, climbing, compass, darkness, dead end, desert, detour, disaster, dorm room, drafted, driver's license or ID card, driving, Easter, elephant, fairy, feet, ferry, finding something, fishing, foreign language, forest, gods, goddesses, hallway, halo, health, highway, hiking, house, hunting, ice skating, Internet surfing, knitting, lamp, library, map, Mars, maze, meditation, mobile home, movie, nature, net, oven, palm reading, path, pilot, quarry, race, roller skates or inline skates, running, secret code, shipwreck, shortcut, space, stars, street, student, surgery, taxi, tenant, tires, toll booth, train, treasure, trip, trucks and semis, tunnel, turtle, wedding, wheel, wilderness, *X* marks the spot.

Karma: circle, Ferris wheel, fetus, wheel.

Knowledge: candle, CDs and DVDs, chalk, chest, college, detective, dorm room, drinking, elephant, escalator, exhibitionism,

Ferris wheel, fireworks, fishing, foreign language, fossil, hanging, Internet surfing, key, lamp, laundry, library, light, light bulb, magnifying glass, manuscript, math, measuring, newspaper, owl, question, reading, roots, snorkeling and scuba diving, stairs, student, teacher, test, time travel, trees, TV, utensils.

Listening: advice; ear; fax machine; gods; goddesses; heart; jaw; mail; mailbox; manuscript; modem; MP3 player; music; mute; noise; piano; question; ringtone; secret; silence; therapist; TV; voice, disembodied; yelling.

Loss: abortion, amputation, bankruptcy, box, cash register, cold, crying, disappointment, dishes, drain, emotional, empty, explosion, failure, falling, finger, fingernails, fired from a job, forest, funeral, glue, grave, hair, hot air balloon, hysterectomy, infertility, injuries, leak, leaves, losing, lost, mastectomy, money, murder, orphan, Ouija board, owl, poker, poverty, power failure, sadness, slide, stairs, storm, thin, ticket, war.

Love: apple, boyfriend, bra, breaking up, brunette hair, candle, carnival, celibacy, circle, corsage, daisy, diamond, disease, divorce, doughnuts, dove, drowning, duck, echo, ecstasy, eloping, emotional, fainting, family, father, feather,

fireworks, fishing, flirting, flowers, forgiving, friends, furnace, girlfriend, gold, heart, heart attack, heat, heaven, heterosexuality, hickey, hole, homosexuality, hugging, husband, incest, infidelity, injuries, jewelry, kissing, kitchen, lesbian, lollipop, love, lust, marriage, matches, mother, office, phone sex, picnic, ring, rose, sex, shaving, stomach, text message, thermometer, tickling, valentine, wedding, wife.

Loyalty: best friend, betrayal, boyfriend, dog, flag, friends, furnace, girlfriend, gossip, government spying, horns, infidelity.

Masculine: bisexuality, boy, boyfriend, bull, circumcision, cross, cross-dressing, dolphin, father, gods, homosexuality, impotence, lesbian, man, phallic symbol, sex change, sex organs, sun, sword, tower.

Medicine and Surgery: amputation, anesthesia, birth, brain, circumcision, dentist, doctor, hospital, hysterectomy, in vitro fertilization, injection or needle, injuries, insane, insane asylum, mastectomy, medicine, midwife, pills, surgery.

Memory: amnesia, camcorder, camera, CDs and DVDs, cemetery, ghost, haunted house, headache, hickey, locker, locker room, museum, past life, perfume, photograph, prom, remembering, school, smell, son, student, Thanksgiving, time travel, tonsils.

Messages: ancestors; answering machine; antiques; Aurora Borealis; author; billboard; birthmark; black; blood; cards; chalk; chat room; computer; cup or glass; dentist; dove; drawing; e-mail; fairy; fax machine; firefly; ghost; glasses; gods; goddesses; grandparents; invitation; jaw; keyboard; knocking; label; letter; library; light; mail; mail carrier; mailbox; manuscript; map; modem; mother; MP3 player; newspaper; noise; numbers; obituary; omen; Ouija board; piano; pigeon; punctuation; reading; remembering; ringtone; secret code; sign; stars; stop signs and stoplights; text message; T-shirt; TV; voice, disembodied; website; writing.

Music and Sound: band, clock, concert, dancing, drum, karaoke, keyboard, MP3 player, music, musical instrument, noise, opera, orchestra, performing, piano, ringtone, silence, singing, siren, thunder, whale, whispering.

Mystery: brunette hair, darkness, detective, digging, dirt, dreaming that you are dreaming and dreaming that you wake up, fairy, fog, foreign language, fortune teller, hole, invisible, key, magic, mask, moon, omen, question, tunnel, veil.

Myths and Legends: aliens, angel, apple, Big Foot, crystal ball, death, devil, fairy, ghost, gods, goddesses, Halloween, heaven, hell, leprechaun, levitation, magic, mandala, Mars, mermaid, monster, moon, Ouija board, past life, saint, siren, skeleton, snake, UFO, unicorn, utopia, vampire, werewolf, zombie.

Nature: alligator or crocodile, animals, ants, Aurora Borealis, autumn, barefoot, bats, bear, bees, Big Foot, bugs, bull, cabin, cactus, camel, camping, carnation, cat, caterpillar, chameleon, chicken, claws, clouds, coastline, cow, cowboy, coyote, crab, crickets, cross, daffodil, daisy, dandelion, dead animal, deer, desert, dog, earthquake, fairy, farm, fire, flowers, forest, fossil, four-leaf clover, garden, goat, grass, green, hail, hiking, hill, hunting, island, jungle, killing, landslide, lava, leaves, lightning, lily, lion, maggots, menopause, meteors and meteorites, moon, mountain, mountain lion, mouse, nature, nest, owl, oysters, palm tree, park, pet, picnic, pig, pigeon, pollution, possum, rabbit, rat, reptiles and amphibians, rip tide, rock, roots of a tree or plant, rose, roughing it, scorpion, shark, sheep, skinny dipping, sky, snake, snow, spring, stars, storm, summer, sun, tent, tidal wave, tides, tiger, trees, tulip, turtle, valley, volcano, water, weasel, whale, wilderness, wildlife, wind, wolf, worm.

Opportunity: adventure, advertisement, astronaut, baby animal, bait, ball, blue, canyon, car accident, cliff, climbing, construction, contest, copy machine, co-worker, crossroads, enter here, extreme sports, fairy, finding something, fishing, four-leaf clover, free stuff, future, gate, graduation, grass, ice skating, interview, invitation, job, ladder, leprechaun, mansion, matches, money, mountain, one-of-a-kind, open door, performing, reptiles and amphibians, saying no, scooter, shiny, space, stairs, ticket, train, treasure, window, worm.

Pain: abdomen, amputation, anesthesia, arthritis, back, bees, braces, breaking something, bruises, crutches, crying, fear, hate, headache, heart attack, hysterectomy, injuries, liver, mastectomy, menopause, menstruation, not invited, pain, scars and scabs, starvation, stomach, torture, wrist.

Peacemaking: arms, dove, drafted, forgiving, military, non-violence.

Peer Pressure: club, cult, friends, gang, karaoke, locker, marching, mob mentality, not invited, possessed by demons, running problems, saying no, smoking, terrorism, wedding, winning.

People: ancestors, archaeologist, artist, assassin, astronaut, audience, author, baby, bachelor, ballerina, best friend, Big Foot, boss, boy, boyfriend, bride, bully, carpenter, celebrity, cheerleader, child or children, chiropractor, city, clown, convict, cousins, cowboy, co-worker, crowd, dangerous person, daughter, dentist, detective, doctor, enemy, ex, family, father, firefighter, foreigner, fortune teller, friends, gang, ghost, girl, girlfriend, government spying, grandchildren, grandparents, groom, grown-up, gypsy, hero, homebody, homeless person, horns, hostage, housekeeper, husband, in-laws, intruder, janitor, king, landlord or landlady, lawyer, leader, lesbian, lifeguard, mail carrier, man, midwife, mother, neighbor, nurse, old person, orphan, parents, party, passenger, patient, pilot, pimp, pirate, police officer, president, prisoner, prostitute, psychic, queen, rebel, religious authority figures, saint, secretary, servant, sibling, slob, soldier, son, stranger, student, teacher, tenant, therapist, villain, wife, woman.

Personal Power: abdomen, adultery, airplane, amputation, applause, assassin, astronaut, audience, Aurora Borealis, author, award, ball, ballerina, balloon, band, baseball bat, bike, bikini, birth, body, bowling, boy, breathing problems, bribing someone, brunette hair, bull, bully, castle, cat, cheerleader, circus, coma, compliment, contest, dandruff, dessert, detective, dishes, dolphin, dragon, election, elephant, engine, erection, exhibitionism, face, fairy, falling, father, feet, flying, four-leaf clover, gods, goddesses, graduation, growing, gun, hand, hang-gliding, happy, hero, hired, horns, hostage, hot air balloon, ice skating, immortality, jail, Jet Ski, jumping, karaoke, king, lawyer, leader, leather, leprechaun, lion, locker room, magic, mansion, mastectomy, masturbation, menstruation, mermaid, mirror, musical instrument, performing, play acting, possessed by demons, power failure, power lines, power tools, president, pride, proposal, purple, purse, quarry, queen, question, race, reality show, rebel, red hair, rehearsal, revolution, rock, roller coaster, roof, salon, saying no, secretary, seduction, servant, sexual harassment, shadow, shaving, shipwreck, skiing, snowboarding, speaking in public, stage, stars, success, summer, SUV, sword, teeth, terrorism, test, thermometer, thin, tiger, tools, tower, train, trampoline, trees, tunnel, underground, utopia, vampire, video game, wallet, wheelchair, winning.

Places: Africa, amusement park, Asia, attic, Australia, bakery, balcony, bank, bar, basement, bathroom, beach, bedroom, border, bridge, cabin, cage, canyon, carnival, castle, cave, cemetery, chat room, church or synagogue, circus, city, cliff, closet, club, coastline, coffin, college, concentration camp, corner, court, crossroads, cruise, desert, dorm room, elevator, enter here, escalator, eviction, exit sign, farm, forest, future, grave, hallway, haunted house, heaven, hell, hiking, hill, hole, home, hospital, hotel or motel, house, insane asylum, island, Jacuzzi, jail, jungle, kitchen, laboratory, library, living room, locker room, mall, mansion, Mars, mobile home, monastery, mountain, museum, neighborhood, nest, nightclub, North Pole/South Pole, office, pantry, park, parking lot or garage, pharmacy, pier, planets other than Earth, playground, quarry, railroad tracks, restaurant, salon, sauna, school, stage, street, time travel, toll booth, tower, trespassing, utopia, valley, volcano, wilderness, zoo.

Plants: cactus, carnation, daffodil, daisy, dandelion, flowers, forest, four-leaf clover, garden, garlic, grass, leaves, lily, onion, palm tree, poison, roots of a tree or plant, rose, trees, tulip, vegetables.

Play: baseball, baseball bat, basketball, bike, bowling, cards, carnival, cartwheels, chess, clown, darts and dartboard, doll, dropping the ball, football, gambling, golf, Jet Ski, juggling, karaoke, kite, play acting, playground, playing hooky, poker, puppet, roller skates or inline skates, scooter, skateboarding, skiing, skinny dipping, slide, snorkeling and scuba diving, snowboarding, surfing, tennis, theater, toys, trampoline, video game, water skiing.

Pleasure: alcohol, bakery, baking, bedroom, beer, berries, blond hair, cake, candy, carnival, cartwheels, champagne, cherry, convertible, cooking, cotton candy, dancing, decadence, dessert, diving into water, doughnuts, duck, eating, ecstasy, exhibitionism, fast food, fireworks, flirting, food, fruit, full, golf, hotel or motel, ice cream, island, jewelry, keg, kissing, laughing, lips, lollipop, love, lust, luxury, manicure or pedicure, massage, masturbation, melons, mouth, nightclub, oral sex, orange, orgy, overflowing, oysters, pear, perfume, phallic symbol, piano, pig, pomegranate, pornography, seduction, sex, shopping, skinny dipping, stranger, taste, wine.

Predictions: crystal ball, danger, dragon, film, fortune teller, future, halo, hanging, hill, midwife, owl, package, palm reading, parachute, pendulum, psychic, sky, soldier, time travel, tuxedo.

Protection: bedroom, bikini, blanket, box, breasts, cactus,

circle, coat, cross, drafted, evacuation, fence, firefighter, freezer, friends, garlic, glass, goldfish, grandchildren, gun, home, Internet dating, intruder, life jacket, lifeguard, lightning, lock, locked out, losing, magic, mask, mattress, military, mother, net, numb, onion, owl, paralyzed, park, parking lot or garage, patient, playing it safe, praying, rabbit, raft, roof, tent, umbrella, vaccination, valley, veil, villain.

Punishment: bad behavior, convict, court, crime, father, hell, jail, mother, not invited, parking ticket, police officer, prisoner, punishment, religious authority figures, saint, stealing, trespassing.

Rebellion: adolescence, Australia, bad behavior, bakery, bus, cowboy, crime, diet, drugs, escape, flag, goat, gypsy, hickey, jail, leather, left hand, marching, motorcycle, passenger, piercing, pirate, playing hooky, rebel, red hair, religious authority figures, revolution, saying no, shortcut, terrorism, trucks and semis, vampire.

Regret: choking, cockroach, confession, contraception, cult, curse, decadence, dishes, drain, film, jail, tattoo, time travel, wedding.

Relationships: abandonment, abortion, abstinence, adoption, anger, argument, arms, asking for directions, assassin, autopsy, axe, baby, bachelor, bar, beer, best friend, betrayal, blaming others, blister, blue, bread, breaking up, breathing, bride, bruises, carnival, celibacy, chain, chalk, chat room, Christmas, circus, city, club, coffee, coffin, cold, contact lens, corsage, couch, coughing, cousins, cow, co-worker, credit card, cremation, dandelion, dangerous person, dating, daughter, dead body, deafness, decadence, diamond, disease, divorce, doll, doughnuts, dropping something, drowning, echo, egg, eloping, e-mail, emotional, empty, enemy, ex, eyes, failure, fainting, family, father, feather, feet, fight, fish, fishing, flexibility, flirting, flood, flowers, following, football, forgiving, freezer, friends, furnace, gang, garlic, gift, glass, glue, gold, gossip, grandchildren, grandparents, groom, gum, gun, happy, healing, heart, heart attack, heat, helping someone, heterosexuality, hickey, hired, homosexuality, horse, hostage, hugging, hunger, hunting, husband, impotence, inaccessible, incest, infertility, infidelity, injuries, in-laws, insult, Internet dating, Internet surfing, interview, jealousy, juggling, kidnapping, kissing, kitchen, knife, knocking, landlord or landlady, laughing, leader, leaves, leprechaun, lesbian, lily, living room, loaning money, lock, locked out, lollipop, loneliness, losing, love, lunch, lust, lying, mail carrier, mall, man, mandala, mannequin, manslaughter, marriage, massage, matches, maternal instinct, menopause, menstruation, mother, mouth, murder, musical instrument, nails, neighbor, neighborhood, nightclub, not invited, numb, office, orchestra, orgasm, parade, party, passenger, pet, phone, phone sex, picnic, pier, piercing, pigeon, pimp, plastic surgery, prom, promise proposal, prostitute, punishment, rabbit, rat, rejection, restaurant, reward, ring, rose, rust, satellite dish, school, science experiment, secret, setting something free, sex, shaving, shunning, sibling, singing, single, son, stiff, surgery, taking responsibility, taxi, teasing, tenant, tennis, text message, Thanksgiving, theater, thirst, tickling, tie, tongue, ugliness, valentine, veil, villain, volcano, wedding, wife, winter, woman, yelling, zombie.

Repression: abdomen, abstinence, acid, Africa, amnesia, anger, animals, aquarium, attic, basement, blaming others, breathing problems, cemetery, closet, crying, decadence, desert, faceless, fear, fish, freezer, ghost, glacier, hate, haunted house, headache, hiding, liver, loneliness, marriage, museum, mute, nausea, past life, plumbing, school, séance, setting something free, sink, snowman, storage, storm, suffocating, temper tantrum, thunder, umbrella, vision problems, water, zoo.

Reputation: AIDs, bank, bankruptcy, bar, celebrity, cleaning, clothes, compliment, co-worker, credit card, crown, decadence, disease, face, faceless, failure, fingernails, flies, grass, hair, insane, insane asylum, interview, jail, lawsuit, legs, lemon and lime, living room, makeup, masturbation, modesty, multiple births, naked in public, neck, newspaper, nose, not invited, obituary, piercing, pimp, pottery, shame, shoes, skin, snowboarding, SUV, tattoo, tie, toes, unemployed, uniform, unraveling, vacuum cleaner, vampire, winning.

Resistance: arthritis, barrier, glasses, glove, husband, itching, mute, rebel, revolution, saying no, sexual harassment, snake, terrorism, wife.

Responsibilities: abduction; back; backpack; bees; bills and debts; blender or food processor; brakes not working; bride; bus; cage; carry; celibacy; chain; child or children; citizen's arrest; claustrophobia; crossword puzzle; danger; dangerous person; deformity; family; fired from a job; flood; groom; hero; hired; housekeeper; husband; immortality; insane; insane asylum; janitor;

juggling; lawyer; lazy; leader; lion; list; loaning money; logs; losing; lost; maze; missing a class, meeting, or appointment; monotony; mouse; multiple births; musical instruments; nest; nurse; panic; parking ticket; playing hooky; playing it safe; police officer; raft; rape; rehearsal; rescue; restaurant; roof; running late; school; seduction; senile; shipwreck; slob; starvation; taking responsibility; teacher; tidal wave; trapped; trucks and semis; uniform; vacation; vegetables; weightless; wife; working hard.

Risky Behavior: adultery, adventure, AIDs, alcohol, ambulance, amusement park, arson, bad behavior, bad habits, beer, betrayal, bingeing, blister, bungee jumping, carnival, club, cockroach, counterfeiting, crawling, crime, crutches, cult, cut, danger, dangerous person, decadence, decapitation, devil, disease, dropping something, duck, extreme sports, fleas, flying, food poisoning, gambling, greedy, gun, Halloween, hang-gliding, health, hero, hijacked plane, hitchhiking, hitting, hostage, injection or needle, insane, insane asylum, intruder, jumping, ladder, lifeguard, lungs, lust, lying, maggots, military, mob mentality, motorcycle, murder, pimp, pirate, playing hooky, playing it safe, poker, pollution, pornography, possessed by demons, prostitute, rape, reality show, red hair, reptiles and amphibians, rescue, rip tide, roof, roller coaster, science experiment, seduction, self-control, sex, shopping, shortcut, siren, skateboarding, skiing, smoking, snowboarding, speeding, stranger, terrorism, tiger, tightrope, trampoline, trespassing, vampire, volcano, werewolf, wildlife, wine.

Rules and Laws: bad behavior, braces, bribing someone, bride, cage, camouflage, carnival, citizen's arrest, claustrophobia, club, convict, counterfeiting, court, crawling, crime, crowd, diet, drafted, drugs, goat, government, hickey, jail, king, landlord or landlady, lawsuit, lawyer, military, mob mentality, parking ticket, passport, pirate, playing hooky, police officer, prisoner, punishment, queen, revolution, speeding, stealing, terrorism, thermometer, toll booth, trespassing.

Sacrifice: blood, cake, carnation, cross, deprivation, dessert, fish, fishing, goat, horse, mother, North Pole/South Pole, roughing it, saint, taking responsibility, ticket.

Secrets: AIDs, amnesia, archaeologist, attic, basement, Big Foot, black, blackout, camouflage, cat, cave, chest, closet, costume, cross-dressing, cut, digging, disguise, fog, haunted house, headache, hiding, hole, key, laundry, lock, locked out, possum, remembering, secret, shadow, skeleton, stairs, storage, tunnel, veil, whispering, worm.

Senses: eating; fear; itching; kissing; laughing; lemon and lime; light; pain; perfume; photograph; piano; piercing; sex; silence; smell; stink; taste; thirst; vision problems; voice, disembodied; yelling.

Sexual Activity: abstinence, adultery, AIDs, air conditioner, amputation, apple, banana, bedroom, belly button, berries, bisexuality, blister, boyfriend, breasts, candle, celebrity, celibacy, cheerleader, cherry, circle, contraception, cross-dressing, cybersex, decadence, disease, diving into water, doughnuts, drought, drowning, duck, emotional, erection, feet, fever, fireworks, flowers, food, fruit, girlfriend, heterosexuality, hiding, hole, homosexuality, hugging, husband, impotence, incest, infidelity, kissing, lesbian, lingerie, lips, locker room, lollipop, love, lust, man, massage, masturbation, mattress, melons, menstruation, mermaid, mouth, neighbor, nightclub, numb, nurse, oral sex, orgasm, orgy, oval, oysters, pear, perfume, phallic symbol, phone sex, pink, pomegranates, pornography, power failure, pregnancy, prostitute, rabbit, rape, red, red hair, refrigerator, reptiles and amphibians, ring, rose, saying no, secretary, seduction, sex, sex organs, sexual harassment, stranger, thermometer, tickling, tongue, tools, underwear, vampire, veil, volcano, water, wife, wine, woman.

Shapes and Symbols: billboard, circle, cross, drawing, hole, key, letter, mandala, math, maze, moon, numbers, Ouija board, oval, phone number, punctuation, ring, secret code, sign, square, stars, straight line, tattoo, tower, triangle, tunnel, wheel, writing.

Social Life: best friend, club, cousins, friends, invitation, karaoke, living room, lunch, neighbor, neighborhood, nightclub, not invited, orgy, party, phone, phone sex, prom, saying no, sex, shunning, shy, singing, single, stove, table, tattoo, villain, wine.

Solutions and Remedies: antidote, axe, backpack, baptism, battery, beach, blister, bribing someone, bridge, chess, chicken, circumcision, cleaning, computer, confession, contact lens, contraception, counterfeiting, crossword puzzle, deprivation, detective, digging, drugs, evacuation, exit sign, Ferris wheel, finding something, fire engine, firefighter, fixing something, forgiving, fortune teller, giving away possessions, glue, gun, hail, hammock, healing, helping someone, hero, hijacked plane, hiking, hitchhiking, hypnotized, invisible, island, janitor, jumping, key, kite, knife, knitting, lawyer, light bulb, lion, loaning money, manicure or pedicure, massage, math, maze, measuring, medicine, meditation, money, onion, orange, orgasm, oven, pajamas, patient, pendulum, pharmacy, pillow, pills, planets other than Earth, punctuation, punishment, quicksand, quitting, relaxation, religious ceremonies, remembering, rescue, reward, roots, running, salad, salon, salt, sauna, saying no, science experiment, séance, secret code, senile, setting something free, sex, shopping, silence, snake, soldier, tent, therapist, vacation, video game, vomiting.

Spirituality: angel, Asia, Aurora Borealis, candle, church or synagogue, cross, cult, devil, dolphin, dove, ecstasy, escalator, Ferris wheel, firefly, fireworks, forest, ghost, giving away possessions, gods, goddesses, gold, grandparents, Halloween, halo, healing, heaven, hell, jungle, kite, levitation, light, lily, love, magic, mandala, meditation, monastery, moon, owl, past life, possessed by demons, praying, psychic, purple, reincarnation, religious authority figures, religious ceremonies, saint, séance, singing, tea, utopia, vegetables, whale, white.

Sports and Games: ball, ballerina, ballet, baseball, baseball bat, basketball, bike, bowling, cards, cheerleading, chess, contest, darts and dartboards, diving into water, dropping the ball, football, Jet Ski, juggling, jumping, karaoke, kite, poker, race, reality show, roller skates or inline skates, running, scooter, shopping, skateboarding, skiing, snorkeling and scuba diving, snowboarding, surfing, swimming, tennis, toys, trampoline, video game, water skiing, yoga.

Stability: ankle, back, bones, cane, chair, chiropractor, crutches, dinner, family, floor, furnace, home, homebody, husband, in-laws, insane, insane asylum, laughing, legs, mattress, meat, mother, neighborhood, nest, old-fashioned, playing it safe, rock, roller coaster, roof, roots, silver, spine injuries, square, trees, tulip, valley, wife, winter.

Stasis: cage, ceiling, chair, cobwebs, coma, drain, jail, machinery, monotony, parking lot or garage, pillow, valley, waiting.

Subterfuge: acid, acne, amnesia, archaeologist, autopsy, axe, black, blackout, blaming others, blanket, boots, camouflage, cave, closet, coffin, costume, cross-dressing, curtains, cut, darkness, digging, disappearing, disguise, escalator, faceless, fog, hanging, haunted house, headache, hickey, hiding, key, lamp, lock, locked out, lying, magic, marriage, mask, storage, tunnel, veil, water, whispering.

Success: applause, audience, award, ballet, baseball, basketball, birds, blender of food processor, bowling, bull, celebrity, club, finding something, football, magic, newspaper, one-of-a-kind, oven, performing, race, rehearsal, running problems, saying no, student, success, test, treasure, winning.

Support: advice, alone, audience, boyfriend, bra, floor, friends, girlfriend, hugging, in-laws, lifeguard, neighbor, praying, religious authority figures, teacher, text message, Thanksgiving, therapist, wife.

Taking Action: eviction, forgiving, invitation, karaoke, moving, murder, newspaper, package, packing for a trip, parking, patient, power tools, president, proposal, remodeling your house, rescue, saying no, sculpture, setting something free, sex, sky, speaking in public, stalling, straight line, student, success, surgery, telling the truth, tent, terrorism, tires, tonsils, tools, torture, underground, vaccination, walking, waves.

Technology: answering machine, astronaut, battery, blank screen, brakes not working, breaking something, camcorder, camera, CDs or DVDs, cell phone, chat room, computer, copy machine, cybersex, elevator, e-mail, engine, escalator, fax machine, future, Internet dating, Internet surfing, keyboard, machinery, modem, MP3 player, nuclear power, office, phone, phone sex, power tools, satellite dish, science experiment, shopping, text message, time travel, tools, TV, video game, website.

Threats: aliens, alligator or crocodile, bats, bear, bugs, cactus, claws, cockroach, convict, curse, danger, dangerous person, desert, enemy, escape, fear, fleas, forest, government spying, gun, horns, hunting, inanimate objects coming to life, infidelity, insane, insane asylum, intruder, jungle, losing, love, monster, mountain lion, museum, naked in public, neighbor, net, nightmare, noose, omen, pain, panic, playground, poison, possessed by demons, rabies, rage, rape, revolution, scorpion, screaming, self-control, sexual harassment, shark, smell, smoking, snake, stink, storm, stove, stranger, sword, tent, terrorism, tidal wave, tiger, trespassing, UFO, volcano, werewolf, whale, wilderness, wildlife, wind, winter, wolf, yellow.

Time: clock; future; immortality; missing a class, meeting, or

appointment; old-fashioned; parking meter; past life; portal; race; running late; sand; school; stalling; time travel; waiting.

Transformation: abnormal, abortion, adolescence, adventure, airplane, amnesia, arson, ashes, audition, autumn, birth, border, bride, brunette hair, butterfly, carpenter, caterpillar, CDs and DVDs, chameleon, cleaning, cliff, corner, costume, crickets, cross-dressing, dating, dead animal, death, destruction, dirt, disappearing, disguise, divorce, earthquake, electrocution, end of the world, fairy, fetus, fire, funeral, future, garbage, grave, health, killing, laboratory, lamp, landslide, lightning, magic, magnifying glass, menopause, meteors and meteorites, microwave, moon, moving, nuclear bomb, obituary, old-fashioned, old person, omen, oven, packing for a trip, possessed by demons, reincarnation, remodeling your house, revolution, sculpture, sex change, showers and baths, snake, snow, spine injuries, spring, storm, street, summer, thin, tides, UFO, unicorn, upside-down, weather changes, werewolf, whale, winter, worm.

Travel: accelerator, adventure, Africa, airplane, archaeologist, Asia, asking for directions, Australia, barrier, bike, birds, boat, bus, camel, car, compass, cruise, dead end, desert, detour, disaster, ferry, foreign language, gas, gypsy, highway, hiking, hitchhiking, lost, map, motorcycle, nausea, North Pole/South Pole, packing for a trip, palm tree, passenger, passport, path, pilot, pirate, planets other than Earth, portal, railroad tracks, shortcut, street, suitcase, taxi, tea, time travel, tires, toll booth, traffic, train, trip, trucks and semis, U-turn, vacation, walking, wilderness.

Trust Issues: abduction, adultery, attacked, betrayal, boyfriend, breaking up, cheating, cross-dressing, dangerous person, friends, girlfriend, gossip, government, government spying, infidelity, intruder, jealousy, knife, lifeguard, lust, lying, magic, mask, motorcycle, neighbor, nuclear power, poison, promise, rape, rat, setting something free, sex, sexual harassment, shaving, stealing, stiff, stomach, stranger, teasing, telling the truth, therapist, tickling, trespassing, unemployed, weasel.

Vehicles: accelerator, accident, airplane, airplane crash, bike, boat, brakes not working, bus, camel, car, convertible, disaster, driving, engine, ferry, fire engine, flying, gas, highway, hijacked plane, Jet Ski, limousine, mobile home, motorcycle, parking lot or garage, passenger, race, railroad tracks, roller coaster, roller skates or inline skates, running out of gas, scooter, shipwreck, skateboarding, speeding, street, SUV, taxi, time travel, tires, traffic, train, trucks and semis, UFO, wheel, wheelchair.

Violence: aggression, anger, argument, assassin, attacked, axe, bad behavior, bar fight, bear, bite, disaster, drafted, explosion, fight, gun, hitting, hunting, injuries, insane asylum, intruder, killing, knife, manslaughter, meat, murder, noose, nuclear bomb, pirate, possessed by demons, rabies, rage, rape, red, revolution, soldier, sword, terrorism, thunder, torture, villain, war, werewolf, wildlife, wolf.

Vulnerability: abdomen, axe, baby, baby animal, baldness, barefoot, bikini, bite, blanket, booing, cane, chest, coat, cradle, crutches, cult, danger, dangerous person, deer, depression, devil, drowning, erection, fainting, fear, fleas, forest, hair, handcuffs, home, hunger, injuries, insane, insane asylum, intruder, locker room, naked in public, nausea, neck, not invited, nurse, oral sex, paralyzed, patient, possessed by demons, prostitute, rape, sex, sexual harassment, shaving, stomach, storage, storm, torture, trespassing, underwear, weightless.

War: drafted, nuclear bomb, prisoner, soldier, sword, war.

Water: bathroom, blue, boat, diving into water, drought, drowning, fish, fishing, flood, fountain, goldfish, Jacuzzi, Jet Ski, leak, life jacket, mermaid, moon, oysters, pier, plumbing, raft, rain, rip tide, shark, showers and baths, sink, skinny dipping, snorkeling and scuba diving, snow, surfing, swimming, tidal wave, tides, underwater, water, water skiing, waves, whale.

Weather and Seasons: autumn, black, Christmas, clouds, cold, danger, disaster, drought, Easter, fog, hail, Halloween, heat, leaves, lightning, moon, nature, New Year's Eve, North Pole/South Pole, omen, rain, sky, snow, snowman, spring, storm, summer, sun, Thanksgiving, thermometer, thunder, tidal wave, tornado, umbrella, weather changes, wind, winter.

Wishes: balloon, birds, candy, carnival, celebrity, chasing, cheating, decadence, fairy, gift, jewelry, love, lust, midwife, movie, old-fashioned, one-of-a-kind, Ouija board, past life, rich, ring, *X* marks the spot.

Work: ankle, ants, author, axe, bees, bike, boots, boss, camel, co-worker, cruise, desk, dropping the ball, engine, farm, fired from a job, hammer, hand, hired, job, juggling, knitting, lazy, logs, lunch, office, oven, painting, parade, playing hooky, secretary, toll booth, tools, unemployed, unraveling, vacation, working hard, working out.

Yin-Yang: androgyny, banana, bisexuality, black, cross-dressing, darkness, light, man, mandala, moon, sex, sex change, sex organs, sun, utopia, wheel, white, woman.

Tuck-in Time

To sleep, perchance to dream ... or, to put it another way (with all due respect to William Shakespeare), to dream, you first have to go to sleep! Here are some tips and suggestions to encourage your nightly journey to dream world.

Bedtime Basics

Your bedroom—the environment in which you sleep—sets the stage for your night's dream time. Your bed, the room's temperature, your jammies, and even what you eat and drink in the hours before slipping between the sheets all influence the quality of your sleep. Sounds, lights, and even smells register with your brain during sleep and may weave themselves into your dreams.

Seven Changes for Better Sleep

1. Give your body good support. Sleeping surfaces that hold your spine in its natural alignment—no matter your sleeping position—allow your muscles to relax. Invest in a quality mattress, and you're investing in a good night's sleep.

2. Surround yourself in comfort. Select fabrics for your sheets and nightclothes that feel good against your skin and keep you warm or cool enough. Make your bed every morning so that getting into it at night is a refreshing, welcoming experience.

3. Choose colors that calm, sounds that soothe, and smells that pacify. Subdued colors such as light blues, pinks, and grays with darker (not brighter) colors for furnishings

and accents give the bedroom a sense of retreat. Quiet music and gentle fragrances help relax your mind … and where your mind goes, your body follows.

4. Turn off the lights. All of them. The darker your bedroom, the better you'll sleep. If necessary, install room-darkening shades or blinds to darken the room when it's still light outside.

5. Moderate the temperature. Most people sleep best when the room is cool enough to need a light blanket. A room that is too hot or too cold distracts your body from sleep by keeping it busy trying to keep itself comfortable.

6. No work, computers, television, research, or snacking in your bedroom! But if you enjoy reading or journaling as a way to relax and unwind, this can be a great way to get sleepy.

7. Establish a bedtime routine. Go to bed at the same time each night. Begin preparing for bed about 20 minutes before your bedtime so you're ready to snuggle in for a night of sweet dreams.

Do you have health problems that may interfere with your ability to fall or stay asleep? Talk to your doctor about ways to help ease pain and discomfort so you can sleep. Your body can't relax enough for you to drift into a sound dreaming sleep when it hurts or otherwise suffers.

Ease into Sleep

Your days are hectic, filled with activities that tax your body, mind, and spirit. Wouldn't it be great to just turn all that off and fall right asleep when it's time for bed? You can give yourself a transitional off-ramp to gear down and ready yourself for dreamland, and you can even do a few things to make dreams come more easily and stay with you longer when you wake up. Here are seven practices to help you relax so you can drift into sleep. Use the same method every night, or vary the practice to fit the kind of transition you desire.

Practice	What to Do	Purpose
Massage	Gently rub your muscles (or have a partner rub them), starting with your toes and moving up your body to finish with your face and head.	Relieve physical tension in the body, relax muscles, and improve blood circulation
Meditation	Choose a point of focus, such as a beloved object or the image of a favorite place, that makes you happy or peaceful. Keep bringing your attention back to this focus when your mind wanders.	Clear and calm the thoughts and mind
Prayer	Engage in communion with the divinity of your beliefs.	Establish a sense of inner peace
Visualization	Create and hold in your thoughts a vision of your muscles relaxing and your mind allowing the day's thoughts and tensions to fade away.	Provide a consciously constructed "map" of your desired sleep and dream experiences
Dream intent	Hold in your thoughts a clear and specific purpose for the night's dreams, such as a question to answer.	Prepare for lucid dreaming
Breathe	Breathe in slow, measured breaths. Count breaths, or count lengths of inhalation and exhalation, gradually lengthening each to slow counts of 10.	Profoundly relax your body and prepare both body and mind for sleep
Journaling	Keep a journal next to your bed and jot down thoughts of what you would like to dream about. Also use this journal to record dream images.	Sculpt your own dream landscape and remember your dreams better

Herbs, Essences, and Oils

Many herbs are calming to the body. Warm herbal teas feel and taste good. Other herbs activate the senses of smell and touch for relaxation and to encourage peaceful dreams. Herbal sachets are great under the pillow for soothing fragrances; essential oils work well in a warm bath.

Herb	Common Forms	Effects
Catnip	Tea, tincture, essential oil, sachet	Relaxation, sedative
Chamomile	Tea, tincture, essential oil, sachet	Mild sedative, calms and relaxes
Clary sage	Tea, tincture, essential oil, sachet	Sedative
Hops	Tea, tincture, sachet	Muscle relaxant, sedative
Lavender	Tea, essential oil, sachet	Mild sedative, calms and relaxes
Lemonbalm	Tea, essential oil	Soothes anger, sedative
Passion flower	Tea, tincture	Sedative
Skullcap	Tea, tincture, extract, tablets, capsules	Muscle relaxant, antianxiety, sedative
St. John's wort	Tincture, tablets, capsules	Acts on brain neurotransmitters
Valerian	Tea, tincture, tablets, capsules	Antianxiety, sedative, shortens length of time to fall asleep

Remember, even though most herbal preparations available in stores are safe for most people, herbs cause biochemical changes in your body and may interact with medications you're taking. If you take regular medications, have ongoing health conditions, or are pregnant, always check with your doctor or pharmacist before adding herbal products to your bedtime routine.

Rock-a-Bye Baby ...

Why do babies fall asleep when their mothers rock them and sing to them? The gentle, rhythmic motions and sounds are soothing and comforting, gradually blocking the effects of other stimuli. Several devices help you re-create this experience in an adult context.

Sleep Aid Device	How to Use	Effects
Blackout shades	Install window coverings to block outside light	Darkens the room, reducing stimuli
Eye mask	Place over the eyes to block light	Gives the perception of a darkened room
Music	Play softly	Helps relax the body and mind; obscures noise
Noise blocker	Play softly	Obscures noise
White noise machine	Play softly	Obscures noise

The Flow of Energy: Feng Shui

The ancient practice of feng shui manipulates the flow of energy, or *chi*, within rooms to support the activities that take place within those rooms. You can use feng shui at home by making simple changes in the arrangement, decor, and clutter in your bedroom, to keep energy moving smoothly and in a healthy way. This is conducive to good sleep and dreams.

- Avoid doors and windows opposite one another, and never sleep facing a door. These placements cause chi to rush between the openings, and to drag your own energy out the door, so you don't get a restful sleep. Locate your bed so it is not in such an energy pathway. If you can't avoid such placement, use soft folds of draperies or decorative room screens to redirect the chi.

- Tip the balance of the elements toward the *yin*, the softer, feminine side of the yin-yang balance. Water, Earth, and wood are *yin* elements; metal and fire are *yang* (masculine, sun, active energy) elements. Put a fountain in your bedroom to further soften the chi.

- Don't arrange your bed under any beams or rafters, or with any corners of the room pointing at you. Beams that cut across you horizontally can cause health problems, according to feng shui, and beams that divide couples can result in relationship problems. Corners send arrows of negative energy at you while you sleep. If your bed must be located under beams, drape a soft cloth over the beams to hide their shape, and place objects in front of corners.

- Keep all dead or dying plants out of your bedroom. These encourage poor health, low energy, and depression. According to feng shui, beautiful fake plants are preferable to wilting live plants.

- Don't locate any mirrors so that you can see yourself in bed. This can cause anxiety, if you should wake up in the middle of the night and see yourself. Mirrors reflecting the bed are a feng shui taboo!

- Clear the clutter. Clutter—lots of furniture crowded into the bedroom, clothing piled on chairs, overflowing closets—causes chi to stagnate, catching it like a dirty drainpipe. This results in a sense of staleness in the room. Less is more when it comes to freshening the energy in your bedroom: clear off surfaces, and keep the space under your bed clean and clear of junk.

- Stand in the doorway to your bedroom, looking in. From where you are standing, the upper right corner of the room is the relationship and marriage corner. If you want a healthy relationship, keep this corner free of junk and beautifully decorated with symbols of love and passion: red and pink flowers or pictures of flowers, wind chimes, and representations of couples.

Dream Interpretation Checklist

Because you're holding this dictionary in your hands, we know you are curious about your dreams and what they mean. Maybe you're a dream analysis pro: you've kept a dream journal for years, and now you're looking for an unexpected slant on a dream, something that gets you thinking in a new way. Maybe you're eager to understand a dream that seems to have come out of nowhere, but you know it has come out of *you* and you want to know what that dream signifies and what message it holds. Maybe you've only begun to look at your dreams, or perhaps you struggle even to recall that you've been dreaming, much less what you've been dreaming about. We've developed some easy-to-use, step-by-step strategies for remembering and interpreting your dreams. We're hoping that all dreamers can find something useful in the suggestions, and we wish you good dreams for your sleeping self and higher awareness for your waking self!

❏ **Having difficulty remembering your dreams?**

- Examine whether you welcome your dreams fully. Maybe you are afraid, uneasy, or skeptical. Make a decision to welcome your dreams.

- When you lay your head on the pillow and close your eyes, repeat a simple affirmation to yourself to remember your dream upon waking. Inhale, say "I will remember my dream and welcome its message," exhale, and allow your mind to relax into sleep.

- Keeping pen and paper by the bedside can be a powerful tool to focus your intention on dream recall. You'll find that if you get into the habit of writing down your dreams right away upon waking, you'll have a more coherent and detailed dream "story." Don't worry if you feel like you're writing in your sleep—that's okay. Read it later, in the morning.

- Practice concentration. As you begin to work on recalling your dreams, take 10 minutes a day to meditate on the dream images or story. Don't worry about interpreting the dream; just meditate and begin to concentrate on how you feel and respond to the dream.

❑ **Are you eager to recall your dreams more fully?**

- Begin to keep a dream journal. Start by simply writing down dream words or images that are powerful parts of your dream: the sun, running fast, a green hat. Over time, think about the Dream Themes that emerge from these Dream Words, and use this dictionary to explore possible connections and dream meanings.

- Make your dream journal a dream story journal. Take the notes you scrawl at bedside and type them out in narrative form. Do this over a period of time and see if the stories have connections. Do they recur? Continue? Where is your dream story going?

- For more sophisticated dream recall, begin to write not only the dream story in your journal, but also the events of your waking day before the dream. Look for unexpected or completely obvious resonances between your waking and sleeping selves.

❑ **Do you want to use your dreams to become more self-aware?**

- If a dream you've had is puzzling you, when you lay your head on the pillow and close your eyes, invite a dream that explains the meaning further. Even if the two dreams don't seem to be related, they are, *somehow*. Meditate on it and see what comes to you.

- If you have a problem or issue in your waking life, you can ask your dreams to help supply answers and strategies for action. Ask your question before sleep, and see what arises in your dream.

- Don't assume anything! Dreams are sometimes *so like us*, and sometimes *so not like us*. Open yourself to the idea that you are a beautiful mystery, wrapped in an enigma (where have we heard that before?), and that you may still have a lot to learn about who you are and who you dream of becoming. Just as you welcome your dreams, welcome the opportunity to let them transform your waking life.

- If your dreams are frightening or violent and they worry you, consider seeing a licensed therapist to explore dream meanings. Most of the time, though, these dreams have the purpose of provoking you or getting your attention—fast. And they do! As you meditate, ask the dream to explain itself to you. For example, if you are being chased by a polar bear, turn and ask the bear, "Why?" If this doesn't work, then invite a dream in which the bear appears to you in a calm way, where you are protected, and helps you to understand why it chased you. Even if you dream about something completely different, the answer will be in there, we guarantee.

The most important thing to remember in interpreting your dreams is to recognize that you have your own, very personal, dream world. As you begin to recall and look at your Dream Words and Dream Themes, you will learn a lot about what you dream about and how those dreams inform and transform your life. Imagine yourself as an explorer about to embark on a journey to map an unknown territory, but this territory is yourself and your dreams. What could be more exciting on the path of life than to think and dream with awareness, insight, and curiosity?